D1562652

REMEMBER THE FUTURE

REMEMBER THE FUTURE

The Pastoral Theology of Paul the Apostle

Jacob W. Elias

Foreword by Reta Halteman Finger

Herald Press
Scottdale, Pennsylvania
Waterloo, Ontario

Library of Congress Cataloging-in-Publication Data
Elias, Jacob W., 1941-
   Remember the future : the pastoral theology of Paul the Apostle /
Jacob W. Elias.
      p. cm.
   Includes bibliographical references and index.
   ISBN 0-8361-9323-7 (pbk. : alk. paper)
   1. Bible. N.T. Epistles of Paul—Theology. 2. Bible. N.T. Epistles of
Paul—Criticism, Narrative. 3. Pastoral theology—History of
doctrines—Early church, ca. 30-600. I. Title.
   BS2655.P3E45 2006
   227'.06—dc22
                                                2005031496

REMEMBER THE FUTURE
Copyright © 2006 by Herald Press, Scottdale, Pa. 15683
   Published simultaneously in Canada by Herald Press,
   Waterloo, Ont. N2L 6H7. All rights reserved
Library of Congress Catalog Card Number: 2005031496
International Standard Book Number: 0-8361-9323-7
Printed in the United States of America
Book design by Sandra Johnson
Cover by Gwen Stamm

12 11 10 09 08 07 06 10 9 8 7 6 5 4 3 2 1

To order or request information, please call
1-800-759-4447 (individuals); 1-800-245-7894 (trade).
Web site: www.heraldpress.com

To our children, Laurel, Morlin, and Joylin,
and their families,
with appreciation and love.

ABBREVIATIONS

KJV   King James Version
LXX   Septuagint
NAB   New American Bible
NIV   New International Version
NRSV New Revised Standard Version
RSV   Revised Standard Version

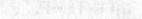

CONTENTS

9

FOREWORD

A generation ago I watched Sesame Street with my two preschool sons. Grover, the skinny blue Muppet who is slightly more academic than Big Bird or Cookie Monster, would hold forth on the nature of stories. "A story," he earnestly intoned while dancing around the screen, "always has a beginning, a middle, and an end." Having delighted in stories since my earliest memories, I recognized Grover's truth, although I never thought of it quite that way. Only later did I realize that his analysis came straight from the ancient Greek philosopher, Aristotle.

Think about it. We must begin somewhere, a once-upon-a-time moment when the setting is described, the characters introduced, and a problem or tension established. The middle of the story involves heroic adventures, the joys and disappointments of the main characters, the search for the Holy Grail or the white whale or the dragon's gold, or finding clues to the mystery, or the struggle against evil. The ending is just as essential. The hero wins the struggle, or the lovers live happily ever after, or the mystery is solved. We understand how stories work from the time we are three years old. And yet our scriptures and our theology are too often stripped of the high drama embedded in them, and are abstracted into systems of doctrines or principles of ethics. Thus we often misinterpret and misapply the very texts we deem authoritative.

Considering the wild excitement over the Harry Potter books and movies and the renewal of interest in the rich story imaginations of J. R. R. Tolkien and C. S. Lewis, this book by Jacob Elias is very timely. By coupling Paul's letters with careful research of the Greco-Roman world in which he lived, Elias creatively reconstructs Paul's own story and the stories of each congregation he planted around the Mediterranean world. Most chapters begin with an imaginative narrative about one or two characters connected to a particular church. This sets the stage for the content and argument of the letter or letters to that congregation. Priscilla and Aquila, Andronicus and Junia, Onesimus, Philemon, and many others remind us of the huge cast of characters that launched the story of the church in which we ourselves are current actors.

In these concrete settings, Paul's pastoral theology makes sense. In his debates and dialogues with local Christian believers, we see him less as a judgmental conservative and more like a daring liberal bringing the gospel of a Jewish savior to Gentiles—and not requiring them first to become law-observant Jews. As one of my students commented at the end of a college course on Paul, "Paul is so *human*. It seems like he's making things up as he goes along!" At some level that student is exactly right, for Paul had to confront issues in a pagan world that the Palestinian Jesus never did.

But Paul's letters also shine light on the larger story— or stories—of Jesus. Just as the Gospels tell one story of Jesus but with four different plots carrying four different theological emphases, so Paul sometimes tells Jesus's story as the royal son of David, sometimes as the new Adam, and sometimes as the eternally existing Wisdom incarnated in human form.

As a writer, actor, and stage director, Paul sees himself as only a small part of the greater drama of human history now beginning to be consummated in Jesus as the crucified and risen Lord. Elias's title, *Remember the Future*, reminds the reader that both we and Paul are characters living and acting in the extended "middle" of the greatest story ever told on earth. Grover's "end" has not yet arrived. Paul's story is shaped and driven by his hope of the future: hope grounded in *past* actions of God's creative power, of God's *present* mercy through the faithfulness of Jesus Christ, and of God's raising Jesus to eternal life as the guarantee of the *future* resurrection of all believers.

Remember the Future reminds me of the ending of the seventh and last book of C. S. Lewis's Narnia stories, *The Last Battle*. In this narrative, the lion Aslan and the children watch and participate in the cataclysmic events at the end of Narnia as they knew it. The new Narnia is dawning, and Aslan appears to them no longer as a lion. Lewis concludes: "For [the children] it was only the beginning of the real story. All their life in this world and all their adventures in Narnia had only been the cover and the title page: now at last they were beginning Chapter One of the Great Story which no one on earth has read; which goes on for ever; in which every chapter is better than the one before." Elias helps us articulate our own hope for a similar future through Paul's inspired vision.

Though not everyone will agree with all the details of Elias's reconstruction—or of Lewis's, for that matter—both are products of fertile imaginations leading us deeper into the bedrock of the story of the people of God and their hope of truly "living happily ever after."

Reta Halteman Finger
Assistant Professor of New Testament
Messiah College, Grantham, Pa.

PREFACE

At the Sunday dinner table with family and friends, I've heard it. During academic advising sessions with students and in class sessions dedicated to introducing Paul's letters, I sometimes hear it: "I don't like Paul."

Explanations vary for the reluctance to include Paul in an active personal canon. Several dominate: "Paul is down on women." Translated: "Anyone who silences women is no friend of mine." Another: "His letters are hard to understand." In elaborated form: "I can't follow Paul's thinking. His theology is too abstract. And I don't find his theology and ethics relevant to my daily life."

Among pastors I am aware of a similar ambivalence toward Paul. Some pastors are quite reluctant to preach from Pauline texts, because Paul's theology seems too complicated for people who want sermons to be practical. Preachers struggle with how to compete with readily available, fast-paced entertainment. In a culture that values stories, preachers are drawn to narrative biblical texts, or they share stories from their own experience, with isolated Scripture texts thrown in as support. It goes without saying that preachers inclined toward narrative preaching will be less likely to choose texts from Paul's letters than passages from the Gospels.

So even though people appreciate some popular texts in Paul's letters, the letters themselves are often neglected. The "love chapter" (1 Corinthians 13) has inspired many wedding meditations, but the Corinthian letters themselves do not enjoy that kind of attention. The triumphant climax in Romans 8 provides reassurance at funerals to families in their grief, but again the rest of the epistle to the Romans rarely receives equal coverage.

Similarly, there are a few passages that have become known as problem texts. Among these have been the texts that silence women, especially 1 Corinthians 14:34-35 and 1 Timothy 2:11-12. In the upheaval over homosexuality, several passages in the Pauline corpus have been debated by people on all sides of the struggle: Romans 1:26-27; 1 Corinthians 6:9-11; 1 Timothy 1:10. Romans 13 has been a problematic text as well, because it has sometimes been interpreted as sanctioning unquestioned obedience to governments, including those that act in oppressive and violent ways.

What then should one do with Paul? Judged to espouse an abstract and irrelevant theology and a socially conservative ethic, Paul is suspect among many postmoderns. Except for several favored or hotly contested passages, Paul and his letters seem at times to be better shoved off to the side.

Yet thirteen of the twenty-seven documents in the New Testament are written by or in the name of Paul. Any dismissal of these letters from the operative canon disregards a major resource within the New Testament, the church's living tradition.

My writing of this book has been motivated by the premise that Paul's contribution to the church in the first century needs to be heard anew by the church at the beginning of the twenty-first. Paul was a missionary whose preaching of the gospel led to the formation of new assemblies of believers. He was a pastor caring for and teaching and encouraging and warning these communities of faith. His theology was pastoral. He sought to relate the good news of the gospel of Jesus Christ to the social, cultural, political, and religious contexts in which these congregations found themselves. In these and many other ways this first-century apostolic missionary pastor continues to speak the gospel to the church for the sake of her participation in God's mission to the world.

As a pastor and theological educator on behalf of the church, I seek to identify with this first-century pastoral theologian in his ministry to various congregations in the Mediterranean world. I also desire to do some of the interpretation necessary to ease Paul's letters onto the mental and spiritual horizons of pastors, Sunday school teachers, college and seminary students, and other Bible readers in this later era. Paul's pastoral theological endeavors in his time need to have their analogs in ours.

Two methodological commitments significantly shape my approach.

During the transition into the third millennium there has been a pronounced tendency in some circles toward accenting a predictive reading of apocalyptic texts, including some in the Pauline corpus. My intention is to bring out the future-oriented, though not predictive, character of Paul's pastoral interventions. Paul longs for the congregations in his care to remember the future toward which God is pointing them through Jesus Christ. Paul provides a roadmap, not a calendar, into the future.

A second commitment is to pursue a narrative approach to Paul's pastoral theology and ethics. Even though Paul utilized the letter form as his medium for engaging the real-life issues of the congregations in his orbit, he is profoundly shaped by story. The stories arise from Paul's own life experiences, especially his turnaround from persecutor of the church to proponent of the gospel. The macro-narrative of Jesus's cosmic career supplies a focal dynamic for his theology. The earlier story of the

Israelite people, up to and including their exile among the nations, forms the backdrop within which Jesus's story emerges and shapes meaning. And each of the congregations has its own story as well. Part of the strategic intent in this volume is to trace the underlying narratives out of which Paul's theology and ethics function.

In pursuing a future-oriented narrative approach to Paul's theology, I am profoundly influenced by the work of other Pauline scholars. I mention several whose interpretive work has deeply shaped my own understanding of this first century apostle to the Gentiles. J. Christiaan Beker and J. Louis Martyn, among others, have helped me to explore the apocalyptic framework of Paul's pastoral thought. As this book's bibliography illustrates, books and articles by N. T. Wright and Richard B. Hays feature strongly in my repertoire, especially in their contribution to an understanding of Paul's appropriation of the biblical texts and their theological and ethical themes.

Narrative approaches to Paul's theology have begun to appear on the scene with some regularity. Richard B. Hays' dissertation on the narrative substructure of Galatians 3:1–4:11 (first published in 1983) illustrates this approach as applied to a particular letter. The 1994 book by Ben Witherington III *Paul's Narrative Thought World: The Tapestry of Tragedy and Triumph* (Westminster John Knox Press) provided an early model for a thoroughgoing narrative approach. A. Katherine Grieb's *The Story of Romans: A Narrative Defense of God's Righteousness* (Westminster John Knox Press, 2002) illustrates well the fruitfulness of the effort to delineate narratives underlying Paul's major theological treatise addressed to the churches in Rome. A collection of papers edited by Bruce W. Longenecker under the title *Narrative Dynamics in Paul: A Critical Assessment* (Westminster John Knox Press, 2002) represents an attempt to assess the pros and cons of a narrative approach, with focus especially on Galatians and Romans. Michael J. Gorman entitles his book *Cruciformity*, but it is the subtitle that announces his intention: *Paul's Narrative Spirituality of the Cross* (Eerdmans, 2001). Gorman's later book, *Apostle of the Crucified Lord: A Theological Introduction to Paul and His Letters* (Eerdmans, 2004) enlarges on this narrative theme by surveying the entire Pauline corpus, always beginning his treatment of a given letter with a section entitled "The Story Behind the Letter." During the final stages of moving my manuscript toward publication I acquired Douglas A. Campbell's *The Quest for Paul's Gospel: A Suggested Strategy* (T. & T. Clark International, 2005); this book also accents the narrative dimensions of Paul's gospel.

My interpretation of Paul's theology and ethics has also been shaped significantly by my interactions with other contemporary readers of his letters. Particularly important to me have been my students at Associated Mennonite Biblical Seminary, Elkhart, Indiana, among whom I have been studying Paul's letters since the 1980s. Members of my Pauline Theology and Ethics class in 2000, 2002, and 2003 read the manuscript-in-process and reflected affirmatively and critically on it.

In my congregational ministry as co-pastor with my wife Lillian I frequently take the opportunity to feature Pauline epistle texts in my sermons. These preaching assignments always pose a key test: Does the approach to Paul's letters that I advocate in the classroom and in this book preach? A related crucial test is whether younger generations (including our children and grandchildren to whom this book is dedicated) will find themselves drawn into the gospel Story and the personal and congregational stories underlying these letters.

A group of eight interested adults in the Parkview Mennonite Church, Kokomo, Indiana, met with me during the summer and fall of 2002 to discuss what I was writing and to offer feedback from their perspectives. I acknowledge with gratitude the evaluation and advice that these persons shared with me. They reassured me that a narrative approach to Paul's letters does make them more intelligible for motivated readers.

I have been keenly aware as well that, in continuity with the Jewish apostle to the Gentiles, I need to take the plunge cross-culturally. Several teaching experiences have aided me in this effort. I am indebted to my students at Union Biblical Seminary in Pune, India (1991), and Good News Theological College and Seminary, Accra, Ghana (1999), where I had the privilege of reading Paul's letters in cultures not my own. In April and May, 2005, I taught and preached from Paul's letters in South Korea and Japan.

My half-year sabbaticals from my normal teaching responsibilities at Associated Mennonite Biblical Seminary in 1999 and 2005 afforded me the time first to launch and then to complete the work on this manuscript. Some research units between those sabbaticals also gave me opportunity to continue this project. I am grateful to my administrators and colleagues who made this time available. In addition I acknowledge the contribution of my faculty colleagues who devoted two Faculty Teaching and Research Seminars in critical engagement with several early chapters. This included some discussion about what I mean by "pastoral theology" in the subtitle of the book. I had not thought carefully about what kinds of expectations this description might raise among people active professionally within the discipline of practical or pastoral theology. My colleague Daniel Schipani, professor of pastoral care and counseling, helped me to articulate more clearly.

I am attempting to discern Paul's "middle-level theology" as apostle and pastor engaging the real-life dynamics of actual congregations in their contexts. In his letters Paul is not a systematic or philosophical "professional" theologian thinking abstractly. Nor is he a grassroots local "lay" theologian trying to understand what God is doing and what kind of life choices are faithful. Within his calling as apostle Paul draws on his own experience of the risen Christ, his training and background in the Scriptures, and his acquaintance with various faith communities to offer them theological counsel and communicate a vision for their faithfulness in light of God's still emerging future. That too is our calling as pastors, teachers, missionaries, and other followers of Jesus in our day.

Jacob W. Elias
Advent 2005

AN OVERVIEW

The organization and content of this book reflect the fruit of my attempts to balance several agendas.

One of my primary goals is to hear the stories that surface in Paul's pastoral letters. Dynamic listening to the interwoven narratives needs to include discernment of how these narratives intersect with the life and mission of the various communities of faith being addressed by Paul's letters. A propositional approach to Paul's theology and ethics cannot do justice to such a dynamic phenomenon. Surveys of Paul's foundational doctrines of faith tend to rely on a more flat reading of his letters, a reading that often pays inadequate attention to the contextual factors that shape their content.

Closely linked to my goal of hearing the formative stories that are imbedded within Paul's pastoral correspondence to scattered congregations is my desire to deal in a focused way with each of his letters. When tracing the contours of Paul's pastoral theology in the chapters that follow, I make an effort to give careful attention to each of the Pauline letters. However, I also needed to decide in what order I would deal with these letters. Many such treatments of the Pauline epistles take them in canonical order. In a narrative approach, I decided, it would make more sense to deal with them in their chronological order, insofar as that sequence can be established.

In significant tension with this commitment to pursue a narrative approach and to focus on each letter separately in their historical sequence is another goal, namely, to articulate Paul's major theological and ethical themes in a more systematic fashion. Each chapter beyond the introductory one includes several essays on the overall theme that is emphasized in the earlier narrative-based discussion of the featured letter.

After weighing a variety of possible patterns, I settled on an eclectic organization that attempts to accommodate a thematic survey of Paul's pastoral theology within a narrative paradigm. Each reader of this book will have the opportunity to assess how well the competing priorities have been managed.

Part 1, Paul's Vision of the Future, is made up of two chapters. The first chapter features Paul's recollections of his own story, his upbringing in the traditions of his Jewish ancestors, his experience as a Pharisee, and his climactic encounter with the living Christ and call to be an apostle to the Gentiles. Also included in chapter 1 is the reminder that Paul's life needs to be viewed within first-century Jewish experience with the dominant Greco-Roman cultural and political realities. Further allusions to Paul's story and the story of first-century Judaism appear occasionally throughout this study.

The story of Jesus is our focus in chapter 2. Paul's letter to the Philippians receives primary attention, in particular the hymn that he quotes in Philippians 2:5-11. Given the transformative impact of Paul's encounter with Jesus Christ, it seems important to begin a survey of his theology with an exploration of his Christology. More powerfully in Philippians than anywhere else, Paul explicitly articulates the normative character of Christ's life and obedience for all who confess Jesus as Lord. It is also significant that Jesus's story as poetically recounted in Philippians 2:5-11 is part of the tradition that Paul receives from the church and its worship. Having received this character-shaping narrative from the church, Paul passes it on by way of encouragement and reminder to the congregation in Philippi.

Paul's choice to quote a christological hymn that had come to him from the life and worship of the earlier church also suggests rationale for my decision to feature Philippians as the first letter to be surveyed. The fact that Philippians was written while Paul was in prison would suggest that our treatment of this letter should appear later alongside the other captivity epistles, Philemon, Colossians, and Ephesians (treated in chapters 10–12). However, it seems appropriate to follow the discussion of Paul's apocalypse of Jesus Christ in chapter 1 with an exploration of how Paul joins the early church in its worshipful telling of the story of Jesus and its celebration of Christ's lordship.

Throughout this survey of Paul's pastoral theology we note the normative function of the story of Jesus in Paul's correspondence with the churches. The story of Jesus is, of course, often assumed as the shared formative narrative for each of the communities he addresses, and therefore it is normally not explicitly recited by Paul in his letters. However, the story of Christ crucified and raised is the paradigmatic narrative that shapes community identity, theology, and ethics for Paul.

In the five chapters of part 2, God's Unfolding Story, we examine Paul's telling of that story as narrated in Scripture. As becomes evident in any reading of his pastoral correspondence to the churches, Paul has not cut himself off from the traditions of his ancestors. He regards the story of his people Israel as recounted in the Scriptures as foundational for the church, even as he interprets these traditions and these Scriptures in light of God's climactic revelation in Christ.

The five chapters in part 2 deal with foundational theological themes: creation and redemption, call and prom-

ise, covenant and law, Israel and the nations, and salvation
and judgment. In each chapter, the beginning focus is on a
particular letter where the identified theme is developed,
and then the scope is broadened to include the rest of the
Pauline corpus. The epistles examined here in a primary
way are 1 Corinthians (chapter 3), Romans (chapters 4
and 6), 2 Corinthians (chapter 5), and 1 and 2
Thessalonians (chapter 7). I have chosen here to follow the
grand story, God's own story from creation to consummation, instead of seeking to treat Paul's letters in a chronological order or in the canonical sequence. This is the holy
history of the one God, the creator of all, the God who
chose the descendants of Abraham and Sarah to be chan-
nels of blessing and salvation available potentially to all. It
is the story of the God who entered into covenant with
Hebrew slaves rescued from Egypt and gave them the law
at Sinai, the God who chose Israel to be a light to all the
nations. It is the expansive narrative of the God who will
yet restore Israel from their exile, vindicate the faithful,
and triumph over all enemy powers.

The five chapters that make up part 3, A Community
Shaped by the Future, explore the dynamic shaping of the
community of faith in light of what God has already done
and will yet do in Christ. Discernible in Paul's letters are
the stories of grace and disgrace among first-century congregations and individuals, who worship and struggle and
make decisions and cope with conflict and deal with life's
issues. In his letters Paul offers pastoral care to these persons and congregations located in Asia Minor, Macedonia
and Achaia, and even Rome.

Theological and ethical themes approached from a
narrative perspective in part 3 include God's righteousness,
and justification; the Spirit and participation in Christ;
faithfulness, freedom, and love; sexuality and holiness; and

the church and the powers. The chapter titles in part 3 are framed so as to provide a generic narrative template of Christian communal experience: Freed by an invasion of God's grace, and participating with Christ in the empowerment of the Holy Spirit, the various communities of faith live within transformed relationships in households of a new order that engage the surrounding culture as warriors with God.

The letters receiving primary attention in part 3 are Galatians (chapters 8 and 9), Philemon (chapter 10), Colossians (chapter 11), and Ephesians (chapter 12). The order in which the letters in this section are discussed is chronological. We begin with the earliest letter, Galatians, and then dedicate a chapter to each of the captivity letters: Philemon, Colossians, and Ephesians.

In part 4, Therefore, Remember the Future! I give attention to the Pastoral Epistles, which supply a natural conclusion to our tracing of the developing story of Paul's pastoral theological enterprise. Throughout this entire exploration of Paul's pastoral theology, a basic premise is that Paul is deeply shaped by the conviction that what God has done in Christ is a preview of the future. In the concluding chapter, which deals with suffering, death, and hope, this premise is made explicit. The three letters to Paul's delegates, the Pastoral Epistles (Titus, 1 Timothy, and 2 Timothy), are given specific attention here.

Part 1

Paul's Vision of the Future

INTRODUCTION

Paul grew up in the eastern region of the vast Roman Empire. Living in a Jewish community in the Roman province of Cilicia, he learned Greek language and culture firsthand. Paul was also educated in the Torah. As a young man he affiliated with the Pharisees, becoming a zealous advocate for that brand of Judaism.

But then the course of Paul's life took a radical turn. The ardent Pharisee encountered the risen Christ. In the person and work of Jesus of Nazareth, the Jewish rabbi who was executed on a Roman cross but was acknowledged by groups of his followers around the Mediterranean to be the cosmic Lord of the universe, Paul caught a vision of the future. And his contribution as apostle of Jesus Christ dramatically influenced the course of subsequent history.

In part 1 of this study we intend to get in touch with the story of Paul, the Pharisee who became the apostle to the Gentiles. And we want to listen to the witness of the church concerning Jesus, the crucified Lord. In his character-shaping pastoral letter to the congregation in Philippi Paul recalls one of the early church's hymns concerning Jesus the Messiah.

Christians need frequent reminders that, like Jesus, Paul was a first-century Jew. Among scholars who have tried to understand Paul there have been fellow Jews who do not share Paul's conviction that Jesus is the Messiah.

Joseph Klausner lamented Paul's reading of Judaism; according to Klausner, Paul represented a contaminated Hellenized form of his ancestral religion (1943:450-66, 600-10). Alan F. Segal describes Paul as a mystic whose departures from traditional Judaism made him "painfully close to apostasy" (1990:277). Daniel Boyarin regards Paul as a radical Jew whose universalizing message moved him to a vigorous cultural critique of his inherited faith (1994:52-6). Mark Nanos has focused especially on a rereading of the underlying ethnic tensions behind Paul's letters to the Romans (1996) and Galatians (2002b).

Some Jews have accepted Jesus as the Messiah, but only rarely do writings about Paul by messianic Jews come to public attention. One such is Menahem Benhayim, whose slim volume on alleged anti-Semitism in the New Testament includes a brief treatment of Paul's contribution (1985:49-64). Most of Paul's interpreters over the centuries have not been Jewish. And many Gentile students of his letters have not adequately recognized Paul's roots in Scripture and first-century Judaism.

There may be numerous reasons for the common portrait of Paul as severed from his Jewish origins. Paul himself bears part of the blame. His vigorous testimony to his transforming vision of Christ crucified and exalted leads him at times to develop stark contrasts between his present experience with God through Jesus Christ and his earlier understanding of God. So eloquent are some of Paul's acclamations about Jesus Christ that the points of continuity with his roots within Judaism seem significantly diminished or even dismantled.

There are, however, significant continuities between Paul's theological roots as a Pharisee and his career as apostle to the Gentiles. Paul's roots in the Hebrew Bible will be explored in part 2, God's Unfolding Story. For now, as we begin our exploration of the pastoral theology of Paul the apostle, we focus on his testimony to his life-transforming personal experience with Jesus Christ.

In a dramatic apocalypse of Jesus Christ, Paul had glimpsed the future, and that future is now breaking in! This vision generated Paul's passion as apostle to the Gentiles and as itinerant pastor, who resorted to writing letters to scattered congregations in the first-century Mediterranean world when he could not be personally present with them.

1

PAUL'S STORY:
FROM PERSECUTOR TO PROCLAIMER

Before we hear Paul tell his own story, we can gain a larger picture by listening to how a fellow Jew of his day might have pondered the circumstances in which the Jewish people find themselves. Let us imagine an individual (we'll call him Ehud) living in the Judean hills adjacent to the city of Jerusalem in about the year A.D. 33. Ehud does not personally know Paul but he has heard about how Paul first persecuted a new Jewish sect and then became an active leader and advocate within it.

Paul's letter to the Galatians (1:11-24), 1 Maccabees chapters 1 and 2, and Flavius Josephus' The Wars of the Jews (2:117-166; 7:409-19) supply some of the primary background material for this brief narrative. Numerous scholars (among them Robert Jewett, Jerome Murphy-O'Connor, Rainer Riesner, and Ben Witherington III) have attempted to reconstruct the dates of Paul's life within the context of his times. The following narrative builds on this scholarly work without seeking to resolve numerous issues that continue to baffle the specialists.

A STORY: What Is the Story Behind Paul's Story?

What did it take for a Jew living in the Roman world to be faithful to the living and true God?

This question seemed urgent whether one lived in the Judean hills close to Jerusalem or one was a diaspora Jew settled in lands far away from the Holy City. Ehud realized that Tiberius was like all the Roman emperors before him. Through governors, such as Pontius Pilate in Judea, and puppet kings, such as Herod Antipas in Galilee, the emperor imposed taxes and tried to keep subject populations in line. He clearly expected allegiance.

For Ehud and other Jews living under the thumb of pagan rulers, the dilemma became acute. How could a person remain faithful to the one true God? Could one recite the Shema (Deuteronomy 6:4) in the synagogue on the Sabbath, confessing that God is sovereign, then during the week declare loyalty to Caesar within the imperial cult? Given that God is supreme over all powers, what kind of allegiance could one offer to Caesar?

The virtues and attractions of the dominant Greco-Roman culture also had strong appeal, even among subject minority groups like the Jews. This was especially the case with the youth. Ehud's own children sometimes asked him, "Why can't we take part in athletic events in the Roman gymnasiums?" He often responded by retelling the story of Daniel, who at great risk to himself resisted the pressure to conform to the ways of people around him. Or he told his children about the Maccabean revolutionaries.

In the revolutionaries' day, a sinful king named Antiochus Epiphanes had demanded that the Jews live like everyone else. A gymnasium was built in the holy city Jerusalem, and some Jewish boys even tried to remove the marks of their circumcision in order to participate in the games without drawing attention to themselves as different or strange. Other families stayed firm in their commitment to the holy covenant; their children did not participate in the games. Pressure on the Jewish people to con-

Paul the Pharisee

Paul characterizes his former life within Judaism as that of a zealot passionately committed to the traditions of his ancestors. His zeal moved him to a fierce and violent persecution of the church with the intention of getting rid of this heretical sect:

> You have heard, no doubt, of my earlier life in Judaism.
> I was violently persecuting the church of God and was
> trying to destroy it. I advanced in Judaism beyond many
> among my people of the same age, for I was far more
> zealous for the traditions of my ancestors. (Galatians
> 1:13-14)

When he recalls his past for the believers in the Galatian churches, Paul apparently assumes that they will understand what had earlier motivated him to engage in such frenzied acts of violence against the followers of Jesus. However, later readers of Paul's letter are not privy to this shared knowledge.

As a Pharisee pondering what it means for the Jewish community to be faithful to God, Paul appears to have embraced the more activist stance of the school of Shammai. When weighing what devotion to God entails for Jews living within Caesar's empire, Paul the Pharisee seems ideologically close to the *sicarii*. These were Jewish activists whose fervor for the Torah and disdain for the Roman occupiers led them to murder fellow Jews who were considered to be collaborators with Rome. Paul might also have had empathy for the Zealots who began to plot guerrilla-type military action against the Roman occupiers of Judea. A futile resistance effort actually broke out a few years later in the disastrous Jewish war of A.D. 66-70.

According to Luke, Paul received his rabbinic training

in Jerusalem within the school of the more moderate Hillel (Acts 22:3). Paul testified that Gamaliel had taught him the way of Torah. However, like many students who differentiate themselves ideologically from their teachers, Paul the zealous Pharisee obviously did not assume Gamaliel's "live and let live" posture toward the nascent messianic movement. As portrayed earlier in Acts, Gamaliel had cautioned his comrades in the Jewish council concerning the apostles Peter and John:

> So in the present case, I tell you, keep away from these
> men and let them alone; because if this plan or this under-
> taking is of human origin, it will fail; but if it is of God,
> you will not be able to overthrow them—in that case you
> may even be found fighting against God! (Acts 5:38-39)

Paul the Pharisee did not share this lenient sentiment. A zealot for God's law, Paul knew beyond any doubt that this messianic minority group was displeasing to God, and it needed to be eradicated before such heresy infected the whole community of Israel. Not only were these messianic Jews treating the Torah's clear guidelines for faithfulness to God with contempt; by flirting with godless Gentiles they compromised the boundaries between God's covenant people and their neighbors.

Paul's Personal Apocalypse

It was while he engaged in this relentless pursuit of the followers of Jesus that Paul experienced firsthand the sovereign intervention of God. In his epistle to the Galatians Paul calls this tumultuous event in his life "a revelation of Jesus Christ" (1:12). The more literal rendering, "an apocalypse of Jesus Christ," communicates more forcefully what Paul claims to have experienced. Paul knew that the protagonist had been none other than God, "who had set me apart before I was born and had called me through his grace" (1:15). In describing this transforming moment Paul uses language that echoes the call of the Old Testament prophets (see Jeremiah 1:4-10; Isaiah 49:1-6). But, unlike these prophets, Paul experienced God's preemptive strike in an apocalypse, a dramatic revelation of God's Son: "[God] was pleased to reveal his Son to me" (1:16).

Face-to-face with the risen and exalted Christ, Paul the persecutor came to a screeching turn in his vocation. The substance and direction of God's call on his life became clear: "that I might proclaim him [Christ] among the Gentiles" (1:16). Still zealous for God, Paul began to preach the faith he had once sought to eradicate. By the time he writes Galatians, possibly in about A.D. 49, Paul had already been actively involved for up to three years in Arabia (1:17-18) and for some fourteen years in the regions of Syria and Cilicia (1:21; 2:1). Paul himself says next to nothing about these years, and Acts provides but scant information (Acts 9:26-30). Presumably he was proclaiming the gospel during this time, along with the work of theological reframing which his transforming encounter with Christ had thrust upon him. Later his evangelistic activity led to the founding of a church in the Galatian region in Asia Minor, as his letter to the Galatian churches attests. In a moment of disarming candor in his letter to the Galatians, Paul recalls that time in a way that gives testimony to how his life has become enfolded by the crucified and risen Christ, whom he now preaches:

> You know that it was because of a physical infirmity that I first announced the gospel to you; though my condition put you to the test, you did not scorn or despise me, but welcomed me as an angel of God, as Christ Jesus. (4:13-14)

Paul's pastoral letters to other congregations also contain occasional allusions to his life-changing encounter
with Jesus Christ. When he writes to the church at
Philippi, Paul feels compelled by circumstances to describe
his impeccable Jewish credentials:

> If anyone else has reason to be confident in the flesh, I
> have more:
> > circumcised on the eighth day,
> > a member of the people of Israel,
> > of the tribe of Benjamin,
> > a Hebrew born of Hebrews;
> > as to the law, a Pharisee;
> > as to zeal, a persecutor of the church;
> > as to righteousness under the law, blameless.
> (Philippians 3:5-6)

Paul does not seem to have been struggling with a guilty
conscience prior to the revelation of the risen Christ to
him. Nor does Paul even hint that he views himself as severed from his roots as an Israelite, a Hebrew, and a zealous
Pharisee. He does, however, point clearly to the fact that,
having come to know Christ Jesus as Lord, he now regards
even his outstanding pedigree as mere rubbish by contrast:

> Yet whatever gains I had, these I have come to regard
> as loss because of Christ. More than that, I regard
> everything as loss because of the surpassing value of
> knowing Christ Jesus my Lord. (Philippians 3:7-8a)

When he addresses the church at Corinth, Paul points
to his vision of the risen Christ as proof of his apostleship:
"Am I not an apostle? Have I not seen Jesus our Lord?"
(1 Corinthians 9:1). In another of his moments of candor
he refers to himself in 1 Corinthians 15:8 as "one untimely

born," perhaps because the appearance of the Lord to him came out of sequence with that of the other witnesses and apostles (15:3-7). Paul also adds his own further explanation: "For I am the least of the apostles, unfit to be called an apostle, because I persecuted the church of God" (15:9).

Paul's Later Recall of God's Work in His Life

In his later letter to the church at Corinth, Paul appears to be reflecting with awe on the mystery of God's ongoing creative and redemptive work in his life:

> It is the God who said, "'Let light shine out of darkness'" who has shone in our hearts to give the light of the knowledge of the glory of God in the face of Jesus Christ. (2 Corinthians 4:6)

Paradoxically this glory shines from the crucified Jesus, and also from the suffering apostle and the suffering church (4:7-12; 6:3-10). This paradox even invites Paul to do some boasting, in which he compares his own credentials with those of his rivals in Corinth:

> Are they Hebrews? So am I. Are they Israelites? So am I. Are they descendants of Abraham? So am I. Are they ministers of Christ? I am talking like a madman—I am a far better one. (2 Corinthians 11:22-23)

Paul's boast accents his hardships (11:23-29) and his close calls (11:30-33). And when he does recount his "visions and revelations of the Lord" (12:1-10), he highlights a struggle with an otherwise unidentified "thorn in the flesh" that keeps him from becoming too elated by such spiritual highs (12:7).

In Romans 7 Paul employs "I" language to speak about another struggle:

> I was once alive apart from the law, but when the com-
> mandment came, sin revived and I died, and the very
> commandment that promised life proved to be death
> to me. (7:9-10)

> For we know that the law is spiritual; but I am of the
> flesh, sold into slavery under sin. I do not understand
> my own actions. For I do not do what I want, but I do
> the very thing I hate. (7:14-15)

This wearying tug-of-war, which involves sin, the law, the
flesh, and the inmost self as combatants in an ongoing
struggle, leads Paul to cry out, "Wretched man that I am!
Who will rescue me from this body of death?" (7:24). Yet
in this struggle, anguish and despair do not have the last
word. Paul blurts out his gratitude to God: "Thanks be to
God through Jesus Christ our Lord!" (7:25).

How are Paul's groans and his gratitude in Romans 7
related to his experience of God's grace? His later readers
have often wondered whether Paul here recalls his own personal struggle, and if so, whether this struggle occurs before
his encounter with the risen Christ or as an ongoing battle
with sin after his life-transforming experience. Likely Paul
here speaks representatively for all of humanity (descendants
of Adam) and not only about his own experience. As Paul
himself testifies from his own personal pilgrimage, Christ has
come into the world, and even though sin still seeks to
enslave, the victory of God's triumphant grace is sure.

Even in his final letters, Paul or perhaps a co-worker
writing on his behalf continues to marvel at God's gracious
calling. As prisoner for Jesus Christ on behalf of the
Gentiles, Paul recalls the revelation of the mystery made
known in Christ. He remembers the commission God had
given him as "the very least of all the saints" to bring to

the Gentiles the news of the boundless grace of Christ (Ephesians 3:1-13). Similarly in 1 Timothy 1:12-14, the former "blasphemer, persecutor, and man of violence" expresses amazement that he had received God's mercy and grace and even a call to apostolic service, despite his former ignorance and unbelief.

A dramatic signal of the momentous consequences of Paul's transformation and apostolic calling comes in what amounts to his final testimony. In 2 Timothy, the former persecutor testifies that ironically he has himself suffered the kind of violence that he had earlier wreaked on others:

> Now you have observed my teaching, my conduct, my aim in life, my patience, my love, my steadfastness, my persecutions, and my suffering the things that happened to me in Antioch, Iconium, and Lystra. What persecutions I endured! Yet the Lord rescued me from all of them. (3:10-12)

Nearing the end of his own life he gratefully gives witness to the Lord's rescuing power in the face of all of the threatening circumstances he had endured.

When Paul Refers to Himself

Besides these occasional autobiographical comments in Galatians, Philippians, and elsewhere, Paul supplies a repertoire of self-descriptions. His letter openings provide glimpses into how he reflects personally and theologically on his identity and calling. Paul frequently employs the term *apostle* when he begins his letters: 1 Corinthians 1:1; 2 Corinthians 1:1; Romans 1:1; Galatians 1:1; Ephesians 1:1; Colossians 1:1; 1 Timothy 1:1; 2 Timothy 1:1; Titus 1:1. He also draws on the image of himself as a servant or slave (the underlying Greek word *doulos* is better translated "slave") in several of the letter openings: Romans 1:1; Philippians 1:1; Titus 1:1. In Philemon 1 Paul refers to himself as "a prisoner for Christ Jesus."

Each of these self-designations also appears within the letters themselves. In Galatians Paul is at pains to qualify the nature of his ministry: "Paul an apostle—sent neither by human commission nor from human authorities but through Jesus Christ and God the Father" (1:1). The struggle for identity taking place in the Galatian Christian community elicits from Paul a posture that emphasizes his authority as apostle (1:6-11). Yet even within the stern rhetoric of his letter to the Galatians Paul draws on maternal imagery to woo his readers away from the choices that he fears will put them at risk: "My little children, for whom I am again in the pain of childbirth until Christ is formed in you" (4:19). As an apostle Paul conveys the tough love of a self-giving and nurturing mother.

Paul does not include any self-designation in his salutations in the two Thessalonian letters, but in 1 Thessalonians 2 he reflects at length on the character of his apostolic ministry. He strikingly uses a series of kinship metaphors to highlight the gentle, nurturing, and encouraging qualities of the apostle of Christ. He had come into Thessalonica on his apostolic mission not as a demanding autocrat but like a child (2:7a), a mother (2:7b), a father (2:11), and even an orphan (2:17). Though Paul nowhere calls himself a pastor, he frequently draws on family images to describe his pastoral relationship with the churches he has established. This is certainly true in his correspondence with the church at Corinth, where he also employs both maternal and paternal images:

I fed you with milk, not solid food. (1 Corinthians 3:2)

In Christ Jesus I became your father through the
gospel. (1 Corinthians 4:15)

Even when he admonishes the Corinthian believers, Paul
conveys warm affection and parental concern:

We have spoken frankly to you Corinthians; our heart
is wide open to you. There is no restriction in our
affections, but only in yours. In return—I speak as to
children—open wide your hearts also. (2 Corinthians
6:11-12)

Having seen the risen Lord and having received a commission to go to the Gentiles (1 Corinthians 9:1; 15:8;
Galatians 1:11-17), Paul recognizes that his calling as apostle has divine authorization. On those occasions when his
apostolic calling was being challenged Paul sometimes
engaged in a spirited defense, especially in 2 Corinthians 10-
13. However, this defense is mounted from within a recognition of the character of his apostolic ministry. As apostle,
Paul has been molded in identification with the suffering and
exalted Christ who had been revealed to him: 2 Corinthians
4:7-8; 6:3-10; 11:23–12:10; cf. also 1 Corinthians 4:9-13.

The character of the one sent as apostle to the nations
is also portrayed through the imagery of slavery. In chapter 2, The Story of Jesus, we will see that in the church's
hymn in Philippians 2:6-11 Jesus is eulogized as one who
was formed in the divine image but became a slave. The
epistle to the Philippians begins with Paul and Timothy
introducing themselves as slaves (1:1), and it includes a
strong appeal for the Philippians to have the mind of the
self-giving Christ (2:5). In Romans, the other epistle in
which Paul gives himself the identifying tag *slave* (1:1 in
NRSV footnote), Paul dwells at length on the conse-

quences of the believer's choice to identify with the crucified and risen Christ. The one enslaved by Christ is ultimately free: free from sin and death, free to do God's will, and therefore free to live in the fullness of God's grace (Romans 6:15-23). Behind Paul's pastoral rhetoric about freedom as Christ's slave there is surely a significant level of apostolic self-disclosure as well.

Closely related to the slavery theme is Paul's identification of himself as *prisoner*. In Philemon Paul twice classifies himself as "a prisoner of Christ Jesus" (Philemon 1, 9), and he also mentions his "imprisonment for the gospel" (13). Ephesians 3:1 refers to Paul'as "a prisoner for Christ Jesus for the sake of you Gentiles." The launching of the ethical appeal in Ephesians 4:1 comes from "the prisoner in the Lord." Significantly the appeal is framed with the qualities of humility, gentleness, patience, love, and eagerness to maintain unity and peace (4:2). Out of his experience of actual imprisonment Paul introduces an eloquent appeal for his hearers to live in conformity to Jesus Christ, in whose service there is freedom.

Paul's Experience as Pattern?

Does Paul commend his "Damascus road experience" to others? Paul's face-to-face encounter with the risen Christ has often been held up as a pattern for conversion, a pattern characterized by a distinct "before" and "after." Those who view Paul's experience not as a conversion to a new religious commitment but as his calling as a Jew to be apostle to the Gentiles understand him to have changed direction within his religious community rather than charting a new direction beyond it. Having been zealous in his devotion to God as a Pharisee, Paul expressed a similar zeal as Jewish apostle now embracing a messianic Jewish mission to Gentiles. Beverly

Roberts Gaventa talks about Paul's transformation and calling (1986:40-6). But the question remains: Does Paul seek to have others experience a similar kind of transformation?

When Paul employs the language of imitation he does not hold up his Damascus road experience as the paradigm of transformation for others to seek to emulate. In his letters Paul nowhere seems to describe his evangelistic approach as that of arousing a sense of personal guilt and advocating an acceptance of Christ for the forgiveness of sins. In his first letter to the church at Thessalonica, Paul does rehearse with remarkable detail the story of the conversion of the Thessalonians:

> Our message of the gospel came to you not in word only, but also in power and in the Holy Spirit and with full conviction; just as you know what kind of persons we proved to be among you for your sake. And you became imitators of us and of the Lord. (1 Thessalonians 1:5-6a)

However, it is not a "Damascus road conversion" that is being imitated. Rather Paul points out to the Thessalonians that in their suffering they became imitators of both Jesus and the evangelists:

> You became imitators of us and of the Lord, for in spite of persecution you received the word with joy inspired by the Holy Spirit. (1:6b)

Paul summarizes:

> You turned to God from idols, to serve a living and true God, and to wait for his Son from heaven, whom he raised from the dead—Jesus, who rescues us from the wrath that is coming. (1:9b-10)

By turning to God and serving God and awaiting the crucified and risen Son the afflicted Thessalonian believers are reliving Jesus's life and anticipating in Jesus's victory over death their own rescue from coming wrath.

In sum, Paul commends not a "Damascus road conversion" experience but the imitation of Christ. He testifies that he and his co-workers aim to live in conformity to the Christ who suffered, died, and was raised. In 1 Thessalonians Paul reassures the suffering believers that their afflictions attest that what had happened to Jesus (1:6), to Paul himself (2:1), and to the churches in Judea (2:15) was also being replayed among them. In their faithfulness to God and their consequent suffering, they, like Paul, were imitators of Christ.

Paul also attests in his other letters that it is in the weakness of Christ crucified that God's power is revealed. Such weakness is embodied in apostolic suffering (1 Corinthians 4:8-13), which others are invited to share: "I appeal to you, then, be imitators of me" (4:16). It is expressed in the Christlike readiness to deny personal rights for the sake of others (1 Corinthians 9:1-27; 10:31–11:1). The calling to manifest the mind of Christ involves a self-emptying for the sake of knowing the power of Christ's resurrection (Philippians 3:17).

Paul therefore does present himself as a model for believers to follow. However, this is the model of self-giving love in anticipation of God's vindicating rescue. Jesus and the apostles suffered. So also, in imitation of Christ and the apostles, the church may suffer in testifying to the gospel of the crucified and risen Christ.

Paul's Story and His Theology

Having pondered briefly Paul's own self-conscious reflections about his career as a zealous Pharisee and his transformation and calling through Christ, we pause to ask about implications for our understanding of his theology. Before outlining a narrative approach to Paul's pastoral theology we do well to give some attention to the chronological sequence of events in Paul's apostolic ministry, including the developments that occasioned the writing of his letters. As has been noted, Paul's willingness to share from his personal and spiritual journey is often elicited by the contentious local and regional circumstances of the congregations that he addresses in his pastoral letters. But what is the chronological framework for Paul's ongoing ministry with these congregations?

A Chronology of Paul's Life and Ministry

A narrative approach to Paul's theology requires some awareness of the progression of events in Paul's apostolic career. A definitive calendar, however, cannot be established. There have been major scholarly efforts toward establishing a Pauline chronology, including studies by Robert Jewett, Jerome Murphy-O'Connor, Rainer Riesner, and Ben Witherington III (see bibliography). It is impossible within the scope of this study to reconcile the differences among them. For the purpose of this study I will work with the following sequence of ministry events, including approximate dates for letters. This chronology has been adapted from Witherington's *The Paul Quest* (pp. 304-31):

Date	Event	References
About A.D. 5	Paul is born in Tarsus of Cilicia.	Acts 22:3 Philemon 9
15-20	Paul studies in Jerusalem under Gamaliel. Some suggest that his family might have moved to Jerusalem during his childhood, but this cannot be established.	Acts 22:3; 26:4

Date	Event	References
30	Jesus is crucified during the time that Pontius Pilate was procurator of Judea.	Luke 23
31-33/34	Paul persecutes the church.	Galatians 1:13-14
34/35	On his way to Damascus, Paul encounters the risen Christ.	Galatians 1:15-16
34-37	Paul in Arabia and Damascus	Galatians 1:17; 2 Corinthians 11:32-33
37	Paul's first visit to Jerusalem as apostle	Galatians 1:18
37-46	Paul preaches in Syria and Cilicia	Galatians 1:21; 2 Corinthians 11:23-29
48	Paul makes his second visit to Jerusalem and enters into an agreement with the Jerusalem leaders.	Galatians 2:1-10
48	During a missionary trip Paul visits south Galatia.	Galatians 4:13-16
49	The Antioch episode: Paul confronts Peter in Antioch. After hearing upsetting news about rival missionary activity, Paul writes GALATIANS.	Galatians 2:11-14
49/50	The Jerusalem conference	Acts 15
50-52	Paul is involved in ministry in Asia Minor and Macedonia and Achaia. In Corinth Paul writes 1 and 2 THESSALONIANS.	1 Thessalonians 2:1-2; 3:1
53-55/56	Paul is based in Ephesus. He writes 1 CORINTHIANS from Ephesus, and 2 CORINTHIANS from Macedonia, possibly Philippi.	1 Corinthians 16:8 2 Corinthians 2:12-13

Date	Event	References
56/57	Paul is in Corinth, anticipating his journey to Jerusalem and Rome on the way to Spain. Paul writes ROMANS.	Romans 1:8-15; 15:14-33
60-62	Paul is in captivity in Rome. He writes PHILIPPIANS, PHILEMON, COLOSSIANS, and EPHESIANS	
62-64	Paul is released, and he engages in further missionary work. It is not clear whether he ever reached Spain.	Romans 15:22-27
65-68	Paul is in prison again, until his execution. The Pastoral Epistles (TITUS, 1 TIMOTHY, and 2 TIMOTHY) are written.	

The besetting problems that continue to plague the effort to develop a chronology of Paul's life and ministry cannot be enumerated here, let alone resolved. Which letters did Paul write and when did he write them? Some judgments on these matters have been made in the chart above. But a few of my underlying assumptions deserve to be noted briefly, without entering into the arguments.

First, Galatians may be the earliest of Paul's extant letters, written before the Jerusalem conference described in Acts 15. The Thessalonian letters are also early, but I am not convinced by Jerome Murphy-O'Connor who dates 1 Thessalonians as early as A.D. 41 (Murphy-O'Connor, 1996).

Second, I have concluded that likely all of the four captivity epistles (Colossians, Philemon, Philippians, and Ephesians) come from Paul's imprisonment in Rome, rather than other times when he was held as prisoner in Caesarea or possibly Ephesus.

Third, I view the Pastoral Epistles as having been written during Paul's lifetime. An amanuensis or a Pauline disciple probably wrote 1 Timothy and Titus, but Paul himself likely wrote 2 Timothy, his final recorded testimony.

A Narrative Approach to Paul's Pastoral Theology

Though he does not share his life story in its entirety anywhere, Paul clearly demonstrates that he recognizes where he has come from and what influences and experiences have shaped him. Yet his own experience is not the primary story that shapes his understanding of God. Paul is mindful of multiple narratives, all interwoven into the theology that informs his missionary activity and pastoral practice. Paul's personal story has a crucial though not paradigmatic function within his pastoral theology and ethics. More important are the Hebrew Scriptures, the holy tradition transmitted by the church concerning Jesus Christ, and his own dramatic personal apocalypse with Jesus Christ.

Evidence of Paul's wrestling with the Scriptures in light of his experience with Christ can be seen in all his letters. However, Paul nowhere publishes a systematic summary of the theology that emerges from this intersection of his study of Scripture, his traditional upbringing as a diaspora Jew, his reasoning, and his experiences. What Paul has left behind are occasional letters addressed primarily to congregations.

In Paul's letters to a handful of congregations scattered from Galatia to Corinth and all the way to Rome itself, the church from the first century onward has observed this missionary pastor as he engages in theological reflection. Paul's pastoral care emerges in interaction with the real-life stories of these congregations. Any attempt to discern Paul's pastoral theology therefore needs to be attuned to his own lived apostolic experience and the pastoral concerns that preoccupy him in relation to specific church situations.

How then might one represent Paul's theology and ethics?

Scholars utilizing narrative approaches to Paul's theology and ethics do so from a variety of points of departure. N. T. Wright repeatedly speaks, in one form or another, about Paul's operative narrative as compressed in the life, death, and resurrection of Jesus: "The story of God and the world, he believed, was focused on and encapsulated within the story of Jesus of Nazareth" (1997:46).

In similar fashion, Ben Witherington III talks about an overarching macro-story, which encompasses four distinct substories:

> (1) the story of a world gone wrong; (2) the story of Israel in that world; (3) the story of Christ, which arises out of the story of Israel and humankind on the human side of things, but in a larger sense out of the very story of God as creator and redeemer; and (4) the story of Christians, including Paul himself, which arises out of all three of these previous stories, and is the hinge, crucial turning point, and climax of the entire larger drama, which more than anything else affects how the Story will ultimately turn out. (1994b:5)

James D. G. Dunn sees five interwoven narrative elements arranged in layers:

> We could readily speak of the substructure of Paul's theology as the story of God and creation, with the story of Israel superimposed upon it. On top of that again we have the story of Jesus, and then Paul's own story, with the initial intertwining of these last two stories as the decisive turning point in Paul's life and theology. Finally, there are the complex interactions of Paul's own story

with the stories of those who had believed before him and of those who came to form the churches founded by them. (1998:18)

The articles gathered together in *Narrative Dynamics in Paul,* edited by Bruce Longenecker, have taken Dunn's five elements as a template for assessing the narrative approach, using Galatians and Romans as primary texts (2002:12-13).

Michael Gorman compares reading Paul's letters to the way that a symphony conductor reads music:

> Like listening to music, reading the letters of Paul requires constant attention to both small details and grand themes, and the careful reader is constantly going back to see how the themes inform the details and the details create the themes. This back-and-forth movement—what is sometimes called the "hermeneutical (interpretive) circle"—eventually yields a framework within which one hears and reads the music, or the text.
>
> Such a framework is seldom, however, simple, reducible to one descriptive word. For this book, six key words describe the frame of reference within which Paul is understood: "Jewish," "covenantal," "narrative," "countercultural," "trinitarian," and especially "cruciform." (Gorman, 2004:xi)

For Gorman, the realm of narrative includes the story of God from promise to ultimate fulfillment. Also for Gorman, "cruciformity" describes Jesus's life and the life of the believer living in conformity to the way of Jesus.

My own efforts in this book feature a movement from Paul's own story, as he himself is transformed through a dramatic encounter with Jesus, to the story of Jesus, through whom all else is viewed with new eyes. This includes the Scriptures themselves, which are reread from the perspective of God's self-revelation in Christ. Paul ministers to various congregations from his own experience of the Scriptures, which are now read through Christ. The stories are multiple and interlocking, but Jesus Christ forms the dynamic center.

Remember the Future!

An interpretive comment about the title of this book may be helpful here.

J. Louis Martyn (1997b:280-84) talks about the bifocal vision that characterizes the Christian apocalyptic theology of Paul and other New Testament writers. Paul invites his hearers to gaze simultaneously, as it were, through bifocal lenses, which enhance both near vision and far vision. The "near vision" focuses on the cross, which is God's dynamic invasion of grace and peace into the world; the "near vision" part of the lens also reveals that the violence and corruption of the present age still continue. However, the believers' "far vision" provides reassurance that God's triumphant reign already inaugurated through Christ will yet be consummated in the future.

A geometrical metaphor has also sometimes been proposed. Instead of seeking to find the "center" or "core" of Paul's theology in Christology or justification by faith, one might propose the concept of an ellipse, with two foci. These foci are, again, the death and resurrection of Christ and the future coming of Christ as the consummation of God's victory over the powers of this age. The church lives within the dynamic space formed by these past saving events and their anticipated future climax.

Another metaphor occurred to me while traveling by car along seemingly endless miles of highway. This image is obviously anachronistic but it may have potential for clarifying Paul's pastoral approach. In his pilgrimage as apostle Paul constantly checks his rearview mirror, in which he beholds the cross of Christ as the climax of God's redemptive initiative toward Israel and all of humankind. But Paul's field of vision through the windshield, as it were, takes in the present and the future of God's ongoing work through Christ by the Spirit among those who align themselves with God. And, strikingly, Paul sees the future already unveiled in the rearview. God will yet consummate what has been inaugurated in Christ.

The church in its worship and life and witness needs to remember that guaranteed future, and live already in the present in light of God's final victory.

2

THE STORY OF JESUS CHRIST: OBEDIENT EVEN UNTO DEATH

We have heard Paul share his testimony about his trans-forming encounter with Jesus. Now we tune our ears to some of the ways in which Paul reflects on the story of Jesus the risen Christ. Our attention shifts toward a church in the Roman colony of Philippi, because Paul's pastoral word to this congregation includes a dramatic telling of Jesus's story. What is it in the life of the church at Philippi and in Paul's relationship to it that moved him so deliber-ately to recall Jesus's story for them?

Epaphroditus was one of the members of the church at Philippi who kept in contact with Paul even during his imprisonment. In the following story we join Epaphroditus during his visit with Paul in prison before he returns to Philippi with a letter from the apostle. This story is based on what is generally known about ancient Philippi, plus a reading of the epistle to the Philippians, especially some texts that supply clear hints about the underlying circumstances: 1:1, 7, 12-14, 27-30; 2:14-18, 19-24, 25-30; 3:2, 17-19; 4:2-3, 15-19, 22. Acts 16:11-40 and 2 Corinthians 8:1-5 also add to our information about the situation in Philippi.

The inscription concerning Caesar Augustus (adapted from Lewis & Reinhold, 1955 [vol. 2]:64-5) reflects the language of a decree issued in the Assembly of Asia sever-

al decades before Paul's ministry in Philippi. Essays in
Richard Horsley's Paul and Empire demonstrate that the
ideology of the emperor cult, which this decree expresses,
was widespread in the first century (Horsley, 1997; cf. the
article by Graham N. Stanton [2002:131]).

A STORY: A Colony of Heaven in Philippi

In the year A.D. 60, at a prison in Rome, Epaphroditus,
a representative from the Christian congregation in
Philippi, visited Paul, the imprisoned apostle. Epaphroditus
had come to deliver another in a series of congregational
love gifts to the apostle. His journey had been long and
arduous, but Epaphroditus felt duly rewarded when he
located Paul and was greeted with a welcoming embrace.

Epaphroditus and Paul had a lot to talk and pray
about during their few precious days together in Rome.
Occasionally Paul reminisced about his first contacts in
Philippi. With gratitude to God he remembered how in the
year 49 the congregation emerged in that city, where a
Gentile businesswoman named Lydia, a worshiper of God,
was among the first to say yes to the gospel of Jesus Christ.
She and her whole household were baptized. For a time
Paul and his partner Silas made Lydia's home the base of
their ministry in Philippi. On one occasion Paul and Silas
had been thrown into jail because their ministry to a
soothsaying slave girl released her from an oppressive spirit. But while praying and singing hymns to God, Paul and
Silas had been dramatically and mysteriously freed.

Praying and hymn-singing also unified and energized
the congregation in Philippi. As they recited psalms and
sang new songs, the Spirit of God regularly inspired their
worship with new expressions of joyful praise. Visitors
from other churches in Macedonia and beyond also intro-

duced new hymns that offered adoration and praise, not only to God as sovereign creator but also to Jesus Christ as Lord.

More than ten years had passed since those beginnings. Epaphroditus remembered that on several occasions, Paul had traveled through their city. Each time the congregation provided him the opportunity to pause for fellowship and refreshment in their company. During these years the congregation was generous in their giving toward one of Paul's major causes: a relief effort on behalf of the poor in Jerusalem. He was quick to testify with gratitude how he received support from Philippi throughout his mission efforts.

Paul and Epaphroditus recalled some of the distinctive historical, social, and political circumstances that continued to shape the congregation in Philippi. Epaphroditus reminded Paul about the prevailing political mood. It was obvious to any visitor that, even though Philippi was in the province of Macedonia, the city was unabashedly pro-Roman in its civic attitudes and public expressions of patriotism. About a hundred years earlier (42 B.C.E.) the Roman general Octavian, who later became Emperor Caesar Augustus, had established Philippi as a military colony and arranged for an infusion of Roman war veterans into its population. The reign of Caesar Augustus was hailed as the birth of a new era of peace and prosperity. Inscriptions on monuments and readings in the public square regularly memorialized Augustus and solicited loyalty toward his successors:

> Providence has filled Augustus with divine power for the benefit of humanity, and in her beneficence has granted us and those who come after us a Savior who has made wars to cease. . . . And Caesar, when he was

> manifest, transcended the expectations of all who had
> anticipated the good news. . . . The birthday of our
> god signaled the beginning of good news for the world
> because of him.

Expressions of loyalty and patriotism toward Rome
were commonplace in public festivals, ceremonies, speeches, and parades. Quite clearly, "the gospel of Caesar" promoted by the ruler cult provided the dominant cultural
ethos for citizens and residents of Philippi.

Surveying his own personal circumstances as a political captive in a Roman prison, Paul realized that he had
fallen victim to the same forces holding sway in Philippi.
He was quite uncertain concerning the outcome of legal
proceedings against him, unsure whether he would live or
die. In the meantime he was letting his prison guards know
that his captivity was for Christ. And some of them had
come to faith, including several members of Caesar's
household.

Epaphroditus also shared with Paul bits and pieces of
news from Philippi. By and large, the congregation was
doing well and was solidly supportive of Paul's missions.
From what Epaphroditus shared, however, it struck Paul
that there were subtle pressures on the church and opposition similar to the kind he was himself experiencing.
Roman citizens and officials tried to persuade believers to
join in giving homage to the emperor, and in both Philippi
and Rome, witness to the Jesus as savior and Lord had
come in direct conflict with this imperial gospel that promoted Caesar as savior and Lord.

Epaphroditus told Paul how the congregation was
showing signs of selfish ambition in their life together.
There was arguing and murmuring, and even Euodia and
Syntyche, two valued partners in the ministry of the gospel

in Philippi, were entangled in a misunderstanding. Paul felt concern that this internal unrest would hinder the ongoing witness of the church.

Paul questioned Epaphroditus about the missionary efforts of some other evangelists in Philippi, and he wondered whether or not their message and lifestyle conformed to the way of Christ. He listened for indications that rival Jewish Christian missionaries might be influencing members of the Philippian congregation to be circumcised and come under the law. Epaphroditus suspected that some who desired more security, like that enjoyed by Jews related to the synagogue, were especially vulnerable to such persuasion.

As their visit neared its end, Epaphroditus became gravely ill. His departure to Philippi was delayed, but concerned that his people back home would worry about him, he soon—perhaps too soon—began to prepare for the long journey home.

Paul began to dictate a letter to the congregation. Though in prison and unable to travel freely to the various churches on his circuit, he could still write letters. Joining him in this communication was his co-worker and scribe, Timothy, who was himself preparing to make a journey to Philippi. For now Paul was grateful to have Timothy by his side. But with his friend and companion, Epaphroditus, about to set sail again for Philippi, Paul and Timothy crafted the letter.

Singing and Living in Harmony with the Story of Jesus

> Let each of you look not to your own interests, but to the interests of others. Let the same mind be in you that was in Christ Jesus. (Philippians 2:4-5)

Paul is not among the first-century evangelists who write gospels telling the story of Jesus. As missionary and pastor he writes letters to congregations. Nowhere in his letters does he provide an account of Jesus's life and teachings, nor does he include stories about Jesus's passion and death and resurrection. Some people have therefore wondered whether the life and teachings of Jesus matter to Paul.

Aspects of Jesus's story do surface in several places in Paul's pastoral correspondence to his churches, but the details of Jesus's life, ministry, and teaching seem to be assumed as adequately known. One cannot conclude from the lack of information in Paul's letters about Jesus's life and teaching that he regarded it as unimportant for the church's ongoing life and mission. One would not expect that shared common knowledge would be reiterated in occasional letters.

In Philippians 2:5-11, however, we find one narrative about Jesus. This story does not trace his career, as a child born in Bethlehem, who became a rabbi in the region of Galilee, a teacher of parables, a healer of the sick. Rather it is the story of Jesus's cosmic journey from equality with God to his exaltation as Lord by way of the cross.

In this chapter we identify with Paul and the church at Philippi and explore how this crucial gospel narrative intersects with their lives.

"Gospel narrative" may not be the most appropriate description for Philippians 2:5-11. There is a widely shared conviction among interpreters that Paul is here citing a hymn, likely one familiar to the Philippian believers. Paul was passing on what he himself had received as a sung confession concerning Jesus Christ, whom he had met in his own life-changing encounter on the Damascus road.

Paul exalts Jesus throughout his letter to the Philippian congregation, but especially in 2:5-11. He lifts up Jesus both in adoration and praise, and as ethical norm for the church. Paul senses that the church in Philippi needs pastoral encouragement and friendly admonition. He also longs to say a hearty "thank-you" to his friends for their loyal partnership, their prayers, and their financial support of the mission. But primarily, Paul feels compelled to share with them the story of Jesus and how the gospel of Christ seeks to take shape in their life as a community.

Living Is Christ

After warm expressions of thanksgiving to God and fervent assurances of his prayers for the church (1:3-11), Paul shares intimately with them concerning his own circumstances as a prisoner awaiting an unknown future (1:12-26). Already in the salutation (1:1-2), where he mentions Christ three times, it is obvious that he wants to present the story of Jesus to this congregation as central for their life and faith. The thanksgiving section (1:3-11) shows that Paul longs for the congregation to be oriented toward the future, "the day of Christ Jesus" (1:6). He also prays that in their present realities they will live faithfully in harmony with the gospel of Christ:

> And this is my prayer, that your love may overflow more and more with knowledge and full insight to help you to determine what is best, so that in the day of Christ you may be pure and blameless, having produced the harvest of righteousness that comes through Jesus Christ for the glory and praise of God. (1:9-11)

Paul's reflections on his imprisonment (1:12-14, 19-26) also indicate that he views his own life and, as it increasingly appears likely to him, his imminent death, from within his lived experience with Christ. As he says, "For to me, living is Christ and dying is gain" (1:21).

This focus on the story of Jesus continues when Paul turns his attention to their situation as a congregation (1:27–2:18). He opens this pastoral exhortation section by appealing to the congregation to conduct their life together in a way that is "worthy of the gospel of Christ" (1:27). First he urgently admonishes them to remain firm in their commitment to the gospel in the midst of the opposition they are facing. Their struggle, he reminds them, is similar to his own; indeed, by trusting in Christ they are also suffering with and for Christ (1:27-30). Paul is pointing to the clash between two competing gospels, the cult of Caesar and the gospel of Jesus Christ, a clash leading to opposition against the Philippian believers and imprisonment for Paul.

Next Paul issues a moving appeal that addresses what appears to be some internal lack of harmony and mutual goodwill within the congregation. He urges the Philippians to be united in mind, love, and commitment, and he calls on them to abstain from selfish ambition and conceit (2:1-3). He longs for them to cultivate the communal qualities of humility and readiness to serve each other (2:4). And the prime exemplar of this humility and servanthood is Jesus Christ. With the plea, "Let the same mind be in you that was in Christ Jesus," he shares with the congregation a powerful poetic rendition of the life and vocation of Jesus in Philippians 2:5-11.

Paul shares this dramatic narrative of Jesus's journey from heaven to earth and back again to address the situation in the church at Philippi. The congregation may well have been quite familiar with this confessional recital about Jesus. They had probably sung it as a hymn in worship. Paul recalls this version of the story of Jesus because of the way it intersects with the ongoing life of this community in Christ.

Before we explore further how this story relates to the life and witness of this congregation we ask, What is the plot of Jesus's story?

A Hymn About Jesus

As already indicated, a widely shared view among interpreters is that in Philippians 2:5-11 Paul quotes an early hymn of the church. Modern Bible translations such as NIV and NRSV therefore typically set this material in poetic form. If this scholarly judgment is correct, Paul does not just tell the story of Jesus; he sings a hymn in honor of Jesus Christ the Lord. In a Philippian jail, according to the record in Acts 16:25-34, Paul and Silas prayed and sang hymns to God. When Paul encourages the church at Philippi to conform to the mind and way of Christ he does so using the evocative imagery of a hymn.

As an exalted poetic narrative about Jesus Christ, Philippians 2:5-11 does not feature Bethlehem and Nazareth, or Jerusalem and Bethany, or other places and events that are significant in the Gospels. The story Paul shares describes the pilgrimage of Christ in three dramatic acts played out on a cosmic stage: from his preexistence to his incarnation (Act 1), including his life as a slave and his death on the cross (Act 2), to his exaltation as risen Lord (Act 3).

Hymns normally invite worship, adoration, and confession within a faith community, rather than critical analysis. However, some interpretive comments about this majestic passage are in order. The exegetical discussions of this hymn have been quite complex (see Fowl, 1990; Martin and Dodd, 1998; Wright, 1992:56-98; Fee, 1995:191-229). In our effort at explanation we will cite a few of the underlying Greek words, because their meaning has often been vigorously contested.

Act 1: This christological hymn begins with a reference to the earliest phase of Jesus's vocation. Philippians 2:6 as translated by NRSV and NIV illustrates the fact that Jesus's vocation prior to his incarnation is variously described:

> Who, though he was in the form of God (*morphe theou*), did not regard equality with God as something to be exploited (*harpagmon*). (NRSV)

> Who, being in very nature God (*morphe theou*), did not consider equality with God something to be grasped (*harpagmon*). (NIV)

Traditionally 2:6 has been understood as testimony to the prior existence of Jesus Christ with God, or as God, before his birth and life as a human being on earth. The Philippians commentary by Gordon Fee, for example, argues this interpretation. The earthly Jesus is therefore God incarnate. Stated in terms of later trinitarian formulations, the human Jesus is the second person of the Godhead. Having existed from the beginning as the coequal partner with the sovereign creator God, Jesus took on flesh as a historical person living for a brief lifetime on the earth (Fee, 1995:202-10).

Some other interpreters, notably James D. G. Dunn, view the term *morphe* (the Greek word underlying *form*) as equivalent to *image*. As the new or second Adam created in God's image, the earthly Jesus was "in the form of God." In this view, Jesus of Nazareth was the human whose glorious reflection of God's image undoes the damage done through the disobedience of the first Adam (1998:281-8).

Debates about the meaning intended here may reflect

an ongoing tendency to interpret the poetry of worship as though it were the language of doctrinal formulation. Worshipers singing or hearing this hymn may actually have recalled not doctrines but multiple metaphors and themes from Scripture, including the story of Creation (Genesis 1:26-27) and the role of wisdom in creation (Proverbs 8:22-31). Later readers need to hear this material in the same way, as the poetry of adoration and praise rather than dogmatic propositions.

Debates also abound concerning the meaning of the word *harpagmon*, which is used in this hymn with reference to Christ's "equality with God" (2:6). If this ancient hymn views Jesus prior to his earthly mission as having had the nature and essence of God, the question is, How did Jesus prior to his incarnation regard this *equality*? If it reflects Jesus's glorious imaging of God as the new Adam, what lies behind this reference to "equality with God"?

Is "equality with God" something Christ already possessed? Then the main issue is whether he should make use of his divine status. The NRSV translation represents this phrase in that way: "who . . . did not regard equality with God as something to be exploited."

Or is "equality with God" something Jesus might find desirable and worth pursuing? If so, the hymn is asserting that, like Adam and Eve in the garden (Genesis 3:1-7), Christ was tempted to seek the status of "equality with God" (NIV: "something to be grasped"), but, unlike the primeval couple, he chose not to seek divine status. In fact, as the next strophe of the hymn points out, instead of seeking to become like God, Christ as the new Adam, though equal with God, became incarnate as a human being.

When seeking to understand and convey the realities glimpsed in the realm of divine mystery, the human mind fails to comprehend and language can never convey even that which is glimpsed. However, the message here is clear enough. Christ's attitude is characterized as unselfish and non-grasping, as ready to give up his own rights and to deny himself for the sake of others. Caesar sought after divine honors, but Jesus did not. Though he was equal with God, Jesus Christ did not exploit his inherent power and status to further his own ambitions or goals. He emptied himself of his divine status in order to serve others.

Act 2: The hymn continues by describing this process of Christ's self-emptying, or *kenosis*. Christ's mindset moves him to demonstrate the depth of God's love through humbling himself, through being poured out, through servanthood, through self-sacrifice for the sake of others, in short through obedience even unto death on the cross (2:7-8):

> But (he) emptied himself, taking the form of a servant,
>   being born in human likeness.
> And being found in human form, he humbled himself
>   and became obedient to the point of death—
>   even death on a cross.

Again the interpretive issues are complicated, but the import of this part of the hymn is indisputable. In his incarnation Jesus Christ came to identify with and to serve needy humanity. Jesus's vocation as servant led him all the way to the cross.

The servant songs in Isaiah 42–53 probably provided some of the language whereby the early church pondered the mystery of Christ's identification with humanity. By his obedience all the way to the cross, the most ignominious of Roman instruments of death and torture, Christ dramatically demonstrated the character of God. In fact, the meaning of "equality with God" is expressed in this radical willingness to give up status and rights in favor of the interests and needs of others. Such sacrificial love reflects the character of God. The cross brings Paul and the church at Philippi and elsewhere face-to-face with the utterly self-giving love of God.

Act 3: The hymn reaches its climax in 2:9-11 with the triumphant announcement of God's vindicating rescue of the obedient slave who gave his life on the cross. So far in this poetic narrative of his life and death, Jesus has been the actor. At this point the initiator of the action is God:

> Therefore God also highly exalted him and gave him
> the name that is above every name,
>   so that at the name of Jesus every knee should bend,
>   in heaven and on earth and under the earth,
>   and every tongue confess that Jesus Christ is Lord
>   to the glory of God the Father.

God reverses the sentence of death pronounced by the earthly rulers over Jesus, and God gives him the name that is above all other names, whether earthly or heavenly or under-worldly, even above the name of Caesar.

Once again the hymn utilizes language from the servant songs in Isaiah. This time the allusions come from Isaiah 45, where the prophet declares the supremacy of the one God, the God of Israel, over all contenders:

> By myself I have sworn,
> from my mouth has gone forth in righteousness a
>   word that shall not return:
>   "To me every knee shall bow, every tongue
>   shall swear." (Isaiah 45:23)

In concert with this ancient divine declaration through the prophet to Israel in exile, the church at Philippi is invited to join in the acclamation of Jesus Christ as Lord. And by exalting Christ as Lord they are joining in the affirmation

of the one supreme God, the creator of all. They are uniting their hearts in the worship of the one true God.
Adoration and praise addressed to Jesus is not understood
to be in conflict with Jewish monotheism. Jesus Christ the
Lord is no rival vying for the veneration appropriate only
for God. Within the mystery and majesty of God, the worship of God includes adoration of the Son.

Living Within the Story of Jesus

How does this lofty hymn speak to the Philippian church?
Paul keeps before these believers the prospect of God's ultimate vindication of all who, like Jesus the incarnate Lord,
trust God, even when obedience is accompanied by persecution and suffering. Certainly the acknowledgment that one
day every knee will bow and every tongue shall confess that
Jesus Christ is Lord must have struck a responsive chord with
believers in Philippi. They were suffering public rejection or
overt persecution because of their unwillingness to participate
in the civic cult, which called upon citizens to confess Caesar
as Lord. This hymn about Jesus's journey from "form of
God" to "form of slave" to "highly exalted Lord" provided
reassurance for this community. The time would yet come
when all "in heaven and on earth and under the earth" would
acknowledge the truth of the radical claim being made by
these beleaguered citizens of the Roman colony of Philippi.
Paul reminds them all, including those among them who, like
Paul himself, are Roman citizens, that their ultimate allegiance is as citizens within the kingdom of God:

> But our citizenship is in heaven, and it is from there that
> we are expecting a Savior, the Lord Jesus Christ. (3:20)

As citizens of a heavenly commonwealth they already
know and confess what would yet become abundantly

transparent to all, namely, that "Jesus Christ is Lord."

Paul's ultimate aim in recalling for the Philippian believers what they themselves confess when singing this hymn is to encourage them to conform to the way of Christ in their relationships with each other and in their response to the surrounding culture. As part of his pastoral strategy Paul testifies concerning his own life and experience as one whose vocation echoes the Christlike pattern.

In the following table we note several points of correspondence between Paul's apostolic experience, as he reflects that experience in this letter, and the story of Christ, as presented in the first two movements of the hymn (Act 1 and Act 2):

The Story of Christ	Paul's Apostolic Experience
Jesus's incarnation is seen as "taking the form of a slave" (2:7).	In the greeting, Paul and Timothy describe themselves as servants (Greek: *slaves*) of Jesus Christ (1:1).
The hymn depicts Jesus's non-grasping self-denying *kenosis*: Christ "emptied himself" (2:7).	After listing his topflight credentials as a Pharisee (3:4-6), Paul declares that he regards them all "as loss" (3:7, 8), "as rubbish" (3:8).
In the hymn Christ is portrayed as one who "became obedient to the point of death" (2:8)	Paul refers to his own imprisonment and coming death as participating in Christ's suffering and death (1:29-30; 3:10).
The language of the hymn says concerning Jesus: "He humbled himself" (2:8).	Paul describes his present state of existence in prison awaiting likely execution as life within "the body of our humiliation" (3:21).

The Story of Christ	Paul's Apostolic Experience
There are sacrificial overtones in the hymn's brief telling of the story of the crucifixion of Jesus: "even death on a cross" (2:8).	Using the language of religious sacrifice, Paul talks about the probability that his life will soon be "poured out as a libation over the sacrifice and the offering of your (the Philippians') faith" (2:17).

Clearly Paul intends to highlight the parallels between his own life, including his suffering and imminent death, and Jesus's life and obedience unto death. But the symmetry between Paul's experience and that of his Lord pertains to the last part of the hymn (Act 3) as well:

The Story of Christ	Paul's Apostolic Experience
The hymn refers not to the resurrection but to the exaltation of Jesus who was obedient even unto death on the cross: "Therefore God also highly exalted him" (2:9a).	While expressing his intention "to know Christ and the power of his resurrection and the sharing of his sufferings by becoming like him in his death" (3:10), Paul also articulates his longing: "if somehow I may attain the resurrection from the dead" (3:11).
In the hymn there is a "prize" for the obedient son: "God . . . gave him the name that is above every name" (2:9b).	Paul admits that the struggle continues (3:12-13) but he anticipates ultimate victory in Christ: "I press on toward the goal for the prize of the heavenly call of God in Christ Jesus" (3:14).
The final strophe of the hymn sounds a triumphant note: "So that at the name of Jesus every knee should bend, in heaven and on earth and under the earth, and every tongue confess that Jesus Christ is Lord to the glory of God the Father" (2:10-11).	Paul declares his confidence, rooted in the mission of Jesus Christ, that his imprisoned and humiliated body will yet be glorified by the power of the One who will ultimately bring all things into submission (3:21).

In sum, Paul testifies in a variety of ways to the reality that his own life conforms to the model and promise of the supreme exemplar, the servant Jesus who in humble obedience even unto death gave himself for others and was exalted as Lord (3:2–4:1).

The story of Jesus's journey is therefore not only sung in worship; it is also replicated in the lives of faithful believers and in the life of the Christian community. Paul offers testimony to the ways in which his co-worker Timothy and the Philippian delegate Epaphroditus lived within the model of Jesus's self-giving service. Unlike others seeking their own interests rather than those of Christ (cf. 2:4), Timothy is genuinely concerned for the welfare of others, including both the congregation in Philippi and the prisoner Paul himself (2:19-24). Epaphroditus nearly died in carrying out his ministry in the name of Christ (2:25-30).

For the church in Philippi, therefore, Jesus's pilgrimage as rehearsed in this hymn offers consolation in their suffering and encouragement for them to stay the course. Their choices matter. Paul urges, "Work out your own salvation with fear and trembling, for it is God who is at work in you" (2:12-13). Amidst competing claims for their loyalty and allegiance, they are summoned to live in conformity to Christ. Rather than yielding to the peer pressure of fellow citizens aligned with the imperial cult, they are commended to the lordship of Christ. Instead of giving in to pressure to be circumcised as proselytes, they are invited to know the power of the righteousness of God, which comes through faith, both the faithfulness of Jesus even to death on the cross and their faith response. And, rather than bickering and arguing among themselves, they are summoned to live in harmony with one another. Their life as a community is a witness in the midst of "a crooked and perverse generation" (2:15). In the Roman colony of

Philippi they are to live as citizens of the colony of heaven, as Christlike, Spirit-empowered children of God.

When Paul concludes his letter to the church at Philippi, he urges them, "Stand firm in the Lord in this way, my beloved" (4:1). He pleads with Euodia and Syntyche "to be of the same mind in the Lord" (4:2). He urges them all, "Rejoice in the Lord always" (4:4). And he adds the assurance that "the peace of God, which surpasses all understanding, will guard your hearts and your minds in Christ Jesus" (4:7). Right up to the end of the letter, Paul commends the example and model of Jesus Christ, the crucified and exalted Lord.

In addition, in a deliberate reminder that the glory of the way of Jesus vastly outshines the paltry pleasures that Caesar has to offer, Paul acknowledges their support for his apostolic mission:

> I have received from Epaphroditus the gifts you sent, a fragrant offering, a sacrifice acceptable and pleasing to God. (4:18)

Then he adds a promise and speaks the doxology:

> And my God will fully satisfy every need of yours according to his riches in glory in Christ Jesus. To our God and Father be glory forever and ever. Amen. (4:19-20)

Not Caesar but God deserves the glory. As if to underscore the fact that even in Rome, and even within the household of Caesar himself, there are people who have joined the chorus in affirming Christ as Lord, Paul appends a striking final greeting. "All the saints greet you, especially those of the emperor's household" (4:22).

The Story of Jesus in Paul's Other Letters

Having focused on the letter of Paul to the church in Philippi, we turn now to a survey of the ways in which Paul draws on the story of Jesus in his other letters. Whether singing in adoration and praise or confessing the faith in creeds or engaging in polemic or debate, he alludes to Jesus many times. One can normally assume that Paul and his readers are drawing on their common familiarity with a story about Jesus. Because this story is nowhere narrated at length in any of Paul's letters, we cannot be sure how widely known it was. As in Philippi, so also with the church in every region, Paul portrays the Christ event, and especially Jesus's death and resurrection, as the climactic revelation of God's salvation and the paradigm for their relationships with each other.

The ways in which the Jesus story surfaces in Paul's correspondence will be noted throughout this study of his pastoral theology.

We noted in chapter 1 how the direction of Paul's life changed radically after the revelation of God's Son to him. Early in Galatians he alludes to his encounter with the risen Christ (Galatians 1:15-16); near the end he advocates a lifestyle of mutual burden-bearing in fulfillment of the law of Christ (6:2). In several key passages (2:16; 3:22) Paul also alludes to Jesus's faithfulness, which elicits a response of faith. (See chapters 8 and 9 for a discussion of Paul's letter to the Galatians, including an elaboration of the theme of Jesus's faith and the response it elicits.)

When appealing to Jews and Gentiles in Rome to live and worship in harmony with each other (see chapters 4 and 6) Paul again gives testimony concerning Jesus's faith and human responsive faith (Romans 1:16-17; 3:21-26). In the concluding climactic appeal of the main body of his letter to the Romans, Paul presents Jesus's self-giving way as the norm for relationships within the faith community: "Christ did not please himself" (Romans 15:3). Paul prays,

> May the God of steadfastness and encouragement
> grant you to live in harmony with one another, in
> accordance with Christ Jesus. (Romans 15:5)

In his epistles to the church at Corinth (see chapters 3 and 5) Paul incorporates abundant testimony to Jesus Christ, especially his cross, as defining relationships within the body (1 Corinthians 1:18–2:5). In 1 Corinthians 15:3-5 Paul enumerates key moments in the gospel narrative that he in turn had received:

> that Christ died for our sins in accordance with the
>   scriptures,
> and that he was buried,
> and that he was raised on the third day in accordance
>   with the scriptures,
> and that he appeared to Cephas, then to the twelve.

When encouraging the church to give sacrificially toward the gift to the church in Jerusalem, Paul cites the example of Jesus Christ in ways highly reminiscent of the Philippians 2 hymn:

> You know the generous act of the Lord Jesus Christ,
> that though he was rich, yet for your sakes he became
> poor, so that by his poverty you might become rich.
> (2 Corinthians 8:9)

Even in the short epistle to Philemon (see chapter 10), the narratives concerning Jesus, glimpsed only in several code expressions, demonstrate the normative character of Jesus's life, ministry, death, and resurrection for Paul and the community of faith. Similarly the story of Jesus supplies the dynamic framework for interpreting what the household codes in Colossians and Ephesians have to say about relationships within the household and attitudes toward the powers (see chapters 11 and 12).

In letters addressed to the church in Thessalonica (chapter 7) and to Paul's pastoral delegates, Titus and Timothy (chapter 13), the life and ministry of Jesus and particularly his death and resurrection are presented as comfort for the afflicted and hope for the suffering. The church's confessions and hymns concerning Jesus shape the life and witness of individuals and congregations in their circumstances of confusion from within and oppression from beyond.

In addition to these confessional allusions to the Jesus story, Paul shares a key historical remembrance and a few of Jesus's ethical and eschatological teachings. The narrative in 1 Corinthians 11:23-25 of Jesus's last meal with his disciples on the night when he was taken into custody is probably the most notable because it is widely cited during celebrations of the Lord's Supper. Jesus's ethical instructions also seem to be echoed in several moral maxims cited by Paul: on divorce (1 Corinthians 7:10-11; cf. Mark 10:11-12), love for enemies (Romans 12:14, 21; cf. Matthew 5:39, 44), payment of taxes (Romans 13:7; cf. Matthew 22:21), and love as the fulfillment of the law (Romans 13:8-10; cf. Matthew 22:34-40). Similarly several of Jesus's similes and metaphors reappear in Paul's writings. For example, in 1 Thessalonians 5:2-3, when Paul highlights the eschatological urgency of the times, he employs imagery also found in Jesus's eschatological teachings in the Gospels. The coming of the day of the Lord will be as sudden as the clandestine activity of a thief in the night (cf. Matthew 24:43) and as inevitable as the onset of birth pangs for a pregnant woman (cf. Matthew 24:8).

The texts listed above indicate that indeed Paul was interested in the earthly Jesus and his teachings. However, an audit of Paul's epistles against the vivid biographical detail supplied by the Gospels reveals clearly that he places the emphasis elsewhere. He apparently assumes that stories about Jesus need not be rehearsed in letters addressed to people who already know at least some of them. More significantly, he places the accent on another kind of telling of the story of Jesus, one that tracks the cosmic pilgrimage of God's Son from heaven to earth and back again. The hymn in Philippians 2 is one such exalted narrative. We now focus on a survey of several related Jesus narratives as glimpsed in the titles that Paul ascribes to Christ.

The Stories Behind the Titles Ascribed to Jesus

Soon after Jesus's death, his followers began to include his name in their worship of God. A variety of titles, some of which were normally reserved for God, came to be used for Jesus. What happened to bring about this remarkable shift among a people usually adamantly resilient in reserving their devotion to God?

Many scholars have attempted to trace this evolution. In his essay "Hymns and Christology" Martin Hengel suggests that the community of Jesus's followers was moved by the Spirit of God in their worship to go beyond the exegesis of Scripture into bold new songs and hymns to Christ. Divinely inspired singing in the context of worship led the community of faith to confess Christ and to venerate him as Lord, even though they did not view the honor bestowed on Jesus as compromising their worship of God alone (1988:78-96).

In *One God, One Lord*, Larry W. Hurtado describes what he calls a "Christian mutation" in the Jewish monotheistic tradition, the readiness to exalt Jesus along-side God, as an innovation that arose early in the messianic movement (1988:93-124). In his later book, *Lord Jesus Christ: Devotion to Jesus Christ in Earliest Christianity*, Hurtado abandons the image of "mutation" and talks instead about an emerging variant form of monotheism (2003:50-53). He enumerates several striking developments in the early messianic Jewish community: the singing of hymns about Christ, praying to Christ, invoking the name of Christ at baptism, commemorating Jesus at the Lord's Supper, inviting converts to confess Jesus as Lord, and prophesying in the name of the risen Christ (2003:134-51). What led to these startling developments within these Jewish assemblies of people who acknowledged Jesus as Messiah? Hurtado mentions several contributing factors. Clearly the earthly Jesus made a deep impression on his followers during his pre-Easter ministry. Furthermore, Jesus's disciples and his later followers (notably Paul) experienced dramatic revelatory visions of the risen Christ (2003:29-78).

In *Jewish Messianism and the Cult of Christ*, William Horbury also notes the acclamation of Jesus in hymns, confessions, prayers, and the celebration of the Lord's Supper. Horbury comments on the way that this "cult of Christ" parallels the contemporary practice of honoring heroes, sovereigns, and divinities within the Greco-Roman world, particularly in the imperial cult and its veneration of Caesar. However, he does not posit that the early church copied the practices of the imperial cult and applied them to Jesus. He suggests rather that the worship of Jesus is rooted in Jewish messianic hopes, specifically in a royal theology that is expressed in praise of rulers both present and future (1998:109-52).

By the time that Paul writes the pastoral letters, he has

inherited the hymns and confessional statements about Jesus that emerged within the early church's worship. Paul therefore prays with the Palestinian Jewish believers using Jesus's own address for God, *Abba*, Father (Mark 14:36), and incorporates this Aramaic prayer in his letters to the churches in Galatia (Galatians 4:5) and Rome (Romans 8:15). Yet, again in company with the messianic Palestinian Jews, Paul also prayed to Jesus in Aramaic, *Maran atha*, "Our Lord, come!" and he concludes one of his letters to the Gentile church in Corinth with that prayer (1 Corinthians 16:22). Paul is heir to the rich and (from the perspective of many of his peers within Pharisaic Judaism) risqué early practice of adoring devotion addressed to Jesus Christ.

Of course, Paul also made his own significant contribution to this developing practice of worship that honors Jesus. He did not have the opportunity to see Jesus perform healings or to hear Jesus teach. Paul may have heard from Jesus's disciples about their deep pain and bitter disappointment when Jesus died. Likely he learned how the events of Easter moved Jesus's disciples and other believers in their worship and prayers to the veneration of Jesus along with their adoration of God. When he aligned himself with the community of those confessing Jesus as Lord, Paul felt moved to join them in prophetic inspiration, expressions of religious ecstasy, singing, and praying in the Spirit, the exercise of various spiritual gifts, and apocalyptic visions. These heady worship experiences, alongside their study of the Psalms, the prophets, and the Torah, led Paul and other messianic Jewish believers as well as a growing number of Gentile converts to sing new hymns and to articulate their beliefs in new ways.

We turn then to several of the titles employed by Paul when he refers to Jesus: Son, Messiah, and Lord. What are the underlying narratives that help us to understand these titles?

God's Son

In several of his letters Paul refers to Jesus as God's Son, who is sent on a mission:

> But when the fullness of time had come, God sent his Son, born of a woman, born under the law, in order to redeem those who were under the law, so that we might receive adoption as children. (Galatians 4:4-5)

> For God has done what the law, weakened by the flesh, could not do: by sending his own Son in the likeness of sinful flesh, and to deal with sin, he condemned sin in the flesh. (Romans 8:3)

> He who did not withhold his own Son, but gave him up for all of us, will he not with him also give us everything else? (Romans 8:32)

> For our sake he made him to be sin who knew no sin, so that in him we might become the righteousness of God. (2 Corinthians 5:21)

When Paul pictures God as launching Jesus on a divine errand he draws on a variety of images. He uses different Greek words for *send/sending* in Galatians 4:4 and Romans 8:3; however, in both of these texts he presents Jesus as God's Son dispatched on a rescue mission. In Romans 8:32 Paul evokes the memory of Abraham's near-sacrifice of his son Isaac (Genesis 22:1-19) when he says that God did not spare his own Son. In 2 Corinthians 5:21 Paul employs rather startling shorthand to make a similar point: God made the sinless one to be sin. All four of these

texts have in common a narrative sequence involving the
God who sends his own Son into the fray, the God who
does not spare but delivers up his Son on a mission identifying sacrificially with humanity. Using spatial categories
one might talk about Jesus's descent. Jesus is sent down
from the heavenly realm outside of human history into the
sinful realities on earth. The divine Son is portrayed as
descending from heaven to earth.

Another specific set of images of Jesus as God's Son is
on display in Paul's salutation in Romans. Paul introduces
himself by offering a synopsis of the gospel,

> the gospel concerning his Son, who was descended
> from David according to the flesh and was declared to
> be Son of God with power according to the spirit of
> holiness by resurrection from the dead, Jesus Christ
> our Lord. (Romans 1:3-4)

Here Paul views Jesus in the lineage of the kings of Israel,
specifically as a king within the Davidic line. As son of
David, Jesus is now declared to be Son of God through his
resurrection from the dead.

Jesus as the royal Son comes on stage, as it were, from
within history. In a fashion not unlike the inauguration of
a king, he is enthroned as Son of God with power. *Son of
God* is therefore a royal title within a longstanding tradition reflected in Psalms, such as 2 and 89, as in this citation where we hear a report of God's words of coronation
for the king:

> I will tell of the decree of the LORD: He said to me,
> "You are my son; today I have begotten you. Ask of
> me, and I will make the nations your heritage, and the
> ends of the earth your possession." (Psalm 2:7-8)

And in Psalm 89 we hear first the new king's affirmation of filial loyalty to God and then God's installation of the king as firstborn son:

> He shall cry to me, "You are my Father, my God, and the Rock of my salvation!" I will make him the first-born, the highest of the kings of the earth. (89:26-27)

Paul presents Jesus as God's Son in this sense: as the descendant of King David, whose coming reign was eagerly awaited in Israel.

Yet this son of David has also been marked out as Son of God in a way that dramatically demonstrates his uniqueness. Through his resurrection from the dead Jesus has been appointed or designated as "Son of God with power according to the spirit of holiness" (Romans 1:4). This exaltation or ascent of the obedient Son into the realm of sovereign supremacy is reminiscent of Philippians 2:9, "Therefore God also highly exalted him."

God's Son, the Crucified Messiah

Paul's twofold designation of Jesus as Son of God in Romans 1:3-4 culminates in the use of the full name "Jesus Christ our Lord." Jesus as king is the anointed one, the Messiah, the Christ.

Herein lies the scandal, however. Jesus of Nazareth had been nailed to a Roman cross, where he died as one accursed (Deuteronomy 21:23; 27:26; as reflected in Galatians 3:13). How then does he qualify as the royal Son, the Messiah? Paul testifies in his letter to Corinth that a crucified Messiah was "a stumbling block to Jews and foolishness to Gentiles" (1 Corinthians 1:23). Yet in the same letter Paul reiterates his commitment: "For I decided to know nothing among you except Jesus Christ, and him crucified" (2:2). Similarly he recalls his initial proclamation of the gospel among the Galatians as featuring the Messiah languishing and dying on a cross: "It was before your eyes that Jesus Christ was publicly exhibited as crucified!" (Galatians 3:1).

Paul interprets the scandalous execution of Messiah Jesus on a Roman cross as the revelatory moment when God intervened to liberate Israel from exile and to save all humanity from bondage to sin. The apostle deploys numerous metaphors and images in the effort to elucidate the dramatic meaning of this event. In Romans 3:24-25 he draws on several of these images when he narrates the benefits which accrue to those who recognize God's justice revealed in the faithfulness of Jesus Christ even unto death on the cross:

> They are now justified by his grace as a gift, through
> the redemption that is in Christ Jesus, whom God put
> forward as a sacrifice of atonement by his blood, effective through faith. (Romans 3:24-25)

Jesus's death is pictured using the language of cultic sacrifice, specifically the Day of Atonement rituals, as well as redemption or ransom imagery rooted in the practice of the release of slaves or prisoners of war. In Colossians Paul depicts Jesus the victim as the one who in his death paradoxically overturns the very powers that killed him:

> And when you were dead in trespasses and the uncircumcision of your flesh, God made you alive together
> with him, when he forgave us all our trespasses, erasing
> the record that stood against us with its legal demands.
> He set this aside, nailing it to the cross. He disarmed the
> rulers and authorities and made a public example of
> them, triumphing over them in it. (Colossians 2:13-15)

The gospel concerning Jesus the Messiah therefore turns the existing power relationships upside down, with the victim victorious and the rulers and authorities defeated. In 1 Corinthians 2:8 Paul comments that, if the rulers of the present age had realized what was actually going on, "they would not have crucified the Lord of glory."

Paul's story of Jesus announces a surprising twist in the path taken by God's Son. The Messiah is killed. Yet this tragedy and its sequel, the resurrection, turn out to release the liberating power of God both for Jews in their ongoing diaspora among the nations and for Gentiles in their idolatry. The resurrection of Jesus reverses the verdict of death by crucifixion and opens the path of victory to all who trust in God.

God's Son, the Crucified Messiah, the Exalted Lord

In Romans 1:3-4 Jesus is the anointed one, the Messiah, the Christ. He is also "our Lord." Hence the more complete designation is given: "Jesus Christ our Lord." The title *Lord* (Greek: *kurios*) occurs frequently in Paul's letters as a reference to Jesus and can also point to God. Often it is not obvious which is which, as the following citation from Romans 10 makes clear:

> If you confess with your lips that Jesus is Lord and believe in your heart that God raised him from the dead, you will be saved. For one believes with the heart and so is justified, and one confesses with the mouth and so is saved. The scripture says, "No one who believes in him will be put to shame." For there is no distinction between Jew and Greek; the same Lord is Lord of all and is generous to all who call on him. For, "Everyone who calls on the name of the Lord shall be saved." (10:9-13)

When Paul seeks support for his assertion that "the Lord of all" graciously responds to all who call on him, he cites Joel 2:3, where *the Lord* denotes the God of Israel, who is God of all. In Paul's mind, however, to "call on the name of the Lord" is also to confess that "Jesus is Lord." The Lord Jesus Christ is now envisioned as fulfilling the role of the Lord God.

This acknowledgment of the lordship of Jesus the Messiah likely goes back to the earliest experiences of worship and scriptural reflection within the community of his disciples and initial followers. Judging from the frequency of citations and allusions to Psalm 110, this psalm must have been high on the list of Scripture texts found to be giving testimony to the lordship of Jesus the Christ. In its opening verse, early Christians heard the Lord God empower the messiah Jesus, whom they honored as "my Lord," to reign in triumph over their enemies:

> The LORD says to my lord, "Sit at my right hand until
> I make your enemies your footstool." (110:1)

Several of the echoes of Psalm 110:1 in Paul's letters emphasize Jesus's position of authority on the right hand of God: Romans 8:34; 1 Corinthians 15:25; Colossians 3:1; Ephesians 1:20. A shorthand articulation of this conviction concerning the reign of Jesus as Lord emerges as a simple yet powerful confession, possibly the earliest Christian confession of all: "Jesus is Lord." In 1 Corinthians 12:3, the confession "Jesus is Lord" serves as the test of the authenticity of inspired utterance. In 2 Corinthians 4:5 Paul summarizes his gospel as the proclamation of Jesus Christ as Lord. And, as we have seen, the hymn in Philippians 2 climaxes by envisioning a future acclamation by every tongue in heaven and on earth: *Jesus Christ is Lord* (Philippians 2:11).

When Paul joins the early church in confessing that God's Son, the crucified Messiah, is Lord of all, they not only speak the language of the Psalms and other Scripture, they make a claim that was recognized as blatantly political. Paul echoes this claim and enlarges on its scriptural grounding. The upshot is clear. Because God is sovereign, the emperor is not supreme. Because Jesus Christ is Lord, Caesar is not. The imperial cult with its announcement of Caesar as the savior and lord and guarantor of peace and security is undercut by the believers' acclamation of the lordship of Jesus the Messiah.

Part 2

God's Unfolding Story

INTRODUCTION

In a life-transforming encounter with Jesus Christ, Paul catches a dazzling vision of the future. He begins to participate in the life, worship, and mission of the community he once zealously sought to destroy. He sings the hymn lauding Christ as Lord of all. He launches an energetic ministry as itinerant evangelist, preaching the gospel of the Lord Jesus Christ. And, wherever he goes, he leaves churches in his wake. As a missionary pastor he tells the story and quotes the hymn, knowing that the story of Jesus forms the character of these communities of faith now springing up throughout the Mediterranean region.

But how does Paul's present experience with the crucified and risen Christ connect with what he knows from his past? How does he understand the Scriptures in light of the coming of Christ? Does his personal experience of call and transformation launch him into a mission that is severed from the Jewish traditions that had shaped him? What message can Paul share with the largely Gentile congregations that emerged as a result of the proclamation of the gospel? Like Paul, each group of believers has glimpsed the future in Jesus Christ. Yet each congregation also knows firsthand that their present circumstances are often marked by difficulty and challenge.

In part 2, we consider how Paul's transforming glimpse of the future relates to what God has done in the past, as attested in the law and the prophets and the writings. In each of Paul's letters to congregations, this view of the future, as linked to God's work in the past, intersects with the life of the people of God in the present.

Perhaps the "auto on the road" metaphor shared earlier can help us to conceptualize our agenda here. With eyes fixed on the road ahead for the congregations scattered around the Mediterranean, Paul constantly checks the rearview as well. In the recent past he sees the cross and the empty tomb, which testify to Jesus as Messiah and Lord. The scenery surrounding the crucified and risen Christ is the landscape of God's handiwork as portrayed by the Scriptures. God creates and rescues. God calls a particular people to be the channel of divine blessing to all. God enters into covenant with that people and gives them the law. God relates to the people of Israel both in judgment and with reassurance in their interactions with other nations, especially during the ongoing experience of Israel's dispersion among the nations. And overall, God demonstrates the sovereign intention both to save those who trust and to judge those who persist in their defiance.

God's story, as this story can be traced in the Scriptures, is not limited to the past. Now focused climactically in the story of Jesus, whom Paul had encountered en route to Damascus, the story of God's dealings also has a future. Along with Paul in his pastoral interactions with churches in first-century Corinth, Rome and Thessalonica we now enter into the mystery and the wonder of God's still unfolding story as the One who creates, calls, covenants, counsels, and consoles a people now enlarged through an apocalypse of Jesus Christ.

3

GOD, FROM WHOM ARE ALL THINGS

We have been in touch with the congregation in Philippi, for whom Paul recalled a hymn in honor of Jesus, a hymn that was apparently sung in various congregations throughout the first-century Roman world. This time we join a delegation from the city of Corinth on their way to visit Paul in Ephesus. His evangelistic efforts in their city a few years earlier led to the emergence of an assembly of the saints.

In 1 Corinthians 16:15-18 Paul commends three individuals who appear to have visited him as representatives of the Corinthian congregation: Stephanas, Fortunatus, and Achaicus. In 16:5-9 he informs the church at Corinth about his own plans to revisit Corinth as part of a tour that would take him first briefly to Macedonia and then for a longer period to Achaia. Paul lets them know that he wants to stay in Ephesus until Pentecost. Elsewhere in this letter Paul alludes to rumors and oral reports he's received about conflict and rivalry among the Corinthians (1:11-12). There is also a blatant case of sexual immorality (5:1-13) and discord at the Lord's Supper (11:17-22). A particularly vexing issue for Paul is a question of whether it is appropriate to eat food that has been offered to idols (8:1-13; 10:25-30).

Our opening narrative attempts to portray the situation in the Corinth congregation based on the texts enumerated above. This narrative also uses the term "to corinthianize," which entered popular usage of the day to describe a lifestyle of sexual immorality and materialism for which Corinth had a particular reputation (see Adams & Horrell, 2004:7n42; Gorman, 2004:228).

This story features, first, Stephanas, Fortunatus, and Achaicus and their memories and reflections as they make their way from Corinth to Ephesus and, second, the meeting of the three leaders from the congregation in Corinth with the apostle in Ephesus.

A STORY: A Delegation, Their Congregation, and the Apostle

As they sailed out of the port of Cenchreae onto the gulf leading toward the Aegean Sea, Stephanas, Fortunatus, and Achaicus instinctively turned their gaze back toward their home, the city of Corinth. In their minds they recalled some of the tumultuous history of their region. The emperor Julius Caesar had established Corinth as a Roman colony in 44 B.C., about a hundred years ago. Approximately a hundred years before that, the Roman army had destroyed the Greek city that was previously located at that site. Many of the original Roman colonists in Julius Caesar's time who made the newly reestablished Corinth their home were former slaves who, upon achieving their freedom, welcomed a setting like Corinth where they could get a new start. Fortunatus recalled for his traveling companions some of the stories in his own family about their roots as former slaves who had come from Rome to settle in Corinth. "My life certainly is easier now than it was for my great grandparents," he commented.

Stephanas and Achaicus looked at Fortunatus and nodded. Each of them had done well within the economic environment in Corinth and the surrounding region. Certainly by the time the Jewish evangelist Paul arrived on the scene in Corinth early in the 50s, descendants of freed slaves were getting ahead. Corinth, situated on an isthmus linking the region of Achaia to the mainland of Greece, provided businesspeople and other travelers convenient access to the major harbors of the Aegean Sea and the Ionian Sea. As host of the Isthmian games, Corinth periodically attracted athletes and spectators, who added another source of revenue. Pulsing with merchants, sailors, military people, and other travelers, Corinth was known for its services to the traveling public. These amenities included the availability of prostitutes to satisfy the sexual appetites of both wayfarers and locals. As a city, Corinth had gained something of a shady reputation for its sexual promiscuity. One poet, Aristophanes, even coined the verb "to corinthianize" to refer to the penchant toward immoral sexual behavior. However, other observers of national morality mused that in the area of moral attitudes and practices Corinth was actually no different from any other seaport city.

In their rambling conversation, Stephanas, Fortunatus, and Achaicus turned to the theme of religious life in Corinth. They agreed that their city offered a veritable smorgasbord of religious options. The cults of Aphrodite, the goddess of love, and Asklepios, a god with reputed healing powers, plus a host of other traditional and mystery religions attracted many pilgrims to the numerous temples situated in Corinth. The temple of Apollos had become especially prominent in the life of the community. Some visitors educated in philosophy came looking for opportunity to debate and discuss with others. Some traveled to Corinth primarily to pursue their business interests. All visitors, whether they came on business or for pleasure, were keenly aware that the temple of Apollos was a gathering place not only for religious ritual but also for social interaction.

The main topic of conversation for the three travelers
en route to Ephesus had to do with what had happened to
them after they met with a Jewish missionary named Paul.
All three recalled vividly the time when Paul arrived in
their lively urban center, set up shop as a tentmaker in the
marketplace, and began to share the gospel of Jesus Christ
with his customers. Initially Stephanas, Fortunatus, and
Achaicus could not believe their eyes when people started
to respond to Paul's message about a crucified Jew named
Jesus. They had known that among the many religious
expressions in Corinth was a Jewish synagogue. They regularly noticed local Jews gathering in the synagogue for
Sabbath worship observances. Sometimes they would hear
their Jewish neighbors reciting what they called the Shema:
"Hear, O Israel: The LORD is our God, the LORD alone.
You shall love the LORD your God with all your heart, and
with all your soul, and with all your might."

But this Jew from Tarsus of Cilicia exuded a boldness
that surprised them. To their utter amazement Paul's message of the crucified Christ took root and an assembly of
believers emerged, even in their wild Roman outpost on the
isthmus. After hearing what Paul had to say, each of them
personally accepted the gospel of Jesus Christ as well.
Stephanas recalled that Paul baptized him and several other
members of his household. Fortunatus and Achaicus also
remembered their decision personally to accept Paul's gospel
of the crucified Messiah and their subsequent call, along
with Stephanas, to give leadership to this congregation.

Several days later, their boat entered the port near
Ephesus. After a brief search, Stephanas, Fortunatus, and
Achaicus discovered Paul deeply immersed in ministry in
the city of Ephesus but eager to hear of recent developments in the Corinthian church. The visitors presented the
letter written by leaders of the congregation, only to learn

that Paul was already puzzling over rumors and reports that had reached him. He was visibly perplexed. "What is happening there?" he asked.

Some time earlier Paul had written a letter to the church, urging them to discipline those members whose immorality was contaminating the whole congregation and leaving a negative witness in the city. Among other things he now heard that what he had written in that first letter had been flagrantly misrepresented, and he would need to write again to correct the misreading. What made this doubly urgent was the fact that the church seemed to be paralyzed in responding to a particularly disturbing case of sexually improper behavior. Apparently a man was living with his father's wife.

But Paul caught wind of other upsetting developments as well. Some people had been lining up behind their favorite leaders in ways that created a divisive spirit within the congregation. Even the Lord's Supper had led to division, this time between wealthy and poor people in the congregation.

Among the many questions raised and assertions made in the letter, Paul fixed on the matter of whether or not it was appropriate for the believers to eat meat that had been previously offered to idols. Indeed, he mused, in cities like Corinth it was difficult to find meat that had not had some previous history with the temple. Reading this part of their letter he sensed that the most important question may have been not whether to eat such meat but where and with whom it was proper to do so. The temple with its festivals had become the primary setting for social networking for anyone seeking to move up the social and economic ladder. It was especially tempting for the wealthier members of the church to frequent the temple to make contact with potential business clients or cultivate relationships with important community leaders.

Was it fitting for Christians to have fellowship, to eat and drink with others, in a setting dedicated to the worship of pagan gods and goddesses? Paul sensed the need for some pastoral searching, of both his heart and the Scriptures, to discern what God might be saying to these blemished and threatened saints in Corinth.

While Stephanas, Fortunatus, and Achaicus busied themselves with other matters in Ephesus and other places in the region, Paul devoted his prayerful attention to the writing of another letter to the church at Corinth.

One God, One Lord, Creator and Redeemer!

> Indeed, even though there may be so-called gods in heaven or on earth—as in fact there are many gods and many lords—yet for us there is one God, the Father, from whom are all things and for whom we exist, and one Lord, Jesus Christ, through whom are all things and through whom we exist. (1 Corinthians 8:5-6)

During visits to cities like Corinth Paul realized with gripping clarity the need for prayerful reflection on the "big story" of God's grand intention. He had had a dramatic face-off with the living Christ and joined in the church's sung confession of Christ as Lord. He also felt compelled to engage in ongoing careful study of Scripture. How do his experiences with Christ and the church's veneration of the risen Lord fit with what God has done in the past? Further, what is God doing, and what does God still want to do?

In his study and prayer Paul finds that his thoughts often turn to the scriptural narratives about God's work as creator, sustainer, and redeemer. Paul's Scripture citations and allusions within his Corinthian correspondence suggest that he has been pondering the biblical Creation story in Genesis and the Psalms:

> For "the earth and its fullness are the Lord's."
> (1 Corinthians 10:26; citation of Psalm 24:1)

> For it is the God who said, "Let light shine out of darkness," who has shone in our hearts to give the light of the knowledge of the glory of God in the face of Jesus Christ." (2 Corinthians 4:6; a quotation from Genesis 1:3)

Judging from the predominance of wisdom themes in 1 Corinthians, especially in 1:17-2:16, Paul appears also to have been influenced by what the book of Proverbs affirms about wisdom's role in creation. Similar themes are also found in Wisdom of Solomon 7:22b–8:1 and Sirach 24:1-22. In Proverbs 8:22-31, wisdom speaks about her beginnings, when God created all things:

> The LORD created me at the beginning of his work, the first of his acts of long ago. Ages ago I was set up, at the first, before the beginning of the earth. When there were no depths I was brought forth, when there were no springs abounding with water. Before the mountains had been shaped, before the hills, I was brought forth—when he had not yet made earth and fields, or the world's first bits of soil. (Proverbs 8:22-26)

Having been created by God, wisdom worked as God's partner in the creation of the heavens, the seas, the earth, and all their inhabitants:

> When he established the heavens, I was there, when he drew a circle on the face of the deep, when he made firm the skies above, when he established the fountains

of the deep, when he assigned to the sea its limit, so
that the waters might not transgress his command,
when he marked out the foundations of the earth, then
I was beside him, like a master worker; and I was daily
his delight, rejoicing before him always, rejoicing in his
inhabited world and delighting in the human race.
(8:27-31)

These affirmations about wisdom, both created by God
and co-creator with God, have likely shaped how Paul
views Jesus Christ and his work: "He [God] is the source
of your life in Christ Jesus, who became for us wisdom
from God" (1 Corinthians 1:30).

However, the affirmations about God's creating and
sustaining work in texts like these from Genesis, the
Psalms, the Proverbs, and elsewhere soon bump into the
realities of life for the church within its cultural context.
Each congregation presents a challenge to Paul as he offers
pastoral nurture and admonition. Certainly the church at
Corinth is no exception. What Paul undoubtedly notices in
Corinth is rampant idolatry, a flagrant display of images in
temples and elsewhere, clearly abhorrent to any Jew. Paul
recognizes that Jewish people have needed to find an
appropriate balance between accommodation and resistance in negotiating their relationships with the dominant
Roman political and religious culture. Nowhere is this
agenda more critical than for the community of the saints
in Corinth.

Wherever Jews like Paul encounter a culture like the
one in Corinth, they are always reminded that the Torah
strictly prohibits idolatry. Their worship and allegiance
belong to God alone, as the beginning of the Decalogue
clearly shows:

Then God spoke all these words: I am the LORD your
God, who brought you out of the land of Egypt, out of
the house of slavery; you shall have no other gods
before me. You shall not make for yourself an idol,
whether in the form of anything that is in heaven
above, or that is on the earth beneath, or that is in the
water under the earth. You shall not bow down to
them or worship them; for I the LORD your God am a
jealous God, punishing children for the iniquity of parents, to the third and the fourth generation of those
who reject me, but showing steadfast love to the thou-
sandth generation of those who love me and keep my
commandments. (Exodus 20:1-6)

Dispersed among the nations, the Jewish people found
abundant indications of idolatrous behavior among the
Gentiles in whose midst they lived. How then were the
Jews to relate to these neighbors, their idols, and their
gods?

For Paul, the Jewish apostle to the nations, the question is similar: How are the Jews and Gentiles within the
community confessing the sovereignty of God and the
lordship of Christ to define their relationship with pagan
neighbors, their idols, and their gods?

God Is at Work!

From the beginning of 1 Corinthians, Paul advances frequent reminders concerning God's work in their lives and
God's grand intention for their present and future. Already
in the opening salutation Paul reminds them that they are
"the church of God" (1:2; cf. 3:9), and he extends to them
a wish for God's grace and peace in their life as a congregation (1:3). He also thanks God for this grace, which has
been made known to them so richly (1:4-5). And he assures
these believers that "God is faithful" (1:9). This reassurance

is later echoed in 10:13 in the context of his pastoral admonition on the issue of the eating of meat offered to idols.

Paul's affirmation of the faithfulness of God leads him directly into reflections on the message of the cross of Jesus Christ as manifestation of God's power and God's wisdom (1:18–2:5). Paul says that the message concerning a crucified Messiah "is foolishness to those who are perishing, but to us who are being saved it is the power of God" (1:18). He exults in the mystery of God's surprising reversal of the world's wisdom. Paradoxically, the message of "Christ crucified" has become a demonstration of "the power of God and the wisdom of God" (1:23-24). The believers in Corinth will have heard clearly that, even though by standard criteria within their culture they were seen as foolish and weak and low and despised (1:26), the God of surprises has called them. Paul writes, "You were called into the fellowship of his Son, Jesus Christ our Lord" (1:9; cf. 1:27-31).

In a word, God has chosen to create a community composed of people often scorned by the world. This is the work of the God who both creates and redeems. The God who in the beginning created the world and its inhabitants out of nothing has now acted through Christ to redeem and shape a motley group of "nobodies" into a community of saints whose only boast is in the Lord. When he considers what God as creator and redeemer has done, Paul gives voice to a rush of lofty thoughts:

> [God] is the source of your life in Christ Jesus, who became for us wisdom from God, and righteousness and sanctification and redemption, in order that, as it is written, "Let the one who boasts, boast in the Lord." (1:30-31)

The language of creation here underscores the fact that God is the source of the life of the Corinthian congregation. The same God who formed the world has brought them into being.

Here is a theologically loaded declaration, which Paul shaped as the climax to his reflections on the scandalous and foolish message of the cross. When viewed from the perspective of God's cosmic intention, the scandal and foolishness of the cross has been paralleled in the emergence of a people, low and despised in the world, who now know their life to be rooted within God's creative and redemptive work in Jesus Christ. In a culture that prizes wisdom, this minority community of "nothings" has experienced in the crucified Christ the very wisdom of God, manifest in righteousness, sanctification and redemption.

Paul employs a variety of images to describe "the church of God that is at Corinth" (1:2), including several that draw on creation themes:

> I planted, Apollos watered, but God gave the growth.
> So neither the one who plants nor the one who waters
> is anything, but only God who gives the growth. So
> neither the one who plants nor the one who waters is
> anything, but only God who gives the growth (3:6-7)

Paul also talks about the church as "God's building" (3:9), more specifically as "God's temple" (3:16, 17). And in summing up these reflections about the church as God's project, Paul breaks out with doxological flourish:

> So let no one boast about human leaders. For all
> things are yours, whether Paul or Apollos or Cephas or
> the world or life or death or the present or the future
> —all belong to you, and you belong to Christ, and
> Christ belongs to God. (3:21-23)

Rebuking the Corinthian proclivity toward boastful favoritism, Paul points them toward each other as coparticipants with Christ and ultimately therefore as people under the sovereign care of the one true God.

As he engages the Corinthian church about their attitudes and behavior in the area of sexuality and marriage in 1 Corinthians 5–7, Paul also builds on his understanding of God's creation. He commends normal sexual relations between a man and a woman within marriage (7:1-7), even though personally he favors singleness because of the urgency of the times ("The present form of this world is passing away," 7:31). Paul affirms the goodness of the body as created by God, and he urges the Corinthians to recognize that sexual behavior needs to be guided by the Creator's intention.

> The body is not meant for immorality, but for the
> Lord, and the Lord for the body. And God raised the
> Lord and will also raise us up by his power. (6:13-14)

Paul therefore prohibits sexual intercourse with a prostitute, citing the Creation story in Genesis 2:24, "The two shall be one flesh" (6:16). He also recycles the temple imagery employed earlier in a reference to the church body (3:16, 17) by applying it to individual bodily behavior:

> Or do you not know that your body is a temple of the
> Holy Spirit within you, which you have from God, and
> that you are not your own? For you were bought with
> a price; therefore glorify God in your body. (6:19-20)

God's creative, sustaining, and redeeming work therefore results in God's claim on the believer to conform to a lifestyle that gives glory to God. (For further discussion of 1 Corinthians 5–7, see chapter 11.)

One God, One Lord

The creative and redemptive work of God in Christ is the first point of appeal when Paul begins to address the difficult issue of food sacrificed to idols (1 Corinthians 8:1–11:1). As we now turn to an analysis of Paul's pastoral response to this issue raised in the Corinthian's letter to him, we notice that he focuses first on what it means to "know" something. Apparently their letter asserts, and Paul basically agrees, that "all of us possess knowledge" (8:1). Anticipating the ethical counsel developed later (8:9-13; 10:23-32), Paul commends this group of believers to the way of love, which builds up, rather than the pursuit of knowledge, which puffs up (8:1-2). Then Paul adds a statement that provides a strong clue about how he approaches the issue of food offered to idols. When he says that "anyone who loves God is known by him" (8:3) he seems to be alluding to the Jewish Shema, especially its second half:

> Hear, O Israel: The Lord is our God, the Lord alone.
> You shall love the Lord your God with all your heart,
> and with all your soul, and with all your might.
> (Deuteronomy 6:4-5)

Paul combines this primary Jewish confession acknowledging the one supreme God with stock Jewish polemic against idols: "We know that 'no idol in the world really exists' and that 'there is no God but one'" (1 Corinthians 8:4).

When he launches his major response to the question of whether to participate in eating food that has been previously offered in sacrifice to idols, Paul cites the central Jewish confession of faith. But he does not stop with that. He expands the Shema, the standard Jewish affirmation of the sovereignty of God, by adding a parallel assertion concerning Jesus Christ.

Deuteronomy 6:4	1 Corinthians 8:6
The Lord is our God,	There is one God, the Father, from whom are all things and for whom we all exist
The Lord alone	and one Lord, Jesus Christ, through whom are all things and through whom we exist.

Scholars generally agree that in 8:6 Paul is quoting a creed or confession commonly affirmed within the early church. In 8:5 he comments sardonically about the many religious options available in Corinth: "In fact there are many gods and many lords." Paul confronts this religious variety by remembering both the Shema's assertion of the sovereignty of God and the church's declaration concerning the lordship of Christ. In doing so, he significantly develops the plot of the underlying theological narrative out of which he relates pastorally to this church.

This theological narrative has roles for both God the Father and the Lord Jesus Christ. The confession employs different prepositions when narrating the respective roles. God the Father is the one "from whom are all things, and for whom we exist." The Lord Jesus Christ is the one "through whom are all things and through whom we exist." God is the source and the goal of both creation and redemption; Jesus Christ the Lord is the mediator in both creation and redemption. In the mystery of God's working the two are one! And strikingly, for Paul and generally for the church, affirming the lordship of Jesus Christ neither contradicts nor diminishes their convictions about the sovereignty of God.

For the congregation upset by divisions concerning the issue of idol-dedicated food, Paul sees ethical consequences arising from this theological narrative. The question of how one knows God is not answered by a process of logical deduction or through a mystical infusion of insight. Rather, those who acknowledge the one God and enter into a relationship with this God through Jesus Christ truly know and love God, and they do so only because God knows them. This covenant relationship with God is initiated by God, but it also requires a response: the recipients of God's love are enabled to love others. Paul's challenge to the Corinthians in 8:7-13 is that they should demonstrate the loving and self-giving character of God in their relationships to each other. By insisting on their personal rights to hobnob in the temple, some of the Corinthian believers were actually destroying other brothers or sisters (8:11), persons who were also created in God's image and redeemed through Christ's death on the cross.

In 9:1-23 Paul reinforces this encouragement by referring to his own example. Even though as apostle he has the right to receive financial support from the church, he renounces that right and works for his own support, so that he might be able to win more people to the gospel. His use of athletic imagery in 9:24-27 also underscores this call for self-denial and self-discipline, not for the sake of individual glory but for the overall welfare of the community of faith, especially its weaker members. (See chapter 10 for further discussion of 1 Corinthians 9.)

No Flirting with Idolatry

The knowledge that idols and the gods they represent actually have no real existence (8:4) does not adequately equip believers to deal with what Paul sees as the sinister reality of the spiritual realm of demons. Idolatry, he believes, can actually lead to destruction. As Paul's further admonition in 10:1-22 points out, their gravest peril is not the ignorance of those lacking knowledge but the bondage of those who cavort with demons. By the end of this section Paul pulls no punches. He asks, "Are we provoking the Lord to jealousy? Are we stronger than he?" (10:22).

To drive home the grave danger inherent in participating in the local temple festivals and social meals, Paul in 10:1-13 offers a creative rereading of a formative chapter in the story of ancient Israel. Previously he had quoted the church's reformulation of the Shema in light of the exaltation of Christ as Lord (8:6). Now he tells the story of Israel's exodus out of Egypt and her experiences in the wilderness in ways that serve both as reminders of God's grace extended to all and as warnings of judgment when some squander this legacy of grace.

It is striking that even when addressing a Christian community composed mostly of Gentiles, Paul refers to the exodus and wilderness generation of Israelites as "our ancestors" (10:1). The church of God in Roman Corinth is rooted in the story of Israel, the people created and called by God, rescued by God from their bondage in Egypt, and led through the wilderness to the land of promise. Paul narrates what happened to the people of Israel in order to supply an example and to instruct that later generation, the congregation in Corinth, "on whom the end of the ages has come" (10:11).

The following table demonstrates that Paul sees significant parallels between what happened to the wilderness generation of Israel and the situation transpiring in the Corinthian church. The Corinthian's experience of God's grace is prefigured in that earlier story, which serves as an important reminder to them (10:1-4).

What Happened to the Israelites	Reminders to the Corinthians
"Our ancestors were all under the cloud, and all passed through the sea, and all were baptized into Moses in the cloud and in the sea." (10:1-2; cf. Exodus 13:12-22; 14:21-23)	Reminders of their baptism in the Spirit and with water
"All ate the same spiritual food and all drank the same spiritual drink. For they drank from the spiritual rock that followed them." (10:3, 4; cf. Exodus 16–17; Numbers 20)	Reminders of the Lord's Supper "The rock was Christ." (10:4)

Paul also views God's judgment on the wilderness generation as a warning for the present generation of believers in Corinth (10:5-10). The following table shows how he saw the biblical narratives about the people of Israel wandering in the wilderness as analogous to what could happen to the congregation in Corinth unless they heed warnings implicit in the Israelites' story. Some of Paul's references to what happened to the wilderness generation Israelites are clearly recognizable, while others cannot be established with any certainty.

What Happened to the Israelites	Warnings to the Corinthians
"Nevertheless, God was not pleased with most of them, and they were struck down in the wilderness." (10:5)	"Now these things occurred as examples for us, so that we might not desire evil as they did." (10:6)
"Do not become idolaters as some of them did; as it is written, 'The people sat down to eat and drink, and they rose up to play.'" (10:7; cf. Exodus 32 story of eating and drinking, and dancing around the golden calf)	"Do not become idolaters like some of them did." (10:7)

What Happened to the Israelites	Warnings to the Corinthians
"We must not indulge in sexual immorality as some of them did, and twenty-three thousand fell in a single day." (10:8; cf. the story in Numbers 25:1-9 about Israelite men having sex with Moabite women, also eating with them and bowing down to their gods)	"We must not indulge in sexual immorality as some of them did." (10:8)
"We must not put Christ to the test as some of them did, and were destroyed by serpents." (10:9; cf. the story in Numbers 21:4-9 about complaining against God and being destroyed by serpents)	"We must not put Christ to the test." (10:9)
"Do not complain as some of them did and were destroyed by the destroyer." (10:10; possibly a reference to the complaints of the people, and their desire to return to Egypt, as narrated in Numbers 14:2-4, although there is no mention of the destroyer.)	"Do not complain as some of them did." (10:10)

Anyone hearing Paul's lively retelling of the story of Israel in the wilderness would have come away with a vivid sense that indeed God is a jealous God with a policy of zero tolerance for idolatry. Most grievously at risk are those who offer allegiance to other gods and confidently think their enlightened knowledge about idols will keep them safe: "If you think you are standing, watch out that you do not fall" (10:12). Though "God is faithful" and provides strength in times of testing (10:13), God also requires clear discernment of the role of the spiritual powers that are aligned against God and God's people.

This recognition of the spiritual peril of flirting with demons leads Paul to plead tenderly with the believers in

Corinth, "Therefore, my dear friends" (Greek: *my beloved*), "flee from the worship of idols" (10:14). Referring to the Lord's Supper (10:16-17) and sacrificial meals in the Jewish temple (10:18) and pagan ritual meals (10:20), he drives his point home. During all of these occasions of eating and drinking in the presence of a deity, a partnership is formed between the worshiper and the god being worshipped. In 11:25, with reference to the Lord's Supper, Paul uses the language of covenant. For Paul the upshot of the argument is clear:

> You cannot drink the cup of the Lord and the cup of demons. You cannot partake of the table of the Lord and the table of demons. (10:21)

After what feels like a categorical prohibition of participation in meals in the pagan temples Paul recapitulates his earlier more conciliatory ethical counsel on buying marketplace meat or eating such meat in private homes (10:23-30). It is clear that he expresses his adamant opposition only against taking part in actual temple meals or festivals. On one hand, he cites Psalm 24:1 to affirm that everything created by God is good:

> Eat whatever is sold in the meat market without raising any question on the ground of conscience, for "the earth and its fullness are the Lord's." (10:26)

The enjoyment of God's good gift of food should, therefore, be accompanied by thanksgiving (10:30). On the other hand, enjoyment of God's creation should not jeopardize what is the higher good, namely, seeking the welfare of others: "Do not seek your own advantage, but that of the other" (10:25).

Paul wraps up his pastoral response to the question about food sacrificed to idols by extending a general appeal and by urging the Corinthians to follow his example. The appeal is stated with reference to God: "So, whether you eat or drink, or whatever you do, do everything for the glory of God" (10:31). The example is articulated in terms of Christ: "Be imitators of me, as I am of Christ" (11:1). Once again he integrates theology and Christology. All of life is to glorify the one God who creates and redeems. This God has been made known in Christ, whose servant stance in his life and death calls for imitation. Relationships within the community of the faithful need to glorify God the creator and echo God's character as made known in Jesus Christ.

God as All in All

After dealing with the food issue, Paul provides pastoral counsel about other matters, including relationships between women and men in worship (11:2-16), economic disparity manifest during their celebrations of the Lord's Supper (11:17-34), the exercise of spiritual gifts within the faith community (12:1–14:40), and the resurrection of the dead (15:1-58). In a variety of ways he alludes in these sections to the grand themes of God's work as creator.

In 11:3 Paul advocates what has often been understood as a hierarchy of relationships rooted in his understanding of the Genesis creation narratives:

> But I want you to understand that Christ is the head of
> every man, and the husband is the head of his wife,
> and God is the head of Christ. (11:3)

The NRSV translation cited here understands this to be a description of an order of relationships in which God is the head of Christ, Christ is the head of every man, and the husband is the head of his wife. The NIV suggests a more generic reading regarding the latter: "The head of the woman is man." Because the underlying word for *head* can also mean "source," some interpreters see reflected here the Genesis 2 Creation story about God fashioning the woman out of a rib taken from the man (see Fee, 1987:501-5).

That Paul has the Creation narratives in mind is apparent in 11:7 where he seems to regard the image of God to be localized to the man: "He is the image and reflection of God; but woman is the reflection of man." The NRSV rendering of Genesis 1:27 suggests that both male and female reflect God's image: "So God created humankind in his image, in the image of God he created them; male and female he created them." Paul appears to be intent on emphasizing gender difference, perhaps because of a threatened blurring of such distinctions in Corinth. However, even here Paul also underscores the interdependence between men and women in the Lord:

> Nevertheless, in the Lord woman is not independent of
> man or man independent of woman. For just as
> woman came from man, so man comes through
> woman; but all things come from God. (11:11-12)

Ultimately God is the one from whom all things come. Since "all things come from God" the community in its worship and in their relationships with each other needs to honor God in ways that reflect the new relationships now made possible "in the Lord." (For more discussion of this text, see chapter 10.)

In his "resurrection chapter" (1 Corinthians 15) Paul also draws on explicit creation themes, especially in 15:20-28, where he articulates his ringing affirmation of Christ's resurrection and the implications of this eschatological event for the believing community. Recalling the Israelite practice of bringing the first of the harvest in thanksgiving to God (Deuteronomy 26:1-11; Leviticus 23:9-14), he calls the resurrected Christ "the first fruits of those who have died" (15:20). God who raised Jesus pledges an abundant future harvest in the resurrection of the dead. Paul envisions God's life-restoring activity at the resurrection as parallel in significant ways to God's work at Creation. Furthermore, God's creative life-restoring work is made necessary by the power of death unleashed through the sin of humanity. In terms of the biblical narrative of Creation and idolatry in the first three chapters of Genesis, death entered the world through Adam acting as representative of sinful humanity. Paul describes the resurrection of Jesus as reversing the death spiral begun in Adam:

> For since death came through a human being, the resurrection of the dead has also come through a human being; for as all die in Adam, so all will be made alive in Christ. (15:21-22)

This Adam/Christ analogy recurs elsewhere in Paul's letters, and will be discussed further under "First Adam and Last" below. For now we note that to Paul, Adam symbolizes the beginning of the (old) creation and Jesus embodies and launches the new creation in which the powers of sin and death are ultimately defeated.

This defeat of death as *the last enemy* is what Paul sees as the outcome of the eschatological drama of liberation begun in Christ and still to be consummated: "Christ the first fruits, then at his coming those who belong to Christ" (15:23). This drama reaches its intended goal in the transfer of the kingdom to God the Father after the destruction of "every ruler and every authority and power" (15:24), including, climactically, the last enemy, death (15:25-26). In addition to Psalm 110:1, with its reference to the vanquishing of all enemies, Paul quotes from Psalm 8:7: "For 'God has put all things in subjection under his feet'" (15:27). Strikingly, Psalm 8 echoes the Genesis Creation story, especially the theme of humanity's dominion over the animals and other works of God's hands (8:6-8; cf. Genesis 1:27). Paul's exegesis of Psalm 8 and the underlying Creation account concentrates the exercise of dominion in Jesus Christ, who subjects all things to God. But Paul clarifies that the Son is also included among "all things" ultimately subject to God. What then is the final result? Paul envisions the consummation of all things through Christ, in order that "God may be all in all" (15:28).

In 15:35-49 Paul speculates about the nature of the resurrection body. He does so, first, by drawing attention to readily observable phenomena in the natural world. A remarkable transformation takes place when a naked seed is planted in the ground and germinates (15:36-38). Human and animal life forms have many different kinds of flesh (15:39). Earthly and celestial bodies differ in their glory (15:40-41). Similarly there is a dramatic metamorphosis that occurs between the lowering of the perishable body into the ground at death and its resurrection in glory (15:42-43).

Having noted analogies from nature, Paul adds a second type of argument, the exegesis of Scripture. To give scriptural support to conclusions drawn from his reflections on the world of nature, both earthly and celestial, Paul offers an interpretation of Genesis 2:7:

> Thus it is written, "The first man, Adam, became a living being"; the last Adam became a life-giving spirit. But it is not the spiritual that is first, but the physical, and

> then the spiritual. The first man was from the earth, a
> man of dust; the second man is from heaven. As was the
> man of dust, so are those who are of the dust; and as is
> the man of heaven, so are those who are of heaven. Just
> as we have borne the image of the man of dust, we will
> also bear the image of the man of heaven. (15:45-49)

Here Paul points to both continuity and contrast between
"the first man, Adam," and "the last Adam" Jesus Christ.
Christ as "a life-giving spirit" identifies him as having a re-
creative role at the consummation of all things, a role that
corresponds to the life-giving activity of God at Creation.
When God breathed life into the lump of clay, "a living
being" (Greek: *psyche*, "soul") emerged, a being that is
physical (Greek: *psychikos*, "soulish"), "a man of dust."
When God raised Jesus from the dead, "a life-giving spirit" came into being. Paul summarizes with commentary
that employs the language of "image," echoing and building on the Creation narrative ("image of God," Genesis
1:26-27). Humanity bears God's image as imprinted at creation: "we have borne the image of the man of dust."
Humanity through Christ also anticipates the consummation of the new creation: "we will also bear the image of
the man of heaven."

As we will see in chapter 13, Paul's climax in this letter to the church at Corinth underscores God's victory
through the resurrection of Christ. He assures them that
"in the Lord your labor is not in vain" (1 Corinthians
15:58). He instructs them on how to participate in the love
gift to the saints in Jerusalem (16:1-4). He notifies them
concerning his upcoming travel plans (16:5-9), prepares
them for Timothy's visit (16:10-11), and explains Apollos's
delayed return (16:12). Paul wraps up with counsel for
their ongoing labor in the Lord:

Keep alert, stand firm in your faith, be courageous, be strong. Let all that you do be done in love. (16:13-14).

Stories of God's Creating and Redeeming Work in Paul's Other Letters

Having followed Paul's "big picture" theological reflection in his pastoral conversations with the church in Corinth, we now examine several texts and discuss several themes related to God's creating and redeeming work in his other letters.

Paul nowhere in his letters recounts the big story of God's work in creation. Some of his interpreters suggest that his implicit story line includes the traditional systematic theological categories of Creation and the Fall. God created the world and everything in it, but the disobedience of the first couple leads all humanity and therefore also the entire cosmos to fall into sin. The Fall then sets the stage for the story of redemption, which culminates in the work of Jesus Christ. This results in the following sequence:

$$\text{Creation} \longrightarrow \text{Fall} \longrightarrow \text{Redemption}$$

Often the emphasis in this telling of the story is on the fallen nature of humanity and the entire created order. Witherington, for example, entitles the opening section of *Paul's Narrative Thought World* "The Darkened Horizon" and includes "Paradise Lost" and "The Human Malaise" as subcategories (Witherington, 1994b:9-35). In this view, the goodness of God's creation seems to have been thoroughly eclipsed by human disobedience and the influence of demonic powers.

Other interpreters of Paul see a different beginning and therefore also a different kind of continuation of God's activity with reference to the world and humanity.

Creation can be viewed from within Paul's understanding of God's apocalyptic intervention in Jesus Christ. Jesus is the dramatic incarnation of God's power and wisdom. Jesus inaugurates the alternative community, a new creation, which gives testimony in its life to God's sovereign power to save. This power is already evidenced in God's creative and redemptive activity in the past (See Hays, 1996:383-7; Wright, 1997:77-94).

Within this view, the created order is declared good and continues to be positive testimony to God's sovereign power. Idolatry is the development that has cast a pall over God's sovereignty. The good news is that the one God and Father of all, the creator and redeemer, has climactically intervened through Christ to overpower all gods and other claimants to sovereignty, including the images that represent them. Through Jesus Christ and the transformed community, the witness to the sovereign God and Father of all, the creator and redeemer, is shared with the world. This telling of the story therefore features a different plot sequence:

Creation —> Idolatry —> Bondage —> Liberation

In Romans 1:18-32 Paul offers a theological diagnosis in which the big picture comes into view. He comments about God's creative handiwork, human idolatry, and divine wrath in ways that conform more to the second of these two plot sequences. According to Paul God's redemptive activity unfolds within a narrative plot featuring creation, chronic idolatry and rebellion, and God's consequent wrath.

God Known but Not Acknowledged

Paul clearly articulates in Romans the conviction that God has been made known through the handiwork of the created world:

> For what can be known about God is plain to them,
> because God has shown it to them. Ever since the cre-
> ation of the world his eternal power and divine nature,
> invisible though they are, have been understood and
> seen through the things he has made. (Romans 1:19-20)

Yet despite the grand display of God's power and character in the natural world in a panorama sufficient to inspire
basic knowledge about God, the typical human response
has been to refuse to honor the Creator and to express
thanksgiving to God. Rather than acknowledging as God
the One made known to them in creation, people have
chronically chosen to worship creation itself, or to bow
down to the works of their own hands—idols and images
of people, animals, birds, even reptiles. Paul employs the
language of "exchange" to tell this story:

> For though they knew God, they did not honor him as
> God or give thanks to him, but they became futile in
> their thinking, and their senseless minds were dark-
> ened. Claiming to be wise, they became fools; and *they
> exchanged* the glory of the immortal God for images
> resembling a mortal human being or birds or four-
> footed animals or reptiles. (1:21-23, emphasis added)

In 1:25 Paul renders his "bottom line" diagnosis in a
poignant summary of what has gone wrong in the relationship between God and humanity.

> They exchanged the truth about God for a lie and
> worshiped and served the creature rather than the
> Creator, who is blessed forever! Amen.

What had gone wrong was that people worshipped the
creature rather than the Creator. They traded their rela-

tionship with the living and true God for phony replicas of creatures that God had made. Idolatry deflects the adoring gaze and obedient devotion of the people whom God brought into being away from the One who is blessed forever, even God the creator.

In this theological analysis Paul expresses himself in ways similar to other contemporary Jewish writers, particularly the one who speaks in the apocryphal Wisdom of Solomon. The premise in the following assertion is that people take on the status of what they worship. God abhors idols. God also declares those who worship idols and the gods they represent to be accursed:

> But the idol made with hands is accursed, and so is the one who made it—he for having made it, and the perishable thing because it was named a god. For equally hateful to God are the ungodly and their ungodliness; for what was done will be punished together with the one who did it. Therefore there will be a visitation also upon the heathen idols, because, though part of what God created, they became an abomination, snares for human souls and a trap for the feet of the foolish. (Wisdom of Solomon 14:8-11)

This statement is typical of Jewish polemic against idolaters, primarily Gentiles. It also serves as warning to fellow Jews who might be tempted to participate in such practices in order to fit in with their Gentile neighbors.

Paul in Romans 1 appears to join this kind of polemic and implicitly warns about the risk of being swept along by such heathen inclinations. His rhetoric, however, also functions to set a trap for Jews in Rome who may be inclined to regard themselves as immune from such temptations and their consequences. He lets it be known that a general if not universal tendency is at work here:

> For the wrath of God is revealed from heaven against
> all ungodliness and wickedness of those who by their
> wickedness suppress the truth. So they are without
> excuse. (Romans 1:18)

At this point Paul has not yet indicated whom he pictures
as the ungodly and the wicked. Precedent would suggest
that he has the Gentiles in mind. But is that the case?

Three times in this passage he uses the poignant
expression "God gave them up" to talk about God's grieved
response to the exchanges people have made:

> Therefore God gave them up in the lusts of their hearts
> to impurity, to the degrading of their bodies among
> themselves. . . . For this reason God gave them up to
> degrading passions. Their women exchanged natural
> intercourse for unnatural, and in the same way also the
> men, giving up natural intercourse with women, were
> consumed with passion for one another. Men commit-
> ted shameless acts with men and received in their own
> persons the due penalty for their error. And since they
> did not see fit to acknowledge God, God gave them up
> to a debased mind and to things that should not be
> done. (Romans 1:24, 26-28)

The chronic pattern of human refusal to honor
God leads to a pattern of consequences. In grieved compassion God abandons humanity to experience the legacy
of their individual and collective choices to align themselves with powers other than God. No longer honoring
God as God they are given over to lusts, passions, and various other abusive inclinations in their relationships with
each other. In 1:32 Paul summarizes the outcome of this
downward spiral:

> They know God's decree, that those who practice such
> things deserve to die—yet they not only do them but
> even applaud others who practice them.

The question still remains open, however: Who is
included by the pronoun *they*? Is this the sorry saga of heathen degradation, as viewed by a Jew who is morally superior? Or does Paul here include the Jewish people within a
universal story?

In 2:1-3 Paul offers a surprising conclusion to this theological analysis. Instead of using *they* language to talk
about people, he speaks directly to them using the plural
you:

> Therefore you have no excuse, whoever you are, when
> you judge others; for in passing judgment on another
> you condemn yourself, because you, the judge, are doing
> the very same things. You say, "We know that God's
> judgment on those who do such things is in accordance
> with truth." Do you imagine, whoever you are, that
> when you judge those who do such things and yet do
> them yourself, you will escape the judgment of God?

Paul therefore draws on common Jewish critique of their
Gentile neighbors, their religious practices, and their
lifestyles, but he does so with rhetoric designed to lead all
people, whether Jewish or Gentile, to recognize their complicity both in misplaced allegiances and abusive behavior.

In sum: The plot of Paul's foundational story climaxes
in an indictment. This indictment recognizes that devotion
to powers other than the sovereign God leads people to
come under the sway of passions and lusts. These passions
and lusts in turn lead to the kind of behaviors that elicit
God's judgment. In 3:9, Paul affirms that the power of sin
leaves both Jews and Gentiles vulnerable to being seduced.

All therefore need God's liberating and restoring power
unleashed through Christ:

> What then? Are we any better off? No, not at all; for
> we have already charged that all, both Jews and
> Greeks, are under the power of sin. (Romans 3:9)

In Romans 7 Paul retells the story of human plight
under the power of sin in ways that also echo the Creation
story. Sin is pictured as a hostage-taking power always
seeking an opportunity to cultivate attitudes and actions
that violate others. "But sin, seizing an opportunity in the
commandment, produced in me all kinds of covetousness"
(7:8). This appears to be a retelling of the Genesis 3 story
of creation's first couple desiring and then eating the for-
bidden fruit. Sin is here portrayed as the protagonist in a
cosmic and personal drama that leads to covetousness and
other violations of others. At the culmination of his
anguished wrestling with the reality of the power of sin,
Paul cries out, "Wretched man that I am! Who will rescue
me from this body of death?" (7:24).

When in Romans 8 Paul begins to spell out the liberating consequences of the arrival of God's Son in human
likeness (8:3), the liberation he has in view is freedom, not
only for humanity but ultimately for all creation. The curs-
ing of the ground in Genesis 3:17-19 appears to be understood as having led not just to thorns and thistles which
thwart agriculture but also to bondage and decay for the
entire created order. With reference to the world and all
that is in it, Paul essentially says, "God gave them up."
The entire creation has been abandoned to the forces of
decay and corruption unleashed through idolatrous
human choices. Creation, however, is not left groaning in
hopeless despair, for it too looks in hope toward a glorious

future when it will participate in the liberation awaiting the children of God:

> For the creation waits with eager longing for the
> revealing of the children of God; for the creation was
> subjected to futility, not of its own will but by the will
> of the one who subjected it, in hope that the creation
> itself will be set free from its bondage to decay and
> will obtain the freedom of the glory of the children of
> God. We know that the whole creation has been
> groaning in labor pains until now; and not only the
> creation, but we ourselves, who have the first fruits of
> the Spirit, groan inwardly while we wait for adoption,
> the redemption of our bodies. (8:19-23)

Within Paul's cosmic vision, therefore, God's work as creator continues in the redemption and restoration made possible through Christ, not only for humanity but also for the entire world. Even chronic human propensity toward idolatry, leading to divine wrath, does not ultimately thwart God's sovereign restorative initiatives unveiled in Christ.

Wisdom

After wrestling in Romans 9 through 11 with issues related to Israel's election as God's people and Israel's rejection of the gospel, Paul includes a declaration about God's hidden wisdom and unfathomable ways (11:33-35). He also appends a doxology (11:36) that echoes the creation language of the creedal statement "from whom are all things and for whom we all exist" in 1 Corinthians 8:6. In this concluding declaration and doxology, Paul supplies further confirmation that he sees an intimate relationship between wisdom and creation:

O the depth of the riches and wisdom and knowledge
of God!
    How unsearchable are his judgments and how
    inscrutable his ways!
"For who has known the mind of the Lord?
    Or who has been his counselor?"
"Or who has given a gift to him, to receive a gift in
return?"
For from him and through him and to him are all things.
    To him be the glory forever. Amen.
      (Romans 11:33-36)

Here Paul appears to be reflecting texts within the
Wisdom genre (Job 5:9; 9:10; 41:3; Wisdom of Solomon
17:1) as well as the lofty declarations by the major prophets
about the incomparable character of creator God (Jeremiah
23:18; Isaiah 40:13). The prophetic oracle in Isaiah 40 is
especially powerful in its exaltation of the God whose powerful grandeur trivializes the claims of any and all contenders, including the nations and all their idols. In Romans
11:34 Paul cites Isaiah 40:13: "Who has directed the spirit
of the LORD, or as his counselor has instructed him?"

Within the Jewish literature apparently available to
Paul there are passages that present a personified Wisdom
characterized as co-creator with God. Paul apparently
views Jesus Christ as the "master worker" of Proverbs
8:30, who works beside God the creator when mapping
out the earth's foundations. In 1 Corinthians 1:30 he sums
up his reflections on God's wisdom and power by affirming that God "is the source of your life in Christ Jesus, who
became for us wisdom from God."

The poetic narrative in Colossians 1:15-20 enlarges on
this emphasis of Jesus as co-creator. Here Paul makes a
twofold profession concerning Christ, describing him first
of all as the agent of creation:

> He is the image of the invisible God, the firstborn of
> all creation; for in him all things in heaven and on
> earth were created, things visible and invisible, whether
> thrones or dominions or rulers or powers—all things
> have been created through him and for him. He him-
> self is before all things, and in him all things hold
> together. (Colossians 1:15-17)

Wisdom's role as God's companion in creation articulated in Proverbs 8:22-31 and Wisdom of Solomon 7:22b–8:1 appears to have shaped this confession about Jesus as pre-existent with God, as cosmic agent of creation and as sustainer.

But Paul continues in this hymn-like confession to portray Christ as creator in another sense. Jesus's resurrection signals his identity as the vanguard of the new creation. The church as Christ's body in the world is the ongoing incarnation, God's indwelling and embodiment for the sake of the world:

> He is the head of the body, the church; he is the begin-
> ning, the firstborn from the dead, so that he might
> come to have first place in everything. For in him all
> the fullness of God was pleased to dwell, and through
> him God was pleased to reconcile to himself all things,
> whether on earth or in heaven, by making peace
> through the blood of his cross. (Colossians 1:18-20)

There is a striking parallelism here: Christ is both agent of creation and the advance guard for the new creation. The redemptive work of Christ as the first to be raised from the dead results in a new creation in which the church, as Christ's body, serves advance notice of a reconciled cosmos.

First Adam and Last

Paul makes explicit reference to the Genesis 1–3 narrative about creation and rebellion in several passages that refer to Adam. The power of death invaded the world in Adam, who represents all humanity (1 Corinthians 15:21-23). Viewed from the perspective of the coming of Jesus Christ as climactic revelation of God's sovereign intention, Adam, the representative human who falls victim to the power of sin and death, turns out also to be a witness to God's liberation through Christ. In Jesus's resurrection from the dead, the spiral of death begun in Adam is reversed: "for as all die in Adam, so all will be made alive in Christ" (15:22). The (old) creation had its beginning in Adam. In Jesus the new creation in which the powers of sin and death are ultimately defeated has begun: "the last Adam became a life-giving spirit" (15:45).

In Romans 5:12-21 Paul develops most fully this comparison and contrast between Adam and Christ. Here Adam is explicitly tagged as "a type of the one who was to come" (5:14). Sin is characterized as a contagion whose influence spreads to all people through the trespass of one person. As a result, death extends its oppressive reign over all humanity. Paul envisions sin and death as tyrannical powers that leave humanity in bondage. Liberation from this universal captivity comes as a consequence of Christ, whose obedience released the conquering power of grace into the world: "Just as sin exercised dominion in death, so grace might also exercise dominion through justification leading to eternal life through Jesus Christ our Lord" (5:21).

There is a remarkable narrative sequence behind Paul's allusions to Adam. When Paul draws on the creation narratives with their allusions to Adam as representative of all humanity he does so in ways that reflect the awareness of a power struggle in which humans and the entire cosmos are enmeshed. This plight has come about through idolatry. The peoples of the world have fallen under the sway of sin, manifest in various powers antagonistic toward God or at least unwilling to honor God as sovereign. Under the power of idolatry many Gentiles in their rebellion have slid down the slippery slope into social, moral, and spiritual disorder. Despite the covenants, the Torah, and the temple, some Jews have also fallen under the spell of the gods and their idols. But there is good news! Through the new Adam, Jesus Christ, the Creator's ambitions that all people might have life in its fullness are now in the process of coming to fruition.

4

GOD OF JEWS AND GENTILES

We now move into the letter that Paul addressed to house churches in Rome. Because he conveys greetings from Gaius, who is described as "host to me and to the whole church" (Romans 16:23; cf. 1 Corinthians 1:14), he appears to have written Romans from Corinth. Phoebe, from Corinth's sister city Cenchreae, apparently delivered the letter (Romans 16:1-2). Even though Paul has not yet been to Rome, he gives his later readers some glimpses into the underlying story, especially in the opening and the closing sections (1:1-15; 15:14–16:27). He comments about his earlier thwarted efforts to visit the city and announces his current travel plans. But he also greets some twenty-five persons by name, often with brief annotations, and offers tantalizing clues about their lives and stories.

The following story picks up on two of Paul's acquaintances in Rome, Andronicus and Junia, whom he describes as relatives (16:7). What might this Jewish couple have experienced among people in the house churches in the imperial capital? Our sources will include texts from the Acts of the Apostles, especially 6:9 and 18:1-5, along with a citation from the Roman historian Suetonius in his Life of Claudius *25:4. Significant evidence is available for the historical data included here (see Wiefel, 1991:85-101). However, this reconstruction from the perspective of Andronicus and Junia is fictional.*

A STORY: Will the House Churches in Rome Support Paul's Mission?

Andronicus and Junia were born and raised in Jewish families actively involved in the life and worship of two of numerous synagogues in Rome. Jews living in the capital city of the empire frequently hosted traveling Jews who found synagogues to be natural settings for meeting each other. The couple had consequently grown up with an awareness of the Jewish diaspora living throughout the Mediterranean world.

Both of their families had endeavored to make pilgrimages to the holy city, Jerusalem, for some of the annual festivals. Andronicus recalled the solemn observance of Yom Kippur, the Day of Atonement, followed by the joyful celebration of Succoth, the feast of Tabernacles, during a memorable family sojourn when he was twelve, shortly after his bar mitzvah. Junia remembered the journey their family had made to Jerusalem for the Passover when she was ten. For several years her parents and other adults had concluded the Seder saying, "Next year in Jerusalem!" How exciting it had been to finally celebrate the feast in the holy city! That was the year, Junia recalled, that she first met her distant cousin Paul, who had also come from Tarsus of Cilicia with his family.

When Andronicus and Junia were married, they left Rome for Antioch in Syria. Here they established themselves in business, raised their children, and participated in synagogue life. But even this move had not severed their ties with their relatives or other Jewish people. Andronicus and Junia occasionally remarked to each other: "Isn't it remarkable how closely related we are as Jewish people, even though we are scattered throughout the world!" Like many Jews in the diaspora, Andronicus and Junia maintained their religious life as Jews through travel and letters and a focus on festivals and rituals in the Jerusalem temple. The couple and their children made pilgrimages to Jerusalem whenever possible, often arranging the trips so that they would double as family reunions.

Andronicus and Junia's children loved extended visits with their grandparents from Rome, who told the children stories from their childhood and from Jewish history. After repeated tellings, the children learned the story of their people and could recount many parts of it. Sometimes when their play turned to mimicking family life, they told these stories to each other—or to their dolls:

"Even though some Jews lived in Rome previously, their numbers increased dramatically in 62 B.C. when the Roman general Pompey settled Judean prisoners of war in that city. When these Jewish captives later received their freedom, many of them chose to stay in the capital. Several synagogues therefore became established in Rome in the course of the years. These synagogues were somewhat diverse in their style and they were only loosely connected to each other. Some of these Jewish freed persons from Rome and elsewhere in the Mediterranean world even spawned daughter colonies back in Judea. Their synagogues, which came to be known as 'synagogues of the Freedmen,' each had the distinctive flavor and culture of their home area."

Andronicus and Junia also retold their memories, especially about the unique challenges they had faced as Jews living in Rome. When they were growing up they did not have Gentile playmates until some Gentiles found their way to the synagogues. Though they accommodated themselves to some Jewish customs, the Romans and Greek-speaking people from various parts of the Mediterranean world continued to be viewed as visitors. Some Gentile adherents converted fully to Judaism. Others did not. Though they appreciated the monotheistic worship and resonated with the wholesome ethic and lifestyle of the Jewish people, they could not abide some of the traditional rituals, such as circumcision and food purity laws. They came to be called "God-fearers." For observant Jews the question became acute: How should the faithful view these new non-Jews who were involved in synagogue life?

Another stimulus for change came from the emergence of a messianic Jewish movement in Judea and Galilee. It began with Jesus of Nazareth, who was crucified by the Romans in Jerusalem during Passover around the year 30. Soon after his death, some of his followers reported that he had been raised from the dead. Enthusiastic followers started meeting in his memory and broadcasting the good news wherever they went.

In the decades after the death of Jesus, messianic Jews traveling as artisans and merchants came from Jerusalem to Antioch and Rome. Wherever they went they gave testimony concerning Jesus. Andronicus and Junia were among the early converts to this movement in Antioch. They began to share the gospel of Jesus Christ wherever they traveled, including Rome, and eventually they moved back there.

Another couple, Priscilla and Aquila, also visited the synagogues in Rome and shared the gospel of Jesus Christ with the people there. Soon there were God-fearers and some Jews in Rome who acknowledged Jesus as Messiah and Lord. At first these converts continued to worship in the synagogue. Soon conflict erupted, in some cases leading to shouting matches and public demonstrations in the streets. The furor within the Jewish community inevitably attracted the attention of officials in Rome, and in A.D. 49 Emperor Claudius expelled Jewish leaders from the city and forbade assembly in the synagogues. Once more,

Andronicus and Junia left Rome, as did Priscilla and Aquila and numerous others.

With many of the Jews gone, the gatherings of believers who professed Jesus as Messiah became predominantly Gentile. The groups began to meet under mainly Gentile leadership and in new settings, such as private homes or common areas in tenement houses, because the synagogues were no longer available to them.

When Claudius died in 54, the new emperor, Nero, repealed the expulsion edict. Many deported Jews—Priscilla, Aquila, Andronicus, and Junia among them, along with other messianic Jews—returned to Rome. The returnees found that patterns of worship and life they once knew had changed during their absence. Andronicus and Junia, once in the leadership, found themselves in the minority and within a congregational reality severed from synagogue life.

The situation provoked deep feelings, especially among the Jewish leaders who were also back in Rome, but powerless. Andronicus and Junia managed to keep calm, but other Jews demanded that certain rituals be more strictly maintained. Gentile boys were not being circumcised, which was an issue for some Jews, even though before the expulsion they had been content to let individual Gentile families decide for themselves. There were also some strong calls for the Gentile believers to pay more attention to ritual purity and to eating kosher food.

These calls for more diligent preservation of the Jewish ways of life came to be viewed by Gentile believers as symptomatic of Jewish attitudes of moral superiority. Some Gentile believers felt denigrated by Jews, especially on lifestyle and morality issues.

In A.D. 56, a circular letter to the churches in Rome arrived from Corinth. It was written by Junia's distant cousin from Tarsus, Paul, who had in recent years gained a reputation as an ambitious missionary and church planter. It was apparent, even at initial glance, that Paul had his eye on Rome as a place to launch a mission westward to Spain.

Andronicus and Junia recognized that Paul would want a support base in Rome, but they wondered if the house fellowships in Rome would assist Paul's mission. They also wondered if there was not a deeper question to be answered: Are Gentiles welcome among God's people or not?

Whom Does God Call? For Whom Is the Promise?

> What then shall we say? Have we found Abraham to be our forefather according to the flesh? (Romans 4:1; translation by Richard B. Hays, 1989:54)

Paul's letter to the house churches in ancient Rome provides an expansive window into his pastoral theology. Though sometimes considered Paul's systematic theology, his compendium of Christian doctrine, this document is instead yet another of his pastoral letters in which he wrestles with real situations arising in the life of the church. The letter also serves as a vehicle for Paul as apostle to the Gentiles to promote the expanding mission of the church within the Roman world.

One of the primary matters that Paul deals with in the epistle to the Romans is the issue of election. Who all is included within the community of God's chosen people? Whom does God call? For whom are God's promises intended?

The issue of election connects in significant ways with our previous theme of creation and redemption. Since the one God as creator has made all things, humanity experiences a universal kinship in relation to their common creator. Yet the Scriptures also tell the story of God's choice, first, of the family of Noah, and second, of the family of

Abraham and Sarah. The one God, though God of all, spared a particular people from universal destruction and chose a particular people to be the channel of blessing to all the world. How then are God's universal intentions as God of all to be reconciled with God's particular actions and choices as the God of Israel? In sum, whom does God call, and on what basis?

Of particular importance for Paul is the story of Abraham. The call narrative in Genesis 12, echoed by him in Romans 4:11 and Galatians 3:7-8, lies in the background:

> Now the LORD said to Abram, "Go from your country
> and your kindred and your father's house to the land that
> I will show you. I will make of you a great nation, and I
> will bless you, and make your name great, so that you
> will be a blessing. I will bless those who bless you, and
> the one who curses you I will curse; and in you all the
> families of the earth shall be blessed." (Genesis 12:1-3)

The part of the Abraham story that piques Paul's interest theologically comes at the point when it seems apparent that God's promise was not becoming reality and time was running out (Genesis 15:1-6). Abram complains that a slave born in his house would end up becoming his heir. Then Abram is shown the star-studded heavens, and he is told, "So shall your descendants be" (15:5). What follows is the text that Paul regarded as key: "And he believed the LORD; and the LORD reckoned it to him as righteousness" (15:5-6; cited in Romans 4:3, 9, 22; Galatians 3:6). A covenant ceremony follows (Genesis 15:7-21). Abraham is told that his family would in the future be enslaved as aliens in a foreign land but in time would be delivered by God. However, circumcision as sign of the covenant was not introduced until some time following the promise of an heir and the promise of land (Genesis 17:1-14).

The issue of inclusion was not just of theoretical interest to Paul. Nor did he deal with this only because he was pastorally concerned for the welfare and the unity of the believers in Rome. This was also an issue of interest to Paul himself when he developed strategy for his next major push as a missionary to the Gentiles. As he plans toward an evangelistic thrust into Spain, he naturally considers Rome as a strategic center from which to launch that effort. Ethnic conflict among the house churches in Rome raises questions about how solid this base for missionary expansion would turn out to be. Can the Jewish and Gentile believers in Rome find unity and harmony in a common understanding of the gospel?

Paul's awareness of ethnic diversity within the Roman house churches is apparent right from the beginning of the letter. Also evident is his expressed desire to develop a uniting theological vision for people historically separated from each other. Can Jews and Gentiles be united in their commitment to God now that the Messiah has come?

The Jews First, and Also the Greeks

Already in the salutation of his epistle (Romans 1:1-7), Paul deliberately frames his initial description of the gospel in a way that seeks to appeal both to Jews and to Gentiles. The Son, who is the subject of the gospel, is "descended from David according to the flesh and was declared to be Son of God with power according to the spirit of holiness by resurrection from the dead" (Romans 1:3, 4). The first declaration reflects the Jewish expectation of a Davidic king. The second employs language familiar in Roman circles, where the emperor was hailed as a son of the gods.

Both Davidic and Roman imperial conceptions are also transcended in ways that critique both of these understandings.

The extended salutation in Romans functions as Paul's self-introduction to a church community in a region where he is not well known. He openly declares his own special apostolic calling to reach out to Gentiles: "to bring about the obedience of faith among all the Gentiles" (1:5). When he describes his desire to visit Rome (1:8-15), Paul seems to be highlighting his primary mission toward Gentiles, especially when he asserts, "I am debtor both to Greeks and to barbarians, both to the wise and to the foolish" (1:14). However, when Paul articulates the essence of his understanding of the gospel in what is often considered to be the letter's "thesis" (1:16-17), he does so in terms of Jewish priority: "to the Jew first and also to the Greek" (1:16). What God has launched in the gospel of Jesus Christ is rooted in a particular story ("the Jew first"). However, these roots develop and flourish into a movement that invites participation among all peoples ("also to the Greek"). Paul's references to "the Jew" and "the Greek" here and elsewhere in Romans (2:9, 10; 3:9; 10:12) set up both the ethnic plurality and the salvation-historical dynamic within which his pastoral initiative toward the Roman house churches operates.

In the opening chapters of this letter, Paul moves back and forth between these universal and particular emphases within the gospel. Like an orator appealing to an ethnically mixed audience, he utilizes anecdotes, metaphors, questions, and various other rhetorical strategies in ways that alternately appeal to and confront the Jewish and Gentile subgroups. He tells the stories that his fellow Jews would consider to be evidence of Gentile debauchery (1:18-32), but then he turns the tables on judgmental people, including Jews, who do similar things (2:1-16). He caricatures those Jews whose behavior contravenes both their ritual correctness and their verbal profession (2:17-24). Paul alludes to Isaiah 52:5 and Ezekiel 36:20-1 to underscore the gravity of the consequences of Jewish lifestyles that do not conform to their calling as God's people: "For, as it is written, 'The name of God is blasphemed among the Gentiles because of you'" (2:24).

Paul even defines true Jewishness in a universalizing fashion as an inner and spiritual rather than external and physical quality:

> For a person is not a Jew who is one outwardly, nor is true circumcision something external and physical.
> Rather, a person is a Jew who is one inwardly, and real circumcision is a matter of the heart—it is spiritual and not literal. Such a person receives praise not from others but from God. (2:28-29)

When he asks, "Then what advantage has the Jew? Or what is the value of circumcision?" (3:1), the presumed audience is expected to say, "No advantage!" However, once again Paul turns the table with the words, "Much in every way." And then he raises the theological questions arising out of the tension between the particular and the universal: Is God faithful to promises made to the covenant people? If so, how then can anyone claim that God is fair and impartial to all (3:1-9)?

After what Richard Hays has called a "jackhammer indictment," emphasizing the universality of human sinfulness in 3:10-18 (1989:50), Paul offers his second thesis-like statement summarizing the gospel (3:21-26). As in 1:16-17, he asserts both Jewish priority and the all-encompassing inclusiveness of the gospel. God's righteousness has been disclosed, Paul says, "apart from the law." But this righteousness now made known through Jesus Christ has also been "attested by the law and the prophets" (3:21). Paul also underscores the universality of the gospel by his use of the notion of *all* when describing both salvation and judgment. God's righteousness has been manifest "for all who believe, for there is no distinction" (3:22). Universal experience with the power of sin and the resulting culpability of all humanity also leads to the conclusion that there is no distinction: "all have sinned and fall short of the glory of God" (3:23).

(More on the "thesis statements" of 1:16-17 and 3:21-26 in chapter 8.)

In 3:27-31, Paul reaches a climax in this pastoral rhetoric, with its dialectic emphases on the two poles: Jewish priority, and universal relevance. His opener here is an attack on ethnic exclusiveness and pride, especially, as the context suggests, Jewish boastfulness, rooted in a particular understanding of the law and of works:

> Then what becomes of boasting? It is excluded. By what law? By that of works? No, but by the law of faith. (3:27)

Paul then enlarges on this notion of "the law of faith" by expressing a conviction that is still to be developed in his interpretation of the biblical stories about Abraham and Sarah (4:1-25) and his theological treatment of the theme of justification (5:1-21). He asserts, "For we hold that a person is justified by faith apart from works prescribed by the law" (3:28). To ground this conclusion, which definitely favors a universal claim over an exclusively Jewish claim, Paul turns to the central Jewish confession, the Shema: "Hear, O Israel: The LORD is our God, the LORD alone" (Deuteronomy 6:4). Strikingly, Paul marshals this Jewish affirmation of the sovereignty of God in support of his declaration of the universality of the gospel. The God of the Jews is also God of the Gentiles:

> Is God the God of the Jews only? Is he not the God of Gentiles also? Yes, of Gentiles also, since God is one; and he will justify the circumcised on the ground of faith and the uncircumcised through that same faith. (3:29-30)

After asserting that God justifies both the circumcised and the uncircumcised on the same basis, namely faith, Paul articulates the question that naturally arises from this universalizing emphasis: "Do we then overthrow the law by this faith?" His response, again surprising given the rhetorical thrust of the current argument, reasserts the priority of the Jewish experience: "By no means! On the contrary, we uphold the law" (3:31).

These competing themes of Jewish priority and yet universal application of the gospel have therefore been running concurrently throughout the first three chapters of Romans. The Jews are the elect, the chosen people, but the gospel is intended for all people on the basis of faith.

In Romans 4 Paul turns to an extended scriptural exposition designed to undergird his assertions that the one God justifies both Jews and Greeks on the basis of faith and that the Jewish law is thereby upheld. Paul recalls specific strands of the story of Abraham and Sarah as narrated in the book of Genesis. These stories have been consciously selected to highlight theological themes such as call and promise, election and mission, and grace and hope. They have also been developed with the Jewish and Gentile ethnic mix of the Roman house churches clearly in mind.

But What About Abraham?

Paul opens his argument in Romans 4 by raising yet another rhetorical question. There is some lack of clarity, however, about the nature of his opener. The NRSV translates 4:1 in this way: "What then are we to say was gained by Abraham, our ancestor according to the flesh?" (4:1). However, Richard B. Hays has made a convincing case for construing Paul's question in 4:1 differently (1989:54). As in various places elsewhere in Romans, Paul introduces his rhetorical question by asking, "What then shall we say?" (cf. 3:5; 6:1; 7:7; 9:14), followed by another question that names one possibility: "Have we found Abraham to be our ancestor according to the flesh?" Speaking to a community of Jews and Gentiles, Paul inquires, "How is Abraham our ancestor? Is Abraham our ancestor according to the flesh?" He raises a question he knows must be on the minds of his hearers, perhaps in this case especially his Jewish audience. In this case, however, Paul does not immediately offer the rhetorical retort, "By no means." Instead he recalls some of the Genesis narratives about Abraham and Sarah. And the fundamental question is, "Who all is to be reckoned as included among their descendants?"

In many circles within the Judaism of Paul's day, Abraham was viewed as the exemplary patriarch. His faithfulness to the point of being ready to sacrifice his only son (Genesis 22:1-14) was considered as a model of ultimate obedience to God. Some of Paul's Jewish contemporaries believed it was this obedience that made Abraham righteous in the sight of God. We can illustrate from the Jewish apocryphal writings, 1 Maccabees and Sirach. In 1 Maccabees 2:51-52, a dying Mattathias encourages his sons as leaders of the Maccabean revolt with these words:

> Remember the deeds of the ancestors, which they did
> in their generations; and you will receive great honor
> and an everlasting name. Was not Abraham found
> faithful when tested, and it was reckoned to him as
> righteousness?

In Sirach 44:19-21 a hymn in praise of the ancestors features Abraham and his descendants:

> Abraham was the great father of a multitude of
> nations, and no one has been found like him in glory.
> He kept the law of the Most High, and entered into a
> covenant with him; he certified the covenant in his
> flesh, and when he was tested he proved faithful.
> Therefore the Lord assured him with an oath that the
> nations would be blessed through his offspring; that he
> would make him as numerous as the dust of the earth,
> and exalt his offspring like the stars, and give them an
> inheritance from sea to sea and from the Euphrates to
> the ends of the earth.

Within these readings, therefore, Abraham would have grounds for boasting (cf. Romans 3:27). Abraham was found faithful when God tested him. He even observed the law of God before it had been delivered.

In Romans 4 Paul enters into a debate with this prevailing interpretation of Abraham. First of all, no one, not even Abraham, has any grounds for boasting before God: "For if Abraham was justified by works, he has something to boast about, but not before God" (4:2). What then does commend people before God? Paul focuses on Genesis 15:6: "Abraham believed God, and it was reckoned to him as righteousness" (4:3). In the story in Genesis this quotation comes immediately prior to the covenant ceremony in which Abraham is promised a large family. This family,

Abraham is told, will be enslaved as aliens in a foreign
land and delivered by God (Genesis 15:7-14). Paul draws
on this foundational story from the Torah to remind his
hearers, especially the Jewish members of the Roman
house churches, that righteousness is a gift of God's grace.

Paul emphasizes the primary importance of establishing and maintaining a relationship with God that is based
on trust. The relationship between humans and God cannot be achieved by working for wages but by trusting God
for a gift (4:4-5). Obviously wages earned while working
are not reckoned as a gift. Those who believe God are
counted as righteous. It is important to note that to believe
God is not just to give mental assent to propositions about
God but to trust in the living God. The relationship
between God and humanity is rooted in a deep sense that
life itself is a gift, since God is creator, and also that righteousness comes as a gift to those who believe. As the quotation from Psalm 32:1-2 attests, this gift includes God's
readiness to justify the ungodly:

> "Blessed are those whose iniquities are forgiven, and
> whose sins are covered; blessed is the one against
> whom the Lord will not reckon sin."

A God of Grace Even Desists from Counting Sin.

Where does this double divine gifting leave humans?
Paul declares that no one can boast before God. This
includes even Abraham the faithful one, who is himself
presumed also to be among "the ungodly" (cf. 4:5) whom
God justifies on the basis of their faith. Life lived as grateful recipients of God's grace can countenance neither
boasting before God about human achievement nor the
flaunting of status before others.

In 4:9-12 Paul answers his opening question, "Have we found Abraham to be our ancestor according to the flesh?" (4:1). In his reading of the story of Abraham and Sarah in Genesis, he realizes forcefully that the children of Abraham and Sarah are not limited to those whose genealogy connects them as biological descendants within this ancestral clan. The descendants of Abraham and Sarah are defined differently. Their children include both the uncircumcised who believe (4:11) and all the circumcised who "follow the example of the faith that our ancestor Abraham had before he was circumcised" (4:12). It was while Abraham and Sarah were Gentiles that they received God's promise of many descendants. It is only on the basis of their faith (that is, their trust) that both Gentiles and Jews share in that promise. First came faith, as a response to God's promises; later the rite of circumcision was added as a sign of God's covenant faithfulness. Faith, as trust in God, predates the law. For Paul, therefore, Abraham has a representative function as a Gentile who trusted God and was counted among the righteous even though at the time he had not yet been circumcised.

Through Faith the Fulfillment of God's Promise

What it means to exercise faith is developed in 4:13-25. God's promise of many descendants was not fulfilled during the lifetime of Abraham and Sarah, even though they began to glimpse the fulfillment of that promise when, against all odds, their son was born. Nor does this promise come to fruition through the law, which came years later. The realization of God's promises comes through a stance of trust and obedience toward God, who is faithful.

Paul characterizes the faith demonstrated by Abraham and Sarah as trust that God would deliver on promises made, even though humanly speaking it seems impossible.

God's promissory guarantee rests on grace, and its benefits extend "not only to the adherents of the law but also to those who share the faith of Abraham (for he is the father of all of us, as it is written, 'I have made you the father of many nations')" (4:16-17).

The story of Abraham and Sarah illustrates God's sovereign power and fidelity. God is shown to be one who creates "out of nothing" and gives life to the dead (4:17). Like Abraham and Sarah, therefore, God's people can trust in God. Paul emphasizes the dimension of hope within this stance of trust. "Hoping against hope" (literally, "from hope out of hope") Abraham believed the divine promise that "he would become 'the father of many nations'" (4:18). Abraham was too old to have children ("as good as dead") and Sarah's womb was barren (4:19), yet God delivered! This God "who gives life to the dead," as the story of Abraham and Sarah dramatically demonstrates, is none other than the Creator who "calls into existence the things that do not exist" (4:17). This God who creates is also one who calls and who delivers on promises. This God invites and calls all humanity into a relationship of trusting obedience.

In wrapping up his retelling of the story of Abraham and Sarah, Paul casts the net wide enough to include all who believe, regardless of ethnic background. Writing to a mixed community of Jews and Gentiles, Paul reassures them that the promise of Genesis 15:6 applies not only to Abraham but to all who manifest the faith of Abraham: "Now the words, 'It was reckoned to him,' were written not for his sake, but for ours also" (4:23-24). How this becomes reality is spelled out with reference to the story of Jesus crucified and raised. The God who brought life to the barren womb of Sarah and to Abraham's aged body also raised Jesus the faithful one, "who was handed over for our trespasses and was raised for our justification" (4:25).

Paul reminds his Roman readers that they too are invited to place their trust in this life-giving and life-restoring God. If they believe in the God "who raised Jesus our Lord from the dead," they too will be counted righteous (4:24).

What lesson does Paul derive from the Genesis narratives about Abraham and Sarah for the Jewish and Gentile believers in Rome? The children of Abraham and Sarah, Paul insists, are not only Jews, or Jews plus circumcised Gentiles. Jews and Gentiles, on the basis of their faith, their trust in God, are the true children of Abraham and Sarah, regardless of whether or not they have been circumcised. Because God is the creator who calls all to be heirs on the same basis, there are no grounds for one group, either the Gentiles or the Jews, to be boasting over the other. All are related to the same God! Like Abraham and Sarah, both circumcised Jews and uncircumcised Gentiles are admonished to grow strong in their faith and to give glory to God (4:20), rather than flaunt their own status in ways that depreciate or exclude others.

Hope of Sharing God's Glory

A "therefore" at 5:1 signals that Paul is beginning to articulate the consequences of God's death-reversing intervention in Abraham and Sarah's life and climactically in Jesus. Here Paul begins to employ "we" statements. Justified by faith, "we have peace with God through our Lord Jesus Christ" (5:1). Through Jesus Christ "we have obtained access to this grace in which we stand." As a consequence, "we boast in our hope of sharing the glory of God" (5:2). Themes like hope and faith, which Paul has been highlighting from the story of Abraham and Sarah, are now elucidated universally. The *we* in Paul's assertions encompasses humanity as a whole rather than only the Jewish people.

In reflecting about generic human experience Paul includes both diagnosis of the human dilemma under sin and the salvific consequences of God's initiative in Jesus Christ. In 5:3-4, he offers a stair-step list of experiences and virtues, a list which climaxes with the theme of hope: "suffering, endurance, character, hope." Hope, Paul adds, will not disappoint us, because "God's love has been poured into our hearts through the Holy Spirit that has been given to us" (5:5). He may be alluding to Abraham's hope against all odds (cf. especially 4:18). In several parallel declarations, Paul refers both to the human dilemma under sin and to God's remedy in Christ: "while we were still weak, at the right time Christ died for the ungodly" (5:6); "while we still were sinners Christ died for us" (5:8); "while we were enemies, we were reconciled to God through the death of his Son" (5:10). Each of these statements provides windows into the world of human need: *weak, sinners, enemies.* In each of these statements Paul also points to God's intervention in Jesus Christ as the solution. Christ died "for the ungodly" (5:6); "for us" (5:8); "we were reconciled to God through the death of his Son" (5:10). An event in the past, the death of Christ, imparts a remedy for sin, and this remedy is potentially available to all humanity.

However, Paul also announces future salvation. Two assertions accentuated by the words *much more surely* point to the assurance of future rescue from wrath. This future deliverance is guaranteed not only by Christ's death but especially by his resurrection life:

> Much more surely then, now that we have been justified by his blood, will we be saved through him from the wrath of God. For if while we were enemies, we were reconciled to God through the death of his Son,

much more surely, having been reconciled, will we be
saved by his life. (5:9-10)

In light of that assured future salvation, the believer,
whether Jew or Gentile, can live confidently in the present:

But more than that, we even boast in God through our
Lord Jesus Christ, through whom we have now
received reconciliation. (5:11)

As Paul's argument unfolds in 5:12-21, he chronicles
the invasion of sin into the world through Adam's unfaithful and disobedient choices. God's redemptive counterpoint to the contagion of sin through Adam comes in the
"second Adam" Jesus Christ, though this title does not
occur here. (See "First Adam and Last" in chapter 3 for a
discussion of this theme.) The outcome of this onslaught of
sin and this invasion of grace is that grace outdoes sin:
"Just as sin exercised dominion in death, so grace might
also exercise dominion through justification leading to
eternal life through Jesus Christ our Lord" (5:21).

Paul's burden in Romans 6 is to correct the presumption, already anticipated in 3:7-8, that, since grace overwhelms sin, one has license to sin all the more. In his
response to this slur on his theological and ethical views,
he articulates what is for him a central theme. Through
baptism believers participate in the death and resurrection
of Jesus Christ by dying to sin and being raised to newness
of life. (See chapter 9 for a discussion of this section of
Romans.)

In Romans 7:1–8:17 Paul focuses squarely on the law
and the Spirit. Questions lurking behind his wrestling here
have to do again with the interplay between the particular
and the universal, specifically the ongoing role of the

Jewish Torah and the ethical sufficiency of life lived under the empowerment of the Spirit. Is the Torah given to the Jewish people to be abandoned, or does it continue to function as an ethical norm now that the Messiah has come? In his argument in 3:27-31 Paul trumpets universal themes ("Yes, of Gentiles also, since God is one"), but he also affirms the particular Jewish claims: "We uphold the law." In 7:1-25 Paul enlarges on how this is the case. But what then is the role of the Spirit of God in the believer's life? In 5:1-5 Paul mentions the Holy Spirit through whom God's love is poured into the hearts of believers. Given the ongoing warfare with the powers of sin and death, does the indwelling Spirit adequately empower humans to live a life that pleases God? In 8:1-17 Paul articulates his passionate conviction that indeed the Spirit of the God who raised Jesus from the dead will also through that same Spirit give life to mortal bodies (8:11) and guarantee all the children of God a common inheritance through Christ (8:12-17). (These themes from Romans 7:1–8:17 are explored further in chapter 9.)

Having focused on how the story of Abraham and Sarah has functioned within Paul's own gospel narrative in Romans, especially in 4:1-25, we need to acknowledge another specific echo of this patriarchal story. In 8:31 Paul launches his climactic and triumphant coda with another series of questions. His opener sounds familiar, because he employs similar rhetorical questions elsewhere: "What then are we to say about these things?" (8:31; cf. 4:1). Having signaled that he has reached a transition in his pastoral reflections about both God's particular calling of the Jews and God's universal intention of including all people, Paul invokes the memory of Abraham's near-sacrifice of his son, Isaac (cf. Genesis 22:1-14):

> If God is for us, who is against us? He who did not
> withhold his own Son, but gave him up for all of us,
> will he not with him also give us everything else?
> (8:31b-32)

Abraham was willing to sacrifice his son, despite his long and anguished wait for the fulfillment of God's promise of a descendant. What Abraham was ready to do, God actually did. And the beneficiaries of God's gracious giving of the Son potentially include people from all backgrounds and walks of life ("all of us").

Strikingly, this broad compass of God's embrace elicits from Paul a reiteration of God's elective choice:

> Who will bring any charge against God's elect? It is
> God who justifies. Who is to condemn? (8:33-34)

Yet, this avowal of God's choice of a particular people is complemented by yet another universal declaration. Paul speaks a resounding affirmation, namely, that ultimately nothing separates humankind from God's love made known in Christ:

> No, in all these things we are more than conquerors
> through him who loved us. For I am convinced that
> neither death, nor life, nor angels, nor rulers, nor
> things present, nor things to come, nor powers, nor
> height, nor depth, nor anything else in all creation, will
> be able to separate us from the love of God in Christ
> Jesus our Lord. (8:37-39)

With the climactic triumph of this chorus still ringing in his (and his reader's) ears, Paul proceeds in 9:1–11:36 to explore what might be the limits, if any, of the conquering love of God in Christ. Specifically the question that is raised for Paul is whether the *us* who cannot be separated from God's love includes the people of Israel who fail to acknowledge God's self-revelation in Christ. (We follow Paul's personal and theological wrestling with that pastoral issue in chapter 6.)

"Whom Does God Call?" Reflections from Paul's Other Letters

In his epistle to the Romans Paul has a missional reason for reflecting theologically on the question, "Whom does God call for participation in the community of faith?" As apostle to the Gentiles Paul desires a unified base in Rome among Jewish and Gentile believers willing to support his ongoing mission westward to Spain. Various stories within the patriarchal narrative material help him to establish a scriptural argument for the unity of Jews and Gentiles in Christ.

Turning to Paul's other letters we now note how the story of Abraham and Sarah has been appropriated there. We sense immediately that in his correspondence with churches in Galatia and Corinth, he was not primarily a missionary planning strategy but a pastor embroiled in congregational conflict, including debates about who are the true descendants of Abraham.

We will also broaden our exploration of election in Paul's thought by examining several related themes, especially the people of God (Israel, the church) as God's elect, the conditions for the inclusion of Gentiles within the people of God, and Paul's theological notion of grace.

Heirs of Abraham in Corinth and Galatia

In what has been dubbed his "fool's speech" to the Corinthian church (2 Corinthians 11:1–12:10) Paul compares himself with other Jewish missionaries active in Corinth. He sarcastically calls them "super-apostles" in

11:5. In 11:13 he less charitably exposes them as "false apostles, deceitful workers, disguising themselves as apostles of Christ." Paul takes on the guise of a fool and, with dripping irony, boasts first about his weaknesses (11:16-21), briefly about his pedigree (11:22), and then about a whole series of hardships, setbacks, and disappointments (11:23–12:10). Imbedded in all this foolish boasting is a rhetorical barb aimed at his critics:

> Are they Hebrews? So am I. Are they Israelites? So am I. Are they descendants of Abraham? So am I. (11:22)

Here Paul echoes what must have been the claims of Jewish teachers in Corinth, who were flaunting their credentials in ways that put Paul in an unfavorable light. They were also actively promoting a rival understanding of the gospel. In his defense and for the benefit of fellow missionaries who were putting on airs, Paul points out that he too is a Hebrew, an Israelite, a descendant and heir of Abraham. In this correspondence with the predominantly Gentile church in Corinth, he does not develop more fully the argument that he makes in Romans and Galatians that believing Gentiles are also Abraham's children.

In Galatians 3:1–4:31 we find Paul's liveliest retelling of elements of the Abraham story. In many ways his use of this story in Galatians parallels that in Romans 4. But his objective in Galatians is not primarily to unite Jews and Gentiles in Christ for the sake of the church's ongoing mission. Rather it is to persuade Gentile believers not to heed the pleas of rival teachers who are urging the men to be circumcised and place themselves under Jewish law. We'll discuss the overall narrative framework of Paul's pastoral counsel to the churches of Galatia in chapters 8 and 9. Here we focus on Paul's use of the Abraham and Sarah stories in Galatians.

As he did in Romans, Paul cites Genesis 15:6 in his arguments in Galatians: "Just as Abraham 'believed God, and it was reckoned to him as righteousness,' so, you see, those who believe are the descendants of Abraham" (Galatians 3:6-7). Paul's main point here is to undergird his conviction that through faith Gentiles receive the promised blessing from God. In 3:8-9 he cites Genesis 12:3, a text not explicitly quoted in Romans 4, and substitutes "Gentiles" for the underlying "families of the earth":

> And the scripture, foreseeing that God would justify
> the Gentiles by faith, declared the gospel beforehand to
> Abraham, saying, "All the Gentiles shall be blessed in
> you." For this reason, those who believe are blessed
> with Abraham who believed.

In 3:10-14 Paul offers exegetical reflections on several other scriptural texts: Deuteronomy 27:26; Habakkuk 2:4; Leviticus 18:5. He concludes this section with an enlarged statement about the basis for the inclusion of Gentiles within the church family. He testifies concerning the redemption accomplished through Christ (3:13) and the outcome of that redemption (3:14) "that in Christ Jesus the blessing of Abraham might come to the Gentiles, so that we might receive the promise of the Spirit through faith." God's promise of blessing through the family of Abraham and Sarah is therefore explicitly seen as fulfilled for Gentiles who through faith receive the gift of the Spirit. In Paul's mind, therefore, there are no grounds for requiring Gentiles to meet any additional entrance requirements.

Another distinctive feature of Paul's interpretation of the story of Abraham and Sarah in Genesis is his exegetical musing about whether the promise to Abraham foresees many descendants or just one. He concludes that the

promised blessing envisions one offspring, namely, Christ
(3:16). As Paul's exegetical and theological argument
unfolds, however, he underscores the believers' participation in Christ through faith (3:26) and baptism (3:27).
Within this community, ethnic, gender, and social distinctives ultimately do not count (3:28). Speaking primarily to
Gentiles Paul throws open the door of welcome to all,

> for all of you are one in Christ Jesus. And if you
> belong to Christ, then you are Abraham's offspring,
> heirs according to the promise. (3:28-29)

Having expressed his conviction that Jesus Christ is the
singular offspring viewed in the Genesis 12 promise of
blessing to all nations, Paul adds that in Christ all who
participate through faith and baptism are Abraham's corporate offspring. All those who belong to Christ are heirs
with Christ of the promised blessing on the nations.

Paul deploys several family images in Galatians to
describe these heirs. They are "children of Abraham" (3:7)
but also "children of God" (3:26; 4:6, 7), and therefore
their relationship to each other is that of "brothers and sisters" (3:15; 4:12, 28, 31; 5:11, 13; 6:1, 18). In 4:1-7 he
also employs the adoption metaphor. God's sending of his
Son results in redemption, here described as a process of
adoption whereby former slaves are incorporated into the
family of God. As adopted children they receive the gift of
the Spirit and address God using the intimate family name,
"Abba," the Aramaic term for father:

> And because you are children, God has sent the Spirit
> of his Son into our hearts, crying, "Abba! Father!" So
> you are no longer a slave but a child, and if a child
> then also an heir, through God. (4:6-7)

Our most vivid glimpse into Paul's interpretation of stories about Abraham and Sarah comes in Galatians 4:21-30. He includes the story of the birth of two sons of Abraham, namely, Ishmael, son of Hagar (Genesis 16:15-6), and Isaac, son of Sarah (Genesis 21:1-7). In his retelling of these stories Paul focuses not on Abraham but on the two women who bore these sons. He identifies his reading as an allegory in which the two women represent two covenants (4:24). It becomes clear from the outset that Paul's selective use of these stories intends to subvert an interpretation offered by rival missionaries, for whom Genesis 21 would have given convincing support for their insistence on circumcision as a mark of the inclusion of Gentiles into the church. Strikingly Paul puts the pro-circumcision missionaries in the Hagar column and his own gospel proclamation in the Sarah column:

Hagar	Sarah
Abraham had two sons, one by a slave woman >	and the other by a free woman. (4:22)
One, the child of the slave, was born according to the flesh (4:23a); >	the other, the child of the free woman, was born through the promise. (4:23b)
One woman, in fact, is Hagar, from Mount Sinai, bearing children for slavery. Now Hagar is Mount Sinai in Arabia and corresponds to the present Jerusalem, for she is in slavery with her children. (4:24-25) >	But the other woman corresponds to the Jerusalem above; she is free, and she is our mother. For it is written, "Rejoice, you childless one, you who bear no children, burst into song and shout, you who endure no birth pangs; for the children of the desolate woman are more numerous than the children of the one who is married." (4:26-27; citing Isaiah 54:1)

Hagar	Sarah
	Now you, my friends, are children of the promise, like Isaac. (4:28)
But just as at that time the child who was born according to the flesh persecuted the child who was born according to the Spirit, so it is now also. (4:29) >	But what does the scripture say? "Drive out the slave and her child; for the child of the slave will not share the inheritance with the child of the free woman." (4:30; citing Gen. 21:9)
	So then, friends, we are children, not of the slave but of the free woman. (4:31)

Paul's creative retelling of the stories of Hagar and Sarah and their sons speaks to his intention to convey a clear message to Gentile believers. They belong to the family of Sarah and Abraham not on the basis of either physical lineage or the rite of circumcision but on the basis of God's promise. In a bold interpretive move Paul describes "the present Jerusalem" as being enslaved with her children (4:25). This is likely a reference to the Jerusalem church, and especially the pro-circumcision faction (note 2:12), not Judaism as a whole. By way of contrast, Paul labels the church that has emerged among Gentiles through the proclamation of the crucified and risen Christ as "the Jerusalem above" (4:26). This is an apocalyptic depiction (cf. Revelation 21:2) of that community birthed through the preaching of the gospel of Christ. Paul seeks to ground in Scripture his conviction that with the coming of Christ the promised blessing on the nations comes through faith and without the addition of any ritual requirements from the Jewish law. When he emphasizes that those of the flesh persecute those of the Spirit (4:29) and that the inheritance is restricted to the children of the free woman (4:30), Paul is responding in a bluntly dismissive tone to rival messianic Jewish missionaries advocating circumcision as a ritual of inclusion. His intention here is not to draw contrasts between Judaism and Christianity. Nor is he commenting about relationships between Arabs and Jews. Rather, he is contrasting two approaches to evangelism among Gentiles: a law-observant mission and his own circumcision-free mission. (See J. Louis Martyn, 1997b:191-208; cf. also Richard Hays, 1989:111-21)

Inclusion of Gentiles in the People of God

Our discussion of how Paul treats the Abraham stories from Genesis has focused especially on the question, Who is included within God's people and on what basis? A brief historical comment about how Jews in the first century viewed Gentiles and their admission into Jewish life may help cast further light on Paul's theology and his missionary and pastoral practices.

In *Paul and the Gentiles*, Terence Donaldson enumerates several of the prevailing Jewish views of Gentiles, including whether and on what basis they can be admitted into the religious community defined by the Torah (1997:51-78).

The strictest understanding simply dismisses Gentiles as aliens without hope. For example, Ephesians 2:12 speaks about the former status of the recipients of this letter in this way. They had earlier been "aliens from the commonwealth of Israel, and strangers to the covenants of promise, having no hope and without God in the world."

Another view is that Gentiles can become proselytes if they abandon idolatry, devote themselves exclusively to the God of Israel, and become ritually incorporated into the community of Israel, including circumcision for males. This appears to have been the position articulated by Paul's rivals, especially in Corinth and Galatia. In 1 Thessalonians 1:9-10 Paul reflects a comparable understanding, although without the necessity of circumcision. He summarizes what had happened to the Thessalonians: "You turned to God from idols, to serve a living and true God, and to wait for his Son from heaven."

Yet another position is evidenced among more philosophically oriented Jews, such as Philo of Alexandria, for whom conformity to the natural law of refined Hellenism is counted as comparable to observance of the Torah. Among some Jews contemporary with Paul, Gentiles who rejected idolatry, worshipped God, and observed a moral code of behavior were deemed to be acceptable to God and welcome as participants in synagogue life. The category "God-fearers" is applied in the Acts of the Apostles (13:16, 26) for these Gentiles affiliated with the Jewish community but not incorporated into it through the rituals of proselytism. In Romans 2 Paul appears to be thinking about such God-fearing Gentiles:

> When Gentiles, who do not possess the law, do instinctively what the law requires, these, though not having the law, are a law to themselves. They show that what the law requires is written on their hearts, to which their own conscience also bears witness; and their conflicting thoughts will accuse or perhaps excuse them on the day when, according to my gospel, God, through Jesus Christ, will judge the secret thoughts of all. (Romans 2:14-16)

Some efforts were made within various Jewish communities to define a lesser set of Torah regulations whereby Gentiles could be counted as righteous. "Righteous Gentiles" embraced monotheism and observed the moral law but did not become proselytes. They were welcome in many synagogues and Jewish homes. There are some indications, including Luke's account of the Jerusalem conference in Acts 15, that certain minimal moral requirements were implemented as guidelines to regulate the inclusion of Gentiles (Acts 15:20, 29; 21:25). These are linked to the Noachian commandments (Genesis 9:4-6), which were given to all humanity after the flood and therefore were considered binding for both Jews and Gentiles.

Yet another Jewish view regarding the incorporation of Gentiles into the community is expressed within "Zion eschatology," that is, the anticipated future restoration of Jewish exiles back to Jerusalem. Major biblical texts expressing this hope include Isaiah 2:2-4 and its repeat in Micah 4:1-3, plus Isaiah 25:6-10a; 56:6-8, and Zechariah 8:20-23. In some later interpretations of Jewish restoration eschatology, Gentiles who worship the one God of Israel and bring their gifts to the temple are visualized as full participants in this glorious pilgrimage to Zion. In a word, Jews and pious Gentiles potentially share in the blessings of the dawning new age. Paul's ardent project of collecting relief from predominantly Gentile churches for the poor among the saints in Jerusalem (1 Corinthians 16:1-4; 2 Corinthians 8–9; Romans 15:14-33) may be rooted in this eschatological pilgrimage tradition. Might Paul have envisioned the entourage of Gentile delegates accompanying him with the love offering for the Jerusalem saints in this way? Did he view himself and his Gentile companions as representatives within an anticipated end-time procession of dispersed Jews and God-fearing Gentiles to the holy city at the dawning of the messianic new age?

Elements of the above contemporary Jewish views

about the inclusion of Gentiles might have entered into Paul's thinking. But Paul's dominant conviction centered on what God had done through Christ to make it possible for Gentiles also to join God's covenant people.

A People Called

As Paul's mission as Jewish apostle to the Gentiles led to the formation of new groups of believers throughout the Mediterranean world, he also needed to help them understand their identity. Are they a new Jewish sect? Are they still Gentiles? Had they been transformed into a new entity, the church?

Speaking to predominantly Gentile churches Paul at times lets it slip that he views them as no longer Gentile. He warns believers in Thessalonica not to live in lustful "passion like the Gentiles, who do not know God" (1 Thessalonians 4:3). He recalls for the Corinthians stories from the time when the Israelites, whom he calls "our ancestors," wandered in the wilderness (1 Corinthians 10:1). But does Paul visualize these communities of faith in continuity with the biblical people Israel?

Further discussion of the connection between Israel and the church occurs in chapter 6. For now we take note of several of Paul's identity signals to the groups of believers with whom he corresponds. In 1 Thessalonians 1:4 he asserts that this group, which is predominantly or exclusively Gentile, is part of the elect: "We know, brothers and sisters beloved by God, that he has chosen you." The same underlying word is used in Romans 11:28 regarding Israel as God's chosen people. God's calling of the believers in Thessalonica is emphasized elsewhere in the letter: "God . . . calls you into his own kingdom and glory" (2:12; cf. 5:24). One of the marks of the called is holiness: "For God did not call us to impurity but in holiness" (4:7). Here Paul reflects the Holiness Code of Leviticus: "You shall be holy, for I am holy" (Leviticus 11:45: 9:2; 20:26). Paul seems to be extending to these groups of Gentile converts the status and corresponding obligations comparable to those in place for Israel.

During the time when Paul writes pastoral letters to Christ-confessing groups in the Mediterranean region there is still considerable fluidity in the names he uses for them. The category *saints* (literally "holy ones") appears frequently, especially in the opening salutations of Romans, 1 and 2 Corinthians, Ephesians, Philippians, and Colossians. In 1 Corinthians 1:2 he employs the expression "called to be saints." In Romans 1:7 he enlarges on this identification by addressing his letter "to all God's beloved in Rome, who are called to be saints." Ephesians refers to the "saints" on multiple occasions besides the salutation: 1:18; 3:5, 18; 5:3.

Paul frequently addresses his communities by using the Greek word *ecclesia* (usually translated "church"). It is difficult for later readers of Paul's letters to let go of their own perceptions in order to visualize a time when the structures were still quite fluid. Paul may have been familiar with the secular usage of *ecclesia* to describe an official meeting of a town's citizens. However, his term *ecclesia* seems to be derived from the biblical phrase "the assembly" (Hebrew: *qahal*), a reference to a formal gathering of all the tribes of ancient Israel (Deuteronomy 23:2,3; Judges 20:2; Nehemiah 13:1). Paul can use *ecclesia* for a household group (Philemon 2), a local gathering (1 Thessalonians 1:1), or an assembly of several groups from a given city (1 Corinthians 11:18).

Consisting of both Jews and Greeks, the ecclesia, for Paul, embodies the calling and the mandate of Israel, the assembly of the Lord. In 1 Corinthians 1:24 he refers to this body as "those who are the called, both Jews and Greeks." Later in the same letter he urges, "Give no offense to Jews or to Greeks or to the church of God" (1 Corinthians 10:32). God's ecclesia, though made up of both Jews and Greeks, is charged with the mission of living in harmony with the promised blessing to all the nations. Social, national, and gender differences have been transcended in Christ. As Paul says in Colossians 3:11: "There is no longer Greek and Jew, circumcised and uncircumcised, barbarian, Scythian, slave and free; but Christ is all and in all!"

Paul's assertion that God calls the church, viewed as made up of both Jews and Gentiles, to carry the role of Israel as God's people raises an acute question: What is the ongoing status of Israel? Having followed Paul's theological articulation of the gospel's universal embrace of all people, we will need also to wrestle with Paul about the significance of God's particular covenant with the Jewish people. That question will preoccupy us in the next two chapters.

For now we need a word about Paul's notion of the grace of the God who calls people to participate in the divine mission.

God's Grace

The question, "Whom does God call?" elicits from Paul the answer, "God calls all, both Jews and Gentiles." The next question, "On what basis?" normally invites the response, "By God's grace."

Essentially *grace* is Paul's shorthand for the gospel of salvation, with God or Christ as the subject acting with undeserved mercy and compassion toward humankind. Paul's benedictions mention "the grace of God" or, with variations, "the grace of Christ." (See Romans 16:20;

1 Corinthians 16:23; 2 Corinthians 13:13; Galatians
6:18.) His greetings at the beginning of his letters typically invoke God's "grace and peace." Occasionally Paul also
uses the word *grace* to mean gospel (see 2 Corinthians
4:15; Colossians 1:5-6; Titus 2:11).

The story of God's embracing grace has often been told
in evangelistic testimony and sermons echoing Pauline texts:

> For by grace you have been saved through faith, and
> this is not your own doing; it is the gift of God—not
> the result of works, so that no one may boast.
> (Ephesians 2:8)

Grace, as God's love in Christ, comes as a gift received by
all who believe: "They are now justified by his grace as a
gift, through the redemption that is in Christ Jesus"
(Romans 3:24). Grace also overpowers the malevolent
powers, sin and death (Romans 5:21). And grace,
supremely modeled by Jesus Christ, elicits a response of
gratitude. In 2 Corinthians 8:9 Paul talks about the grace
of Christ in ways that invite the church to be generous in
their giving for the needs of others:

> For you know the generous act of our Lord Jesus Christ,
> that though he was rich, yet for your sakes he became
> poor, so that by his poverty you might become rich.

The NRSV here translates the underlying word *charis* as
"generous act." Notably Paul employs the same word in
2 Corinthians 8:6, 7, 19 (in the NRSV translated "this generous undertaking") to refer directly to the collection project itself. People who have experienced the grace of God in
Jesus Christ reciprocate in grace. In fact, expressions of
gratitude and thanksgiving to God also participate in this

character of grace. Often the word *charis* simply means "thank you": "Thanks be to God for his indescribable gift!" (2 Corinthians 9:15).

The story of God's grace made known in Jesus potentially embraces all. God's grace invites responsive grace, both in gratitude and in giving.

5

GOD'S LAW AND THE SPIRIT

In chapter 3 we followed Paul's pastoral counsel in his first letter to the Corinthians, in which he responded to oral and written reports of conflict and divisions in the church at Corinth. We focused in a special way on one concern raised in this letter: "May believers eat meat that has been offered to idols?"

Having moved into the orbit of Paul's appeal to Jewish and Gentile groups in Rome in chapter 4, we now turn our spotlight back onto the Corinthian congregation. What has transpired in Corinth in the intervening period?

In 2 Corinthians Paul leaves a significant number of clues. In 1:1–2:13 and 7:2-16 he recalls a near-death experience, a painful visit to Corinth, another letter to the church, and a visit by Titus. In chapters 8 and 9 he advocates for generous participation in the collection project and makes judicious arrangements for its administration. There are hints in chapters 10 to 13 concerning Paul's ongoing relationship with the congregation, a relationship that is troubled by the efforts of rival teachers who are, in his opinion, seriously undermining his own efforts.

The narrative below features Paul's trusted colleague, Titus, who recounts the still unfolding events in Corinth and prepares for a rendezvous with Paul.

A STORY: More Issues on the Isthmus

Titus knew that the church in Corinth had been much on Paul's mind. His major letter to them had dealt with a heady mix of issues and questions raised by its leaders. These included a case of blatant immorality, differences of opinion about marriage and singleness, the divisive issue of meat offered to idols, divisions along economic lines at the Lord's Supper, and the proper exercise of spiritual gifts in worship. Another of Paul's partners, Timothy, had delivered that letter and was present when it was read to help to interpret it. He stayed in Corinth for a while, and it soon became clear to him that Paul's letter had not settled matters. Timothy soon returned to Paul in Ephesus.

The next chapter in Paul's relationship with the Corinthian church was a deeply painful one. Timothy reported that the contentious party spirit within the group had dissipated somewhat, but now rival missionaries from outside the congregation were criticizing Paul and advocating a different understanding of the gospel. Some in the congregation were persuaded.

Like Paul, these missionaries were Jews who had accepted Jesus as Messiah. Unlike Paul, they emphasized that the covenant established with Israel at Sinai, including the law and its prescription of circumcision and other rituals, needed to continue to guide the life of the people of God, including the Gentile believers.

Paul decided to make a pastoral visit to the Corinthian church, but it was a disaster. He was publicly ridiculed before the whole church by his most vocal critic and left angry and disgraced. A short time later, he wrote a blistering letter calling on the church to deal with the offending individual. This time he summoned Titus to deliver the letter. Titus mused that Paul could have chosen him for an easier job. Serving as Paul's envoy and representative had its down side!

With knots in his stomach Titus made the trip back to Corinth and anxiously delivered the letter to the congregation. He had witnessed Paul's anguish and tears while drafting the document and wondered how the church would receive it and respond to his stern tone.

In the meantime, Paul carried on with his evangelistic work, this time in Troas. Though there was an openness to the gospel in Troas, Paul's anxiety about Corinth left him preoccupied and unable to give himself freely to the ministry there. He wondered how the Corinthian believers were accepting his tear-stained letter. Would they heed his reprimands and respond to the calls for firm action?

He decided to rendezvous with Titus. When Titus finally arrived in Troas he immediately sensed Paul's apprehension. Titus had come with good news and bad news. When he finished his report, Paul felt a mix of both tremendous relief and continued grave concern.

First the good news. The letter had moved the Corinthians to grief that led to genuine repentance. Even Paul's nemesis in Corinth, the person whose public criticisms had left him feeling stabbed in the back, expressed remorse. Whether this change of heart came as a result of Paul's letter, the congregation's disciplinary action, or some combination of the two, the important thing was that there has been a change. A spirit of reconciliation was in the air!

Then for the bad news. Some itinerant missionaries were continuing to assert an alternative vision of what it takes to be faithful to the gospel. Flashing their letters of recommendation from certain church leaders in Jerusalem, they were asking where Paul got his credentials for apostolic ministry. In contrast to Paul, they came certified to speak God's message. They projected an image of themselves as faithful Hebrews, authentic Israelites, legitimate descendants of Abraham and Sarah. Among other things, they seemed to be depicting themselves as being in the spiritual lineage of Moses, the glorious lawgiver and intercessor who met face-to-face with God and conveyed God's instructions to the people.

"Some people in the church at Corinth see you to be nothing at all like Moses, whom these other teachers hold up as their model," Titus told Paul. "Let's face facts. You have a major image problem in Corinth. The other missionary teachers don't get themselves beaten up like you do. They come recommended. And they offer clear guidelines for faithful living."

Paul shifted restlessly but listened intently. Titus knew Paul was grieved and angry, and eager to correct such perceptions. Paul signaled for Titus to continue.

"These other teachers promote the Jewish law as normative guidance for life. You preach a gospel that appears to deny that the law of Moses has any validity for them, even though you have urged them to recognize themselves as accepted by Israel's God into the covenant people."

Titus summarized. "You regularly get yourself into tight corners, Paul. Your ministry seems anything but glorious. Word has even come back to Corinth that you nearly died here in Asia. Some in Corinth are beginning to say, 'If this guy Paul is an apostle of the Lord Jesus Christ, why does he get beaten up and thrown into prison all the time? Can a battle-scarred jailbird be a true apostle?'"

Titus waited for Paul's reaction to the news from Corinth. Deeply relieved at the positive outcome within the Corinthian congregation, yet grieved and aggravated by the outsiders meddling in the life of this congregation, Paul began to write another letter. Titus was relieved that in this letter Paul did not come across as angry, but rather struck a more conciliatory tone. In it Paul was able to celebrate the reconciliation that was in progress. It was also apparent that he was committed to shoring up support for his ministry and his understanding of the gospel.

Ministers of the New Covenant

> You show that you are a letter of Christ, prepared by us, written not with ink but with the Spirit of the living God, not on tablets of stone but on the tablets of human hearts. (2 Corinthians 3:3)

In 2 Corinthians Paul continues his ministry to a community he addresses as "the church of God that is in Corinth"; he also has his sights on "all the saints throughout Achaia" (1:1). As we concentrate our attention on this letter (or edited collection of letters), we continue to explore Paul's pastoral theology with attention on how he interprets Scripture, this time on themes related to covenant, the law, and the work of the Spirit of God.

We recapitulate briefly what Paul has recalled from the biblical story.

As creator of all, the one God called a particular people, the descendants of Abraham and Sarah. God's covenant with this couple included a promise of descendants, a promise made incredible, even ludicrous, by the fact that they were well past the normal years for bearing children. Yet God proved worthy of their trust, and Abraham was reckoned righteous because of his faith in the God who creates life and restores life. A son and heir was born, and the family through whom God's blessing was to flow to all peoples had its beginning. But who all was to be included in this family?

Paul's reading of the story of Abraham and Sarah emphasizes that all those who share in the faith of Abraham inherit God's promise of blessing. The scope of

God's redemptive intention is not limited to those who can biologically trace their lineage back to Sarah and Abraham. Yet God's strategy is to begin by calling a particular people and channeling through them the promise of a blessing that is potentially available to all.

The biblical story of God's covenant at Sinai and the giving of the law heightens still further the tension between God's universal promise and God's particular strategy. What is the nature of the agreement that God establishes with the chosen community, and what are the requirements that this covenant imposes on those so called? Now that Jesus the Messiah has come, what is the significance of the covenant at Sinai? In what way does that covenant now encompass the Gentiles? How does the law fit into God's ongoing purposes? These and related questions repeatedly occupy Paul the former Pharisee, the apostle to the Gentiles, in his pastoral engagement with the congregations in his care.

Titus's report to Paul about developments in Corinth poses these questions sharply. Paul realizes anew how important it is to read the Scriptures carefully, indeed to reread them in light of Jesus Christ. How should believers in Jesus Christ, especially Gentile believers, view Moses, the Sinai covenant, and the Torah?

Judging from what Paul writes in 2 Corinthians, especially in 2:14–4:6, he has been pondering several biblical stories, texts, and themes. He comes to these biblical texts in part because it appears that his opponents have appealed to them to buttress their arguments. In light of his own life-transforming encounter with Jesus Christ, Paul also seeks fresh inspiration for himself and guidance for the Corinthian believers. What biblical narratives does he have on his mind? In 2 Corinthians he quotes or echoes a number of biblical stories. We will name some.

Paul does not explicitly cite the Ten Commandments,

but he assumes acquaintance with the narrative about the giving of the Torah to the Israelites at Sinai (Exodus 20:1-17; Deuteronomy 5:6-21). Paul makes a point of emphasizing that the commandments were inscribed on tablets of stone (2 Corinthians 3:7). Both Exodus and Deuteronomy report that the finger of God wrote these inscriptions:

> When God finished speaking with Moses on Mount Sinai, he gave him the two tablets of the covenant, tablets of stone, written with the finger of God. (Exodus 31:18; cf. 24:12; also Deuteronomy 9:10.)

In Paul's reading of this story, however, the fact of the divine inspiration of the written Torah recedes into the background. He appears to focus more on what the covenant people need to enable them to obey God's law. In 2 Corinthians 3:5-6 it is apparent that Paul is reminded of the following text from Jeremiah, which promises a new covenant and holds forth hope that God will yet write the law onto human hearts:

> The days are surely coming, says the LORD, when I will make a new covenant with the house of Israel and the house of Judah. It will not be like the covenant that I made with their ancestors when I took them by the hand to bring them out of the land of Egypt—a covenant that they broke, though I was their husband, says the LORD. But this is the covenant that I will make with the house of Israel after those days, says the LORD: I will put my law within them, and I will write it on their hearts; and I will be their God, and they shall be my people. (Jeremiah 31:31-33)

Similar themes from the prophet Ezekiel also echo in Paul's mind (2 Corinthians 3:3). Ezekiel speaks about a heart transplant in which a stony heart is replaced by a fleshly one:

> I will give them one heart, and put a new spirit within
> them; I will remove the heart of stone from their flesh
> and give them a heart of flesh, so that they may follow
> my statutes and keep my ordinances and obey them.
> Then they shall be my people, and I will be their God.
> (Ezekiel 11:19; cf. 36:26-28)

Closely related for Paul may have been Ezekiel's vision of dry bones becoming alive again through the life-giving infusion of God's breath:

> Thus says the Lord GOD to these bones: I will cause
> breath to enter you, and you shall live. I will lay
> sinews on you, and will cause flesh to come upon you,
> and cover you with skin, and put breath in you, and
> you shall live; and you shall know that I am the LORD.
> (37:5-6)

Jeremiah's forecast of the new covenant and Ezekiel's vision of a new heart and renewed bones appear also to have led Paul to new creation and new exodus themes in the book of Isaiah. In 2 Corinthians 6:2 Paul explicitly cites from Isaiah 49:8:

> Thus says the LORD: In a time of favor I have
> answered you, on a day of salvation I have helped you;
> I have kept you and given you as a covenant to the
> people.

However, judging from the upbeat new creation themes in 2 Corinthians 5:16-17 immediately before this citation, Paul may also have had some other Isaiah passages in mind, especially the following texts from Isaiah 43 and 65. One evokes memories of the exodus and Israel's time in the wilderness, and the other employs apocalyptic new creation imagery to inspire hope for Israel in exile:

> Do not remember the former things, or consider the things of old. I am about to do a new thing; now it springs forth, do you not perceive it? I will make a way in the wilderness and rivers in the desert. (Isaiah 43:18-19)

> For I am about to create new heavens and a new earth; the former things shall not be remembered or come to mind. But be glad and rejoice forever in what I am creating; for I am about to create Jerusalem as a joy, and its people as a delight. (Isaiah 65:17-18)

Paul's scriptural reflections therefore seem to navigate freely from the story of God's giving of the law at Sinai to various prophetic oracles longing for God's life-giving work to be done on stony hearts and dry bones, oracles anticipating a new creation and new exodus. Yet Paul gives sustained attention to a particular moment in Israel's early formation as a covenant people. He ponders at some length the stories of Israel's worship of the golden calf in the wilderness, and the renewal of covenant, as recounted in Exodus 32–34.

As Moses lingers on Mount Sinai, awaiting the two tablets of the covenant, the people grow weary of waiting for him and they persuade Aaron to forge a golden calf (Exodus 32:1-6). God becomes angry and threatens to destroy this rebellious people, but Moses intercedes with God, recalling the promises that God had made to Abraham and his descendants (32:7-14). When Moses descends the mountain and surveys the scene at the base of the mountain, it is his turn to be angry. In his rage at the Israelites' blatant unfaithfulness to God, Moses smashes the stone tablets and destroys the golden calf (32:15-20).

In the next scenes, Moses continues to intercede before God in behalf of the people (32:31-32; 33:12-23). In 33:20 God warns Moses about the dazzling glory: "You cannot see my face." After God reissues the two tablets of stone and renews the covenant (34:1-28), Moses descends the mountain again with the two tablets of the covenant in hand. His face radiates God's glory, so that he needs to put a veil over his face. This rhythm of Moses's encounters with God, with face unveiled, and his reporting to the people, with face veiled, features strongly in Paul's selective recollection of this dramatic story (34:29-35). Paul demonstrates his special interest in God's glory and its effect on Moses's face (2 Corinthians 3:12-18).

There are some hints in 2 Corinthians that Paul has also been pondering some other texts from the biblical narratives featuring Moses and the law. When encouraging the Corinthians to participate generously in the collection for the saints in Jerusalem, he recalls the experience of the Israelites gathering food in the wilderness. There was always enough (Exodus 16:18; quoted in 2 Corinthians 8:15). As he anticipates his third and particularly difficult visit to Corinth, he quotes from the Deuteronomic legislation: "Any charge must be sustained by the evidence of two or three witnesses" (Deuteronomy 19:15; cited in 2 Corinthians 13:1).

Paul's Ministry Like Moses's

Reflecting on what the rival missionaries have been preaching in Corinth, Paul considers some of the biblical stories that are apparently influencing them. They count

Moses to be their glorious hero and role model, and they point out that Paul's career as apostle is not similarly characterized by glory.

But Paul might well have asked, What was Moses's actual situation?

It is clear that Moses's career also included setbacks and reverses. He experienced suffering, and he questioned his own competence for the task to which he felt God was calling him. That Paul has been pondering Moses's ministry, as the story is told in Exodus, is suggested by his question, "Who is sufficient for these things?" (2 Corinthians 2:16). As Scott Hafemann has argued, Paul knows that God called all of the prophets, including Moses, despite their personal inadequacies. What matters is that God is sufficient (1995:100-5). When Moses, during his exile in Midian, is assigned the mission of pleading Israel's plight before Pharaoh (Exodus 3:1-12), he asks, "Who am I that I should go to Pharaoh, and bring the Israelites out of Egypt?" (3:11).

Paul opens 2 Corinthians by recalling his own suffering, particularly an experience in Asia: "We were so utterly, unbearably crushed that we despaired of life itself" (1:8). We cannot know what actually had happened to Paul, because he does not disclose the details. However, we can take note of the lesson he draws from his painful experience:

> We felt that we had received the sentence of death so that we would rely not on ourselves but on God who raises the dead. He who rescued us from so deadly a peril will continue to rescue us; on him we have set our hope that he will rescue us again, as you also join in helping us by your prayers. (2 Corinthians 1:9-11)

Paul has learned that his sufficiency comes not from himself but from God, "the God and Father of our Lord Jesus Christ, the Father of all mercies and the God of all consolation" (1:3). The deprivations and obstacles in Paul's way simply serve to accentuate God's mercy and abundant compassion. Confidence in the God who raises the dead leads to a joyful participation in prayer whereby many more are blessed (1:11).

This sense of adequacy rooted in the God who rescues the afflicted and raises the dead helps Paul not only to deal with personal reverses but also to cope with misunderstandings and opposition in the church. In 1:15–2:13 he alludes to several disheartening situations in his ongoing pastoral relationship with the saints in Corinth. He made a disastrous pastoral visit to Corinth, wrote a scathing follow-up letter, decided against another trip to Corinth, dispatched Titus as his emissary instead, and then waited anxiously for Titus to return. In the midst of all of these developments, Paul also became increasingly aware of the undermining influence of his detractors in Corinth.

Confronting a dizzying set of troubling circumstances, Paul realizes powerfully that his competence is not his own. His competence is derived from the one whose gospel he has been called to preach. Paradoxically, his weakness turns out to be a witness to the power of the gospel of Jesus Christ, the one who was crucified in weakness yet raised in power.

In 2:14-17 Paul draws on the image of a triumphal procession to make this point. When a general and his soldiers experience victory in a war abroad, they typically compel prisoners of war to parade through the streets of their capital city. For the victorious army this is a triumphal procession, but for the captives and their nation it is an experience of humiliation. Paul says,

Thanks be to God who in Christ always leads us in triumphal procession, and through us spreads in every
place the fragrance that comes from knowing him.
(2:14)

There is some question about how Paul applies this
image. Is he comparing himself to the victorious general in
such a triumphal parade? Or does he envision himself as
the prisoner of war forced to march in chains? Given his
overall argument in this letter, the latter seems more likely.
Paul is employing this image to make the same point that
he emphasizes at the beginning of 1 Corinthians. The message of the cross, proclaimed by a weak and trembling
evangelist and incarnate in a congregation of "nothings,"
announces God's strategy of foolishness and weakness to
overcome worldly wisdom and power (1 Corinthians
1:18–2:5). The image of the triumphal procession in
2 Corinthians 2:14-17 underscores the paradox that the
suffering apostle preaching the message of the crucified
Christ announces the triumph of God's grace over the
powers of sin and death. Paradoxically, what seems to
those who are perishing to be the stench of defeat (a fragrance from death to death) becomes the sweet aroma of
victory (a fragrance from life to life) to those who are
being saved (2:15-16).

Paul's application in 2:17 reveals clearly that he has in
his mind the rival missionaries' challenge to his ministry:

For we are not peddlers of God's word like so many;
but in Christ we speak as persons of sincerity, as persons sent from God and standing in his presence.

Strikingly Paul refers to himself and his partners in terms
that recall Moses's call and his ministry as mediator and

intercessor on behalf of the people of Israel. As Moses was commissioned by God for a particular mission and as Moses stood in God's presence as intercessor and mediator, so also Paul is seeking to be faithful to his commission from God.

The Old and the New

In 3:1-3 Paul turns to the challenge brazenly being raised by some of the intruders into the church at Corinth. They have apparently been asking questions about Paul's authority and credentials. They inquire, "Where are Paul's letters of recommendation?" Apparently these "super-apostles" (as Paul sarcastically calls them later in 11:5) have been flashing letters of recommendation, possibly from some Jerusalem church leaders, to back up their own ministry. And they point out that Paul has no such recommendations.

Paul's rebuttal picks up on this matter of "letters of recommendation." He appeals to the Corinthian church to recognize that as a body of believers they are themselves a letter "to be known and read by all" (3:2). Paul insists that the fact that the congregation in Corinth exists at all is itself living testimony to his legitimacy and authority as apostle.

In 3:3 Paul enlarges on this metaphor of the church as a living letter by recalling the story of Moses and the stone tablets of the covenant:

> You show that you are a letter of Christ, prepared by us, written not with ink but with the Spirit of the living God, not on tablets of stone but on tablets of human hearts. (3:3; cf. Exodus 24:12; 31:18; Ezekiel 36:26)

The preachers whom Paul calls peddlers of God's word may have used the Sinai story to support their understanding of

the gospel for the Corinthian believers. The language of sufficiency and competence demonstrates that Paul is engaging
in a spirited defense of his ministry over against their claims.
"Our competence is from God," he asserts (3:5).

Paul is eager both to portray his own ministry and
message positively and to shore up the church's loyalty to
himself over against the insinuations of some outsiders. He
attempts to achieve both goals by evoking the prophet
Jeremiah's new covenant theme:

> Not that we are competent of ourselves to claim any-
> thing as coming from us; our competence is from God,
> who has made us competent to be ministers of a new
> covenant, not of letter but of spirit. (3:5-6)

The "new covenant" is mentioned once earlier in the
Corinthian correspondence. In Paul's recollection of the
memory of Jesus's last meal with his disciples, Jesus says,
"This cup is the new covenant in my blood" (1 Corinthians
11:25).

Paul's mention of a new covenant in 2 Corinthians 3:6
echoes his remembrance of Jesus's final Passover meal. But
Paul here articulates what appears to be a sharp contrast
between the new covenant and that which preceded it. The
old and the new are described respectively as *letter* and
spirit. The new covenant within which Paul has been called
into ministry is "not of letter but of spirit; for the letter
kills, but the Spirit gives life" (3:6).

But how exactly does Paul envision the relationship
between the old and the new covenants? In 3:7-11 Paul
proceeds to compare two ministries. (The word *diakonia*,
utilized four times in these verses, is correctly translated as
"ministry" in NIV and NRSV; cf. RSV, which offers the
misleading term "*dispensation.*") One notices at once that

he describes the old and new ministries in starkly contrasting terms. However, his "from lesser to the greater" type of argument makes it apparent that, even though he is contrasting the old with the new, he also sees the former as preparing the way for the new:

The Old Ministry	The New Ministry
Now if the ministry of death, chiseled in letters on stone tablets, came in glory so that the people of Israel could not gaze at Moses's face because of the glory of his face, a glory now set aside, >	how much more will the ministry of the Spirit come in glory?
For if there was glory in the ministry of condemnation, >	much more does the ministry of justification abound in glory!
Indeed, what once had glory has lost its glory >	because of the greater glory;
for if what was set aside came through glory, >	much more has the permanent come in glory!

Because these comparisons are articulated so sharply the tendency has been to interpret these two ministries respectively as an inferior plan A, which God has abolished in favor of a totally revised and superior plan B. But is that Paul's point?

Because of the polemical situation in which Paul finds himself in relation to the Corinth church, he does emphasize the contrast between the old and the new. Yet he is clear in describing both the old and the new as glorious. The Sinai covenant also came with glory, in fact with such glory "that the people of Israel could not gaze on Moses's face" (3:7). Paul is comparing two glories, the law and the gospel.

Yet he also alludes to a dramatic change that has been

introduced by God through Christ, now that the new age of the Spirit has been ushered in. The glory of the former has now been recognized as having been fulfilled in the new. Indeed the splendor of the new outshines the glory of the old. The gospel of Jesus Christ is the reality toward which the law had pointed.

For Paul, the law and the prophets give witness to the gospel. The law foreshadows the good news of Jesus Christ. The transitory character of the law as witness to the gospel is conveyed by means of the Greek word *katergeo* (3:7, 13), often translated as "fading" (as in RSV), but more accurately rendered as "set aside" (NRSV). Paul's point is not that the old covenant is fading in its glory but rather that the glory of the ministry of the old covenant is transitory, now eclipsed by a greater glory in the new age, the era of the Spirit. The Torah is a good thing, but its jurisdiction is temporary. The purpose and the goal of the law have now been achieved in Jesus Christ and within the Spirit-empowered community that embodies the way of Christ in the world.

Moses, the People, the Veil, and the Law

In 3:12-18 Paul offers a metaphorical treatment of the veil with which Moses covered his face following each mountaintop audience with God. The veil, he says, was needed for Moses's face so that Israel would not gaze on the *telos*, "end," of that which has transitory splendor. Several vexing translation issues confront us in 3:13, including the meaning of the Greek word *telos*, which is often rendered as "end":

> [Moses] put a veil over his face to keep the people of Israel from gazing at the end of the glory that was being set aside.

The term *telos* has been traditionally understood in a chronological sense to signal that the glow of Moses's face was fading, a sign also that the Mosaic old covenant has been abrogated. The RSV talks about "the end of the fading splendor" in this sense. However, Hays has argued convincingly that *telos* should be understood not in a chronological sense as "end" (termination, conclusion) but in the teleological sense of *end* (goal, purpose, or outcome). The previous glory, namely the law seen within the framework of the Sinai covenant, gives testimony beyond itself to the gospel of Jesus Christ. As Hays puts it,

> Those who turn to the Lord see through the text to its
> *telos*, its true aim. For them the veil is removed, so that
> they like Moses are transfigured by the glory of God
> into the image of Jesus Christ to whom Moses and the
> Law had always in veiled fashion pointed. (1989:137)

In a word, Paul wants to make several interrelated points. We'll summarize concerning Moses, the people, the meaning of the veil, and the view of the law.

Paul attests the interim and transitional character of Moses's contribution but the overall picture of Moses is a positive one. Moses conceals the glory of God from the people, but the reason for this is not to thwart revelation but to spare a people not yet prepared for God's glorious presence. The veiled Moses shields the people from God's judgment, because their hearts were not prepared to receive God's grace and mercy. As Paul puts it, "Their minds were hardened" (3:14). Moses does see the glory of God's image, and he experiences transformation, but the people as a whole are not yet ready to see and be similarly transformed. Moses as mediator between God and the people and as intercessor is therefore a precursor of the new covenant when all with unveiled faces will be enabled to see God's glory.

Paul's portrait of the people of Israel, therefore, is that since their hearts were hardened, they could not yet directly receive the glory of the Lord. Ezekiel's vision of God replacing hearts of stone with fleshly hearts needed to become reality first. The people need to approach God with unhardened hearts. The work of the Holy Spirit in the lives of those who participate in the way of Christ accomplishes such softening of the heart. In other words, the problem is not with the law but with the people. Their inability to keep the law is not a critique of the law itself. Their unfaithfulness to the law does not derive from an inability to understand the law, but rather from their inability to keep it, because their hearts are hardened. Their lives need first to be transformed by the work of the Spirit of God, so that they will desire to be obedient to God. Through the Spirit's ministry all would therefore be able to experience God face-to-face, even as Moses had.

Paul therefore claims that it is not the law but the veil that is removed in Christ and by the freeing Spirit. In Paul's retelling of the narrative about how Moses communicated with God and then reported to the Israelites, the veil moves from Moses's face, where it serves the merciful function of shielding the Israelites from the judgment of God, to a place over the minds of contemporary hearers of the Torah. Paul states his lament in two parallel assertions:

> Indeed, to this very day, when they hear the reading of the old covenant, that same veil is still there, since only in Christ is it set aside. (3:14b)

> Indeed, to this very day whenever Moses is read, a veil lies over their minds; but when one turns to the Lord, the veil is removed. (3:15-16)

Paul likely has in mind especially the messianic Jewish interlopers in Corinth who find his credentials inadequate. In their reading of the Mosaic old covenant, in a way comparable to that of their Jewish contemporaries in the synagogues, they seem still to be blind to the freeing truth of that toward which the law points: the gospel of Christ. Of course, Paul is not addressing these missionaries directly. Rather he is appealing to the Corinthian believers not to be persuaded by their rival interpretation of the story of Moses and the covenant. And so Paul gives testimony to God's transforming work through Jesus Christ and by the empowering presence of the Spirit: "Now the Lord is the Spirit, and where the Spirit of the Lord is, there is freedom!" (3:17).

Paul's exultant concluding coda celebrates the fact that what Moses experienced in his glorious transforming encounters with God on the mountain has now become a possibility for all:

> And all of us, with unveiled faces, seeing the glory of
> the Lord as though reflected in a mirror, are being
> transformed into the same image from one degree of
> glory to another; for this comes from the Lord who is
> the Spirit. (3:18)

Here is a vision of what Paul sees as the outcome of the transformation already underway. This transformation perpetuates what happened to Moses himself. It also goes beyond what Moses experienced, and it is a change that continues. And because, as Paul says, "the glory of the Lord" is accessible to all ("all of us" includes Paul and the Corinthians), it is also mediated toward each other as believers within the church. As a congregation, they are, after all, "a letter of Christ" (3:3), a letter "to be known and read by all" (3:2). The mirror in which these believers see reflected the glory of the Lord is not only Jesus Christ or just the gospel of Christ. The community, the body of Christ, also mirrors the glory of the Lord. As N. T. Wright puts it:

> Those who belong to the covenant are, by the Spirit, being changed into the glory of the Lord: when they come face to face with each other they are beholding, as in a mirror, the glory. (1991:185)

The new age has dawned. The believing community already experiences and reflects the glory of God as made known in the face of Jesus Christ and mediated by the ministry of the Holy Spirit. The covenant at Sinai was also glorious. This includes the law as mediated by Moses, who met God face-to-face on the mountain. Yet the Sinai covenant has prepared the way for the new covenant. The Sinai covenant is a precursor and advance witness to the new covenant ushered in by God through Christ.

In sum: When Paul talks about the metamorphosis "from one degree of glory to another," he has in mind the eschatological process of individual and communal transformation through Christ and the Spirit. Given the ways in which he has narrated the story of Moses's encounters with God and interpreted that story to underscore both continuity and difference, he may also be referring to two glories, the law and the gospel, of which the latter outshines the first. The law within the Sinaitic covenant possessed—and still possesses—"one degree of glory." The gospel as made known in Christ, climactically through his suffering and death on the cross, testifies to another brighter glory.

New Covenant, New Creation, the Day of Salvation

Paul's "therefore" in 4:1 signals that he is picking up again his appeal to the Corinthian church concerning his commission from God. His biblical ruminations in 3:7-18 have been complex. Even his original readers may have needed a fresh reminder that these forays into Scripture are elicited by Paul's desire to shore up his support base in Corinth.

In 2:17 Paul introduced his explorations into the new covenant theme: "in Christ we speak as persons of sincerity, as persons sent from God and standing in his presence." Having compared and contrasted his own ministry with that of Moses in 3:1-18, he now revisits the motifs established earlier: his personal suffering, the opposition he encounters, and what these experiences say about his credentials for apostolic ministry.

As Paul recalls his struggles he also views the existence of the church as reassurance that his calling is from God: "Therefore, since it is by God's mercy that we are engaged in this ministry, we do not lose heart" (4:1). He differentiates himself from those who practice cunning and those who falsify God's word, vowing rather to speak the truth openly (4:2). And in 4:3-4 he invokes the veil metaphor yet once more, this time to say that just as Israelites failed to understand God's message through Moses, so also in Corinth in their own time the gospel is veiled for some people:

> And even if our gospel is veiled, it is veiled to those
> who are perishing. In their case the god of this world
> has blinded the minds of the unbelievers, to keep them
> from seeing the light of the gospel of the glory of
> Christ, who is the image of God. (4:3-4)

Once again the veil conceals. In this case, however, the veil does not protect people with unready hearts from the dazzling radiance of God's glory. Paul asserts that the veiling effect of "the god of this world" keeps unbelievers from glimpsing the glory of the gospel in Jesus Christ, who is God's luminous image. Some people remain unreceptive to gospel glory, even though the light of the gospel shines forth through Christ, the apostle, and the church as a whole. Yet the faith community, as letter of Christ, as mirror of the glorious gospel, continues to narrate the story and reflect the light of God.

Paul's theological vision here takes a wide-angle view. He sees God's glory, made known in the present and anticipated more fully in the future, as reaching all the way back to the time of creation:

> For we do not proclaim ourselves; we proclaim Jesus Christ as Lord and ourselves as your slaves for Jesus' sake. For it is the God who said, "Let light shine out of darkness," who has shone in our hearts to give the light of the knowledge of the glory of God in the face of Jesus Christ. (4:5-6)

As he basks in the light of God's glory Paul ponders the fact that his own suffering as apostle participates in the paradoxical glory of the crucified Christ, who was vindicated by God through his resurrection from the dead. That is where his competence as apostle rests, and not in any external credentials. To emphasize this point Paul changes his metaphor:

> But we have this treasure in clay jars, so that it may be made clear that this extraordinary power belongs to God and does not come from us. (4:7)

In 4:7-5:10 Paul then shares some of his most intimate thoughts about his life and his death, and his confidence in the midst of his suffering. The themes and images in this section will be explored further in chapter 13. For now we can note that Paul is still considering his apostolic commission from God. As a participant in Jesus's suffering (4:8-12) he anticipates being raised with Jesus (4:13-15). In the meantime the Spirit has been given as a guarantee (5:5). And, aware of the prospect of appearing before the judgment seat of Christ, Paul reminds himself and others that what ultimately matters is whether one is living in faithfulness to God (5:10).

Another "therefore" at 5:11 signals the continuation of Paul's pastoral comments in yet another direction. Having contemplated the ways in which ministry within the "new covenant" compares and contrasts with Moses's ministry, Paul enters into a particularly dense set of theological pronouncements centered on the theme of "new creation." However, he also continues to articulate his desire for the Corinthian believers to side with his understanding of the gospel:

> Therefore, knowing the fear of the Lord, we try to persuade others; but we ourselves are well known to God, and I hope that we are also well known to your consciences. We are not commending ourselves to you again, but giving you an opportunity to boast about us, so that you may be able to answer those who boast in outward appearance and not in the heart. For if we are beside ourselves, it is for God; if we are in our right mind, it is for you. (5:11-13)

Furthermore, Paul reveals again in a variety of ways that, because of what God has done in Jesus Christ, the past and the present can now be viewed through new eyes, and a radically new future is breaking into the present. In 5:14 he shares about the compelling power of Christ's love, a love expressed supremely in Christ's sacrificial death:

> For the love of Christ urges us on, because we are convinced that one has died for all; therefore all have died. (5:14)

In 5:15 Paul enlarges on the power of Christ's self-denying love. Christ's death "for all" evokes imitation on the part of those who are gripped by the redemptive power of selfless love. People who are drawn into the orbit of Christ's self-giving love are transformed into a way of life that conforms to the same pattern:

> And he died for all, so that those who live might live no longer for themselves, but for him who died and was raised for them. (5:15)

In Jesus Christ, therefore, a new era has dawned. Power for selfless living has been unleashed among those who in Christ have caught the vision for the future already taking form in the present. Paul celebrates a new way of perceiving reality, including a new way of knowing Jesus Christ himself (Martyn, 1997b:89-110) (5:16). For those who are in Christ, he exults, a new age has begun: "there is a new creation" (5:17):

> From now on, therefore, we regard no one from a human point of view; even though we once knew Christ from a human point of view, we know him no longer in that way. So if anyone is in Christ, there is a new creation: everything old has passed away; see, everything has become new! (5:16-17)

With the dawning of the "new creation," all has been made new. "All this is from God," Paul says (5:18). The God who is the creator of all things has accomplished a new exodus and announced a new day of salvation. As suggested earlier, Jeremiah's anticipation of the new covenant and Ezekiel's vision of the fleshly heart may have also connected in Paul's mind to Isaiah's picture of the new heavens and new earth, climaxing in the joyous announcement of the "now" of the day of salvation in the quotation from Isaiah 49:8 (6:2). Within the lavish grace of God, new creation and new exodus lead to a salvation that outdoes even the glory of God's initial creation and the drama of Israel's liberation out of Egypt.

Such grace dare not be received in vain, Paul urges (6:1). Indeed such grace invites participation with God, both Paul's ("we work together with him," 6:1), and the Corinthians' partnership along with Paul.

To portray this dynamic partnership Paul develops another metaphor from the realm of diplomacy and economics:

> All this is from God, who reconciled us to himself
> through Christ, and has given us the ministry of recon-
> ciliation; that is, in Christ God was reconciling the
> world to himself, not counting their trespasses against
> them, and entrusting the message of reconciliation to
> us. So we are ambassadors for Christ, since God is
> making his appeal through us; we entreat you on
> behalf of Christ, be reconciled to God. (5:18-20)

Reconciliation involves an exchange: enmity is traded for friendship. Within this metaphor God is portrayed as transforming estrangement into gracious hospitality and acceptance. Broken relationships have been restored in

Christ between God and the world and therefore potentially also between people. Like an ambassador representing his nation abroad, Paul declares God's message of release from previous enmity, and he urges those who have been reconciled to join with him in the ministry of reconciliation. Within the economy of God's dealings with humanity, debts are no longer reckoned, and erstwhile enemies now are at peace.

Paul's use of the reconciliation image is reminiscent of the role of Moses as intercessor appealing for God not to count Israel's grievous sin in the wilderness against them. Yet, as Paul proceeds to say, within the now of the new creation, the day of salvation, God has in Christ achieved release through the supreme offering for sin:

> For our sake he made him to be sin who knew no sin,
> so that in him we might become the righteousness of
> God. (5:21)

The new covenant provision for liberation from the power of sin is likened to the Mosaic legislation of sacrificial offerings to atone for sin. Within the new creation the community of people who are in Christ will become an incarnation and embodiment of the justice of God.

In 6:3-10 Paul speaks eloquently from his own experience about what it means for him as the battered apostle to be part of the community that incarnates God's righteousness. And in 6:14–7:1, a section often regarded as having been inserted from a previous letter (perhaps the one mentioned in 1 Corinthians 5:9, 11), Paul amplifies how the righteous community lives within a culture marked by lawlessness, darkness, and idolatry (6:14-16). It is striking that the communal values advocated within the Torah are to be embodied in those who through Christ have become

the righteousness of God. In a rich conflation of Scripture
texts, Paul depicts the covenant people as God's temple
(6:16; cf. Ezekiel 37:27-28), he announces the rescue of
God's people out of their exile among the nations (6:17; cf.
Isaiah 43:5-7; 52:9-12), and he reaffirms God's covenant
promise (6:18; cf. Leviticus 26:11-12):

> For we are the temple of the living God; as God said,
> "I will live in them and walk among them, and I will
> be their God, and they shall be my people. Therefore
> come out from them, and be separate from them, says
> the Lord, and touch nothing unclean; then I will wel-
> come you, and I will be your father, and you shall be
> my sons and daughters, says the Lord Almighty."
> (2 Corinthians 6:16-18)

With these marvelous assurances of God's fidelity ringing
in their ears, the predominantly Gentile community of
believers in Corinth hears Paul pledge that the ancient
promises for the people of God also apply to them. Paul
therefore also summons them to holy living, to purity in
body and spirit:

> Since we have these promises, beloved, let us cleanse
> ourselves from every defilement of body and of spirit,
> making holiness perfect in the fear of God. (7:1)

This admonition to holy living comes within the gracious provision of reconciliation through Christ and
empowerment through the Spirit. Within the new era now
launched in Christ the requirement of obedience and holiness as defined by the Torah continues but the power of
the Spirit of God enables a holy and obedient lifestyle.
Even though struggles and temptations continue, faithfulness is now made possible.

In 2 Corinthians 8 and 9 Paul expresses how the boun-
teous grace of God enlists even impoverished churches in a
demonstration of God's overflowing generosity through
the offering for the saints. He alludes to the wilderness
generation experience of receiving manna to point out that
within God's provision there is enough (8:15, citing
Exodus 16:18). He quotes Psalm 112:9 and interprets it to
accent God's bounty and to urge cheerful giving (9:8-10):

> You will be enriched in every way for your great gen-
> erosity, which will produce thanksgiving to God
> through us; for the rendering of this ministry not only
> supplies the needs of the saints but also overflows with
> many thanksgivings to God. (9:11-12)

The final section of his letter (chapters 10–13) clearly
suggests that Paul later encountered intensified opposition
in Corinth. In a reprise of his earlier reflections about his
sufferings as apostle, Paul testifies that paradoxically the
power of God made known through the crucified Christ is
abundantly made known despite his weakness:

> Three times I appealed to the Lord about this, that it
> would leave me, but he said to me, "My grace is suffi-
> cient for you, for power is made perfect in weakness."
> So, I will boast all the more gladly of my weaknesses,
> so that the power of Christ may dwell in me. (12:8-9)

Once more Paul sounds the note of sufficiency, not his own
but that which comes through the indwelling Christ.

The Covenant, the Law, and the Spirit of God

Second Corinthians is not the epistle in which Paul's perspectives on the Torah are most prominent. In fact Paul

seems to have studiously avoided the words "law" and "commandment" in this part of the Corinthian correspondence. However, our discussion has demonstrated that covenant provides an essential framework for his understanding of the Jewish law. The prophetic promise of the new covenant broadcasts a vision for how the law can be fulfilled.

We now turn to a more focused treatment of Paul's understanding of the Jewish law. In Galatians and Romans he has the most to say on this topic. These are also the letters where Paul deals most intensively with relationships between Jews and Gentiles within the church. (See chapters 4 and 6 for a treatment of Romans and chapters 8 and 9 for Galatians.)

The Torah Story

Traditional Christian understandings have been steeped in deeply ingrained assumptions about the character of Judaism and the nature of the Torah. Ancient Judaism has often been regarded as a legalistic and ritualistic religion whose adherents sought to attain salvation through their own efforts. The 1977 book *Paul and Palestinian Judaism* by E. P. Sanders prompted a major shift away from this kind of thinking. Some of this rethinking can be summarized here before we examine specific Pauline texts and themes. Sanders explains his conclusions about what he calls "covenantal nomism" within the Judaism of Paul's day:

> The pattern or structure of covenantal nomism is this:
> (1) God has chosen Israel and (2) given the law. The law
> implies both (3) God's promise to maintain the election
> and (4) the requirement to obey. (5) God rewards obedi-
> ence and punishes transgression. (6) The law provides
> for means of atonement, and atonement results in
> (7) maintenance or re-establishment of the covenantal

relationship. (8) All those who are maintained in the covenant by obedience, atonement and God's mercy belong to the group which will be saved. An important interpretation of the first and last points is that election and ultimately salvation are considered to be by God's mercy rather than human achievement. (1977:422)

Even after his Damascus Road encounter with the risen Christ, Paul shares these convictions, with one major exception: for him entrance into the community is gained by faith. He affirms the validity of the commandments of God although he differentiates between them:

Circumcision is nothing, and uncircumcision is nothing; but obeying the commandments of God is everything. (1 Corinthians 7:19; cf. also Galatians 5:6; 6:15)

Paul's convictions about covenant and Torah continue to be vigorously debated. (See the essays in Dunn, 1999.) That debate will not be described here. We can, however, explore the basic plot of Paul's story of the Torah, a story that involves him deeply because he shifted from zeal as Pharisee to zealous apostle. What is Paul's rendering of the story of the law?

First, God gave the law. Paul can say, "So the law is holy, and the commandment is holy and just and good" (Romans 7:12), and he adds, "The law is spiritual" (7:14) and "I delight in the law of God in my inmost self" (7:22). Even righteous Gentiles give evidence through the prompting of their consciences that in some ways the law is innate: "What the law requires is written on their hearts" (2:15). God graciously provided the law and it continues to be God's good gift.

Second, the law came not before but after God had ratified the covenant of promise with Abraham and Sarah and their descendants. The law is embedded within God's gracious covenant. Obedience to the law is not the condition for entrance into a covenantal relationship with God or for the promises included within that relationship. The sequence, first covenant then the law, is important to Paul:

> My point is this: the law, which came four hundred thirty years later, does not annul a covenant previously ratified by God, so as to nullify the promise. For if the inheritance comes from the law, it no longer comes from the promise; but God granted it to Abraham through the promise. (Galatians 3:17-18)

Third, faith has precedence over works of the law such as circumcision. For Paul entrance into the new covenant community is gained on the basis of justifying faith like that of Abraham, who trusted God despite the apparent futility of such trust (Romans 4). Faith as entrance requirement raises vexing questions about the relationship between Jews and Gentiles, given what the Torah says to Jews about maintaining appropriate boundaries between themselves and the nations. Paul's references to "works of the law" in Galatians 2:16 (three times), Galatians 3:2, 5, 10 and Romans 3:20, 28 visualize not obedience to the Torah in general but adherence to those rituals such as circumcision that define boundaries and separate people within the community of faith from each other.

Fourth, the law was given to be obeyed, and obedience to the law is possible. In fact, Paul declares that

> it is not the hearers of the law who are righteous in God's sight, but the doers of the law who will be justified. (Romans 2:13)

However, the ability to live in accordance to the law is crippled by the weakness of the flesh and by the power of sin, which has taken the law hostage. Paul laments:

> For I delight in the law of God in my inmost self, but I see in my members another law at war with the law of my mind, making me captive to the law of sin that dwells in my members. (Romans 7:22-23)

The problem does not lie with the law itself. The problem is with sin as the occupying power that has hijacked the law and with human inability to comply with the law's righteous requirements.

Fifth, the law has several positive functions in relation to the human struggle against the power of sin. The law defines and measures sin (Romans 5:13; 7:13), brings it to consciousness (Galatians 3:19), even increases sinfulness (Romans 7:8), all with the intention of warning, guiding, and instructing God's people concerning their response within their covenant with God. One of the word pictures Paul uses for the law is that of tutor or disciplinarian with temporary protective custody over a child until the time of maturity:

> Now before faith came, we were imprisoned and guarded under the law until faith would be revealed. Therefore the law was our disciplinarian until Christ came, so that we might be justified by faith. (Galatians 3:23-24; also 4:1-7)

Sixth, Christ brings the law to its fulfillment. Paul himself, a zealous Jew who at one time in his life persecuted followers of Jesus, testifies that he needed to die to the law so that he might live to God: "For through the law I died to the law so that I might live to God" (Galatians 2:19).

His earlier zeal paralleled that of his Jewish kin, for whom he longs that they might know Christ, who is the "end of the law" (again *telos*, as the end or goal of the law, not the abrogation of the law). Jesus Christ is the *telos*, the end, goal, or outcome toward which the law points:

> Brothers and sisters, my heart's desire and prayer to God for them is that they may be saved. I can testify that they have a zeal for God, but it is not enlightened. For, being ignorant of the righteousness that comes from God, and seeking to establish their own, they have not submitted to God's righteousness. For Christ is the end of the law so that there may be righteousness for everyone who believes. (Romans 10:1-4)

Paul can even talk about "the law of Christ" (Galatians 6:2). Christ's self-giving love fulfills the law. In Galatians 5:14 he says it succinctly: "For the whole law is summed up in a single commandment, 'You shall love your neighbor as yourself.'" Similarly Paul says in Romans: "Owe no one anything, except to love one another; for the one who loves another has fulfilled the law" (13:8).

Seventh, having given the law, God also makes compliance with the law possible. Those who participate with Christ fulfill Christ's law: "Bear one another's burdens, and in this way you will fulfill the law of Christ" (Galatians 6:2). God's empowering Spirit bears the kind of fruit within the faith community that more than fulfills the law of God. In Galatians 5:22-23a Paul identifies the Spirit's fruit: "love, joy, peace, patience, kindness, generosity, faithfulness, gentleness, and self-control." He adds wryly, "There is no law against such things" (5:23b).

In Romans 8 Paul enlarges on this theme of divine enabling. After his extended lament about human inability

to live in accordance with God's law (7:1-24), he finally
bursts forth with thanksgiving for what God has done
through Jesus Christ (7:25). He adds that there is no condemnation for those who are in Christ (8:1), and he follows with a narrative detailing God's freeing and empowering work through Christ and the Spirit:

> For the law of the Spirit of life in Christ Jesus has set
> you free from the law of sin and of death. For God has
> done what the law, weakened by the flesh, could not
> do: by sending his own Son in the likeness of sinful
> flesh, and to deal with sin, he condemned sin in the
> flesh, so that the just requirement of the law might be
> fulfilled in us, who walk not according to the flesh but
> according to the Spirit. (Romans 8:2-4)

Scholars debate whether Paul is here talking about the
Torah in each of three references to the law in 8:2, or
whether he is using a word play in which the word "*law*"
sometimes means "principle." Fee argues for the latter: the
"law" of the Spirit overcomes the "law" of sin so that the
requirements of God's law are fulfilled (1994:519-27).
Dunn views all three as references to the Torah, the law of
God. He understands "the law of sin" as shorthand for the
law abused and misused by sin to bring about death, and
he sees "the law of the Spirit of life in Christ Jesus" as the
law freed from sin's power so that it can serve again as
guidance for living (1998:642-49).

Paul's clear conviction, articulated above, is that the
law is fulfilled in Christ by those who abide by the law of
Christ; the law is not abolished but fulfilled. The most likely interpretation of Paul's meaning is that the law, though
God-given and spiritual and good, can be taken over by the
power of sin (hence "the law of sin and death"). However,

the law can also be wrapped up in the power of the Holy Spirit ("the law of the Spirit of life in Christ Jesus").

But, regardless of which scenario best reflects Paul's view, one thing is clear: What the law is powerless to bring about, God has made possible in Christ through the indwelling Spirit!

Paul's Own Torah Story

Alongside this attempt at narrating the Torah story from Paul's perspective in Christ, one is inevitably drawn into Paul's own pilgrimage with the Jewish Torah. In chapter 1, we have already noted some of the ways in which Paul reflects on his past life as a Pharisee who was zealously devoted to observing the Torah. In Philippians 3:5-6 he lists his credentials as a Pharisee, climaxing with the claim that he had been blameless "as to righteousness under the law." Yet he also recognizes that this stellar pedigree is loss in comparison to knowing Christ Jesus as Lord (3:7-8a). In Romans 7 Paul repeatedly employs the first person singular "*I*" to reflect representatively about Israel's experience with the Torah. However, in the process he also opens some windows into his own personal pilgrimage with the law.

Paul's several comments about his own earlier zeal (Galatians 1:13) and Israel's unenlightened zeal (Romans 10:2) may provide a clue to his personal story with the Torah. Robert Sloan suggests that Paul came to realize following his encounter with the risen Christ that as a zealous Pharisee he had had a "nearly disastrous experience with the law":

> That is, his zeal for the law had blinded him to the
> very hope toward which his zeal and religious devotion
> in principle and intention drove. . . . Paul came to

believe that his devotion to the law had opened him up
to the powers of evil. As one zealously under the law,
he had (unwittingly) become a victim of the powers of
sin. (Sloan, 1991:55-6)

As one who had become so zealous for the Torah that he
could not see God as revealed in Messiah Jesus, Paul needed
to die to the law so that he could live to God (Galatians
2:19).

Sloan also suggests that Paul came to see his own pilgrimage with the law as paralleling Israel's story with the
law:

I am arguing that Paul could only explain his and
Israel's blindness to Messiah as a function of zeal, i.e.,
their devotion to the law. The powers of evil operating
through the law/their devotion to the law had actually
rendered them incapable of seeing Messiah. (1991:56-7)

Even this co-optation of the law by the power of sin has a
redemptive outcome, both for Paul himself and for Israel.
Within the sovereignty of God, Israel's rejection of the
Messiah, toward whom the law had pointed, actually
opens the door for God's mysterious mercy to be unveiled,
both among Jews and among Gentiles (Romans 11:11-36).

Paul realized that the law could be hijacked by sin.
Those zealously devoted to the Torah could be drawn
along with the law into the sphere of sin and its tyranny.
In retrospect following his Damascus road encounter with
the Messiah sent by God, he knew that to be a possibility.
Yet the problem was not with the law itself; the law is
God's gift. And the law, and those devoted to the law, can
also be drawn into the sphere of influence of the Spirit of
God, thereby leading to faithfulness to God's law. Through

the community of those conformed to Christ and empowered by the Spirit, the just requirements of the law are fulfilled.

6

GOD'S PEOPLE

In chapter 4 we followed Paul's efforts to unite Jews and Gentiles in Rome behind a vision of the gospel that would rally their support for an expanding apostolic mission to Spain. To assure the Gentile believers in Rome that they are welcome as full participants in the family of faith, Paul turns to the story of Abraham and Sarah. Jews and Gentile proselytes to Judaism are not the only heirs of God's promised blessing on Abraham's descendants. Also among the chosen are Gentiles who, like Abraham, are reckoned righteous by faith.

Having joined Paul in his ongoing pastoral interaction with the church in Corinth, as shown in chapter 5, we now connect again to his letter to the house churches in Rome. Our sources continue to be his letter opening and closing (Romans 1:1-15; 15:14–16:27) and the greetings in 16:1-16. We also take special note of several texts in Romans where Jewish perspectives are emphasized, apparently to temper a dismissive tendency among some Gentiles toward Jews: 3:1-8; 9:1-5; 11:1-32; 14:1–15:13.

In the following story we hope to complement the previous one in chapter 4 about Paul's Jewish acquaintances, Andronicus and Junia (16:7). The story here is told from the perspective of Ampliatus, who is mentioned in 16:8. Judging from his Latin name, Ampliatus was a native of Rome, possibly a freedman whose ancestors had been slaves. Once again, the details are fictional, although efforts have been made to develop the narrative in plausible fashion based on data in Romans and in generally available historical sources (see Wiefel, 1991:85-101).

How do Ampliatus and other Gentiles in Rome view the Jews and their religious practices?

A STORY: Will God's People in Rome Accept Each Other?

Ampliatus realized from personal experience that old habits and prejudices do not die overnight. His life had been dramatically turned around as a result of meeting the living and true God through Jesus Christ. The way he viewed himself and others had been transformed by the preaching of the gospel and by the inspired testimony of Priscilla and Aquila, Andronicus and Junia, and others like them. Even so, there were times when Ampliatus wondered how long he would be able to put up with the quirks and idiosyncrasies of his newly discovered friends, the Jews. Would he ever come to understand what makes them tick?

As he reviewed his own family history, Ampliatus recognized that Rome and its economic and social opportunities had been good for his family. His grandparents had been slaves who were granted freedom. With hard work and some luck his grandfather, father, and an uncle had managed to become established in business, and they did well. The family business prospered, and there always seemed to be enough.

Ampliatus recognized that he and his family had pushed their roots deep into the culture and social life of the proud city of Rome. Like others, he felt a certain patriotic sentiment at civic festivals and athletic events. It felt good to be a citizen in the heart of the grand Roman Empire. Claudius

Caesar may have been a jerk, but he was the emperor. Now that Nero was emperor, Ampliatus continued to express his allegiance. He joined his family and friends in publicly showing homage, respect, and support for the empire.

As he associated with Jews in his house church, Ampliatus occasionally thought back to the attitudes of his family toward minority groups in Rome. In particular he remembered opinions and sentiments concerning the Jews living in the city or traveling there on business. The Jewish people tended to congregate in certain areas and liked to maintain a rather segregated community life. Their pagan neighbors regarded some of the Jewish festivals and rituals with puzzled curiosity, and sometimes disdain. Jewish synagogues, though open to outsiders for many functions, were often viewed with suspicion.

The Jews in Rome also tended to be suspect politically. Their loyalty to Caesar and commitment to the values of the empire seemed shaky, because they mostly avoided parades and patriotic festivals. The Jews, in fact, appeared to be generally more in tune with what was happening in Jerusalem than in Rome. Some hotheads in the Jewish community in Rome even advocated a stance of open solidarity with their zealous cousins in Galilee and Judea who were increasingly strident in promoting rebellion against Rome. Ampliatus wondered how long it would be before the revolt simmering in the Jewish homeland broke into the open. If that happened, the full arsenal of the Roman military was sure to be unleashed to suppress it.

Furthermore, the Jews seemed to have constant disagreements among themselves, Ampliatus thought. There had been a major and very public squabble about whether Jesus was the Christ. The arguments attracted the attention of the palace, and in the year 49 Emperor Claudius had sent the whole bunch packing.

Ampliatus was aware, of course, that in some ways all of this was ancient history. Jews like Andronicus and Junia, who were members of house fellowships in Rome, were fully accepted as brothers and sisters in Jesus Christ. Yet Ampliatus at times lost patience with their sensitivity over apparently insignificant questions. Should they eat meat or stay with vegetables? May they drink wine? What is involved in observing the Sabbath faithfully in pagan Rome? Does Sabbath observance have precedence over the celebration of the resurrection of Jesus? In addition, they devoted so much energy to festivals, one after another—Passover, Pentecost, the Feast of Tabernacles, Hanukah. Ampliatus wondered whether it was appropriate to perpetuate these traditional Jewish practices since they now shared faith with Gentiles.

But it was the Jewish rite of circumcision that bothered Ampliatus the most. He found the premise of this ritual offensive, but he knew that to the Jews, circumcision was the mark of belonging to the people of God. Sometimes it seemed more like an expression of Jewish pride in their identity as a separate people.

Ampliatus suspected that God was also frustrated with the Jews. Their expulsion from Rome by Claudius must have been an indication of God's righteous judgment against them. Most of them came back after Nero rescinded the expulsion edict, but did they deserve another chance? Ampliatus mused that God may well have removed the Jewish branch from the tree of the people of God. In fact, both in Rome and throughout the Mediterranean region, the stubborn resistance of the majority of the Jewish people to the gospel of Jesus Christ seemed to point to the kind of hardness of heart that put them beyond God's mercy. Surely God's judgment had fallen on them at last. The Jews had rejected God's messenger, Jesus Christ, whom God had sent in the lineage of their own king, David. The Jews had rejected the gospel, and God had no choice but to turn against them in judgment.

The Mercy of God, the Mystery of God, the People of God

> What if some were unfaithful? Will their faithlessness nullify the faithfulness of God? By no means! (Romans 3:3-4)

Paul's theology is deeply rooted in the biblical story. Our observation of his pastoral interventions in Corinth and Rome has already highlighted certain elements of that story. He knew that God created all things, including all the peoples of the earth. From among all these people, God called Abraham and Sarah and their descendants to be a special family whom God would bless and through whom divine blessing would flow to all the nations of the world. The miracle child Isaac was born to Sarah though she was barren and old. The clan that came into being with the birth of Isaac eventually became enslaved in Egypt. Yet God through Moses graciously rescued these people from their bondage and at Sinai entered into covenant with them, a covenant stipulating the keeping of the law.

In his pastoral interventions with the congregations that emerged as a result of his preaching of the gospel, Paul's recollections of the narrative concerning covenant and the requirements of this law are often colored by the fact that he finds problematic the demands of some fellow messianic Jewish missionaries. This was the case in Corinth and certainly also in Galatia, where itinerant evangelists and teachers insisted that the Gentile believers should observe the ritual aspects of the Jewish law. Paul in response denounces these additional requirements, some-

214 Remember the Future

times doing so in ways that seem to suggest that he views
the Sinaitic covenant and its legal requirements as a colos-
sal mistake, a failure requiring God to take a radically different approach. Yet underlying all of Paul's seemingly dismissive commentary concerning the law is the contention
that the law (and the prophets) serve a necessary role as
witnesses to God's climactic saving intervention in Jesus
Christ. Through Christ the promise made to Abraham and
Sarah was now in the process of becoming a reality.

The epistle to the Romans was written to congregations
not founded by Paul. He wrote the letter to unite them and
to solicit their support for a mission to Spain. Their unity
as Jews and Gentiles in Christ required that they address
the disagreements among them, including their differences
concerning the role of the law. Paul insists that in the
church Gentiles need not become Jews to be accepted.
There are two consequences for the church: Jews need to
accept Gentiles without circumcision. And Gentiles need to
respect Jews in their observance of the law.

In Romans Paul deals directly only with Jews who
have accepted Jesus as messiah. Yet he also asks why so
many Jews have not. Paul's bitter disappointment at the
fact that many of his fellow Jews are rejecting the gospel of
Jesus Christ leads him to a fervent rereading of the
Scriptures. Clearly God's covenant people do not always
abide by the covenant requirements, nor, as has become
painfully evident, do these people accept God's continuing
restorative initiatives, including the coming of Jesus Christ.
So the question is poignantly raised for Paul: Does God
remain committed to the covenant with its promises for
the chosen people? God has called and rescued them, guided and chided them, and sustained them in exile. But will
God abandon them, now that they have largely said no to
the gospel of Jesus Christ?

As a Jew called to be apostle to the Gentiles, Paul has a delicate task when pastorally addressing the house churches in Rome, consisting of both Jews and Gentiles who affirm Jesus as Messiah. Confronting Jewish attitudes of ethnic exclusiveness by emphasizing the impartiality of God, as in Romans 2 (especially 2:11), can also feed a latent and sometimes blatant Gentile antipathy toward Jews. Asserting that true Jewishness is a matter of the heart, as in 2:28-29, can lead to the conclusion that the Jewish people have no ongoing special place within God's future salvation-historical intentions. In the social and political environment of mid-first-century Rome, an instinctive suspicion of the Jewish population living in the city can easily translate into dismissive Gentile arrogance toward the Jews, even those within the church.

Even in 2:1-29, where Paul underscores God's impartiality as righteous judge, he seems aware that this emphasis could heighten feelings among some Gentile believers that the Jewish people have finally been displaced from their privileged role within God's plan. In Romans 3:1 Paul puts the brakes on the rhetorical momentum that he has been building up. He asks a twofold question: "Then what advantage has the Jew? Or what is the value of circumcision?" Given the thrust of the preceding discussion the hearer of the letter would undoubtedly have been surprised by Paul's reply, "Much in every way" (3:2). Having forcefully driven home his conviction that God is impartial as judge of all, both Jew and Greek (2:6-11), Paul now moves to reassert Jewish priority within God's grand intention: "For in the first place, the Jews were entrusted with the oracles of God" (3:2).

This reminder of Israel's responsibility and privilege in her historical relationship to God immediately elicits the question, What happens to God's project when the people chosen as God's agents prove to be unfaithful? (3:3). Does God remain faithful to covenant promises even when the covenant people do not abide by the requisite stipulations? Particularly poignant for Paul the apostle is the question whether the widespread Jewish rejection of Jesus as Messiah means that God will finally also give up on this chosen people.

Does God Still Choose the Jews?

Paul's retelling of the story of Abraham and Sarah in Romans 4 highlights God's call and promise for all who believe. The universal story of all humanity seems to dominate in Paul's reflections on how Christ's faithfulness undoes the consequences of Adam's transgression (Romans 5–6). In Romans 7–8 Paul's deliberations about the crippling grip of sin and the freeing power of the Spirit climax in a thundering affirmation of God's cosmic triumph. This seems clearly to have all humanity in view:

> For I am convinced that neither death, nor life, nor
> angels, nor rulers, nor powers, nor height, nor depth,
> nor anything else in all creation, will be able to sepa-
> rate us from the love of God in Christ Jesus our Lord.
> (8:38-39)

Immediately following this rousing exclamation Paul appears to shift gears dramatically. In 9:1 the soaring chords acclaiming God's ultimate triumph recede. In their place are Paul's personal expressions of anguish provoked by his fellow Jews' unwillingness to recognize Jesus as Messiah.

In 8:31 Paul had asked, "If God is for us, who is against us?" His reply takes the form of another rhetorical question. "He who did not withhold his own Son, but gave

him up for all of us, will he not with him also give us
everything else?" (8:32).

In 8:38-39 he leaves no doubt that the answer is, Yes,
of course! God who gave up his Son for all will also give
us everything else. But now the dilemma, already introduced and addressed in Romans 3, comes crashing into the
center of Paul's consciousness. Does the *us* that God continues to be *for* include ethnic Israel, despite the faithlessness of so many of them in the face of God's new grace initiative in Christ? In 3:3 Paul asked the thorny question:
"What if some were unfaithful? Will their faithlessness
nullify the faithfulness of God?" His rebuttal in 3:4 is formulated with an exuberance that signals how much is at
stake here: "By no means! Although everyone is a liar, let
God be proved true" (3:4). In Romans 9–11 Paul looks to
the Scriptures for confirmation sufficient to persuade himself and others that indeed God is faithful and true even
when the chosen people are not.

What are the biblical texts to which Paul is drawn in his
impassioned quest to read God's mind and intention
regarding the Jewish people? Nowhere in his writings are
Scripture texts and allusions more thickly packed together
than in Romans, especially in chapters 9–11. In 9:6-13 Paul
recalls stories from the period of the patriarchs: Sarah's son
Isaac is chosen over Hagar's son Ishmael (Genesis 18:10;
21:12), and Jacob is favored over Esau (Genesis 25:21-23).
In 9:13 Paul also cites Malachi 1:2-3 as part of his interpretation of the relationship between Jacob and Esau. In
9:14-18 he refers to the story of Pharaoh in a way that
evokes the memory of the plagues on Egypt during the time
leading up to the exodus (Exodus 9:16). In 9:15 he cites
God's word to Moses in Exodus 33:19 about divine choices concerning mercy and compassion; this is part of the narrative in Exodus 32:32 about Moses interceding with God

on behalf of Israel, a story whose themes also echo in Paul's opening lament in 9:3. He cites a text from Leviticus 18:5 about life under God's law (10:5). In 10:6-9 Paul comments on part of Moses's sermon to Israel in the wilderness as recorded in Deuteronomy 30:11-14, and in 10:19 he adapts part of Moses's song (Deuteronomy 32:21) to interpret the level to which Israel comprehended the gospel. In 11:1-6 when Paul looks for instances within the biblical drama when a minority within Israel responds positively to God, he remembers the story of the prophet Elijah in 1 Kings 19:10, 18.

Paul also has direct quotations from and allusions to the Psalms and the Prophets. He quotes Psalm 19:4 in a depiction of the ever-spreading gospel message (10:18). In 11:7-10 Paul cites Psalm 69:22-23 and Isaiah 29:10 to talk about the hardening of part of Israel. In 9:19-24 he employs the metaphor comparing God to a potter, a metaphor that he may have found in Isaiah 29:16; 45:9, and Jeremiah 18:1-11. In 9:27-29 Paul quotes Isaiah 1:9 and 10:22 to remind his hearers that by God's mercy a remnant of Israel has always survived. He uses the metaphor of the stumbling stone in 9:33 in a quotation that combines Isaiah 8:14-15 and 28:16. In 9:25-26 he applies the symbolic names "My People" and "Not my People" from Hosea 1:10 and 2:23 with reference to the welcome for Gentiles within the people of God. In 10:13 he quotes Joel 2:32.

Especially prominent are Paul's quotations from and echoes of texts in the latter half of the book of Isaiah. Isaiah 52:7 gives Paul the words to talk about the proclamation of the gospel, and Isaiah 53:1 provides a description of Israel's unresponsiveness (10:15-16). In 10:20-21 he offers a particularly ingenious reinterpretation of Isaiah 65:1-2 to describe both the Gentiles' receptivity and Israel's resistance to the gospel. He quotes Isaiah 59:20-21, supplemented by Isaiah 27:9, when in 11:26-27 he announces the salvation of all Israel.

Is God Still for Israel?

From the passionate opening to the concluding doxology of this exegetical and theological essay in Romans 9–11, Paul's argumentation clearly attests that he has been prayerfully wrestling with the Scriptures in search of clarity concerning God's ongoing commitment to Israel. As Richard Hays has shown, this central section of Romans has the structure of a lament Psalm (1989:57-64). That Paul has been pondering the laments of Israel in exile is suggested by the quotation from Psalm 44:22 that introduces his ringing declaration of God's ultimate triumph in 8:36:

> As it is written, "For your sake we are being killed all day long; we are accounted as sheep to be slaughtered."

Might Paul be modeling Romans 9:1–11:36 after the pattern of Psalm 44 and other psalms of lament? Hays sees the following overall structure (1989:64):

> 9:1-5: Lament over Israel.
> 9:6-29: Has God's word failed? Defense of God's elective purpose.
> 9:30-10:21: Paradox: Israel failed to grasp the word of faith attested by God in Scripture.
> 11:1-32: Has God abandoned his people? No, all Israel will be saved.
> 11:33-36: Doxological conclusion

Robert Badenas has also shown that between the opening lament (9:1-5) and the concluding doxology (11:33-36), Paul has organized this material into three movements, which are structured as a chiasm (an **A-B-A'** pattern). In **A** Paul focuses on God's intention, in **B** on Israel's disobedience, and in **A'** on God's design for the future:

> **A** God's sovereign intention in relation to Israel and the nations has not failed. (9:6-29)
>> **B** In pursuit of righteousness Israel has stumbled into disobedience. (9:30–10:21)
> **A'** Yet God's design for the future incorporates Israel's disobedience into a plan for salvation that includes Gentiles as well as all Israel. (11:1-32)
>
> (1985:94-9)

The overall flow of Paul's discussion in Romans 9–11 is easier to follow than some of the undercurrents in his exegetical and theological discourse. Our discussion of this material recognizes these three movements in Paul's thought. We will also note his use of rhetorical questions to move his argument along.

Paul opens with an outburst of personal anguish (9:1-3). The fact that the first-person singular pronoun appears numerous times clearly conveys to his readers that he is about to comment personally about an issue that also has deep pastoral and theological significance for him:

> I am speaking the truth in Christ—I am not lying; my conscience confirms it by the Holy Spirit—I have great sorrow and unceasing anguish in my heart. I could wish that I myself were accursed and cut off from Christ for the sake of my own people, my kindred according to the flesh.

There are several other places in this part of Romans where Paul also bares his soul using "I" statements (10:1-2; 11:1-6, 13-14, 25), but nowhere else with this level of pathos.

His initial hearers may not have been aware of it but later interpreters such as Scott Hafemann have pointed out that Paul's cry of the heart in 9:3 is reminiscent of Moses's intercession before God following Israel's sin with the golden calf:

> But now, if you will only forgive their sin—but if not, blot me out of the book that you have written. (Exodus 32:32)

According to Hafemann, this may have been a deliberate allusion. At the very least it points to Paul's impassioned engagement with Scripture as he seeks to comprehend what God is doing through his apostolic work, and it reflects his deep anguish about the lack of response among his own Jewish people (1995:107-10).

The biblical story line is transparent in Paul's catalog of the rich heritage of ethnic Israel:

> They are Israelites, and to them belong the adoption, the glory, the covenants, the giving of the law, the worship, and the promises; to them belong the patriarchs, and from them, according to the flesh, comes the Messiah. (Romans 9:4-5)

As Katherine Grieb shows, this listing cryptically recalls some of Paul's previous allusions in Romans to elements of the inheritance now shared with all the descendants of Abraham and Sarah: adoption (8:15-17); glory (8:18, 28-30); covenants (4:6-8, 17-18, 22-25); the giving of the law (7:12, 22; 8:3-8); the worship (5:2; 8:15-16, 26-27); the promises (4:13-16) (Grieb, 2002:89). Significantly Paul mentions "the patriarchs" as the origin and "the Messiah" as the culmination of the biblical story in which the Israelites have had and continue to have a key role. Beginning with Abraham and his descendants (9:6-13) and culminating with "the Deliverer" who "will come out of Zion" (11:26-27), Paul addresses the wrenching theological problem of God's ongoing relationship with the people through whom the Messiah has come into the world. How durable is God's covenant faithfulness toward Paul's kinfolk by race, the Jewish people, given that so many of them have rejected the Messiah?

Before he moves into his exegetical exploration into God's relationship with Israel now that the Messiah has come, Paul voices his praise in doxology: "The Messiah, who is over all, God blessed forever. Amen" (9:5b). Wrestling with biblical texts, seeking to fathom God's ways, Paul instinctively gives himself first to adoration and worship.

God's Word Has Not Failed!

In the first movement (9:6-29), like an orator before a skeptical or hostile audience, Paul opens with a declaration designed to refute any claim that God has failed to keep faith with the elect people: "It is not as though the word of God had failed" (9:6). In the diatribe style of first-century Roman orators, Paul articulates the proposition, which he then sets out to support by recalling stories from the Scriptures:

> Not all Israelites truly belong to Israel, and not all of Abraham's children are his true descendants. (9:6b-7a)

Paul proceeds by highlighting several moments in Israel's story: the patriarchs (9:7-13), and the exodus from Egypt and the years in the wilderness (9:14-18).

First Paul traces God's elective choices as demonstrated in the patriarchal narratives. He featured the story of Abraham and Sarah in 4:1-25 to document his point that inheritance of God's promised blessing is on the basis of faith. Here Paul recalls the same story but he notes that God chose Isaac, the child of promise, over the other son: "It is through Isaac that descendants shall be named for you" (9:7; citing Genesis 21:12). The son chosen to inherit the promise is the younger of the two sons of Abraham: "About this time I will return and Sarah shall have a son" (9:9; citing Genesis 18:14).

The next story (9:10-13) underscores this point. Even before Isaac and Rebecca's twin sons were born, God chose the younger son, Jacob, over the firstborn, Esau, as the instrument of divine intention. Paul points out that God's choice is never based on merit or physical descent: "so that God's purpose of election might continue, not by works but by his call" (9:11-12). The assumed primacy of the elder son is reversed in favor of the younger: "The elder shall serve the younger" (9:12b; from Genesis 25:23). At 9:13 Paul cites a terse comment from Malachi 1:2-3 to emphasize this point further: "As it is written, 'I have loved Jacob, but I have hated Esau.'" Interpreters offended by such arbitrariness need to remind themselves that Paul is pointing not to the relative merits of these twin brothers but rather to God's intentional calling of one people, the descendants of Jacob, to be the chosen instrument of a blessing that is available to all people.

In the next section (9:14-18), Paul in fact asks, and immediately answers, the question about God's fairness: "What then are we to say? Is there injustice on God's part? By no means!" (9:14). He recalls yet another story in his effort to document the "selective character of God's grace" (Hays, 1989:64). Paul remembers how God responded when Moses interceded on behalf of wayward Israel in the Sinai wilderness: "I will have mercy on whom I have mercy, and I will have compassion on whom I have compassion" (9:15, quoting Exodus 33:19). God did show mercy to the Israelites in the wilderness. And God had hardened the heart of Pharaoh (9:17). The ultimate goal of these divine choices, however, is to proclaim God's sovereignty in all the earth. God has the sovereign freedom to extend mercy or harden hearts whether people deserve it or not:

> So then he has mercy on whomever he chooses, and he hardens the heart of whomever he chooses. (9:18)

In 9:19-26 Paul again anticipates the question that an orator might hear from a dubious audience: "You will say to me then, 'Why then does he still find fault? For who can resist his will?'" (9:19). He replies to this imaginary interlocutor by using the metaphor of God as a potter who has the right to choose what kind of object is shaped from the clay (9:20-21; reminiscent of Isaiah 29:16; 45:9; Jeremiah 18:1-11). Again, God's promise of blessing is dispensed not on the basis of ethnicity or works but rather, like the potter's actions toward her clay, by God's sovereign choice.

In 9:24 Paul announces the identity of the people newly constituted through God's sovereign mercy, "including us whom he has called, not from the Jews only but also from the Gentiles." The people of God are now made up of both Jews and Gentiles. Paul recalls how the prophet Hosea envisions that a wayward Israelite people will be restored to covenant relationship with God. In a bold rereading of Hosea 1:10 and 2:23 Paul views Gentiles as those of whom it had previously been said, "You are not my people." God has promised them, "There they shall be called children of the living God" (9:25-26).

Yet Israel is not thereby excluded from the people of God. At this point Paul introduces the theme of remnant, a theme that he develops further in 11:1-6. He cites two Isaiah texts, the first of which is often construed as a word of condemnation:

> Though the number of the children of Israel were like the sand of the sea, only a remnant of them will be saved; for the Lord will execute his sentence on the earth quickly and decisively. (9:27-28, citing Isaiah 10:22-23)

As Hays points out (1989:68), the NRSV rendering "only a remnant" has no support in the underlying Greek text. This is not a word condemning Israel but Paul's hopeful word from Isaiah concerning Israel's future: "a remnant of them will be saved" (9:27). Paul views the execution of God's judgment as leading to the salvation of a remnant.

The second Isaiah text (Isaiah 1:9, quoted in 9:29) makes a similar claim. However, again the NRSV has partially obscured the point:

> If the Lord of hosts had not left survivors to us, we would have fared like Sodom and been made like Gomorrah.

The underlying text has the Greek word *sperma*, meaning "seed" (NRSV: "survivors"; RSV: "children") to communicate clearly that beyond the destruction of judgment there is "seed." Here is a hopeful word. God provides for a remnant, the heirs of God's promise to Abraham (cf. 4:13, 16). Central to this divine strategy is the Messiah and the Messiah's people.

What Happened? Israel Tripped

The second of the three movements in Romans 9–11 begins again with the orator's rhetorical question, "What then are we to say?" (9:30a). With God's sovereignty clearly in mind, Paul proceeds in 9:30–10:21 to focus on Israel's response, or lack of response, to the gospel of Jesus Christ.

In 9:30-33 Paul employs the metaphor of a race to depict a paradoxical situation. On one hand, Gentiles who had not even been entered into the race after righteousness have reached the finish line, namely righteousness through faith (9:30). Through the faithfulness of Christ and their response of faith in Christ, many Gentiles have become righteous. On the other hand, Israel, vigorously running the race by pursuing a law of righteousness, did not attain to that law because her pursuit came not out of faith but as though it were through certain works of the law (9:31).

This text requires some deliberate unraveling. As Paul has previously said, the law itself is righteous and good (7:13). Israel pursued "a law of righteousness" (9:31, NIV), not "the righteousness that is based on law" (as in NRSV). Israel's problem, Paul says, is that their devotion to the righteous law too often fixated on a few boundary-marking works of the law rather than on faith: "they did not strive for it [i.e. the law] on the basis of faith, but as if it were based on works" (9:32). Furthermore, as Paul goes on to say, they have stumbled in their race toward the finish line (9:33), and in their zeal for the law they have not recognized the Messiah toward whom the law points (10:1-4).

In 9:33 Paul conflates Isaiah 8:14 and 28:16, two passages that utilize the stone metaphor:

> As it is written, "See, I am laying in Zion a stone that
> will make people stumble, a rock that will make them

fall, and whoever believes in him will not be put to
shame." (9:33)

In her dash toward the finish line Israel has tripped over
"the stumbling stone" (9:32-33). In Isaiah the "stumbling
stone" is God, or trust in God. But what does Paul here
consider to be the stone that causes Israel to stumble? Is it
God, or the law given by God, or the Messiah toward
whom the law gives witness, or the gospel about this
Messiah? Toews rightly argues that the immediate context
shows that Paul considers the "stumbling stone" to be the
law itself: "Paul is discussing Israel's failure to achieve the
goal of the law" (2004:260).

In 10:1-4 Paul continues by elaborating his interpretation of Israel's failed pursuit of the law. Zealous for God
but unenlightened regarding God's own righteousness as
revealed in Christ's faithfulness, Israel has sought rather to
establish her own righteousness. Wright suggests that this
reference to Israel's own righteousness points not to a
legalistic pursuit of righteousness through obedience to the
Torah but rather to Israel's reliance on ritualistic boundary
markers such as circumcision and food laws to maintain
favored status with God (Wright, 1991:239-46; cf. Toews,
2004:261-2). It is likely that Paul here is reflecting back on
his own pilgrimage prior to his encounter with the risen
Christ (cf. Philippians 3:6: "as to zeal, a persecutor of the
church"). He realizes from his own life that zealous confidence in particular marks of ethnic identity and privilege
can lead to a dismissive and violent exclusion of those who
enter the people of God through Christ. What is needed
instead is a stance of submission to God through trusting
faith, thereby attaining God's righteousness.

Still following through on the racing metaphor, Paul
talks about the finish line. He says, "Christ is the end of

the law, so that there may be righteousness for everyone who believes" (10:4). In the phrase "end of the law" the underlying word for "end" (*telos*) points not to the termination or abolition of the law but rather to Christ as the "end (meaning *outcome* or *goal*) of the law." Through Christ, to whom the law gives witness, is the possibility of righteousness to all who believe (Hays, 1989:75-7).

According to Paul, therefore, Israel's failure is exposed by her large-scale unwillingness to recognize Christ as the one toward whom the law points. Indeed, that is the main thrust of Paul's extended exegetical treatment in 10:5-21. Moses and an embodied "righteousness from faith" as well as Paul himself and other preachers of the gospel have with one voice announced the good news of Jesus Christ.

In Leviticus 18:5 Paul finds Moses's promising and reassuring word to Israel about the righteousness that is from the law: "the person who does these things will live by them" (10:5). Then in Deuteronomy 30:12-14 he hears the voice of "the righteousness that comes from faith," envisioned as coming from another speaker giving testimony. The intention of the Deuteronomy text is to encourage Israel to realize that the Torah is neither remote from them nor impossible to observe; it is near, in their mouths and hearts, accessible and life-giving. Paul interprets this text in light of Christ (10:6-7), and he sees the word of the Torah as testimony to the gospel that he preaches:

> But what does it say? "The word is near you, on your
> lips and in your heart" (that is, the word of faith that
> we proclaim). (10:8)

What Paul writes in 10:9-13 may well contain echoes of his customary missionary preaching, together with Scripture texts that corroborate these gospel themes:

If you confess with your lips that Jesus is Lord and
believe in your heart that God raised him from the
dead, you will be saved. For one believes with the heart
and so is justified, and one confesses with the mouth
and so is saved. The scripture says, "No one who
believes in him will be put to shame." For there is no
distinction between Jew and Greek; the same Lord is
Lord of all and is generous to all who call on him. For,
"Everyone who calls on the name of the Lord shall be
saved." (with citations from Isaiah 28:16 and Joel 2:32)

But Paul also anticipates the charge that the Jewish people
had not had the opportunity to hear the gospel. A chain of
questions in 10:14-15 begins with the protest, "But how
are they to call on one in whom they have not believed?"
Paul quotes Isaiah 52:7, likely in part at least as a description of his own apostolic role: "How beautiful are the feet
of those who bring good news!" (10:15).

Paul bemoans that not all have obeyed the good news,
and he quotes another Isaiah text to help him voice his
lament: "Lord, who has believed our message?" (10:16;
quoted from Isaiah 53:1). Israel has heard the word of
Christ, Paul claims, citing Psalm 19:4 (10:18). At this point
in his search of the Scriptures to help him understand
Israel's answer of no to the gospel of Jesus Christ, Paul is
left with a bleak observation. Israel has heard the message
but has not received it. The question remains, What will
God do? In 10:19 Paul quotes Deuteronomy 32:21, which
was addressed to Israel as a non-nation in exile, but is now
applied to Gentiles. In this text Paul finds a clue in the
theme of jealousy, a theme that he develops further in
chapter 11:

230   *Remember the Future*

Again I ask, did Israel not understand? First Moses says,
"I will make you jealous of those who are not a nation;
with a foolish nation I will make you angry." (10:19)

For now, however, Paul simply ponders the irony.
Gentiles have responded with acceptance, but many within historic Israel have not believed the message. Paul turns
to yet another prophetic text (Isaiah 65:1-2) to help him
articulate this anomaly. In 10:20 he interprets Isaiah 65:1
to express the Gentiles' acceptance of the gospel:

I have been found by those who did not seek me; I
have shown myself to those who did not ask for me.

And in Isaiah 65:2 Paul finds intimations of Israel's non-
responsiveness to the gospel:

But of Israel he says, "All day long I have held out my
hands to a disobedient and contrary people." (10:21)

God Still Calls and Extends Mercy

Paul again borrows the diatribe style of Roman oratory
in the third major movement of this essay about God, Israel,
and the nations (11:1-32). He reiterates his initial question
(cf. 9:6): "I ask, then, has God rejected his people?" He
immediately replies with a forceful negation: "By no
means!" (11:1). He documents this claim by developing the
remnant motif that was introduced in 9:27. Referring to his
own status as a member of the historic Israelite community
(11:1), Paul asserts, "God has not rejected his people whom
he foreknew" (11:2). Even if the remnant were to consist of
one person—himself—there is proof that God is true.

Paul also retells the story of the prophet Elijah, who com-
plained to God during a period of acute isolation and loneli-

ness: "I alone am left, and they are seeking my life" (11:3). God reassured Elijah that a sizeable group in Israel continued along with him to confess God as supreme (11:4). He affirms: "So too at the present time there is a remnant, chosen by grace" (11:5). And echoing his earlier themes (9:16: not human effort but God's mercy; and 9:32: not works but faith), he says, "But if it is by grace, it is no longer on the basis of works, otherwise grace would no longer be grace" (11:6).

With another "What then?" Paul in 11:7-10 continues to unpack the fruit of his exegesis and theological reflection on God's faithfulness, Israel's disobedience, and the current progress of the messianic mission to Gentiles and Jews. Israel as a whole has not reached the goal. A remnant within Israel ("the elect") has obtained the righteousness they were seeking, but the rest have not:

> Israel failed to obtain what it was seeking. The elect
> obtained it, but the rest were hardened. (11:7)

In 11:8-10 Paul supports this conclusion by means of citations from Isaiah 29:10 and Psalm 69:22-23. These texts speak about the sluggish spirit, the darkened eyes, and the stooped backs that God gives those who refuse to see and hear and obey.

In 11:11a Paul restates his earlier question in 11:1: "So I ask, have they stumbled so as to fall?" and once again he interjects forcefully, "By no means!" Having reaffirmed God's faithfulness to the remnant within Israel, he continues with his theological reflections about how even Israel's stumble has a redemptive outcome. Here he introduces the jealousy motif, a theme that he begins to develop at length: "But through their stumbling salvation has come to the Gentiles, so as to make Israel jealous" (11:11b). Paul wants the Gentile believers in Rome to know that the sov-

ereign God employs even Israel's unwillingness to accept
the gospel. In Paul's view, Israel's nonresponse becomes the
means whereby Gentiles are incorporated into the people
of God. And that development, in turn, leads consequently to salvation for the Jews:

> Now if their stumbling means riches for the world, and
> if their defeat means riches for Gentiles, how much
> more will their full inclusion mean! (11:12)

What then is the plot of this still unfolding story? It has
to do with God's merciful and sovereign care for the
covenant people and through them also all people who
acknowledge God. As the hardening of Pharaoh's heart led
to the deliverance of Israel (9:17), so now the hardening of
Israel results in salvation to the Gentiles. And the Gentiles'
experience of salvation will make his fellow Jews jealous,
so that more of them will also accept the gospel (11:13-
14). Paul glimpses the consequences in dramatic terms:
Gentile receptiveness leads to "the reconciliation of the
world," and the eventual Jewish positive response is
viewed as "life from the dead" (11:15).

In 11:16 Paul introduces the extended metaphor in
which the people of God are compared to an olive tree
(11:17-24). This metaphor may have roots in various passages in the Psalms and the Major Prophets in which Israel
is compared to a tree: Psalm 92:12-15; Isaiah 61:3;
Jeremiah 11:16-17. Paul's major agenda in this part of the
letter is to warn the Gentiles in Rome not to be arrogant.
His distress about the lack of substantive progress in the
mission to the Jews is intensified by the fact that some
among the Gentile believers in Rome have cultivated dismissive theological judgments concerning Jewish people.
In 11:13 he self-consciously addresses himself to a Gentile

audience: "Now I am speaking to you Gentiles." His comments in 11:19-21 suggest that Paul is particularly disturbed by the negative attitudes of some Gentiles toward their Jewish sisters and brothers in the church:

> You will say, "Branches were broken off so that I might be grafted in." That is true. They were broken off because of their unbelief, but you stand only through faith. So do not become proud, but stand in awe. For if God did not spare the natural branches, perhaps he will not spare you. (11:19-21)

Gentile believers are warned that, having recently been grafted into the tree whose roots lie deep in the soil of God's covenant promises toward Israel, they could still be pruned from that tree. Conversely, Paul holds forth the hope that even those who were removed from this tree will yet be grafted back in (11:23-24). Gentiles are not to presume that God will continue to extend kindness toward them, nor are they to forget that God's severity toward Jewish people could also be reversed (11:22).

In 11:25-32 Paul brings his persuasive argument to its climax. Once again he warns about boastfulness, likely especially the presumed wisdom of those who see God as having rejected Jews in favor of Gentiles (11:25a). Paul shares his revelation, which he calls a "mystery." He grounds this "mystery" in Isaiah 59:20-21 and 11:26-27:

> I want you to understand this mystery: a hardening has come upon part of Israel, until the full number of the Gentiles has come in. And so all Israel will be saved; as it is written, "Out of Zion will come the Deliverer; he will banish ungodliness from Jacob." "And this is my covenant with them, when I take away their sins." (11:25b-27)

Clearly God continues to be true to the covenant established with Israel. Paul here specifically articulates the surprising plot progression of the story of God's relationship with the covenant people. This story was told in 11:11-12 and developed further in the olive tree metaphor: a hardening comes upon part of Israel, and this leaves the door open for an influx of Gentiles, and so in this way "all Israel will be saved."

Interpreters have long debated this scenario of the future. Who all is included in this reference to "all Israel"? Is this a reference to all or at least most ethnic Jews, or even to the political entity by that name? Or is this an "enlarged Israel" consisting of Jews who acknowledge Jesus as Messiah plus the Gentiles who have also been incorporated into the people of God through this Messiah? (Bosch, 1991:160-5).

Also debated is whether Paul envisions the future salvation of Israel coming as a result of an ongoing mission to seek the conversion of Jews to Christ. One suggestion is that Paul anticipates that "all Israel" will come to faith in Jesus as the Messiah in the same way that he himself had: without human intervention, through a firsthand personal encounter with the risen Christ (Hofius, 1990:19-39). According to this interpretation, Paul may be anticipating that his fellow Jews will be won through an encounter with Christ at his future triumphant return. Whichever may have been Paul's understanding, one thing is clear: He urges the Gentile believers now grafted into the people of God to remember the future which God still has in store for the original covenant people.

In 11:28-29 Paul summarizes in two parallel declarations and a theological affirmation. Jews are God's enemies for the sake of the Gentiles; yet they remain God's chosen people, still beloved by God (11:28). What remains irreversible is God's abiding faithfulness in election:

Jews as the Gospel's Enemies	Jews as God's Beloved	Theological Affirmation
As regards the gospel they are enemies of God for your sake; >	but as regards election they are beloved, for the sake of their ancestors; >	for the gifts and the calling of God are irrevocable.

Another set of parallel statements (11:30-31), along with the theological rationale (11:32), underscores God's sovereign strategy toward Gentiles and Jews respectively:

Gentiles	Jews	Theological Affirmation
Just as you were once disobedient to God but have now received mercy because of their disobedience, >	so they have now been disobedient in order that, by the mercy shown to you, they too may now receive mercy.	For God has imprisoned all in disobedience so that he may be merciful to all.

At the conclusion of his exegetical and theological reflections concerning God's relationship with historic Israel, now enlarged through the admission of Gentiles through Christ, Paul breaks out into doxology. In this climactic acclamation he echoes themes from Isaiah 40:13 and Job 41:11 concerning God's sovereign wisdom:

> O the depth of the riches and wisdom and knowledge
>   of God!
>   How unsearchable are his judgments and how
>   inscrutable his ways!
> "For who has known the mind of the Lord? Or who
>   has been his counselor?"
>   "Or who has given a gift to him, to receive a gift
>   in return?"

> For from him and through him and to him are all
> things.
> To him be the glory forever. Amen. (11:33-36)

Therefore Welcome One Another

By the time he begins his focused appeals concerning life and relationships in the ethnically mixed community of house churches and synagogue groups in Rome (12:1–15:13), Paul has clearly made his point. God has not rejected Israel, and the Gentile believers in Rome dare not dismiss them either. As latecomers into the family, as branches grafted onto that tree whose roots are Jewish, Gentiles should respond in gratitude to God for the gracious opportunity to participate in God's ongoing mission within the world.

Their participation as God's people now composed of Jews plus the Gentiles who have joined them through Christ calls for them to adopt a stance of nonconformity toward the present age. Paul's pastoral counsel in 12:1–13:14 concerning relationships within the community of faith and their conduct toward outsiders is discussed in chapter 12. As Paul has summarized in 11:30-32, God's mercy has been extended toward the chosen people and it is now extended to others as well. Those who have now experienced the mercies of God climactically through Christ are summoned as a transformed and renewed people to present themselves as "a living sacrifice, holy and acceptable to God" (12:1).

In 14:1–15:13 Paul continues to spell out the ways in which relationships among the members of the people of God are altered through Christ, especially in the direction of mutual acceptance and welcome. This section will get attention in chapter 10. For now we notice that the pattern of the life and the death of Jesus Christ is commended as a model for conduct within the community of faith (15:1-6) and that this pattern has particular implications for relationships between Jews and Gentiles (15:7-13).

With reference to Christ as model, Paul says, "For Christ did not please himself" (15:3a). He adds a line from Psalm 69:9 in elaboration: "The insults of those who insult you have fallen on me" (15:3b). The people of God are therefore also called upon to relate to each other in ways that mirror Christ's suffering in behalf of others:

> Welcome one another therefore, just as Christ has welcomed you, for the glory of God. For I tell you that Christ has become a servant of the circumcised on behalf of the truth of God in order that he might confirm the promises given to the patriarchs, and in order that the Gentiles might glorify God for his mercy. (15:7-9)

Here is a remarkable restatement of Paul's argument in Romans 11. Christ has welcomed Gentiles into the people of God by becoming a servant of the Jewish people, in order that God's promises to the patriarchs might be confirmed by including Gentiles!

In 15:14-33 Paul makes it clear that he longs for a strong base of operations in Rome for his westward mission thrust into Spain. A united church in the capital of the empire, a church in which Jews and Gentiles joyfully worship the one God and relate to each other with mutual recognition and service, would provide such a base.

Beyond the desired local unity of Jews and Gentiles in Christ in Rome, Paul also envisions a kinship between Gentiles in various areas of the Mediterranean and needy Jews in Jerusalem. A collection project elicits his passionate investment (cf. also Galatians 2:10; 1 Corinthians 16:1-4; 2 Corinthians 8–9). Even while preparing himself to travel to Spain via Rome, Paul promotes and interprets the collection of a generous contribution by Gentile churches for the poor among the Jerusalem saints, and he declares his intention first to go to Jerusalem with this love gift (15:25-28).

Paul's View of the People of God

In his letter to the Romans Paul seems intent on avoiding the use of the word *church* to designate God's people. The first occurrence in Romans of the word *ecclesia* (the underlying Greek word for "church") comes in his final chapter, where he employs it three times to refer to local gatherings of believers (Romans 16:1, 4, 5) and twice in the collective sense (16:16, 23). It is anachronistic therefore for later Christians reading this letter to think that Paul is here describing the relationship between Israel and the church as distinct entities. Rather, as has been reiterated in our discussion of Romans 9–11, Paul reflects theologically on the nature of God's elect people, Israel, which has now been enlarged through the incorporation of Gentiles through Christ.

In many of his other letters, Paul does employ the word *church* to refer to the assemblies meeting in various locations as a result of his and other's evangelistic efforts around the Mediterranean. We examined in chapter 4 various terms that Paul uses to designate these groups. In chapter 13 we will look at how Paul views the church as a community whose life intersects with the social and political context.

For now we continue to examine Paul's conscious reflections on God's people from the perspective of his own people by race. The Messiah has come, yet many among his Jewish kin have not acknowledged him. We turn briefly to a passing reference in Galatians 6:16, a troubling aside in 1 Thessalonians 2:14-16, and some concluding thoughts about the people of God in exile.

The Israel of God

In an enigmatic expression in Galatians 6:16 Paul refers to "the Israel of God." When we compare the RSV and NRSV translations of this verse we note how divergent are the exegetical and theological judgments about the meaning of this expression:

> Peace and mercy be upon all who walk by this rule, upon the Israel of God. (RSV)

> As for those who will follow this rule—peace be upon them, and mercy, and upon the Israel of God. (NRSV)

The words "this rule" (Greek: *canon*) refer to what Paul has just summarized in 6:15: "For neither circumcision nor uncircumcision is anything; but a new creation is everything!" What Paul intends his Galatian readers to understand here needs to be discerned within a contextual study of that letter (see chapters 8 and 9). But what might this fleeting reference to "the Israel of God" mean? A pervasive interpretation, which is reflected in the RSV translation, sees this as pointing to the church as a new creation, which replaces (old) Israel. The NRSV offers another interpretation, namely, that Paul pronounces God's peace and mercy also upon ethnic Israel, the people beloved and chosen by God.

In the aftermath of the twentieth-century Jewish holocaust, biblical interpreters have been increasingly aware that even subtle exegetical judgments have a way of betraying anti-Semitic biases. The notion of the church as a new Israel or true Israel has often led to dismissive judgments about ethnic Israel, which is then viewed as having been set aside or superseded. Our reading of Romans 9:1–11:36 has offered a corrective. God does not expropriate Israel by creating the church; rather God through Christ appropriates Gentiles within an enlarged Israel. This perspective can lead to a more faithful understanding of Galatians 6:16 as well. David Bosch says it well:

> Paul never surrenders the continuity of God's story with Israel. The church cannot be the people of God without its linkage with Israel. Paul's apostolate to the Gentiles is related to the salvation of Israel and does not mean a turning away from Israel. The gospel means the extension of the promise beyond Israel, not the displacement of Israel by a church made up of Gentiles. . . . Paul therefore never (not even in Galatians 6:16) explicitly says that the church is the "new Israel," as becomes customary from the second century onward. (1991:164)

To assert continuity from the story of Israel to the story of the church is, however, not to posit a linear progression from one to the other. Ever since his dramatic encounter with the risen Christ, Paul has been affirming that God has indeed done a new thing through the death and the resurrection of Christ. Within this new reality, old categories such as circumcision have receded in their significance: "a new creation is everything" (Galatians 6:15; cf. 2 Corinthians 5:17). A whole new world has been opened up. Paul exults:

> May I never boast of anything except the cross of our Lord Jesus Christ, by which the world has been crucified to me, and I to the world. (Galatians 6:14)

How then can such extraordinary newness introduced through Christ be reconciled with the claim of the continuity of God's covenant with ancient Israel? In a chapter entitled "Israel" Douglas Harink allows this tension to stand within the sovereignty of God:

> God's abiding and effective love toward Israel, that is, Israel's election/calling, is incorporated into and guaranteed by the history of the gospel (the death and resurrection of Jesus Christ), since in that history alone God has defeated all the powers which might threaten to create a final separation. Israel's story line appears on Paul's apocalyptic horizon in only one way: as the story not of its own action (whether good or bad) but of God's action, as the story of its *election* as a corporeal body, which Paul now understands to be preceded by, drawn up into, and finally sustained in God's apocalyptic action in Jesus Christ. (2003:178-79, emphasis added)

In short, God has not displaced Israel in favor of the church. Through the climactic invasion of grace in Christ, God has opened up a whole new world, in which Jews and Gentiles together constitute the people of God, and in which God's covenant with ancient Israel is sustained. These two consequences of God's covenant activity are obviously in significant tension with one another. The human mind cannot fully comprehend how both can be true. Glimpsing the mercy and the mystery of God's sovereign care, one is therefore compelled to join Paul in doxology!

A text that might be construed to contradict this conclusion is found in Paul's first letter to the church in Thessalonica:

> For you, brothers and sisters, became imitators of the churches of God in Christ Jesus that are in Judea, for you suffered the same things from your own compatri-

> ots as they did from the Jews, who killed both the
> Lord Jesus and the prophets, and drove us out; they
> displease God and oppose everyone by hindering us
> from speaking to the Gentiles so that they may be
> saved. Thus they have constantly been filling up the
> measure of their sins; but God's wrath has overtaken
> them at last. (1 Thessalonians 2:14-16)

When writing to the church in Thessalonica, Paul seems to be saying that God is finally done with the Jews. The measuring cup with which God keeps a tally of their sin is full and overflowing. God's wrath has been unleashed upon the Jewish people for their chronic opposition to the prophets, their complicity in the death of Jesus, and now also their resistance to the apostolic proclamation of the gospel among the Gentiles.

Upon closer examination, however, this text displays Paul's anguish about how certain Jews have repeatedly positioned themselves against God's messengers, including Jesus. A recent tragedy among the Jews could have been considered as a sign of God's judgment for such obstinacy and opposition. For example, Jewish historian Flavius Josephus reports the massacre of twenty to thirty thousand Jews at a Passover feast in Jerusalem in the year 48 (*Jewish War* 2.223-7; see Cornfeld, 1982:162). Other disasters occurred during this general time period as well. Even if these tragic events were interpreted by Paul, and others, as circumstances through which God's judgment is expressed, this is not God's final judgment on Israel. The wrath that has come upon them still envisions a future for the chosen people. (Further on the theme of judgment, including discussion of this text, see chapter 7.)

A motif related to the pilgrimage of historic Israel has implications for how we construe Paul's view of the people of God. Some scholars have noted that he understands Jesus's life and death and resurrection as an answer to Israel's ongoing exile. N. T. Wright argues that God concentrates the sin of humanity on Jesus as representative of historic Israel, thereby bringing Israel's exile to an end (1995:30-4).

John Howard Yoder, however, reads the texts quite differently. In Yoder's view, the prophets called on the people of Israel to understand their exile not primarily as God's judgment on their sin but as an opportunity to live out of the vision of their calling from God to be a light to the nations. The story of Israel as God's people thereby becomes, in Yoder's interpretation, a paradigm for the people of God as an alternative to the lifestyle and the idolatry of the nations among whom they dwell (1997:51-78).

In sum, God's covenant with Israel still sustains this historic people, including their life in ongoing exile among the nations. God has now incorporated Gentiles through Christ. Furthermore, the church as part of an enlarged Israel also experiences God's providential sustenance for its life and mission as an alternative community dispersed among the nations. The church with its roots in God's covenant with Israel and its foundation in Jesus Christ continues along with ancient Israel to experience life as a dispersed, rejected, and misunderstood people. A lifestyle of ongoing devotion to God despite continued suffering gives powerful testimony to the sovereignty of God and the lordship of Christ.

7

GOD THE RIGHTEOUS JUDGE

In our congregational stories thus far we have visited Philippi, Corinth, and Rome, and followed Paul's pastoral interventions into churches in each of these communities. We now connect with a group of believers in Thessalonica, the capital city of the Roman province of Macedonia.

Paul's two letters to the church in Thessalonica were among his earliest. He may have written them about A.D. 50 and 51, some fifteen years after his dramatic encounter with the risen Christ and his calling to be an apostle to the Gentiles.

In our next story, we identify with Aegina, whom we imagine to be a member of the small group of believers that emerged as a result of Paul's missionary efforts in Thessalonica. Paul nowhere mentions the name of any of these Thessalonian believers, so we have invented one. As we attempt to tune in to the story of this congregation, however, we are not left entirely to guesswork. In his two letters to this congregation, Paul has included significant recollections of his earlier ministry in this city and his subsequent strategy of sending Timothy back for a visit: 1 Thessalonians 1:2–3:13. He also alludes to subsequent developments in the church: 4:13–5:11; 2 Thessalonians 1:3-5; 2:1-2; 3:11. And throughout these two letters one can hear significant hints concerning the joys and struggles of the fledgling group of believers in this metropolitan region.

The lively account of Paul's ministry in Thessalonica in

Acts 17:1-9 adds to the overall picture gained from read-
ing these letters. Especially pertinent is the reference in
verses 6 and 7 to how Paul and his partners were violating
the decrees of the emperor by preaching another king
named Jesus.

The oath of allegiance to the emperor cited in this nar-
rative is of the kind that was administered in various parts
of the first-century Roman world (quoted from Lewis &
Reinhold, 1955:35; cf. Elias, 1995:367).

A STORY: Patriotism, Persecution, and the Parousia

When she was a child growing up in Thessalonica, Aegina had felt proud to be part of the Roman world. She'd known that Thessalonica was the capital city of the province of Macedonia, and she had a vague awareness that Macedonia had not always been aligned with Rome. Her parents sometimes considered their status as Roman citizens a mixed blessing. Occasionally they recalled a time several generations earlier when Macedonia had been part of the grand Greek empire. Now, however, they were expected to express loyalty to Rome.

For Aegina and her childhood friends it seemed normal to be Roman. Along with her friends and their families, Aegina and her parents had frequently taken part in public rallies at Caesar's temple in the city center. How exciting it had been for Aegina to participate in those public celebrations, where the family had expressed their gratitude for life within the empire and voiced allegiance to the emperor.

Occasionally some of Caesar's deputies came to Thessalonica for official visits. As a child she sometimes imagined what it would be like to welcome Claudius Caesar himself. In anticipation of the imperial visit, the local leaders would mount massive cleanup and redecorating efforts along the parade route. Residents of the city would line the streets and show their adulation and allegiance. On the long-awaited day, city and provincial leaders would wait at the city gates for the regal visitor to arrive. The town crier would position himself on a platform and call out, "Welcome, Caesar! You are the lord of the empire! You are the savior who guarantees our peace and security!" Crowds would echo the chant, as they would have done in rehearsal. Aegina still sensed the excitement she felt as a child when she imagined Claudius Caesar's chariot rumbling through their city along the Egnatian Way.

Her childhood patriotism soon seemed naïve and innocent. As a young adult, Aegina heard a message about another Lord, Jesus Christ. A Jew named Paul had come to the marketplace close to where she lived. He set up shop as a tentmaker and began to share a most remarkable message with his customers and with everyone he met. He told the story of Jesus, a Jew whom the Romans had crucified near Jerusalem. But the most remarkable part of the story was that God had raised this man Jesus and that the risen Jesus had actually appeared to Paul. Aegina was profoundly moved by Paul's testimony. She was inwardly compelled to declare her loyalty to Jesus Christ as Lord and became affiliated with a group of like-minded folk meeting regularly in the courtyard of her tenement house. They gathered to worship God and to receive instruction from Paul and his co-workers, Silas and Timothy.

Unfortunately Paul's message evoked suspicion and opposition, so he soon needed to leave town abruptly. But the young congregation stayed together, and new converts joined them. As believers they began to hold themselves aloof from local festivals and other occasions known for patriotic exuberance. Their lifestyle and witness aroused attention elsewhere in Macedonia and as far away as

Achaia. City leaders became alert to the patterns of private meetings, and they were increasingly vigilant in observing their public conduct.

Aegina was quite familiar with the political history of Thessalonica. The city's story was often told at the rallies she frequented. She knew that ever since 146 B.C., when Macedonia became a Roman province, Thessalonica had been its capital. Having been aligned with the side that in 42 B.C. emerged victorious in the Roman civil war, Thessalonica had gained the status of a free city. This meant that citizens of Thessalonica were immune from paying tribute to Rome. Furthermore, the city won the right to govern itself, at least as long as its leaders promoted a civic culture that honored the empire and its Caesar. It left the city's local officials with a delicate balancing act to perform. Their right of self-government continued as long as they maintained a cordial relationship with Rome. In exchange, the city was promised the peace and security of Roman protection.

It was therefore politically expedient for officials in Thessalonica to support the building of a temple dedicated to the Roman Caesar. There the citizens could do homage to former emperors such as Caesar Augustus, who since his death had been revered as a god. Through public ceremonies in and around this temple, the citizens of Thessalonica could also demonstrate their allegiance to the current emperor, Claudius. Attendance at the temple's rallies and festivals allowed local officials to assure their imperial benefactors in Rome. "Look," they could say, "the citizens of Thessalonica are loyal to Caesar!"

But these political rallies had become distasteful to Aegina's new faith family. How could they participate in such worship of the emperor when they worshipped God as sovereign and acknowledged Jesus Christ as Lord?

Their reticence to publicly worship the emperor was noted. The local officials soon found a way to identify dissidents and make a public example of some of them. They were rounded up and ordered to recite an oath of allegiance:

> I swear by Jupiter, Earth, Sun, by all the gods and goddesses, and by Augustus himself, that I will be loyal to Caesar Augustus and to his children and descendants all my life in word, in deed, and in thought, regarding as friends whomever they so regard, and considering as enemies whomever they so adjudge; that in defense of their interests I will spare neither body, soul, life, nor children, but will in every way undergo every danger in defense of their interests; that whenever I perceive or hear anything being said or planned or done against them I will lodge information about this and will be an enemy to whoever says or plans or does any such thing; and that whomever they adjudge to be enemies I will by land and sea, with weapons and sword, pursue and punish. But if I do anything contrary to this oath or not in conformity with what I swore, I myself call down upon myself, my body, my soul, my life, my children, and all my family and property, utter ruin and destruction unto all my issue and all my descendants, and may neither earth nor sea receive the bodies of my family or my descendants, or yield fruits to them.

Those unwilling to swear allegiance became vulnerable to violent attacks by self-styled vigilantes eager to promote themselves as friends of Rome. At times dissenters were also apprehended and questioned by the police. But how should a follower of Jesus Christ respond when confronted by civil servants who demand, "Swear your loyalty to Caesar"?

With fear and deep sadness Aegina mourned, along with the Thessalonian church, after the deaths of several of their young men. How they died remained a mystery. Had they refused to swear the required oath of allegiance to Caesar when they were singled out for official interrogation? Or had some local militants in their zeal to fulfill their own oaths of loyalty judged them to be enemies of Caesar and deserving of death? All the church knew was that these brothers in the Lord were dead.

News of these and other developments in Thessalonica caught up with Paul, who sent Timothy back to Thessalonica to ascertain how the new converts were faring. After hearing Timothy's report, Paul wrote a letter to commend them for their witness in difficult circumstances and to encourage them to continue in the faith.

Timothy's visit and Paul's letter helped raise spirits, but the persecution only intensified. Many were under pressure to participate in the rituals honoring the emperor, and there was always the potential for more interrogation, continued harassment, and the constant threat of death. Some in the congregation wondered whether God was noticing.

"Is the God in whom Daniel placed his trust able also to rescue us?" they asked. "Will God vindicate us? Will God judge our oppressors?"

There were a few in the congregation who concluded that these were the birth pangs of the dawning messianic age. Some enthusiastically announced that the day of the Lord had already come. These people attracted even more official notice. Their demonstrations in the marketplace were publicly dismissed as obnoxious craziness but were used to justify continued harassment and demands for the death of all those professing Christ as Lord.

Fearful of both further persecution by city officials and harassment by Caesar's zealous defenders, Aegina tried to envision what the future might hold. Bewildered by the noisy claims of some meddlesome insiders who insist that the day of the Lord had come, Aegina wondered, "Where is God in all of this?"

God's Righteous Judgment

> Therefore we ourselves boast of you among the churches of God for your steadfastness and faith during all your persecutions and the afflictions which you are enduring. This is evidence of the righteous judgment of God. (2 Thessalonians 1:4-5)

Several key moments in the biblical saga appear to have been particularly important to the apostle Paul. Certainly the stories of Abraham and Sarah and other patriarchal figures from the past bear significant freight in Paul's theology. Moses does not show up prominently in Paul's stories, nor does the exodus of the Hebrews out of Egypt, but the law that Moses received and delivered to the people at Sinai registers a strong response. The current unfolding of God's relationship to the chosen people Israel moved Paul to an anguished rereading of the Scriptures, in particular the oracles of the prophets who ministered during and after the Babylonian exile.

Paul, however, not only followed these and other particular stories from the past, he was also keenly interested in the overarching divine narrative, which we might call "God's own story." He understands that the story of God's creative and redemptive activity in the world is still unfolding. God's story has its beginning; it also has a goal, and we now focus on Paul's view of where the divine project is headed.

It is the concrete circumstance of a congregation in distress that moves Paul to his reflections about how God is at work. In Athens, involuntarily separated from the threatened congregation in Thessalonica, he had decided to dispatch Timothy for a return visit (1 Thessalonians 3:1). When Timothy caught up with Paul again some time later in Corinth and shared his report (3:6), Paul decided to write this struggling grief-stricken congregation the letter we call 1 Thessalonians.

When he reflects on the big picture of God's grand intention, Paul shares the passionate convictions of apocalyptic prophets and visionaries. In the face of what appears to be incontrovertible evidence to the contrary, these apocalyptic seers affirm that God still has a glorious future awaiting the faithful. The message of Daniel, for example, reassures the oppressed exiles in Babylon that God saves the faithful and judges the wicked. In 1 and 2 Thessalonians Paul nowhere quotes directly from any biblical texts, but convictions like those expressed in the book of Daniel have strongly influenced him. We note the climactic vision in Daniel 12 of a future resurrection of the dead, some to everlasting life, and others to shame and everlasting contempt:

> At that time Michael, the great prince, the protector of your people, shall arise. There shall be a time of anguish, such as has never occurred since nations first came into existence. But at that time your people shall be delivered, everyone who is found written in the book. Many of those who sleep in the dust of the earth shall awake, some to everlasting life, and some to shame and everlasting contempt. Those who are wise shall shine like the brightness of the sky, and those who lead many to righteousness, like the stars forever and ever. But you, Daniel, keep the words secret and the

book sealed until the time of the end. Many shall be
running back and forth, and evil shall increase. (12:1-4)

What do the story and the message of Daniel say to the
people of Paul's day? The situation facing a group of grieving believers in Thessalonica might well have moved Paul
to ponder the experience of Daniel during his exile in
Babylon or to rehearse the apocalyptic visions of other
Jews during their seasons of affliction. Paul rejoices in
God's sovereign intervention as redeemer and judge.

Paul was also aware of the story of the Maccabean
freedom fighters, who against great odds managed to
reverse the tyranny of the Syrian king Antiochus IV
Epiphanes. Whether or not Paul ever read 1 Maccabees, he
had undoubtedly heard the history of that period. In 167
B.C. king Antiochus Epiphanes invaded Jerusalem and
plundered the temple, leaving it defiled and desolate. Three
years later, the temple was back in Jewish hands; it was
cleansed, and worship was restored.

Pondering the situation in Thessalonica, Paul affirms
that almighty God is still able to deliver. Yet, reflecting on
the affliction of Macedonian believers, including the
deaths of some martyrs for their newfound faith, he asks,
"What is the shape of God's redemptive justice for the suffering church in Thessalonica?"

The Big Picture

Through what kind of lenses does Paul view their situation? It is evident right from the beginning of his first letter
to the Thessalonian congregation that Paul views their per-
ilous present in light of the glorious future—a future already
made known to them by God through Jesus Christ. He
addresses them as "the church of the Thessalonians in God
the Father and the Lord Jesus Christ" (1 Thessalonians 1:1),

a striking reminder that their identity is inextricably linked to what God has done in Christ. No longer are they identified primarily in terms of their allegiance to the Roman Caesar and the ancient gods with whom he is aligned.

As Paul opens his letter, he thanks God for the fruit-bearing character of their faith, love, and hope. He remembers with gratitude their past and their present faithfulness and love, and he anticipates already their future hopefulness: "your work of faith and labor of love and steadfastness of hope in our Lord Jesus Christ" (1:2-3). Then he notes how their faith, love, and hope are rooted in the prior activity of God in their lives: "For we know, brothers and sisters beloved by God, that he has chosen you" (1:4). God loves, and God chooses. Paul desires for these beleaguered new converts to know that God has chosen them. They are among God's elect!

As if to document their chosenness, Paul proceeds to describe the ripple effect of their faithful witness. On what basis can Paul say that this besieged minority group in the capital city Thessalonica are part of the elect? How can he say that God has chosen them? Receiving the word in much affliction, yet with the joy inspired by the Holy Spirit, they had become an example to others (1:5-8). Their responsive faithfulness under duress sent a clear message. Their witness sounded forth from them into their home province of Macedonia and even into distant Achaia (1:7-8).

Paul's lenses for viewing this congregation display the large picture of God's redemptive mission for the world. Within this grand view, even this persecuted motley minority group has a role. They are part of God's gracious invitation to the world. Even their suffering has meaning. In their suffering Paul sees an imitation of the model of Christ's suffering as well as his own. In their lives and in

their spoken testimony he sees neither the raw newness of
beginning life in Christ nor the faltering steps of immature
believers but rather the expansive spread of the word of
the Lord. When Paul summarizes their experience he says,

> You turned to God from idols, to serve a living and
> true God, and to wait for his Son from heaven, whom
> he raised from the dead—Jesus, who rescues us from
> the wrath that is coming. (1:9-10)

Past, present, and future are all wrapped into one grand
vision of what God has done and will yet do through this
fragile community of faithful believers.

At the heart of Paul's caring intervention both personally and by letter is the awesome story, the gospel of Jesus
Christ crucified yet raised up by God, the story of Jesus
"who rescues us from the wrath that is coming" (1:10).
This gospel consoles people in their grief. For the grieving
Thessalonian survivors of affliction, Paul paints a dramatic and moving picture. God intervenes in behalf of all who
have turned toward God and away from idols, all who
serve the living and true God, all who await God's Son
from heaven.

In 2:1-12 Paul shares some of his most intimate recollections of the time when he and his partners Silvanus and
Timothy worked among them and preached the gospel.
His intention here is to encourage these new believers. As
missionaries they too had suffered shameful treatment, yet
they had trusted God for the courage to persist in their witness to the gospel:

> You yourselves know, brothers and sisters, that our
> coming to you was not in vain, but though we had
> already suffered and been shamefully mistreated at

> Philippi, as you know, we had courage in our God to
> declare to you the gospel of God in spite of great
> opposition. (2:1-2)

Their apostolic example demonstrates the priority of pleasing God (2:4) and the importance of truthful and honorable speech (2:5-6). Paul describes himself and his co-workers by using family metaphors such as children, mother, and father (which we discuss later in chapter 11), in order to urge the Thessalonian believers also to follow their example (2:7-12). Included here is also Paul's recollection of the way that they had supported themselves during their time as missionaries in Thessalonica:

> You remember our labor and toil, brothers and sisters;
> we worked night and day, so that we might not burden
> any of you while we proclaimed to you the gospel of
> God. (2:9)

In 2:12 Paul paints a word picture of the future guaranteed by a God "who calls you into his own kingdom and glory." The big picture features God's reign and God's glory. This kingdom is not just future nor already totally present but both future and already here. This kingdom has been inaugurated; therefore it is already here. However, God's reign has not yet been fully realized. Because God has launched and will yet consummate the triumphant kingdom, those who trust God are called to live in conformity to the One who has called them.

What then is the big picture for Paul? By now we might suspect that the metaphor of "picture" does not do justice to such dynamic conceptions as "kingdom" or "reign." At least we need to realize that it is a moving picture, a drama, a story, a grand narrative! And snatches of this grand story come through in a variety of ways. What Paul assumes as central is not always emphasized; it is often assumed. Yet we catch glimpses, dramatic views of what God has already done and what God still wants to do.

God Rescues the Perishing

In 2:13 Paul recalls again what he already narrated in 1:2-10, namely that the converts in Thessalonica had aligned themselves with God's word. Furthermore, he remembers that in this process the Thessalonian believers had faced antagonism and suffering similar to what some Judean believers had earlier encountered from their compatriots:

> For you, brothers and sisters, became imitators of the churches of God in Christ Jesus that are in Judea, for you suffered the same things from your own compatriots as they did from the Jews, who killed both the Lord Jesus and the prophets, and drove us out; they displease God and oppose everyone by hindering us from speaking to the Gentiles so that they may be saved. Thus they have constantly been filling up the measure of their sins; but God's wrath has overtaken them at last. (2:14-16)

Paul appears to be referring here to a violent confrontation fomented in Thessalonica by some Jewish leaders, who were joined by militant ruffians in the marketplace (Acts 17:5-10). This uprising had led to the hasty departure of Paul and his party. When recalling this tumultuous end to his initial ministry in Thessalonica, Paul narrates the resistance of fellow Jews to the gospel, and he says, "Wrath has come upon them until the end" (2:16c; author's translation). The Judean believers, among whom Paul himself had once been engaged in persecuting activity, continued to face suffering. The Judean believers and the church in Thessalonica and Paul himself had all experienced divine rescue from wrath (cf. 1:10). Upon unbelieving Jews, however, wrath had come, although not in the form of God's final judgment. Paul may have had in mind some catastrophic event such as the Passover massacre of some twenty to thirty thousand Jerusalem Jews in the A.D. 48 (Elias, 1995:89-98). What Paul hints at here in his phrase "until the end" is developed more fully in Romans 11:25-32. God's mercy continues to be extended "until the end," and, in the end, within the mystery of God's still unfolding plan, all Israel will be saved. (For more discussion of this theme, see chapter 6.)

Yet Paul's agenda here in 1 Thessalonians is not primarily to figure out God's ongoing relationship with Israel. He wants mainly to reassure the Thessalonians that God rescues the faithful. Paul expresses his concern for them as well as his deep affection: "Yes, you are our glory and joy!" (2:20). He explains that he had sent Timothy to encourage them "so that no one would be shaken by these persecutions" (3:3). One can almost hear his sigh of relief at Timothy's good report: "For we now live, if you continue to stand firm in the Lord" (3:8). Paul's closing prayer in 3:11-13 both recapitulates his longing to be back with the Thessalonians to impart encouragement for their faith and anticipates his ethical and pastoral exhortations regarding their love, holiness, and hope:

> Now may our God and Father himself and our Lord
> Jesus direct our way to you. And may the Lord make
> you increase and abound in love for one another and
> for all, just as we abound in love for you. And may he
> so strengthen your hearts in holiness that you may be

blameless before our God and Father at the coming of
our Lord Jesus with all his saints.

In 4:1-12 Paul deals with the themes of sexual ethics
and communal love, discussed further in chapter 11. We'll
focus here on the way that Paul in 4:13-18 consoles the
Thessalonian believers in their grief at the death of their
loved ones.

In 4:13-18 Paul provides a dramatic view of God's liberating work through Jesus Christ when he responds pastorally to the Thessalonian believers' grief following the
death of one or more of their members. He makes explicit
mention in 4:13 of "those who have died," but he provides
no details about how they died. The shock and grief in
Thessalonica is in all likelihood occasioned by the deaths
of some members of their faith community at the hands of
city officials or militant locals who were eager to demonstrate their loyalty to Rome. City leaders sought to maintain their citizens' loyalty to Rome, so that the benefits
would continue to flow into the city; they had reason to
come down hard on dissenters who would not confess
Caesar as Lord. Vigilante individuals also had motivation
for overt, even violent, acts of public support of the
empire, perhaps in hope of a reward for such loyalty.

This reading of the circumstances underlying 4:13-18
cannot be proven. However, support for this reconstruction comes from the frequent references to persecution and
suffering earlier in the letter, especially in 1:6, 2:14, and
3:4, in which Paul recalls that such suffering need not have
come as a surprise:

> In fact, when we were with you, we told you before-
> hand that we were to suffer persecution; so it turned
> out, as you know. (3:4)

Paul also mentions his own dire distress, and he notes that the Thessalonians' faithfulness has encouraged him in the opposition that he has experienced: "During all our distress and persecution we have been encouraged about you through your faith" (3:7).

Paul's purpose here is to comfort these believers in their grief and to give them hope: "So that you may not grieve as others do who have no hope" (4:13). He does so by telling the story of Jesus and pointing to the hope inspired by his death and resurrection:

> Since we believe that Jesus died and rose again, even
> so, through Jesus, God will bring with him those who
> have died. (4:14)

Paul's accent here falls on how what God did for Jesus in raising him following his death on the cross will be replicated for those whose faithfulness to God has led to their deaths. To underscore the certainty of God's vindicating rescue of the perishing faithful, Paul previews a glorious future scenario. He employs powerful images, which betray the influence of biblical and other Jewish apocalyptic literature: "God's trumpet" (Isaiah 27:13; Joel 2:1, 15; Zechariah 9:14) and "the clouds" (Daniel 7:13). Drawing on these and other apocalyptic motifs, Paul gives testimony to the guaranteed future for both those who have died and those who are still alive when the Lord descends from heaven:

> For this we declare to you by the word of the Lord,
> that we who are alive, who are left until the coming of
> the Lord, will by no means precede those who have
> died. For the Lord himself, with a cry of command,
> with the archangel's call and with the sound of God's

trumpet, will descend from heaven, and the dead in
Christ will rise first. Then we who are alive, who are
left, will be caught up in the clouds together with them
to meet the Lord in the air; and so we will be with the
Lord forever. (1 Thessalonians 4:15-17)

Later readers have often scrutinized Paul's words to the
Thessalonian believers in an effort to establish a calendar
of end-time events. Such interpretations neglect to recognize that his primary intention here is to console grieving
believers. God's life-restoring power assures them that
whether they live or die they will be with the Lord forever.
To communicate this reassurance Paul paints a lively picture of the future, employing stock apocalyptic images.

He also uses words and themes that would have been
heard as overtly political, because they echo the rhetoric of
the imperial cult. As believers they were awaiting not the
coming of Caesar but the triumphant coming of Christ the
Lord. As believers they were assured of a future public
meeting with the Lord not on the parade route leading into
the heart of the city but "in the clouds to meet the Lord in
the air" (4:17). As citizens of another realm called "the
kingdom of God" they could anticipate the summons of
the royal trumpet (4:16). They could look forward to a
glorious reunion with the martyrs and then uninterrupted
communion with God through Christ.

This preview of a reunion of resurrected and surviving
believers with the Lord in the air (4:15-17) dramatically
reassures the besieged survivors. Paul's message at its sim-
plest and most profound level is this: "Jesus died, and he
rose again; so we, though we die, yet shall we live!"
Continuity of fellowship in Christ is guaranteed for those
who entrust themselves to the God who raised Jesus from
the dead.

Jesus's story and the believers' stories are thereby interwoven within the drama of salvation. The drama of salvation was portrayed in the events at Calvary and the tomb. This drama was also playing itself out in the public square near the temple dedicated to Caesar, when the oath of loyalty identified those who confessed Christ as Lord and when these dissidents paid with their lives. These believers shared in the suffering of Christ. They became imitators of Jesus Christ (1:6; 2:14). What had happened to Jesus, who had been charged with sedition against Roman authorities, was also happening to them. And, just as Jesus was raised from the dead, so those who died in Christ would also emerge alive!

Armed with Faith, Love, and Hope

In his treatment of the theme of "the times and the seasons" (5:1-11) Paul makes his most direct comment about the Roman power establishment and how God's people should view its role in their lives. The mighty Roman Empire might promise peace and security to its citizens and to its loyal subject peoples, to all those who express their loyalty to Caesar. But Paul assures those who place their loyalty in God that God will triumph even in the face of the might of Rome:

> When they say, "There is peace and security," then
> sudden destruction will come upon them, as labor
> pains come upon a pregnant woman, and there will be
> no escape. (5:3)

Those who say, "There is peace and security!" are people who promote absolute allegiance to Caesar. They shout patriotic slogans in support of the emperor, who is confessed to be the savior and deliverer of the world. But upon them,

Paul says, "sudden destruction will come." Ultimately God will exercise sovereign judgment over the emperor and his supporters. By contrast, those who trust in God as revealed in Jesus Christ are the sober ones who belong to the day (5:4-7).

Those who belong to the day are equipped with God's weapons to resist evil and strive for the good. Paul portrays the believers' participation in God's redemptive mission to the world by using a military metaphor:

> Since we belong to the day, let us be sober, and put on the breastplate of faith and love, and for a helmet the hope of salvation. (5:8)

Through the trusting exercise of faith, love, and hope, believers are invited to take the offensive against idolatry and evil. Believers are God's warriors, armed with faith and love as their breastplate, with hope of salvation as their helmet. In Tom Yoder Neufeld's words, believers are not "passive and worried bystanders awaiting the arrival of the Lord" but "divine combatants, ready to seize every opportunity to exercise the warfare of love" (1997:91). When Paul wraps up this word of comfort he again reassures them with a reminder of the salvation already won through Jesus Christ:

> God has destined us not for wrath but for obtaining salvation through our Lord Jesus Christ, who died for us, so that whether we are awake or asleep we may live with him. (5:9-10)

That Paul longs to reassure and comfort rather than outline an eschatological timetable is again evident: "Therefore encourage one another and build up each other, as indeed you are doing" (5:11).

Paul's first letter to the Thessalonians concludes with some instructions and encouragement about life and worship in the congregation (5:12-21). Also included is a wish prayer that underscores the enduring faithfulness of the God of peace:

> May the God of peace himself sanctify you entirely;
> and may your spirit and soul and body be kept sound
> and blameless at the coming of our Lord Jesus Christ.
> The one who calls you is faithful, and he will do this.
> (5:23-24)

Given the political circumstances prevailing in Thessalonica and the grief among believers there, the language that Paul utilizes in this prayer is remarkable. God (not Caesar) is "the God of peace." In their oath, Caesar's warriors pledge body, soul, life, and children in defense of the empire. In contrast, God's warriors venture forth with the weapons of faith, love, and hope, in the assurance of the faithfulness and trustworthiness of God. Each of God's warriors is assured of the preservation of "spirit and soul and body" within the realm of God's triumphant reign.

But Will the Judge Rule Justly?

Some time elapsed following Paul's first letter to the church in Thessalonica before he wrote the second. In the interim he continued his involvement in Corinth, always alert to any word about further developments in the Macedonian capital. News soon came from Thessalonica, indicating clearly that the congregation needed more reassurance and pastoral guidance. So probably about A.D. 51 Paul writes a second letter, again seeking to show the Thessalonian believers where they fit within the big picture of God's redemptive agenda.

As a missionary pastor continuing to care for this church, Paul appears especially to have been moved by the heart cry of a persecuted people who asked, "Why do the righteous suffer? Where is God's justice?" Strangely Paul begins by giving thanks for their growing faith and love (2 Thessalonians 1:3). He continues by boasting a little:

> Therefore we ourselves boast of you among the church-es of God for your steadfastness and faith during all your persecutions and the afflictions that you are enduring. (1:4)

Then he inserts an interpretive expansion, which in the original continues the previous thought without the kind of paragraph break that Bible translations usually insert here: "evidence of the righteous judgment of God" (1:5a).

What constitutes "evidence of the righteous judgment of God"? Is it the Thessalonians' endurance? Or do their perse-cutions and afflictions supply that evidence? Grammatically and theologically, the most likely reading is that Paul regards their "steadfastness and faith" as proof that God judges justly. As believers they have been enabled to remain stead-fastly faithful to their calling to conduct themselves accord-ing to the values of the kingdom of God. Hence Paul boasts about their continued faithfulness, even when their values and commitments come into direct conflict with loyalty to the empire. They have been counted "worthy of the kingdom of God," even to the extent that they are suffering for it (1:5b).

In 1:6-10 Paul enlarges on the "big picture" premise on which this assertion is based. He explains,

> For indeed it is just of God to repay with affliction those who afflict you, and to give relief to the afflicted as well as to us. (1:6-7)

Faithful endurance under persecution is rooted ultimately in the confidence that God will vindicate the faithful. A providential turning of the tables will occur as part of God's "righteous judgment." When steadfastly and faithfully enduring persecution, the Thessalonians testify to the hope that in the end God's justice will prevail. To those who afflict, God will repay affliction. To those being afflicted, God will grant relief. That is what God deems just.

Although this kind of dramatic reversal of fortunes still lies in the future, the awareness of God's ultimate vindication inspires the faithful to endure their present distress. Paul articulates that future in the vivid language of apocalyptic, talking about the Lord Jesus being revealed from heaven "with his mighty angels in flaming fire, inflicting vengeance on those who do not know God" (1:7-8). God's righteous judgment will be exercised through Jesus the crucified and triumphant Lord. For the disobedient there is the threat of exclusion, but for the faithful there is the prospect of glory. Within the big picture, judgment is left to God. The faithful, though besieged and under threat, can therefore join in praise, giving glory to almighty God.

Evil's Script and God's Triumph

In 2 Thessalonians 2:1-17 Paul continues to offer pastoral care through the medium of dramatic apocalyptic storytelling. His specific agenda includes the need to confront the alarm and confusion created by some people in Thessalonica who claim that "the day of the Lord is already here" (2:2). The story Paul tells features an antagonist, variously described as "the lawless one" and "the one destined for destruction," whose antics include the usurpation of divine status:

> He opposes and exalts himself above every so-called
> god or object of worship, so that he takes his seat in
> the temple of God, declaring himself to be God. (2:4)

Paul was undoubtedly aware that this dramatic portrait would have rung all kinds of bells for all Jews and God-fearers familiar with their recent history. The actions of Antiochus IV Epiphanes in 167 B.C. had come to symbolize the way emperors and kings often put themselves in God's place. The Roman general Pompey in 63 B.C. and the mad Roman emperor Gaius Caligula in A.D. 41 used the same blueprint for their acts of blasphemous defiance. In each case, they entered (or threatened to enter) the Jerusalem temple, a symbolic action which communicates (at least to Jews) that they were taking God's place. During the coming apostasy, Paul warns, a future antagonist will follow the same script. And he wants the Thessalonian believers to know that the emperor, whom they were urged to honor as supreme, was already making such claims.

In 2:6-7 Paul employs cryptic language to continue this dramatic portrayal. The opaque character of the symbols attests his desire to protect the recipients of this letter from unnecessary exposure and subsequent further persecution. That Paul is deliberately employing secretive code language is evident in his side comment: "Do you not remember that I told you these things when I was still with you?" (2:5). It is as though he deftly delivers a gentle kick under the table to alert his readers that they should look underneath the surface, literal meaning of his words for the deeper message that he wishes to share with them.

The key symbolic code that modern interpreters have found difficult to decipher is the Greek participle *katechon*, which occurs once in 2:6 as grammatically neuter and once in 2:7 as grammatically masculine. The underlying word has a range of possible meanings, including "to restrain, hinder, prevail, seize, oppress, or lay legal claim." It is the notion of restraining that has been most prevalent in the translations of these two occurrences of this word. The NRSV has translated these verses as follows:

> And you know what is now restraining him, so that he may be revealed when his time comes. For the mystery of lawlessness is already at work, but only until the one who now restrains it is removed. (2:6-7)

This translation suggests that Paul is depicting a benign or friendly buffer, described once using the neuter participle, pointing to an institution of some kind ("what is now restraining him"), and once with the masculine participle, referring to the leader of that entity ("the one who now restrains it"). This institution and its leader are viewed as having the positive function of restraining the antagonist and protecting the church for an interim against this antagonist. A dominant reading has been that the Roman Empire and the emperor through its laws and social structures are providing protection for the church until the antagonist is let loose. There are, however, major problems with this rendering. For one thing, in the original Greek text neither of these participles has an object; both *him* ("what is now restraining him") and *it* ("the one who now restrains it") have been added by translators.

A reading of these verses that is contextually and grammatically more coherent understands Paul to be referring to an institution (the Roman Empire) and an official (the emperor, through his regional governors) that are suspicious and hostile toward the church. The participle *katechon* therefore refers first to *the oppression* and then to *the oppressor*. (For the exegetical argument, see Elias,

1995:281-85.) The different readings can be viewed in parallel:

	NRSV	My Proposal	An Elaboration
to katechon (neuter participle pointing to an institution)	"what is now restraining him" (often understood to be the Roman Empire)	*the oppression*	The empire and its imperial ideological structures promoted through the imperial cult
ho katechôn (masculine participle pointing to an official)	"the one who now restrains it" (often understood to be the emperor)	*the oppressor*	The emperor working through his provincial and city officials to promote the imperial ideology

The translation of these enigmatic verses (2:6-7) proposed here therefore is as follows:

> And now the oppression you know, so that he may be revealed in his time. For the mystery of lawlessness works already; only the oppressor [works] already, until he is taken from the midst. (author's translation)

What then does this mean?

In their rebellion against God, the Roman Empire and its representatives attempt to control or suppress the believers who confess Christ rather than the emperor as their Lord. Paul testifies, however, that the tenure of the emperor and his provincial and local officials will come to an end. When he refers to an individual who will be revealed ("he may be revealed in his time"), who will be removed ("he is taken from the midst"), Paul is referring to the emperor, the leader who as antagonist exalts himself above God, the lawless one who takes his seat in the temple. But Paul has no clear chronology or timetable in mind. He seeks primarily to reassure the believers in Thessalonica that God will vanquish even those most blatant perpetrators of evil of any period who seek to seduce the faithful. Even if evil seems to triumph, justice will finally be done. In the end, the forces of evil will be defeated and those who remain true to God will be rewarded.

In 2:8-12 the eschatological drama comes to a climax in a graphic depiction of the final holy war. Paul's primary intention here again is to reassure and to warn. Those who remain faithful and steadfast under persecution are reassured that their Lord reigns and will come as righteous judge. On the other hand, those who were being deceived by the arrogant claims of the antagonist hear a warning. Though not just yet, God's righteous judgment will surely come.

The church of the Thessalonians in their suffering is summoned to hear the reassuring message that God has chosen them as "the first fruits for salvation" (2:13). Despite all present signs to the contrary, they are bound for glory (2:14). Paul therefore admonishes them to stand firm (2:15). And he reassures them with the message of God's grace:

> Now may our Lord Jesus Christ himself and God our
> Father, who loved us and through grace gave us eternal
> comfort and good hope, comfort your hearts and
> strengthen them in every good work and word. (2:16-17)

Within the big picture of God's grand design, grace supplies the resplendent background. Paul's second letter to the besieged believers in Thessalonica frequently sounds this comforting theme, not only in the greeting (1:2) and benediction (3:18) but also at key transitions in the letter (1:12; 2:16). God's grace provides the matrix within which their suffering takes on eternal significance.

As in the first letter, so here in concluding this letter Paul reassures his friends in Thessalonica that God is faithful: "But the Lord is faithful; he will strengthen you and guard you from the evil one" (3:3). He also expresses his confidence in their ongoing obedience (3:4) and he commends them to God's love and Christ's steadfastness (3:5). These words of reassurance and expressions of confidence are intended to equip believers to confront the powers of evil aligned against the church in its external environment.

But Paul also feels compelled to address an internal problem within the congregation, a problem that has been getting worse. When introducing the theme of "the day of the Lord" he hinted broadly about the need to confront the alarm and confusion created by some who were claiming that that day had already come (2:2). Active within the Thessalonian church from the beginning were some who caused disruption. Already in his first letter, Paul exhorts them "to aspire to live quietly, to mind your own affairs, and to work with your hands, as we directed you" (1 Thessalonians 4:11). As he concludes this first letter, he urges, "Admonish the idlers" (5:14). Translating the underlying Greek word *ataktoi* as "idlers" has fed the notion that the problem was laziness. The way that Paul revisits the issue in 2 Thessalonians 3:6-15 clearly suggests that these people were a disruptive group of unruly enthusiasts who became a burden on the congregation's resources and created a bad impression among outsiders. Paul recommends that the congregation disassociate themselves from such people (3:6, 14). (For more on 3:6-15, see chapters 10 and 13.)

It is noteworthy that, in a letter underscoring God's righteous judgment enacted in favor of the oppressed, Paul also emphasizes the need for communal judgment within the congregation. Busybodies engaged in meddlesome activity without becoming productively involved are called to account. This judgment, however, is not punitive but redemptive:

> Take note of those who do not obey what we say in this letter; have nothing to do with them, so that they may be ashamed. Do not regard them as enemies, but warn them as believers. (3:14-15)

Firm and loving discipline is needed within the community of faith. Such discipline echoes both God's lavish grace and God's grieved holiness. God will finally judge both the living and the dead. In the meantime, however, God continues to impart peace and extend grace to all, as Paul attests in his two concluding benedictions:

> Now may the Lord of peace himself give you peace at all times in all ways. (3:16)

> The grace of our Lord Jesus Christ be with all of you. (3:18)

When God's Judgment Will Be Revealed

The letters to first-century believers in Thessalonica show us how Paul opens the curtain to unveil God's restorative justice. Those who have died in their faithfulness are assured of life with Christ. The afflicted find comfort, their persecutors face exclusion. God is the judge before whom all must give account on the coming Day.

We turn now to Paul's other letters. In his correspondence with other congregations, how does he convey the perspective of God as judge? Is it possible to piece together a narrative showing how God's judgment works? We focus first on the theme of God's reign and then explore several texts where Paul reflects on God as judge.

The Kingdom of God

In 1 Thessalonians 2:11-12 Paul refers to the kingdom of God as a realm yet to be fully realized but already present. In 2 Thessalonians 1:5 he accents believers' future inheritance but also points out that in their faithfulness to God they are already suffering for the kingdom. Their steadfastness and faithfulness in the midst of suffering constitutes proof of God's righteous judgment, whereby the afflicted are granted relief and those who afflict them face punishment.

In his other letters Paul also portrays God's kingdom as already inaugurated but still to be consummated in the future. We examine several of the pertinent texts.

In 1 Corinthians 15:24 he identifies the kingdom as a present entity associated with Christ. This kingdom will in the future be delivered to God so that ultimately God will be sovereign over all:

> Then comes the end, when he hands over the kingdom
> to God the Father, after he has destroyed every ruler
> and every authority and power. (1 Corinthians 15:24)

The risen Christ is the first fruit of the kingdom, and those who are in Christ participate in this kingdom already.

What such participation in God's kingdom means for believers is described in Romans 14:1–15:13, where Paul articulates how members of the diverse Roman house churches are to relate to each other. Their different traditions with reference to food and drink and holy days are to be viewed as secondary to the larger picture of God's kingdom ways. He summarizes this perspective:

> For the kingdom of God is not food and drink but
> righteousness and peace and joy in the Holy Spirit.
> (Romans 14:17)

The model of Christ's self-giving love (14:15; cf. 15:3, 8-9) expresses itself within the community of faith in justice, peace, and joy, all inspired by the Holy Spirit. Such is the nature of life under the reign of God.

Several of Paul's other references to the kingdom of God include warnings to those whose lives do not conform to these values. Paul waxes sarcastic in 1 Corinthians when he addresses people whose triumphalistic spirituality ignored the "not yet" aspect of their experience of God's kingdom:

> Already you have all you want! Already you have
> become rich! Quite apart from us you have become
> kings! Indeed, I wish that you had become kings, so
> that we might be kings with you! (1 Corinthians 4:8)

Paul proceeds dramatically to enumerate his own weakness, his hunger, his humiliating reverses, and his weariness (4:9-13). He warns the arrogant folk in Corinth that he would come to investigate not their boastful talk but their power (4:19), and he adds, "For the kingdom of God depends not on talk but on power" (4:20). And, as Paul has made explicit in his earlier reflections in this letter (especially 1:18-2:5), the power that characterizes persons who participate in God's kingdom is the power of the cross, of weakness and shame. It is through the foolishness and weakness of the cross that the wisdom and the power of God are made known.

Later in 1 Corinthians Paul speaks explicitly about the requisite lifestyle of persons who have entered the faith community. He makes clear that persons baptized in the name of Christ and in the Spirit of God need to live in certain ways in order to inherit God's kingdom:

> Do you not know that wrongdoers will not inherit the kingdom of God? Do not be deceived! Fornicators, idolaters, adulterers, male prostitutes, sodomites, thieves, the greedy, drunkards, revilers, robbers—none of these will inherit the kingdom of God. And this is what some of you used to be. But you were washed, you were sanctified, you were justified in the name of the Lord Jesus Christ and in the Spirit of our God. (1 Corinthians 6:9-11)

Paul issues a similar warning in Galatians 5:

> Now the works of the flesh are obvious: fornication, impurity, licentiousness, idolatry, sorcery, enmities, strife, jealousy, anger, quarrels, dissensions, factions, envy, drunkenness, carousing, and things like these. I am warning you, as I warned you before: those who do such things will not inherit the kingdom of God. (Galatians 5:19-21)

Final inheritance of the kingdom of God comes, therefore, after experiencing the justifying and sanctifying work of Christ and the Spirit. This implies human participation in the righteousness, peace, and joy that mark the kingdom of God. It also calls for the avoidance of those behaviors that contravene the values of God's kingdom.

In sum: When Paul reaches for the "big picture" of God's grand intention, he speaks about the kingdom of God, the domain of God's sovereignty into which people are invited to enter through Christ. Within this realm God desires active participation in the way of Jesus Christ. People whose lives signal commitments contrary to the way of Christ hear warnings that God will ultimately judge them, and in the final judgment they could find themselves excluded.

God Through Christ Judges

When Paul's later interpreters come to the texts where he deals with the final judgment, they often look for answers to their curious questions about the future. David Aune lists some twenty passages in Paul's letters containing fragments of a chronological scheme of events. He laments: "Clever scholars have tried to 'connect the dots' by coordinating these passages" (2002:70). Aune concludes his article by saying that "such discourse consisted of a pastiche of eschatological convictions which probably could not have been formulated by Paul (even if he wanted to) into a consistent narrative of end time events" (2002:86).

We will not attempt to "connect the dots" that we find in Paul's letters into a coherent eschatological scenario or seek to differentiate neatly between distinct resurrections or among different seasons of judgment. What we can do is identify motifs in Paul's teachings about God's judgment and note how these teachings intersect with the situations in the congregations that he addresses.

Paul communicates clearly in several of his letters that God will judge people on the basis of their works. His most extensive discussion of this theme is in Romans 2, where he emphasizes that God as impartial and righteous judge will reward or punish all people on the basis of what they have done. This section of his letter fits within his overall purpose in Romans: to establish a level playing field on the basis of which Jews and Gentiles in Roman house churches can welcome each other. In 2:5-8 he builds on the self-incriminating stance of those who judge others without examining themselves:

> But by your hard and impenitent heart you are storing up wrath for yourself on the day of wrath, when God's righteous judgment will be revealed. For he will repay according to each one's deeds: to those who by patiently doing good seek for glory and honor and immortality, he will give eternal life; while for those who are self-seeking and who obey not the truth but wickedness, there will be wrath and fury. (Romans 2:5-8)

He drives this point home with reference to Jews, who hear a reminder that what is required of them is doing the law and not just hearing it:

> For it is not the hearers of the law who are righteous in God's sight, but the doers of the law who will be justified. (2:13)

Paul also makes the case for righteous Gentiles who live according to God's moral law without actually possessing the law. Their consciences guide them in the kind of righteous behavior that will acquit them on the day when God through Christ will exercise judgment on all:

> When Gentiles, who do not possess the law, do instinctively what the law requires, these, though not having the law, are a law to themselves. They show that what the law requires is written on their hearts, to which their own conscience also bears witness; and their conflicting thoughts will accuse or perhaps excuse them on the day

> when, according to my gospel, God, through Jesus
> Christ, will judge the secret thoughts of all. (2:14-16)

A text later in Romans also appeals to the Jewish and Gentile believers in Rome to desist from judging each other, because in the end God will judge all of them. Here Paul echoes two Isaiah texts (Isaiah 49:18; 45:23) to underscore the certainty of a future universal acclamation of God as sovereign. He emphasizes that everyone will be called to account before almighty God:

> Why do you pass judgment on your brother or sister?
> Or you, why do you despise your brother or sister?
> For we will all stand before the judgment seat of God.
> For it is written, "As I live, says the Lord, every knee
> shall bow to me, and every tongue shall give praise to
> God." So then, each of us will be accountable to God.
> (Romans 14:10-12)

In this case it is the tendency for some to judge and others to despise that evokes Paul's reminder that God will eventually judge all such behavior that disrupts communal unity.

Another key text conveying Paul's conviction that God through Christ will judge all people on the basis of what they have done is found in 2 Corinthians. In this case, Paul refers to the judgment seat of Christ:

> For all of us must appear before the judgment seat of
> Christ, so that each may receive recompense for what
> has been done in the body, whether good or evil.
> (2 Corinthians 5:10)

This assertion is part of Paul's larger discussion of his own credentials as a minister of the new covenant (as we examined in chapter 5). He has presented his experience of suffering as corresponding to the suffering and death of Jesus, and he derives his confidence and hope from the gospel of the risen Christ. This mention of the final judgment before the eschatological tribunal of Christ serves to undergird his appeal to the Corinthian church to side with his understanding of the gospel and to live in a way that pleases God and will elicit a reward.

In his earlier letter to the church at Corinth Paul also mentions the possibility of reward or loss on the day of judgment, depending on how the various leaders who followed him worked to build up the church on the foundation of Jesus Christ (1 Corinthians 3:11). He develops the building metaphor by referring to various types of construction materials, some durable, some flammable:

> Now if anyone builds on the foundation with gold, silver, precious stones, wood, hay, straw—the work of each builder will become visible, for the Day will disclose it, because it will be revealed with fire, and the fire will test what sort of work each has done. If what has been built on the foundation survives, the builder will receive a reward. If the work is burned up, the builder will suffer loss; the builder will be saved, but only as through fire. (1 Corinthians 3:12-15)

Especially for apostles and church leaders Paul envisions a pattern of reward and loss on a future day of judgment depending on how they have performed their ministries. He is also clearly aware that he is not exempt. His ministry too will receive divine scrutiny. He communicates this awareness in some candid comments that come a bit later in the same letter:

> But with me it is a very small thing that I should be judged by you or by any human court. I do not even

judge myself. I am not aware of anything against
myself, but I am not thereby acquitted. It is the Lord
who judges me. Therefore do not pronounce judgment
before the time, before the Lord comes, who will bring
to light the things now hidden in darkness and will disclose the purposes of the heart. Then each one will
receive commendation from God. (1 Corinthians 4:3-5)

Along these lines we note that near the conclusion of
2 Timothy, Paul expresses himself sadly concerning an individual who had apparently inflicted injury or insult. He says,
"Alexander the coppersmith did me great harm; the Lord
will pay him back for his deeds" (2 Timothy 4:14). Because
God will ultimately judge this man, Paul need not do so.

By way of a brief summation: Paul's assertions about
God's judgment do not supply a neat sequence of events
envisioned as unfolding when an individual dies or when the
end of the age arrives. He draws on a variety of familiar
apocalyptic motifs. His understanding of these themes has
been transformed through his own apocalypse: the revelation of the crucified and exalted Christ to him. When he
offers his brief glimpses into the judgment tribunal with God
or Christ on the throne, he does so primarily not to predict
a future judgment calendar but to provide reassurance to
suffering believers. The consolation of the oppressed with
the message of God's sure vindicating judgment also sends a
clear warning to the unfaithful and the apostate. In mercy
yet with justice, God through Christ already exercises judgment and will in the end be the judge of all.

Part 3

A Community Shaped
by the Future

INTRODUCTION

An encounter with the crucified and risen Christ radically transformed Paul's outlook on his world. In Jesus, nailed to a Roman cross and raised in triumph, Paul received a privileged glimpse of a glorious future guaranteed by God. This cross unveils God's cataclysmic intervention into the life of Israel and into human history.

Yet, as his recollection of the story of God's activity narrated in the Scriptures shows, Paul viewed this future as rooted in the past. We have seen that scriptural stories and themes profoundly shape his pastoral enterprise in relation to the congregations among which he ministers. Israel confessed that there is one God who is sovereign as creator and sustainer, and so did the church when lauding Christ as Lord. Because of their trust in God's promises, Abraham and Sarah were reassured of God's blessing on all their descendants, both Jews and Gentiles, a blessing now recognized as accessible to all on the basis of faith. The covenant at Sinai with the Hebrews whom God had rescued from their slavery has a splendor surpassed only by the new covenant now implemented in Christ and guaranteed by the Spirit. Israel's chronic tendency to lapse into idolatry and disobedience led to her exile among the nations but even that experience becomes another occasion for the unfolding of the irrevocable plan and promises of God for both Jews and Gentiles. The apocalyptic visionaries' dramatic pictures of God's judgment of the wicked and triumph for the faithful have been given explosive manifestation in Jesus, the victorious victim on the Roman cross.

But questions arise. Some questions are deeply theological. How can what God has done in Jesus Christ simultaneously be in continuity with the salvation history of the past and also a radically new creation? Can the announcement that God, through Christ, has invaded the world in unprecedented fashion be reconciled with the claim that this event is continuous with God's past dealings with Jews? What is God doing, and what does God want to do, in the communities of faith popping up like mushrooms throughout the region of the Mediterranean?

Other issues are profoundly practical. As we have already seen, Paul is keenly aware that all of the congregations among whom he travels and with whom he communicates by letter have to deal with conflicts and stressful situations of one kind or another. In various ways he seeks to stay tuned to the ongoing story of each of these faith communities. And he attempts to communicate with them in ways that are heard. What images, stories, and metaphors from the Greco-Roman world can be drafted into service to relate the grand vision of God's invasive grace through Christ to the places where people live, relate to their neighbors, make ethical decisions, and deal with life's tragedies and pain?

As a Jewish apostle relating to Gentile congregations in Galatia and elsewhere in Asia Minor, Paul and his affiliates seem to be wrestling with these and other questions. Here in part 3, we focus on Paul's epistle to the churches in Galatia, the letter addressed by him to believers in Colossae, and the general letter to congregations in and around Ephesus. We will also see that even in the deeply personal memo to Philemon and the church meeting in his house, Paul's pastoral counsel emerges from within an ethical tradition now radically reshaped in Christ.

8

FREED BY AN INVASION OF GRACE

We begin this chapter (and chapter 9) by reconstructing the story underlying Paul's rather contentious letter to churches in Galatia. In his epistle to the Galatians he recounts several anecdotes, but the details of the underlying story behind this letter are far from clear.

As he opens the letter to the churches in Galatia, which were probably made up exclusively of Gentiles, Paul recounts the story of how he was called to become an apostle to the Gentiles. But as we saw in chapter 1, Paul was not the only Jew engaged in missionary activity in that region. In fact, the work of other Jewish teachers among the churches of Galatia provokes Paul to make some rather strong correctives.

In this story we listen to Dorian, whom we imagine to be one of Paul's Galatian converts. Dorian, his wife Felicia, and their sons (ages 4 and 8) are active participants in one of the Galatian congregations. Dorian is bewildered by what he hears from some of the Jewish teachers who came to their community after Paul left.

Our primary sources for this story are Paul's references to the work of some agitators (Galatians 1:6-7), his account of how the Galatians had initially responded to the preaching of the gospel (3:1-5), and his reminiscence about how they had welcomed him during his first visit (4:12-20). In addition we have noted some of Paul's com-

ments about what had been transpiring in Galatia: a ten-
dency to relapse into paganism (4:8-10) or to take on
Jewish rituals (5:2-12; 6:12-13).

How might Dorian have told the story about life in the
churches of Galatia?

A STORY: The Crucified Galilean and Confused Galatians

When Dorian and Felicia married they settled in a
region of Galatia, a Roman province with a number of
Jewish communities and several synagogues. During the
first years of their life as a family, they paid little attention
to the Jews, who stood apart in rather visible ways from
other populations. Their religious activities as a couple,
and later with their children, included occasional involvement in the sacrifices and festivals in the local temples.
They also took part in the festivals and parades in honor
of the Roman emperor.

In his business contacts Dorian occasionally conversed
with foreigners who set up shop in the local marketplace.
Artisans and peddlers often shared interesting tales. They
also brought with them their religious convictions and
philosophies of life. A messianic Jewish evangelist named
Paul, who made a stop in their community as part of his trek
through the province of Galatia, quickly caught Dorian's
attention. As it turned out, when Paul became quite ill and
needed to delay the continuation of his trip, Dorian and
Felicia reached out to him with food and medical help. His
health slowly improved. As he picked up his work schedule
and prepared to resume his journey, he did what he apparently was inwardly compelled to do and shared a remarkable message about a Jew named Jesus, whom he characterized as a special messenger from the one supreme God.

In the market and the public square Paul publicly and passionately proclaimed Jesus to be a holy man who faithfully obeyed God even though his obedience led to death on the cross. Some Galatians who bothered to stop and listen scoffed at the notion that a Jew who had been executed could have any religious significance. Others who heard Paul preach received him as though he were an angel, a messenger from God. A sizeable number of them accepted the gospel of Jesus Christ and felt the dynamic power of God. Paul testified that they were experiencing a powerful visitation of the Holy Spirit of God.

During one of these dramatic encounters, Dorian and Felicia turned away from their traditional pagan gods. They entrusted themselves to the one holy God made known through the story of Jesus hanging on an accursed cross.

Paul soon left Galatia, resuming the itinerary he had been following before he fell sick. Dorian and several others were left to lead the group of converts. Paul inspired them with reassuring words urging them to keep their focus on Jesus, now exalted as the Lord of all.

Soon after Paul's departure from Galatia, other messianic Jewish missionaries came to visit. Dorian was moved yet strangely irked by the teachings of one Reuben of Jerusalem, a winsome and zealous advocate of a perspective concerning life in Christ that was quite different from Paul's vision. Reuben sounded the alarm about the fact that Paul had not introduced his converts to the Jewish law and especially to some of the rituals, which Reuben claimed were needed for them to be fully incorporated into God's historic people. Particularly upsetting to him was the fact that, like many men and boys in Galatia, neither Dorian nor their two sons were circumcised. He pointed out from the ancient story of the first proselyte, Abraham, that both he and his sons Ishmael and Isaac were circumcised. Would this not suggest that proselytes of later periods also need to be circumcised in order to ensure that they and their descendants would inherit God's blessing?

Dorian and others among the believers in Galatia were perplexed. How were they to reconcile these two conflicting presentations of what God requires? In response to the persuasive appeal of these Jewish missionaries, some of the men and boys in the Galatian churches considered circumcision. Some Gentiles—earlier proselytes to Judaism before accepting Paul's gospel—were adamant in their insistence that Reuben was right: Gentiles are welcome into the people of God only if they submit to circumcision and come under God's holy law.

Dorian resisted this step, however. Through contacts with Jews in various cities to which he traveled on business, he sensed that Reuben and missionaries like him were under fierce pressure from ardent Jewish leaders in Jerusalem. In the volatile political climate of Judea and Galilee, zealous Jews were issuing strong calls for a clean separation between Jews and their Gentile neighbors. Any Jewish travelers associating with Gentiles were suspect. Jews living in the Hellenized cities of Palestine at times caricatured their Gentile neighbors as "fornicating idolaters." The hotheads in Judea seemed at times to taunt the Roman soldiers, always resented as the embodiment of the oppressive might of the empire. A Jewish riot against Rome seemed imminent. The news that Paul and other Jewish evangelists were welcoming Gentiles into the faith community without accepting them as proselytes was angrily rebuked. Dorian realized why Reuben wanted to report to leaders in Jerusalem that he had persuaded Gentiles to be circumcised. This would effectively get the zealots back home off his case.

Dorian had other concerns about requirements laid

down by this second wave of Jewish teachers. Not only were they attempting to persuade Paul's converts to "upgrade" their standing by undergoing circumcision, they were advocating other Jewish practices such as the observance of special days and festivals. And there were indications that more obligations would come later. Reuben and other teachers even intimated that the outpouring of God's Spirit in the Galatians' lives would not continue unless they demonstrated their wholehearted obedience to the Jewish law. Dorian worried about the implications if the Galatian believers submitted to all the rituals and demands.

Some of the teachers hinted that Paul was inconsistent on the matter of circumcision and that he avoided reference to the demands of the law in order to make conversion more palatable.

Dorian was confused. Which teaching were they to trust: Paul's gospel or this proposed upgrade?

Agreement and Confrontation, Appeals and Argument

But when I saw that they were not acting consistently with the truth of the gospel, I said to Cephas before them all, "If you, though a Jew, live like a Gentile and not like a Jew, how can you compel the Gentiles to live like Jews?" We ourselves are Jews by birth and not Gentile sinners; yet we know that a person is justified not by the works of the law but through faith in Jesus Christ. (Galatians 2:14-16)

In our story we have attempted to get in touch with the Christian community in Galatia, where Paul proclaimed the gospel of the crucified and resurrected Christ. Now we try to comprehend his response to what developed there following his departure.

Paul's letter to the Galatians may be the earliest of the

epistles in the New Testament, although this cannot be established with any certainty. The exact circumstances facing the believers in the churches of Galatia is also difficult for later readers of this letter to decipher. There can be no doubt, however, that something in the situation had emerged among these converts and touched off an angry and polemical response from Paul. His anger and defensiveness are already evident in the way that he introduces himself in Galatians 1:1:

> Paul an apostle—sent neither by human commission
> nor from human authorities, but through Jesus Christ
> and God the Father, who raised him from the dead.
> (1:1)

By issuing denials about his dependence on human authorities and by claiming direct authorization from Jesus Christ, Paul sets the stage for his hearers to understand what he considers to be at stake. In his mind the character of the gospel is up for grabs if what he has been hearing from Galatia were to turn out to be true. Departing from his customary pattern he appends a synopsis of the gospel to his normal opening greeting:

> Grace to you and peace from God the Father and our
> Lord Jesus Christ, who gave himself for our sins to
> deliver us from the present evil age, according to the
> will of our God and Father; to whom be glory forever
> and ever. Amen. (1:3-5)

Here Paul articulates his conviction that the gospel of Jesus Christ is the announcement of the invasion of God's grace and peace into the world. A decisive victory has been won over the oppressive power of sin in the present age. Even though "the present evil age" continues, God's liberation has begun! The community of those who through Christ are already rescued from sin's grip can therefore raise their voices, giving glory to God forever.

Paul has been hearing reports about what some upstart missionary teachers are advising converts in Galatia to do. He is incensed. Paul is so distressed that when he begins his letter to the churches of Galatia he dispenses with the conventional friendly gesture of an opening thanksgiving. Instead he immediately declares his perplexity about the tendency of the Galatian believers to waver, and he vents his rage about people who disturb the Galatians with some proposed add-ons to the gospel:

> I am astonished that you are so quickly deserting the one who called you in the grace of Christ and are turning to a different gospel—not that there is another gospel, but there are some who are confusing you and want to pervert the gospel of Christ. (1:6-7)

Paul finds the supplementary demands of circumcision and the observance of the laws of *kashrut* and the celebration of Jewish holy days to be dangerous additions to the truth of the gospel. He even pronounces an anathema (not once but twice!) on those who advocate this troubling addendum to their life-transforming appropriation of the gospel of Jesus Christ (1:8, 9). Who were these people? Likely they were visitors from Jerusalem; like Paul, they were messianic Jews. Some Jews and proselytes from Galatia might have joined these visitors in trying to persuade the converts in Galatia to upgrade their credentials by coming under the Torah.

After venting his feelings in this way, Paul moves into a story-telling mode. He shares with the Galatians a suc-

cession of stories, all of which are intended to speak directly to the situation in the churches of Galatia. As we have
seen in chapter 1, Paul narrates his own life story about
how as Pharisee and former persecutor of the church he
had been transformed through a revelation of God's Son
and been called to be an apostle of Jesus Christ to the
Gentiles (1:13-24). This story serves to undergird Paul's
claim that he is an apostle commissioned directly by God
and not in a mediated fashion by way of the Jerusalem
apostles (1:1, 11-12). Paul's story of call also functions to
commend his version of the gospel to the church.

Agreement in Jerusalem, Confrontation in Antioch

Paul's next two stories are more directly motivated by
his plea to the Galatian churches not to yield to the
demands of the Jewish teachers who had followed him into
Galatia.

First he reiterates the concessions and agreements that
were achieved when Barnabas, Titus, and he had conferred
in Jerusalem with the church leaders there (2:1-10). He
underscores the fact that the Jerusalem apostles had not
compelled Titus to be circumcised, even though he was a
Greek (2:3). The implications for Galatia were clear. No
one claiming to represent the Jerusalem leaders should be
permitted to persuade believers in Galatia that it was necessary for Gentile converts to be circumcised. Even fellow
believers can be deceptive and misleading, Paul warns. In
Jerusalem, he said, there had been false brothers "who
slipped in to spy on the freedom we have in Christ Jesus,
so that they might enslave us" (2:4). He and his partners
had not submitted to them (2:5); neither should the
Galatians yield to the people now surreptitiously enslaving
them by committing them to the rituals of the law.

But Paul's other major point when recalling this event is that James, Cephas (who is also called Peter), and John had all recognized the legitimacy of his ministry of preaching the gospel to Gentiles, here called "the uncircumcised" (2:7). The symbolic gesture of extending the right hand of fellowship had sealed an apostolic agreement:

> And when James and Cephas and John, who were acknowledged pillars, recognized the grace that had been given to me, they gave to Barnabas and me the right hand of fellowship, agreeing that we should go to the Gentiles and they to the circumcised. (2:9)

A cordial agreement had been achieved, affirming both the Jerusalem apostles' ministry among the Jews and the apostolic ministry of Paul and his co-workers among Gentiles. There was one provision, and it had nothing to do with circumcision. Only one request was added, namely, "that we should remember the poor" (2:10). Paul quickly adds that he strongly shares this commitment to reach out to the poor. Indeed he reports in 1 Corinthians 16:1 that he gave the churches in Galatia instructions about how they might participate in offering material assistance to the church in Judea. Again the application to the situation in Galatia is clear. They should not accept any further requirements from itinerant teachers supposedly representing the Jerusalem church.

In 2:11-14 Paul recounts another recent episode. Even though the setting is Antioch, it is obvious that he shares this memory of a painful experience in that city in the hope that the Galatians will get the message. Even friends and co-workers sometimes behave in ways that compromise the gospel.

Paul develops this story in several scenes. He recalls

that Cephas at first associated freely with the Gentiles in the Antioch church, including eating with them (2:11). But Cephas's patterns of relating to the Gentiles changed dramatically when some persons, who were characterized as "the circumcision faction," arrived from James (2:12). At that point Cephas withdrew from intimate fellowship with the Gentile believers. Other Jews, likely including Antioch residents, also separated themselves from their Gentile sisters and brothers in the church. And, Paul adds, even his mission partner, Barnabas, joined in this hypocrisy (2:14).

In the next scene we find Paul nose to nose with Cephas. Paul publicly confronted Cephas because in his view Cephas and the other messianic Jews were not "walking the straight line" of the truth of the gospel (2:14). The opening salvo in this public censure puts the question bluntly. Though he is a Jew himself, Cephas has been living like a Gentile, having relaxed his law observance to the point where he associated and ate with Gentiles. Now under pressure from conservative Jerusalem Jews who insist on strict Torah observance, Cephas has essentially compelled Gentile believers in Antioch to begin living like Jews, something that he was no longer consistently doing himself. Once again, beyond reporting this shouting match in Antioch, Paul wants the people in the Galatian churches to hear how this episode informs their situation. Paul is offering the Galatian believers strong encouragement not to abandon their commitment to the gospel of Jesus Christ in favor of another gospel that requires the observance of certain rituals of the law.

In 2:15-21, Paul summarizes what he said to Peter in Antioch. This recital is again framed primarily for the benefit of the Galatian churches. He knows that there are zealots in Judea and agitators in Galatia clamoring that they need to hold the line and observe the Torah. He also realizes that sometimes friends and co-workers, like

Cephas and Barnabas, are swayed into unacceptable compromises. Confrontation therefore becomes necessary at times. However, after confronting the hypocrisy, Paul articulates the beliefs and theological convictions that function as the basis for their unity and ongoing partnership. "We ourselves are Jews by birth and not Gentile sinners," he says to Cephas (and by association also to the other Jerusalem leaders) (2:15). As the ensuing discussion clearly suggests, this distinction between "Jews by birth" and "Gentile sinners" takes on an ironic tone. Both Jews and Gentiles in Christ are justified on the same basis. Distinctions made along an ethnic divide between Gentiles and Jews cannot continue now that Christ has come. And both Paul and Peter know it! In 2:15-16 Paul begins to spell out a uniting vision centered in what he considers to be their common understanding of the gospel.

The Truth of the Gospel

When Paul confronts Peter in Antioch about the issue of the inclusion of Gentiles into the church, what was at stake (at least insofar as Paul read the situation) was "the truth of the gospel" (2:14; cf. 2:5). But what is this truth?

In 2:16 Paul zeroes in on God's relationship-restoring initiative in Jesus Christ. The Protestant Reformation emphasis on justification by faith has often sidetracked the church into a reading of this passage exclusively in terms of how the individual can be restored into a right relationship with God. But Paul's main agenda here is focused more on the communal than the individual dimension. He seeks to define how Jews and Gentiles (later in 3:28 he adds "slave" and "free," and "male and female") can all be incorporated within God's covenant community on the basis of faith. He wrote to articulate the theological basis

on which people who have been justified by faith can be
restored and maintained in their relationship to each other
within a mutually accepting and loving community. The
agitators claiming the backing of Jerusalem leaders were
planting seeds of discord among people who were all saved
by God's grace through faith.

But whose faith? The prevailing reading of 2:16 intimates that humans are justified by their own faith in Jesus
Christ. Even though this assertion is not entirely untrue, it
leaves out what Paul views as the absolutely crucial prior
step, namely the faithfulness of Jesus Christ even to death
on the cross. Hence the text should read, as it does in the
KJV: "the faith of Jesus Christ" (2:16). Taking the NRSV
rendering of this verse, but substituting the minority marginal reading "the faith of Jesus Christ" (instead of "faith
in Jesus Christ"), we observe that Paul here points to the
pattern of grace initiative and human response. God's initiative in Christ, who was faithful even to his death on the
cross, invites all humanity, regardless of ethnicity or economic status or gender, to respond in faith. This initiative-
response pattern in 2:16 can be viewed chiastically:

> **A** We know that a person is justified
> > **B** not by the works of the law
> > > **C** but through the faith of Jesus Christ
> > > > **D** And we have come to believe in Jesus Christ
> > > **C´** so that we might be justified by the faith of Jesus
> > > Christ
> > **B´** and not by doing the works of the law,
> **A´** because no one will be justified by the works of the law.
> (Galatians 2:16)

The desired outcome of God's salvation initiative manifest
in "the faith of Jesus Christ" (C and C´) is that people might

"believe in Jesus Christ" (D), which is how persons are "justified" (A and A′), "not by the works of the law" (B and B′).

What Paul means by the phrase "works of the law" is contested. Here in Galatians Paul uses this expression to refer not to the Torah as a whole but to the boundary-defining observances of the law, such as circumcision, food laws, and special holy days. These are among the practices that distinguish Jews from Gentiles. In other words, Paul is not combating either works righteousness or legalism, which view good works or obedience to the law as the way of gaining salvation. Rather he here confronts an exclusiveness that seeks to limit God's righteousness to a certain group on the basis of their ethnicity. God graciously transforms diverse people into a unified community, not through their observance of rituals of the law, but by the faith of Jesus Christ, who was obedient even unto death on the cross. The death of Jesus on the cross was an act of self-giving faithfulness that elicits a human, responsive faith.

In 2:17 Paul moves to clarify himself further, recognizing that there are different judgments concerning the nature of sin. From a strict Pharisaic perspective based on the law, persons exercising in Christ their freedom from the law's rituals would be categorized as sinners. This in turn would then implicate Christ, who thereby becomes an agent promoting sinful behavior. Paul vigorously denies that Christ is guilty of serving up a diet of sin:

> But if, in our effort to be justified in Christ, we ourselves have been found to be sinners, is Christ then a servant of sin? Certainly not! (2:17)

Paul presents a markedly different understanding of sin. According to him, whoever imposes the law's rituals on Gentiles who are already in Christ would be the transgressor. Such exclusion is sinful, he insists:

> But if I build up again the very things that I once tore
> down, then I demonstrate that I am a transgressor. (2:18)

Though he is still recalling his speech to Peter, he is obviously pleading with the Galatian believers not to allow anyone
ostensibly representing the Jerusalem leaders to persuade
them to accept these rituals of the law, which essentially erect
again the dividing wall between Jews and Gentiles.

In 2:19-20 Paul cryptically recounts his own personal
story of transformation, again to address the situation
within the Galatian congregation:

> For through the law I died to the law, so that I might
> live to God. I have been crucified with Christ; and it is
> no longer I who live, but it is Christ who lives in me.
> And the life I now live in the flesh I live by the faith of
> the Son of God, who loved me and gave himself for
> me. (substituting the marginal reading instead of "by
> faith in the Son of God")

Paul's zeal for the law as a Pharisee had had such a captivating grip on his life that he was nearly strangled by it. He
needed to give up the law, good though it was, so that he
could become alive to God. He now understands that paradoxically his being alive to God has come as a consequence of having died with Christ (2:19). Paul testifies that
the life he lives now has come to him as a gift from God,
specifically because of the faithfulness of the Son of God
(2:20). Again, the more accurate rendering is given in the
KJV: "The life which I now live in the flesh I live by the
faith of the Son of God, who loved me, and gave himself
for me." The pattern is transparent: divine initiative ("the
faith of the Son of God") evokes the human faith response
("I live by faith").

In 2:21 Paul offers yet one more formulation of the point driven home earlier. He points to Jesus's faith, expressed supremely in his death, and the consequent human acceptance of this gracious gift, as the universally accessible gateway into the community shaped by God's righteousness. Indeed that is how God's grace is expressed:

> I do not nullify the grace of God; for if justification comes through the law, then Christ died for nothing. (2:21)

Personal Experience and the Witness of Scripture

To this point in the letter, Paul has given voice to his disappointment and frustration concerning developments in Galatia. He has also told a series of stories as part of his appeal to the Galatian believers not to accept circumcision for the sake of full inclusion into the people of God. In 3:1–4:31 Paul continues to unpack his arsenal of pastoral arguments. He appeals to the Galatians' experience (3:1-5) and his own story (4:12-20). He revisits some of the Scriptures apparently used by the agitators to buttress their teachings among the Galatian believers (3:6-22; 4:21–5:1). And he offers practical theological commentary defining their status in Christ (3:23–4:11).

In 3:1 Paul openly voices his distress concerning the choices some Galatians were apparently considering: "You foolish Galatians! Who has bewitched you?" (3:1a). Before dealing with particular Scripture texts Paul recalls for them what had happened when they first heard the gospel of the crucified Christ. He remembers that his testimonial about Jesus's death on the cross touched the Galatians deeply: "It was before your eyes that Jesus Christ was publicly exhibited as crucified!" (3:1). This had been a profoundly transforming experience for them. They had felt the dramatic moving of the Spirit of God during those exhilarating days, and they had witnessed amazing miracles and signs.

Rehearsing their experience with God's Spirit, Paul wonders out loud whether the Galatians will now continue along the path on which they began or abandon that path in favor of the alternative vision of the gospel now being presented to them by some rival missionaries. Twice he asks his question (3:2, 5). Sandwiched between these two formulations of his question are his further expressions of anguish about the fact that these new believers seem to be waffling in their commitment (3:3, 4). Paul is obviously quite upset:

> The only thing I want to learn from you is this: Did you receive the Spirit by doing the works of the law or by believing what you heard? Are you so foolish? Having started with the Spirit, are you now ending with the flesh? Did you experience so much for nothing?—if it really was for nothing. Well then, does God supply you with the Spirit and work miracles among you by your doing the works of the law, or by your believing what you heard? (3:2-5)

In 3:2 and 3:5 Paul pointedly asks the believers in Galatia how they received the Spirit. He frames two alternatives, the first of which was already mentioned in 2:16: by observing "the works of the law," namely those dimensions of Jewish law observance now being promoted by the agitators, especially circumcision. Obviously he anticipates that the Galatians will truthfully answer: "No! God did not supply the Spirit and work miracles among us because we performed the works of the law." Paul envisions that they will admit that the truth lies elsewhere: God poured out the Spirit in their midst when they heard the story of the crucified Christ. That was the message that had elicited their faith. He hopes that remembering how their life in Christ and their experience of the Holy Spirit began will put the brakes on the apparent readiness of some believers in Galatia to swap such powerful Spirit-empowerment for the paltry guarantees inherent in ritual law observance.

In 3:6-9 Paul launches a creative rereading of several strategic Scriptures, all interpreted in light of both his own encounter with the crucified and risen Christ and the Galatians' experience of the crucified Christ and God's outpoured Spirit. The rival Jewish teachers in their appeals to the Galatians may also have utilized the same or related stories from Scripture. We have already seen how Paul draws on the narratives about Abraham and Sarah to underscore his conviction that God is a God of both Jews and Gentiles (chapter 4; see especially "Heirs of Abraham in Corinth and Galatia").

In 3:6 Paul highlights Abraham's righteousness, which is based on his trust in God's promises (Genesis 15:6). He notes in 3:7 that this inheritance is available to all who believe, including Gentiles: "those who believe are the descendants of Abraham." Paul refers to God's promise of blessing in Genesis 12:1-3 as the gospel preached beforehand: God's blessing is potentially available to all people through the descendants of Abraham and Sarah (3:8). Wishing to underscore his main point (descendants of Abraham are those who believe, 3:7), he repeats himself in 3:9: "For this reason, those who believe are blessed with Abraham who believed."

Paul's interpretive moves when recalling these Scriptures reflect the priority that he gives to his and the Galatians' revelatory experiences of Christ and the Spirit. As Richard Hays puts it:

The unwritten logic of Paul's claim must be something
like this: (a) Scripture promises that Gentiles will be
blessed in Abraham. (b) Gentile Christian communities,
who—like Abraham—have come to believe in Israel's
God apart from the Sinai Torah, have experienced the
blessing of the Spirit, palpably present in their midst.
(c) Therefore, this experienced Spirit must be the promised blessing of which the Scripture speaks. (1989:110)

Having pondered God's promise of blessing, Paul turns
rather abruptly to the theme of God's curse. In 3:10 he
invokes a curse from Deuteronomy 27:26 on all who rely
on observing the works of the law (cf. also his earlier references to works of the law in 2:16; 3:2, 5):

For all who rely on the works of the law are under a
curse; for it is written, "Cursed is everyone who does
not observe and obey all the things written in the book
of the law." (Galatians 3:10)

Sometimes Paul's use of Deuteronomy 27:26 here is
viewed as the citation of a proof text, with no regard for
its context. Actually he appears to have in mind a contextual deuteronomic understanding of the consequences of
unfaithfulness to the Torah. The covenant established by
God and affirmed by the people of Israel specified that disobedience would bring a curse upon them (Deuteronomy
27:11-26). The book of the law warns that failure to keep
the covenant stipulations would result in the nation's exile
(29:19-28). Indeed Deuteronomy as a whole functions as a
witness against Israel when she comes under God's judgment for her idolatry and is taken into exile among the
nations (31:16-22). From this curse, the curse of exile, Paul
says, God has through Christ now provided redemption.

He quotes Deuteronomy 21:23, a text about the curse that falls on a criminal executed and publicly exposed through being hanged on a tree. The corpse of such a criminal was to be buried on the same day, lest the land be defiled. Clearly Paul evokes the memory of Jesus's crucifixion. On a Roman executioner's cross, Jesus took upon himself the brunt of this curse articulated in Deuteronomy:

> Christ redeemed us from the curse of the law by becoming a curse for us—for it is written, "Cursed is everyone who hangs on a tree"—in order that in Christ Jesus the blessing of Abraham might come to the Gentiles, so that we might receive the promise of the Spirit through faith. (3:13-14)

Through Christ's death, therefore, the curse on Israel ("for us" in 3:13 understood as Paul and his fellow Jews) has been defused. The outcome of this transaction is that in Christ the blessing promised through Abraham has potentially become a reality for all (with "we" in 3:14 understood as Jews and Gentiles together in Christ through faith).

Between the two deuteronomic curse citations (3:10, 14) Paul replays his earlier theme: justification is by faith, not by works of the law (2:16; 3:2, 5). In 3:11-12 he cites two more scriptural texts. From Habakkuk 2:4 he quotes God's reply after the prophet laments that pagans seem to be prevailing over God's people: "The one who is righteous will live by faith" (3:11b). This reassurance grounds what Paul declares as self-evident: "No one is justified before God by the law" (3:11a). The law apart from its context within God's gracious covenant does not deliver life. Paul goes on to say, with the aid of Leviticus 18:5, that the law outside of the initiative of God's grace and a responsive faith cannot produce the life that the rival missionaries claim is available through it:

> But the law does not rest on faith; on the contrary,
> "Whoever does the works of the law will live by
> them." (3:12)

In the dense exegetical argument in 3:10-14, therefore, Paul wants to hammer home his rejection of the premises underlying the version of the gospel promoted by the agitators. He insists that the gospel was already proclaimed in the promise of blessing on all nations through Abraham and Sarah and their descendants (3:6; Genesis 12:1-3). This gospel unambiguously summons those who have felt God's liberating grace through Christ's faithfulness and have experienced the empowering Spirit to continue to trust God. Taking on circumcision and Torah observance would be to join those still under the curse of exile rather than to continue in the blessing of liberation now opened up for all.

In a series of further scriptural arguments (3:15-18), Paul continues to plead with the Galatians. He wants them to understand that in Christ, the singular "seed" or descendant of Abraham and Sarah, all who believe will inherit the promise (3:16). The promise of the blessing of Gentiles, now fulfilled in those who are in Christ, cannot be nullified by the Sinai covenant, which came 430 years later (3:17; cf. Exodus 12:40-41). The law has a positive role during the interim period while awaiting Abraham's promised offspring (this includes Christ himself, 3:16, and those who are in Christ, 3:29), but the inheritance comes not by the law but by the promise (3:18).

In 3:19 Paul enunciates the provisional character of the law. He includes an obscure comment about the law's origins through an intermediary. What is more transparent is that here he introduces an image on which he lingers for a

while: The law is a temporary trustee with interim custodial and disciplinarian functions. He also articulates clearly that the law in itself cannot bring life (3:21). In 3:22
Paul recapitulates:

> But the scripture has imprisoned all things under the
> power of sin, so that what was promised through the
> faith of Jesus Christ might be given to those who
> believe. (3:22, substituting the NRSV marginal reading
> instead of "faith in Jesus Christ")

Paul shares both good news and bad news. The bad news:
Sin is an occupying power that continues to take captives,
and the law is helpless to liberate those who are captivated by sin's power. The good news: God's promised blessing
has now come to fruition. Through the faithfulness of
Jesus Christ (echoing the KJV reading, "faith of Jesus
Christ," as given above) God has brought about liberation
from the captivating power of sin to all who believe (this
includes "faith in Christ").

From Slave to Heir

At 3:23 Paul appears to take a few steps back from particular Scripture texts and themes to provide an overarching view. He launches a series of theological reflections
about the status of believers now that Christ has come.

It is important to highlight the fact that in 3:22 Paul
depicts sin as a hostage-taking and dominating power. Sin
is a power that desires to exercise dominion over all things.
In 3:23–4:11, where Paul utilizes the metaphors of minors
coming of age (3:23-29), slaves becoming heirs (4:1-3), and
orphans being adopted into the family (4:4-7), he has in
mind this oppressive power of sin. When he looks for
metaphors to describe liberation from sin as the cosmic

tyrant, he moves quite naturally to themes of enslavement and freedom. As Sylvia Keesmaat has shown, motifs from the history of Israel, in particular slavery and exodus, and exile and restoration, were on Paul's mind. When he narrates the still unfolding story of God's invasion of grace through Christ into the arena of sin's tyranny in the world he instinctively employs images from the story of Israel, her enslavement, and her liberation (Keesmaat, 1996:133-68).

In 3:23-29 Paul refers to the coming of Christ as an event that divides time into two epochs: "before faith came" (3:23) and "now that faith has come" (3:25). This "coming of faith" is correlated with the coming of Christ (3:24). This "before" and "after" can be visualized by laying out the text as follows:

> Now *before faith came*, we were imprisoned and
>   guarded under the law
>   until faith would be revealed.
> Therefore the law was our disciplinarian *until Christ came*,
>   so that we might be justified by faith.
> But *now that faith has come*, we are no longer subject
>   to a disciplinarian,
>   for in Christ Jesus you are all children of God
>   through faith. (3:23-26; emphasis added)

Paul is taking the long view. He recognizes Jesus's life, his faithfulness unto death on the cross, and his vindicating resurrection from the dead, as one cosmic moment ushering in a new age. The faith of Jesus Christ, which elicits human faith in response (cf. 2:16), is presented as that epoch-creating invasion of grace when the custodial function of the law can cease. God has opened the way for women and men, Jews and Greeks, and slaves and free people to participate in the way of Christ, as part of the community whose members are baptized into Christ:

> As many of you as were baptized into Christ have
> clothed yourselves with Christ. There is no longer Jew
> or Greek, there is no longer slave or free, there is no
> longer male and female; for all of you are one in Christ
> Jesus. (3:27-28)

(This baptismal confession is discussed further in chapter
11.)

In 4:1-11 Paul elaborates on the transformative impact
of the coming of Christ. The keynote is sounded in 4:4-6.
He narrates the "big picture" of the sending of God's Son
into the world as a human child born during the jurisdiction of the law, thereby opening up for Gentiles the
prospect of being adopted into the family. He also recalls
some of the intimate memories of the Galatians' dynamic
experience of the infusion of God's Spirit into their midst.
In their worship they had been moved by the Spirit of God's
Son to cry out to God in ways that echo Jesus's own prayer
to God (cf. Mark 14:36). Paul's narrative here unveils both
the coming of redemption through Christ and the
Galatians' experience of their adoption into God's family:

> But when the fullness of time had come, God sent his
> Son, born of a woman, born under the law, in order to
> redeem those who were under the law, so that we
> might receive adoption as children. And because you
> are children, God has sent the Spirit of his Son into
> our hearts, crying, "Abba! Father!" (4:4-6)

Surrounding his telling of this salvation story and the
Galatians' appropriation of it, Paul has deployed a series
of overlapping vivid word pictures: minors receive their
inheritance; a slave is redeemed and becomes a child and
heir. Each metaphor would have evoked associations for
the Galatians, especially for the slaves, or for recently freed

slaves. Each metaphor also dramatizes how Christ brings about a distinct division between "before" and "after":

Before Christ	After Christ
Minors remain under guardians and trustees until the date set by the father. (4:1-2)	"We might receive adoption as children." (4:5)
"While we were minors, we were enslaved to the elemental spirits of the world." (4:3)	"You are no longer a slave but a child, and if a child then also an heir, through God." (4:7)

It is evident in what follows in 4:8-11 that once again Paul's main intention is to appeal to the Galatians. The transformational Christ event not only has implications for the transition from one era to another in God's dealings with humanity. There also needs to be a distinct "before" and "after" in the individual and communal experience of believers in Galatia. Paul describes the nature of their "before" and "after" and he implores them not to slip back into what had characterized them as pagans and idol worshipers before their liberating experience in Christ:

Before	After
"Formerly, when you did not know God, you were enslaved to beings that by nature are not gods." (4:8)	"Now, however, that you have come to know God, or rather to be known by God, how can you turn back to the weak and beggarly elemental spirits? How can you want to be enslaved to them again?" (4:9)

When Paul implores the Galatians not to go back into their slavery again, he may have in mind the story of the grumbling Israelites in the wilderness who longed to go back to the basic pleasures they once enjoyed even while they were still captives in Egypt. This sequence (enslavement, liberation, and the risk of a return to bondage) intimates that Paul views the coming of Christ as God's renewed restorative initiative, a new exodus, a climactic restoration from exile. Strikingly, however, as he seeks to show in his allegory concerning Hagar and Sarah and their sons (4:21-31), the law given at Sinai turns out also to enslave even the people whose ancestors had been freed from slavery. The slave Hagar gets associated with Mount Sinai and present-day Jerusalem, likely referring to the missionaries acting in the name of the Jerusalem church, and Sarah is linked with the freedom of a new Jerusalem. (See the discussion of this allegory in chapter 4.)

Which enslavement does Paul have in mind? Gathering together all of his references in Galatians 3 and 4 to the forces that have held sway over Israel as God's historic people and over humanity in general, we realize that in Paul's view God's dramatic new rescue initiative in Christ became necessary because of several interlocking kinds of captivity:

> All who rely on works of the law are *under the curse of the law.* (3:10, 13)
> Scripture consigns all things *under sin.* (3:22)
> Israel was *under the law.* (3:23; 4:5)
> The law put them *under a disciplinarian.* (3:24-25)
> So that even heirs are *under guardians and trustees.* (4:2)
> And all are *under the elemental spirits of the world.* (4:3, 9)

The good news of the gospel is that in Christ God has redeemed humanity from all these forms of bondage.

Deliverance from the powers of the present evil age (cf. 1:4) has come by means of an invasion of God's grace through Christ.

After having employed multiple metaphors in his theological elaboration of the liberation accomplished through Christ, Paul becomes intensely personal again in 4:10-20. Commenting that the Galatians are "observing special days, and months, and seasons, and years" (4:10, likely a reference to the Sabbath and Jewish festivals), he laments that his labors among them might turn out to have been in vain (4:11). He addresses them as "brothers and sisters" (4:12) and as "my little children" (4:19). He reminisces about how warmly he had been received in Galatia during his initial visit (4:12-15). He hurls broadsides at the opposition (4:17-18) and he tenderly chides his friends (4:19-20).

Clearly this pastor's feelings for the Galatian congregation run deep. As later readers of this letter, we'll take this opportunity to take a break. In chapter 9, we'll resume our visit to Galatia and listen further to what Paul has to say to the Galatian believers. As we will see, in the continuation of this pastoral letter he addresses the question, "Having been freed by an invasion of God's grace through Christ, how are believers to live?"

Justification by Faith and Other Metaphors of Salvation

In Galatians Paul wrangles with unnamed messianic Jewish teachers who promote an understanding of salvation that he finds profoundly troubling. Supported by some local Jews and proselytes these visitors from Jerusalem were trying to persuade the converts in Galatia to upgrade their credentials by coming under the Torah.

These teachers agree with Paul that God has acted in Christ to offer redemption. However, as we have seen, Paul distinguishes himself sharply concerning the necessity for Gentiles to observe the Torah. Underlying this difference, as he sees it, is a profound dispute about the nature of salvation and about how the redeemed shall live.

As we widen our inquiry by looking at how he treats these themes in his other letters we soon become aware of the vastness of this terrain. Given the pivotal significance of the revelation of the crucified and risen Christ to him it is not surprising that liberation through Christ plays such a central role in Paul's pastoral theology.

We begin by reflecting on the theme of God's righteousness and how it is appropriated through faith. We follow by exploring God's plan of salvation, noting the dominant images and metaphors that Paul employs to evoke and enliven human understanding.

God's Righteousness, and Faith

In Romans 1:16-17 and 3:21-26 Paul articulates thesis statements that summarize his understanding of the gospel. These summaries state succinctly what he views as foundational for the churches in Rome. Both emphasize God's righteousness, a theme that is not directly explicated in Galatians, although its underlying dynamic is there also.

In Romans 1:16-17 Paul communicates his comprehension of that gospel which he feels compelled to proclaim:

> For I am not ashamed of the gospel; it is the power of God for salvation to everyone who has faith, to the Jew first and also to the Greek. For in it the righteousness of God is revealed through faith for faith; as it is written, "The one who is righteous will live by faith." (Romans 1:16-17)

Paul makes two parallel claims about that gospel of which he is unashamed. First, the gospel is God's dynamic power moving things toward salvation. Salvation is viewed as still future, although those who trust God are granted present assurance about inheriting it (1:16). Second, the gospel reveals God's righteousness (1:17).

What does Paul mean by the expression "the righteousness of God"? This phrase also occurs three times in Romans 3:21-26, as well as in Romans 10:3, Philippians 3:9, and 2 Corinthians 5:21. A study of its biblical roots in the Septuagint suggests that he has in mind God's faithfulness to the covenant established with the people Israel. This theme is especially prominent in those divine oracles in Isaiah that are addressed to the exiles. Isaiah 51:5, here cited from the NIV, is a good example:

> My righteousness draws near speedily, my salvation is
> on the way, and my arm will bring justice to the
> nations. The islands will look to me and wait in hope
> for my arm. (Isaiah 51:5)

When Paul speaks about "the righteousness of God" he signals both what God is and what God does. It is God's character to be righteous and just. God also acts justly, actively intervening in rescuing the covenant people in their distress. Such rectifying activity also vindicates God, who is thereby shown to be faithful to the covenant established in the past. Surely God will also be true to promises now being made regarding future salvation. Inherent in the phrase "the righteousness of God," therefore, is confidence in the reliability of God. God keeps covenant promises.

Also included in the succinct articulation of the meaning of the gospel in 1:16-17 are Paul's announcements concerning how people can experience the gospel, as God's power and God's covenant faithfulness. In addition to God's reliability, Paul underscores God's moral integrity in offering salvation to all. The power of God toward salvation is available to all, both Jews and Greeks, through faith (1:16). Unfortunately the translation "to everyone who has faith" conveys the impression that the acceptance of the gospel primarily involves mental assent. A better rendering would be to communicate that the human response elicited by God's power and righteousness is dynamic trust. In 1:17 Paul clarifies himself, although he does so in a rather enigmatic expression: "The righteousness of God is revealed through faith for faith." To explain himself he includes a citation from Habakkuk 2:4: "The one who is righteous will live by faith."

In Habakkuk 1–2 Paul finds a clear instance in which the prophet challenges God to act by vindicating the beleaguered exiles against their Babylonian oppressors. Will God be true to covenant assurances of deliverance and protection? In 2:4 we hear the divine reply, which Paul quotes both here and in Galatians 3:11: "The righteous live by their faith" (Habakkuk 2:4).

It is usually assumed that in his three uses of the noun *faith* in Romans 1:16-17 Paul is speaking about human faith as the magic key which opens up the possibility for humans to be declared righteous by God. This interpretive assumption neglects to recognize adequately that it is the power of God that initiates the possibility of human responsive faith (1:16). "The one who is righteous," the one who "will live by faith" (1:17), is first of all Jesus the Messiah, whose faith and trust in God moved him in faithfulness and obedience to die on the cross. God vindicated him by raising him back to life. This righteous one now lives. By identification with Jesus in his faithfulness even unto death on the cross, believers also will live. Life and salvation come not through human effort (by having enough faith) but by God's gracious initiative through Christ. In the compound phrase "through faith for faith" in 1:16, the first phrase ("through faith") testifies to God's faithfulness manifest in Jesus's trust in God even to the point of his death on the cross. The second phrase ("for faith") acknowledges the responsive character of the faith of those to whom God's salvation in Christ has become known.

In Romans 3:21-26 Paul elaborates on his thesis-like summary in 1:16-17. Here he prominently features the theme of "the righteousness of God" (3:21, 22, 25). First he describes how God's justice correlates with the law and the prophets: the law and the prophets testify concerning God's righteousness, although it has been made known apart from the law:

> But now, apart from law, the righteousness of God has
> been disclosed, and is attested by the law and the
> prophets. (Romans 3:21)

Next Paul explicates how God's righteousness has been made known: "the righteousness of God through the faith of Jesus Christ for all who believe" (3:22). This wording reflects the NRSV marginal reading "faith of Jesus Christ," as also in KJV, rather than "faith in Jesus Christ," to underscore the fact that the disclosure of God's righteousness is by divine initiative not by human believing, which is always a response to what God has done.

In his next assertion (3:22b-25a) Paul underlines the gift character of the manifestation of God's righteousness. The universality of sin stresses human helplessness apart from God's saving grace. What God has done through the death of Jesus Christ on the cross is narrated using redemption language and sacrificial imagery:

> For there is no distinction, since all have sinned and fall short of the glory of God; they are now justified by his grace as a gift, through the redemption that is in Christ Jesus, whom God put forward as a sacrifice of atonement by his blood, effective through faith. (3:22b-25a)

The redemption and sacrifice metaphors of salvation are discussed below. For now we note only that the two phrases "through faith" and "by his blood" in 3:25 both refer to Jesus's obedience unto death on the cross, whereby God has provided redemption, an atoning sacrifice for sin. The NRSV addition of the word *effective* is unnecessary; it reflects the presumption that Paul has human faith in mind. His concern here is rather to underline God's initiative: "whom God put forward." Similarly the NIV rendering ("through faith in his blood") is misleading, even though it retains the original word order, since it implies a magical saving quality to Jesus's blood itself rather than to his obedient death by crucifixion.

As he brings this thesis statement to a conclusion Paul summarizes the implications of the redemption made known in Christ's death on the cross. God's vindicating justice has thereby been demonstrated for the past and in the present, and it has been guaranteed for the future:

> He did this to show his righteousness, because in his divine forbearance he had passed over the sins previously committed; it was to prove at the present time that he himself is righteous and that he justifies the one who has faith in Jesus. (3:25b-26)

The final clause in 3:26 as rendered by the NRSV again deserves some correction. Paul affirms the righteous character of God, as proven "at the present time" (cf. in 3:21 the "now" of God's climactic revelation in Jesus Christ). But Paul also declares the future promise of God's vindication of (literally) "the one who is of the faith of Jesus." Those who participate in the faithfulness of Jesus are assured of salvation.

We recapitulate briefly Paul's view of God's righteousness and the nature of faith. God's justice has been climactically disclosed to the world by the faith of Jesus Christ. Not human faith in Jesus Christ but the faithfulness of Jesus Christ opens the vista of God's righteousness. And God's righteousness constitutes the vindicating power which brings justice and sets things right. In trust and obedience Jesus went to the cross. Yet God vindicated Jesus by raising him from the dead. Human faith is therefore a trusting and grateful obedient response to this stunning manifestation of God's redemptive justice made known in Jesus Christ.

God's Plan of Salvation

The clash between Paul and the Jewish teachers who were active in Galatia following his initial visit has roots in two competing narratives. Scholar J. Louis Martyn identifies these as forensic and cosmological. Both of these describe what has gone wrong and what God has done to remedy the problem. The forensic narrative features law court imagery, the other employs cosmic warfare images. This chart compares the two competing views (quoted from Martyn, 1997b:298-9):

The Forensic View	The Cosmological View
Things have gone wrong because human beings have willfully rejected God, thereby bringing death and the corruption and perversion of the world. Given this self-caused plight, God has graciously provided the cursing and blessing Law as the remedy, thus placing before human beings the Two Ways, the way of death and the way of life. Human beings are individually accountable before the bar of the Judge. But by one's own decision, one can accept God's law, repent of one's sins, receive nomistic forgiveness, and be assured of eternal life. For at the last judgment, the deserved sentence of death will be reversed for those who choose the path of Law observance, whereas that sentence will be permanently confirmed for those who do not.	Anti-God powers have managed to commence their own rule over the world, leading human beings into idolatry and thus into slavery, producing a wrong situation that was not intended by God and that will not be long tolerated by him. For in his own time, God will inaugurate a victorious and liberating apocalyptic war against these evil powers, delivering his elect from their grips and thus making right that which has gone wrong because of the powers' malignant machinations.

Martyn claims that the teachers, whom Paul regards as agitators (Galatians 1:7), advocate a forensic view, whereas Paul promotes a cosmological view. In Galatians this may be the case. However, elsewhere in Paul's writings he draws on dimensions of both of these narratives. To be sure, he continues to feature the convulsion that occurred within the cosmos through the invasion of God's saving grace in Christ. And, while he affirms in some ways the law's continuing validity in Christ, he nowhere gives it the prominence described in the forensic scenario.

Paul in fact draws on a significant variety of metaphors as windows into God's salvation initiative through Jesus Christ. Each of these metaphors resonates with the life experiences of the people whom Paul addresses in his letters. None of these metaphors alone is adequate to communicate all that needs to be said. Human comprehension fails to grasp fully the depth of God's gracious salvation through Jesus Christ.

This chart illustrates the variety of metaphors and images that Paul employs. For each image we identify briefly the biblical roots and/or the Greco-Roman framework within which it comes to life. In the final column we quote a representative text and in most cases cite references to other texts featuring similar occurrences of this metaphor.

Image or Metaphor	Biblical and/or Greco-Roman Background	Representative Text, Plus Other References
Warfare, Liberation	Liberation of Hebrew slaves from Egypt in the exodus. A victorious general marches prisoners of war in a triumphal parade.	"And having disarmed the powers and authorities, he made a public spectacle of them, triumphing over them by the cross." (Colossians 2:15, NIV) Ephesians 1:19-22
Vicarious suffering	The Servant Songs of Isaiah, especially Isaiah 52:13–53:12	"For God has destined us not for wrath but for obtaining salvation through our Lord Jesus Christ, who died for us, so that whether we are awake or asleep we may live with him." (1 Thessalonians 5:9-10) Galatians 1:4; Romans 5:6, 8
Sacrifice	Cultic sacrifice, including sin offering; especially the Day of Atonement rituals (Leviticus 16) and Passover (Exodus 12).	"For our paschal lamb, Christ, has been sacrificed." (1 Corinthians 5:7) Romans 3:25; 8:3; 2 Corinthians 5:21

Image or Metaphor	Biblical and/or Greco-Roman Background	Representative Text, Plus Other References
Expiation	A ritual of cleansing from impurities or contamination.	"They are justified by his grace as a gift, through the redemption which is in Christ Jesus, whom God put forward as an expiation by his blood." (Romans 3:24-25, RSV)
Redemption	The manumission of slaves through payment of ransom or other ways.	"You were bought with a price; do not become slaves of human masters." (1 Corinthians 7:23) 1 Corinthians 6:20; Galatians 3:13; 4:5; Romans 3:24
Reconciliation	The restoration of relationships between estranged parties.	"And might reconcile both groups to God in one body through the cross, thus putting to death that hostility through it." (Ephesians 2:16) Romans 5:10-11; 2 Corinthians 5:18-20
Justification	The plaintiff and defendant appear before the judge in a court of law. Who will be declared in the right?	"Therefore, since we are justified by faith, we have peace with God through our Lord Jesus Christ." (Romans 5:1) Galatians 2:15-16
Adoption	A person is received as a member into a new family through a legal transfer and mutual acceptance of responsibilities.	"For you did not receive a spirit of slavery to fall back into fear, but you have received a spirit of adoption. When we cry, "Abba! Father!" it is that very Spirit bearing witness with our spirit that we are children of God." (Romans 8:15-16) Galatians 4:5; Ephesians 1:5; Romans 8:23

A chart like this is surely inadequate to interpret what each of these biblical and Greco-Roman word pictures would have conveyed to recipients of Paul's first-century pastoral letters. As already indicated, each individual metaphor by itself cannot communicate sufficiently the still unfolding story of God's future salvation already announced in Jesus Christ. Yet the texts cited above, plus many others, signal clearly Paul's passionate efforts through metaphorical speech to impart the glorious good news in authentic and gripping ways.

One prominent cluster of Paul's images still missing in this chart centers on the rhetoric of participation with Christ. We feature the image of participation as we continue to explore Paul's letter to Galatians in the next chapter.

9

PARTICIPATING WITH CHRIST

The narrative that opened our initial exposure to life in Galatia featured a young couple with two sons, ages 8 and 4. We told the story in chapter 8 from the perspective of Dorian. This time we feature his wife, Felicia. As a young mother Felicia had been baptized as an expression of her commitment to Christ and her pledge of active participation in the church. But what happens next?

Our sources for this installment of the ongoing story continue to be similar to what we utilized earlier. These include Paul's recollection of what happened among the Galatians when they first heard the gospel of the crucified Christ: Galatians 3:1-5; 4:6-7. We also note hints in 4:12-20 about what has been happening in Galatia since Paul's departure. Especially important for the narrative below are a few indicators in 5:13–6:10 that a contentious and divisive spirit has surfaced among the Galatian believers.

After experiencing the liberating power of the gospel, how is the gospel dynamic sustained in an ongoing way? It's great to be free, but where are the guidelines that ensure faithfulness? Where is the power for holy living? In Galatia these and related questions were apparently raised by the new believers. The fervent counsel of visiting Jewish missionaries, who taught that the Torah contains the remedy, only deepened the urgency of these questions.

A STORY: There Ought to Be a Law!

Like most parents, Felicia and Dorian wanted their children to grow up in a wholesome environment and to find clear direction and purpose for their lives. Occasionally when their travel on business became a family outing they would visit Jewish synagogues, both for the Sabbath-day readings and prayers and for the social activities that often followed. Felicia found such gatherings uplifting, especially because of the edifying teaching and fellowship, the family feeling, and the sense of being rooted in a rich heritage. She welcomed this kind of extension of the home as a positive influence on their children.

When the Jewish evangelist Paul started preaching in their region, Felicia and her husband eagerly embraced the gospel of Jesus Christ, crucified and raised. They had been hungry for deeper meaning in their lives, and in Christ and the community of converts they found it. There was something contagiously exciting about those early days, when the Spirit of God worked extraordinary miracles and signs in their midst. Felicia experienced an exhilarating feeling of freedom. No longer did they need to fear the enslaving power of fate and fortune. Nor did they have to constantly guard against the anger of gods and goddesses. Through Christ they were set free from superstitions and bondage to these powers. The presence of the Holy Spirit in their gatherings provided a tangible guarantee that indeed this was "for real."

After some time had passed, however, Felicia experienced nagging doubts. Even before a few Jerusalem-based teachers arrived in Galatia she wondered whether their freedom in Christ wasn't a bit overrated. Felicia found something quite reassuring in structure, guidelines, and rules. Paul had issued some warnings about certain kinds of behavior that would prohibit participation within the future kingdom of God, but he offered few concrete guidelines for living.

Unlike her husband, Felicia was receptive to what the other Jewish teachers had to say. When these teachers advocated that their sons undergo circumcision, Felicia was inclined to comply. Through this ritual her boys could formally take their place in the rich historical and ethical heritage that shaped the men of the synagogues they had visited previously. What could be better for them as a couple and for their boys? And surely God would honor such obedience by continuing to bless them through the pouring out of the Spirit into their family and their faith community.

There were additional reasons to consider what these teachers from Jerusalem had to say. Several church members were caught up in unhealthy wrangling, as well as some tiresome sniping, competition, and jealousy. A few people had fallen into self-indulgence. Felicia had even heard rumors of sexual immorality among recent converts. How tempting it was after receiving salvation in Christ and experiencing the transforming power of God's Spirit to slip back into previous patterns of immoral conduct. Those people within the church who knew that these things were happening seemed unable to restore upright living.

Felicia suspected that the ritual observances of the law, especially circumcision and the regular cycle of daily, weekly, monthly, and annual festivals, would provide the sense of identity and the moral guidance they sorely needed. If they had a law to guide the good folks and a clear standard for judging the wicked, internal dissension, quarrels, and factions would no longer disrupt the community.

"There ought to be a law," Felicia thought. Surely they would all be more secure about their future if someone would "lay down the law" in their congregation. Paul had not seemed ready to do so before he left. The teachers from Jerusalem just might have the answers that they were looking for.

The Fruit of the Spirit and the Law of Christ

> For through the Spirit, by faith, we eagerly wait for the hope of righteousness. For in Christ Jesus neither circumcision nor uncircumcision counts for anything; the only thing that counts is faith working through love. (Galatians 5:5-6)

We continue to identify with the Galatian churches as they ponder the competing visions presented by Paul and some later Jewish teachers. As we have seen, he reacts angrily to the way rival teachers have disturbed the new believers in Galatia by pressuring them to upgrade their spiritual status through circumcision. He relentlessly denounces this recommended addendum. Righteousness is not achieved through ritualistic law observance but rather through trust in God as made known in the Messiah Jesus, whose faithfulness was dramatically manifest in his death on the cross. On this understanding of what God has done in Christ, Paul claims to have the full agreement of the Jerusalem leaders. Accordingly the Galatian believers dare not be swayed by the divergent teachings of those who claim to be representing the apostles in Jerusalem.

As we listen further we sense however that more is at stake for the Galatian converts than a determination of how they become righteous through Christ and whether they need to be circumcised in order to be fully incorporated into the people of God. They also wonder what they need to do to continue to live in obedience. Beyond entry into life in Christ and the church is the matter of maintaining a life of faithfulness. Is it enough to celebrate the freedom that comes from being adopted as God's children through Christ? Where might one discover guidance for living? Where might one find the power to be righteous? Might there be a need for law, perhaps the law of Christ?

Paul's letter to the Galatians is occasioned primarily by the fact that some Jewish teachers have been infiltrating the Galatian congregations with an alternative vision of the gospel. In the first half of his letter, Paul gives voice to his feelings of anger and frustration, he appeals to both the Galatians' experiences and his own, he discusses various Scripture texts, and he engages in theological reflection. Already in the opening salutation Paul signals the major theme of his gospel: "Christ gave himself for our sins to deliver us from the present evil age" (Galatians 1:4). Deeply perplexed by the potential risk that some Galatian believers would default, he combats these disturbing teachings, emphasizes both his agreement with and his independence from the Jerusalem church leaders, and implores the Galatian believers not to submit to the persuasive arguments of the rival teachers.

Participation in Christ by the Power of the Spirit

Birthing and family images appear to have been on Paul's mind when he thought about how the uncircumcised Gentile believers in Galatia fit into God's scheme of things. As we have seen, in Galatians 4:1-7 Paul metaphorically portrays the coming of Christ in the fullness of time as the liberating moment when minor children come of age and slaves are adopted as children and heirs. His allegorical interpretation of the Genesis stories about Hagar and Sarah and their sons (4:21-31) concludes with a summarizing declaration: "So then, friends, we are children not of the slave but of the free woman" (4:31). Clearly Paul longs for the believers in Galatia to identify themselves as descendants of Sarah; they should associate with the spiritual Jerusalem rather than the earthly one. Sarah is the barren woman who miraculously bears many children (4:27, citing Isaiah 54:1). Among these children of promise who are born of the Spirit are the brothers and sisters in Christ in Galatia (4:28-29).

In 4:12-20, when Paul reminisces about his initial time in Galatia, he employs a striking birthing metaphor. He pictures himself as a pregnant woman in the throes of giving birth:

> My little children, for whom I am again in the pain of childbirth until Christ is formed in you. (4:19)

We may be bewildered about how Paul envisions the physiology here but evidently his eagerness to bring the church to maturity in Christ precipitates his "birth pangs." Remarkably he longs for the Galatian congregations also to become pregnant, with Christ himself being formed anew within them.

Paul's rather forced use of birthing images in 4:19 originates within what E. P. Sanders labels "participationist eschatology" (1977:549). A classic articulation of this perspective is found in Paul's summary of his speech to Peter at Antioch:

> I have been crucified with Christ; and it is no longer I who live, but it is Christ who lives in me. And the life I now live in the flesh I live by faith in the Son of God, who loved me and gave himself for me. (Galatians 2:19b-20)

Paul here employs a representative "I" to speak for Peter and himself and by extension also for all who align themselves by faith and commitment with God's in-breaking into the world through the faithful Christ. Jesus's death is not only an event back then that occurred on a cross outside the walls of Jerusalem. His self-giving faithfulness, expressed climactically in his death by crucifixion and his subsequent vindicating resurrection, is replicated in the lives of individual believers and in the ongoing life of the faith community.

This notion of participation with Christ also helps to explain Paul's exegesis of the references in Genesis (12:2-3; 15:5; 17:8) to Abraham's "seed" (NRSV: "offspring") both as singular, referring to Christ (3:16), and as plural or collective, pertaining to the church as a corporate body (3:29). Through participation in Christ, who is the promised descendant of Abraham and Sarah, the Galatians are also invited to view themselves as heirs of that same promise. Whether Jew or Greek, slave or free, male or female, individual believers are incorporated through baptism into Christ and into the community of faith:

> As many of you as were baptized into Christ have clothed yourselves with Christ. There is no longer Jew or Greek, there is no longer slave or free, there is no longer male and female; for all of you are one in Christ Jesus. (3:27-28)

The church as a corporate body participates in the crucifixion death and the resurrection life of Jesus Christ. Paul utilizes the image of "putting on Christ" to convey the intimacy of the believer's living relationship with Christ within the church as a body.

Closely linked to Paul's mystical understanding of indi-

vidual and corporate participation in Christ is his awareness of the empowering work of the Holy Spirit in the life
of the individual and the community. The parallel assertions in Galatians 4:4 and 4:6 testify that he considers
God's initiatives through Christ and the Spirit to be
dynamically equivalent:

> But when the fullness of time had come, God sent his
> Son. (4:4)

> And because you are children, God has sent the Spirit
> of his Son into our hearts. (4:6)

The God who "sent his Son" in order to adopt former
slaves as children also "sent the Spirit of his Son" into their
hearts so as to authenticate their status within God's family. The Spirit of God powerfully at work in their lives ver-
ifies their status as God's children. Those who receive the
gift of God's Spirit are moved by that Spirit to utter the
same intimate and familiar cry to God that characterized
Jesus's own praying: "Abba! Father!" (4:6).

Set Free in Christ

In Galatians 5:1-12 Paul shifts overtly into the mode of
ethical exhortation. He continues his polemic against the
intruders who were advocating ritualistic Torah observance (5:2-4). He gives voice to his disappointment in the
Galatians (5:7-8). He warns them (5:9), expresses his confidence that they will make the right choices (5:10), and
assures them that the agitating outsiders will be judged
(5:10). In 5:11 he reacts to the absurd charges that he himself had been advocating circumcision for Gentile converts.
And in 5:12 he utters the harshest of his outbursts against
these rival teachers.

Here Paul also issues his strongest warnings yet to the Galatian believers about the hazards inherent in assenting to the teachers' Judaizing addendum to the gospel. Paul's warnings in 5:2 and 5:4 are framed in relation to his conception of the believers' participation in Christ:

> Listen! I, Paul, am telling you that if you let yourselves be circumcised, Christ will be of no benefit to you. (5:2)

> You who want to be justified by the law have cut yourselves off from Christ; you have fallen away from grace. (5:4)

In the strongest of tones Paul alerts the Galatians to the fact that their life-giving relationship with Christ would be at risk if in their desire to achieve righteousness they allowed themselves to be persuaded to add ritual law observance. Clearly he wants these new believers to recognize that they need no ritualistic upgrade for them to be authenticated as full participants within the people of God.

However, Paul not only attacks his Jewish opponents and warns his Galatian friends. He also injects some constructive ethical encouragement and admonition. Likely he has sensed, or possibly been informed, that some Galatian believers are attracted to the message of the Jewish teachers because their teachings provide concrete ritualistic and normative guidance for everyday living. Accordingly he feels constrained to enlarge on his theological emphasis on freedom in Jesus Christ by pointing out how the believers' participation in Christ and the presence of the Holy Spirit in their lives supply the needed ethical guidelines, motivation, and power for faithful living.

To this point in this letter, Paul has in various ways

been bringing out the liberating aspect of the gospel of Jesus Christ. Jews in Christ no longer need to be under the disciplining custody of the law (4:1-7). Gentiles in Christ have been rescued from their enslavement to the rudimentary powers of the universe (4:3, 8-11). In Christ, both Jews and Gentiles, also slaves and free people, and males and females enter into a realm characterized by freedom.

But now Paul wants to address the question, What shape does this freedom take? By means of a summarizing assertion in 5:1, he launches his moral counsel. He begins in the indicative mood and then follows with a command. In other words, Paul both reminds his hearers about what God has graciously provided in Christ and counsels the believers concerning their conduct as persons set free through Christ:

> For freedom Christ has set us free. Stand firm, there-
> fore, and do not submit again to a yoke of slavery.
> (5:1)

Paul urges resolute and steadfast resistance against the Jewish teachers' added requirement of law observance (here caricatured as "a yoke of slavery") among the Gentile converts.

Before he deals specifically with how the freed community behaves, he has incorporated a concise thesis-like declaration. In 5:5-6 he both recapitulates themes already discussed and anticipates the emphases still to follow:

> For through the Spirit, by faith, we eagerly wait for the
> hope of righteousness. For in Christ Jesus neither cir-
> cumcision nor uncircumcision counts for anything; the
> only thing that counts is faith, working through love.
> (5:5-6)

Paul's phrase "by faith" once again signifies both Christ's faith and human responsive faith. The phrase "through the Spirit" recalls the earlier emphasis on the Spirit's role (3:1-5, 14; 4:6) and signals the ensuing major theme of the Spirit's empowerment for righteous living (5:16–6:10). He also acknowledges the eschatological tension within which Spirit-enabled believers eagerly await "the hope of righteousness." Through the work of Christ and the Holy Spirit in their lives, believers already experience righteous standing, not by keeping the law but "by faith." National privilege and ethnic distinctives do not lead to such standing before God. According to Paul, "neither circumcision nor uncircumcision counts for anything," only faith. However, the believers' righteous status has yet to be fully consummated. Such righteousness implies not just status but also commitment and behavior. Their "hope of righteousness" will ultimately be realized only as they continue in faith and rely on the power of the Spirit. Such faith expresses itself in the way people live: "the only thing that counts is faith, working through love" (5:6). Spirit-enabled love expresses itself in self-giving service for others.

Spirit-guided Freedom in the Slavery of Love

Paul's assertion that love is the way that faith works (5:6) functions as a foreword to his admonition and encouragement in 5:13–6:10. Here he comments on specific ways in which love expresses itself within the church community.

In 5:13 Paul articulates an entreaty which demonstrates his awareness that freedom can be wrongly construed as opening the way to a self-indulgent style of life. Freedom gained through Christ is not license to do as one pleases; rather it leads to loving service in behalf of others.

In a striking turn of phrase Paul implores the Galatians to deploy their freedom in the slavery of love:

> For you were called to freedom, brothers and sisters;
> only do not use your freedom as an opportunity for
> self-indulgence, but through love become slaves to one
> another. (5:13)

Such love, in fact, effectively fulfills the whole law:

> For the whole law is summed up in a single command-
> ment, "You shall love your neighbor as yourself."
> (5:14, including a quotation of Leviticus 19:18)

To this point in the letter Paul has been adamant in his warnings to the Galatian believers against taking on circumcision and other aspects of law observance, so this positive assertion concerning the law comes as something of a surprise. Yet he distinguishes between coming under the law (note 5:18: "you are not under the law") and living in Christ empowered by the Spirit in such a way that the law (especially in its moral dimensions) is actually fulfilled.

There are several direct hints in this context that Paul has in his mind some destructive patterns of behavior reportedly occurring in the Galatian congregation. One of these clues concerning the situation in the congregation appears immediately following the Levitical reminder for them to love their neighbor. He urges, "If you bite and devour one another, take care that you are not consumed by one another" (5:15). Instead of chewing each other up they should love each other. Another window into what was happening in Galatia may be the list of the "works of the flesh" in 5:19-21. This list may be somewhat generic in character, but Paul's actual selection is probably shaped by the overt or incipient conduct of at least some people in Galatia:

> Now the works of the flesh are obvious: fornication, impurity, licentiousness, idolatry, sorcery, enmities, strife, jealousy, anger, quarrels, dissensions, factions, envy, drunkenness, carousing, and things like these. (5:19-21)

Following his enumeration of "the fruit of the Spirit" in 5:22-23 Paul appends an admonition, which also appears to have been occasioned by actual or rumored attitudes and behavior in Galatia: "Let us not become conceited, competing against one another, envying one another" (5:26). Furthermore, the comment in 6:1 ("if anyone is detected in a transgression") suggests that there may have been one or more reported cases of moral transgression within the church.

In addition to these warnings and exhortations pertaining to the contentiousness within the congregation and some individual violations of their freedom in Christ, Paul offers constructive guidance regarding the life of faithfulness. However, instead of laying down the law, he points to Christ and the Spirit respectively as providing the pattern and the power for their faithful behavior.

Jesus Christ demonstrates the pattern. God's grace, which is extended to humanity through Jesus's self-giving death on the cross, invites those who receive this grace to participate with Christ in his crucifixion. Reminiscent of both his personal testimony in 2:19 ("I have been crucified with Christ") and his theological reflections about being incorporated into Christ in 3:29 ("if you belong to Christ") Paul declares in 5:24:

> And those who belong to Christ Jesus have crucified
> the flesh with its passions and desires.

Whereas in 2:19 Paul communicates that believers are those who themselves have been co-crucified with Christ, in 5:24 believers are named as active agents in their own crucifixion. They need to take responsibility for their own lives, making choices that reflect the way of Jesus. Once again, God's gracious initiative opens up the possibility for faithful and obedient response.

Christ shows the pattern of obedience and faithfulness, and the Holy Spirit supplies the power. Again with reference to the work of the Spirit in individual and corporate Christian experience, Paul points to both the gracious gift and the corresponding ethical mandate. This can be seen in the two statements that frame his discussion of the works of the flesh and the fruit of the Spirit.

> Live by the Spirit, I say, and do not gratify the desires
> of the flesh. (5:16)

> If we live by the Spirit, let us also be guided by the
> Spirit. (5:25)

Life in the Spirit comes as a gift from God through Christ, but the individual and the community still need to make choices to walk in line with the Spirit. The underlying verb in 5:25, *stoichomen*, is a military term for marching in orderly fashion, expressed well by the NIV translation: "let us keep in step with the Spirit." If personal and collective decisions are made in harmony with God's life-giving Spirit, the life of the Christian community will bear fruit, including "love, joy, peace, patience, kindness, generosity, faithfulness, gentleness, and self-control" (5:22-23a). With more than a touch of irony Paul adds, "There is no law against such things" (5:23b).

The contrast between flesh and Spirit in 5:16-26 has sometimes been understood to suggest that a war rages within the breast of the individual believer between two evenly matched adversaries. Paul's language in 5:17 might be construed in that way:

> For what the flesh desires is opposed to the Spirit, and what the Spirit desires is opposed to the flesh; for these are opposed to each other, to prevent you from doing what you want. (5:17)

However, Paul's purpose here is not to report a relentless and wearying tug-of-war within the individual. Rather he seeks to encourage the individual members of the Galatian churches and the Christian community as a corporate body to live out their commitment against "the works of the flesh" and for "the fruit of the Spirit." As those who live in Christ and desire to walk by the Spirit, believers can be confident that the lingering desires of the flesh will not succeed in setting them endlessly adrift on a sea of moral relativism without any rudder to guide them and without the fuel to propel them along.

The warfare imagery in 5:16-26 (especially verses 16, 17) indicates that here again Paul gives voice to an apocalyptic view of what God has done in Christ. When he talks about life in the flesh and life in the Spirit he is not thinking only along anthropological lines. In other words, he does not have the individual believer primarily in mind. Rather he is reflecting his conviction that a cosmic shift has occurred within the human story. Paul views history as having been rocked by a convulsion, namely God's dramatic invasion through Jesus Christ. God's cataclysmic intervention in Christ has effected a turn of the ages, thereby dividing chronology into "before" and "after." The sphere from which potentially all of humanity has been rescued is "the present evil age" (cf. 1:4). The "kingdom of God" (note 5:22) is the realm inherited by believers who acknowledge Jesus Christ as Lord and live in faithful obedience to God through the empowerment of the Holy Spirit. Later in 6:15 Paul employs the expression "the new creation" for this reconstituted community of Jews and Gentiles, slave and free, men and women, who belong to Christ and walk by the Spirit.

Paul's lively recital of the battle between flesh and Spirit in 5:16-25 demonstrates that he recognizes that these two ages overlap. Life in the flesh is concurrent with life in the Spirit. Through Christ and the Spirit of God the new eon has been inaugurated but the former eon continues. Though believers who walk in line with the Spirit "inherit the kingdom of God" they also need to be aware that the attitudes and practices of the flesh threaten to jeopardize that inheritance (5:22). However, God's gracious intervention through Christ and the gift of the Spirit enable and empower the riches of life within God's triumphant reign. And, as Paul goes on to illustrate in his words of counsel in 6:1-10, the consequences of this divine intervention deeply shape the communal life of the congregation.

Fulfilling the Law of Christ

In a series of moral maxims in 6:1-10 Paul addresses specific situations in the Galatian churches. He does so in a way that illustrates how the Spirit of God guides the practical outworking of individual and congregational life in Christ.

What needs to happen when a member of the church

gets entangled in moral transgression? Paul extends specific counsel to the spiritual people in the congregation. This is not an elite group of the spiritually endowed but all who live by the Spirit and are guided by the Spirit (cf. 5:25). Spirit-guided people should intervene, not with self-righteous condemnation but with gentleness. Their goal should be to restore the lapsed individual to faithful living. And they should take necessary precautions lest they too be tempted:

> My friends, if anyone is detected in a transgression,
> you who have received the Spirit should restore such a
> one in a spirit of gentleness. Take care that you your-
> selves are not tempted. (6:1)

There is no evidence indicating which of the works of the flesh might have been identified in the life of this erring member. Perhaps this was a case of fornication, impurity, or licentiousness. It is more self-evident what fruit of the Spirit is needed for dealing with this individual. One might highlight especially the qualities of love, patience, kindness, gentleness, and self-control.

Paul emphasizes both corporate responsibility and individual accountability. As a congregation they are advised, "Bear one another's burdens, and in this way you will fulfill the law of Christ" (6:2). As individuals they are urged humbly to remember their own vulnerability to temptation and their own responsibility to make choices reflective of their status in Christ (6:3-5).

The phrase "the law of Christ" in 6:2 comes as something of a surprise near the conclusion of this letter, given the fact that earlier in Galatians Christ and the law seem to have been portrayed as polar opposites. Since the coming of Christ there is no more need for the law with its custodial function (3:23-26). What then does Paul mean when he refers to "the law of Christ"? John M. G. Barclay identifies several proposed explanations for this striking expression. Some see a rabbinic notion of the Jewish law renewed or reinterpreted during the new age introduced by the Messiah. Some think that Paul understood Jesus's ethical teaching to be a Christian law. Still others who consider the underlying Greek word *nomos* to mean not "law" but "principle" suggest that, as in 5:14, Paul prescribes love as the operative norm for Christian conduct and relationships (1988:127-31).

Given Paul's repeated emphasis in Galatians on believers' participation in Christ, some variation of the last suggestion resonates best with the data. He points to Jesus Christ, crucified and raised, as the ultimate paradigm for loving and self-giving relationships. With the enabling of the Spirit of God, those who are in Christ replicate such self-denying servanthood. Their life together in Christ fulfills "the law of Christ." This kind of lifestyle also sums up the law as it is now viewed through Christ.

In 6:7-10 Paul reissues his eschatological reminder concerning the flesh and the Spirit (cf. 5:16-26). He employs agricultural imagery about sowing and reaping to underscore the truth that after they have been delivered through Christ and empowered by the Spirit it matters how people behave. Their lifestyle decisions have long-term consequences:

> If you sow to the flesh, you will reap corruption from
> the flesh; but if you sow to the Spirit, you will reap
> eternal life from the Spirit. (6:8)

Because the consequences of human choices can include either corruption or eternal life Paul urges diligence in doing what is right and doing good:

> So let us not grow weary in doing what is right, for we
> will reap at harvest time, if we do not give up. So then,
> whenever we have an opportunity, let us work for the
> good of all, and especially for those of the family of
> faith. (6:9-10)

Evidently with the contentiousness in the Galatian congregations in mind, Paul has added this final statement.
Within the church household, the family of faith, good
works need to be sown like seed, and the resulting harvest
will benefit others as well. Those who belong to Christ
within the family of faith are summoned to Christlike, loving servanthood in the power of the Holy Spirit.

Having vented his feelings and voiced his pastoral counsel for the Galatian churches by dictating this emotional letter, Paul picks up the quill himself for his wrap-up (6:11-18).
He drafts some concluding accusations against the intruders
(6:12-13) and some reminders and words of blessing for the
faith community (6:15-16, 18). In the process he also testifies
candidly regarding his own ongoing commitment (6:14, 17).

Paul's accusations against his rivals continue to be caustic.
He challenges their motivation and questions their integrity:

> It is those who want to make a good showing in the
> flesh that try to compel you to be circumcised—only
> that they may not be persecuted for the cross of Christ.
> Even the circumcised do not themselves obey the law,
> but they want you to be circumcised so that they may
> boast about your flesh. (6:12-13)

Paul insinuates that these rival teachers were experiencing
pressure from their zealous Jerusalem peers, who worried
about Jews having contact with Gentiles. During the build-
up toward a Jewish revolt against Rome it was risky for
traveling Jews to associate with Gentiles. They could be

accused of being "collaborators with the enemy." Paul charges that the visitors who followed him into Galatia took a hard line on Torah observance in order to save their own skins. He tells the Galatian believers that these hard-liners are more interested in a good showing in their flesh (i.e. the Galatians' circumcised foreskins) than they are concerned about being faithful observers of the law.

Paul not only challenges the Galatians to discern what motivates the other missionaries making inroads into Galatia. He also takes the opportunity to articulate his own motives as he knows them:

> May I never boast of anything except the cross of our Lord Jesus Christ, by which the world has been cruci-fied to me, and I to the world. (6:14)

The rhetoric here moves into the lofty realm of the cosmos. Paul's language about the world being crucified, and he with it, is reminiscent of Galatians 2:20: "I have been cru-cified with Christ." The whole cosmos has been caught up in the cataclysmic event of Jesus's crucifixion. Yet for Paul this experience of crucifixion is also intensely personal. He talks about his own "stigmata," the wounds on his own body from his participation in the ongoing struggle: "I carry the marks of Jesus branded on my body" (6:17).

When Paul in closing speaks from his heart to the churches of Galatia, he drops in, without elaboration, sev-eral major themes, each of which cries out for further com-ment. The believers hearing his conclusion might have understood what he meant by circumcision and uncircum-cision, but how would they have taken his passing refer-ence to the new creation?

> For neither circumcision nor uncircumcision is any-
> thing; but a new creation is everything! (6:15)

Paul speaks a traditional Jewish blessing on the readers of his letter; he wishes them God's peace and mercy (6:16). He refers to his readers more specifically in a way that will have nudged them once more toward compliance with his understanding of the gospel: he talks about them as "those who will follow this rule" (6:16). He calls them, literally, "those who march in line with this canon" (cf. his earlier use of the same military term in 5:25). Paul's mention of "this rule" (Greek: "canon") presumably refers back to 6:15: the new creation transcends ritual law observance. But what does he want his hearers to infer from his provocative designation "the Israel of God" (6:16)? He appears to be saying to these Gentile believers in Galatia that they are now members of the historic people of Israel. Through the invasion of God's grace into the cosmos through Jesus Christ, a whole new world has opened up, "a new creation," in which Jews and Gentiles together make up the people of God. (See the earlier discussion of "The Israel of God" in chapter 6.)

In his final benediction Paul addresses these believers as his "brothers and sisters." Their wavering has caused him consternation, but in Christ they are sisters and brothers. He also reminds them of the sustaining matrix of God's amazing grace: "May the grace of our Lord Jesus Christ be with your spirit, brothers and sisters" (6:18). Beyond the disappointment, anger, and confusion inherent in the relationship between this pastor and these people is the all-pervasive sovereign grace of God.

Participating with Christ in the Power of the Spirit

We have had many occasions to note that in Galatians

Paul tangles with some Jewish teachers, whose influence on these new believers he deplores. He regards them as agitators who distort the gospel when they try to persuade converts to add law observance to seal their identification with the people of God. Even though both Paul and these teachers know that in Christ God has ushered in a new era of salvation, he differentiates himself sharply from their prescription of Torah observance for Gentiles. Their primary dispute centers on how the redeemed are enabled to live faithfully. Paul emphasizes participating with Christ in the power of the Holy Spirit. His rivals commend the ritual and moral guidelines of the Jewish Torah.

As we shift our attention to other congregations with which Paul carries on pastoral correspondence, we note that, although he is less polemical than in Galatians, he emphasizes similar themes. We take the occasion here to dwell on texts outside of Galatians where Paul expresses his conception of participation in Christ. We will also explore Paul's image of the church as the body of Christ. And we will attempt to draw together some of what Paul says about the role of the Holy Spirit.

Before we proceed with a survey of these themes, we could visit the question of what social or religious realities within the Greco-Roman world would make the notion of participation in Christ understandable to the audiences for whom Paul wrote. Some scholars early in the twentieth century thought Paul was borrowing vocabulary prevalent in mystery religions, some of which told stories of a dying and rising god and invited adherents to be initiated through rites resembling baptism. Others looked to more Jewish understandings, especially that of "corporate personality." Jews at Passover Seder meals, for example, viewed themselves as direct participants in what their ancestors experienced in the past: "We were slaves in

Egypt," they recalled. Another suggestion is that relationships among members of the traditional Roman household and of the empire as a whole as "the body politic" supplied the backdrop. Yet another possibility is that Paul built on the model of various voluntary associations that were in existence in most communities in the Roman world. Trade guilds, artisan clubs, and other grassroots community groups, whatever their purpose, all had defined procedures for entering and clear expectations for maintaining membership in ways that participated in the mission of the organization.

Elements of some or most of these precursor models might have helped Paul's original readers to connect with his participation language. The social and political models of the household and voluntary associations, however, may have come to the mind of his recipients most readily.

Baptism into Christ, Life in Christ

Paul frequently employs phrases like "in Christ" or "with Christ" to express how the people of God participate in the life, death, and resurrection of Jesus Christ. The frequency of these expressions led Albert Schweitzer to propose that Paul's central convictions take the form of a "being-in-Christ" mysticism. Schweitzer employed the geological image of a small crater situated within a huge volcanic crater to assert that the believer's mystical experience of Christ, rather than the doctrine of justification by faith, dominates Paul's theological thought:

> The doctrine of righteousness by faith is therefore a subsidiary crater, which has formed within the main crater—the mystical doctrine of redemption through being-in-Christ. (Schweitzer, 1931:225)

More recently E. P. Sanders proposed that Paul's "pattern of religion" can be characterized as "participationist eschatology" (1977:549). Sanders does not elaborate on this conclusion to any significant extent, but Paul's notion that believers identify deeply with Christ's dying and rising has increasingly been given scholarly attention. In a 2001 book entitled *Cruciformity: Paul's Narrative Spirituality of the Cross*, Michael J. Gorman has even coined the term "cruciformity" to describe this Pauline emphasis and to expand on its implications for spirituality, ethics, and the life of the church.

Paul's "in/with Christ" references function in a variety of ways. Sometimes the phrase "in Christ" testifies objectively to the Christ-event itself: the life, death, and resurrection of Jesus. For example, Paul begins his story of Jesus in Philippians with this appeal: "Let the same mind be in you that was in Christ Jesus" (2:5). In the thanksgiving section of 1 Corinthians he reminds them about "the grace of God that has been given you in Christ Jesus" (1:4). His theologically dense recapitulation of what God has done through Christ in 2 Corinthians includes this summation: "That is, in Christ God was reconciling the world to himself" (5:19).

In other "in Christ" passages Paul focuses less on the moments in the life and ministry of Jesus and more on believers' subjective experiences with Jesus Christ. The salutation in 1 Corinthians talks about the recipients' status as "those who are sanctified in Christ Jesus, called to be saints" (1:2). Near the end of that letter Paul enlarges on what the implications would be if those who deny the resurrection were to be correct: "Then those also who have died in Christ have perished" (15:18). He can also talk about his partners in ministry by using "in Christ" language: "Greet Prisca and Aquila, who work with me in Christ Jesus" (Romans 16:3).

In some places Paul speaks of his own relationship "in Christ" in a way that is designed to encourage or exhort believers to behave in certain ways or to choose (or avoid) particular kinds of behavior. As he draws his initial chiding of the believers in Corinth to a close in 1 Corinthians, Paul says, "Indeed, in Christ Jesus I became your father through the gospel" (4:15). Quite perturbed by some disorderly folk in Thessalonica who refuse to contribute toward the common cause, Paul pleads, "Now such persons we command and exhort in the Lord Jesus Christ to do their work quietly and to earn their own living" (2 Thessalonians 3:12).

In addition to places where Paul speaks about objective and subjective dimensions of life "in Christ" there are texts about the believer's experiences "with Christ." In his letter to the Colossians Paul recalls what had happened to them in the process of their incorporation into the community of faith. He reminds them:

> And when you were dead in trespasses and the uncircumcision of your flesh, God made you alive together with him, when he forgave us all our trespasses. (2:13)

Some of Paul's reminders have to do with what is still envisioned as the future inheritance of believers. An example:

> We know that the one who raised the Lord Jesus will raise us also with Jesus, and will bring us with you into his presence. (2 Corinthians 4:14)

A related phenomenon that is remarkably common in Paul's correspondence is his use of compound words, both nouns and verbs, which begin with the Greek preposition meaning "with." Translations normally do not adequately convey the dynamic notion that the believer dies, rises, lives, and reigns with Christ. Nor is it possible to describe clearly the communal dimension, the experience of believers sharing with each other by identifying with Christ. Rather than attempting to enumerate some of these "with" compounds in what would turn out to be a lengthy and awkward listing, we'll focus on Romans 6, which contains a cluster of such compound words.

In Romans 6 Paul has just posed what he had earlier identified as a scandalous caricature of his teaching, namely, "Let us do evil so that good may come" (3:8). In 6:1 he asks, "Should we continue in sin in order that grace may abound?" In his rebuttal against the charge that the message of God's boundless grace through Christ encourages people simply to keep on sinning, he comments about Jesus's death, burial, and resurrection and the way believers are incorporated into that sphere in which Christ now lives and reigns. In the following extended quotation, the translations of the "with" compound words are rendered in italics:

> Do you not know that all of us who have been baptized into Christ Jesus were baptized into his death? Therefore *we have been buried with* him by baptism into death, so that, just as Christ was raised from the dead by the glory of the Father, so we too might walk in newness of life. For if *we have been united with* him in a death like his, *we will* certainly *be united with* him in a resurrection like his. We know that our old self *was crucified with* him so that the body of sin might be destroyed, and we might no longer be enslaved to sin. For whoever has died is freed from sin. But if we have died with Christ, we believe that *we will also live with* him. We know that Christ, being raised from the dead, will never die again; death no longer has domin-

ion over him. The death he died, he died to sin, once
for all; but the life he lives, he lives to God. So you
also must consider yourselves dead to sin and alive to
God in Christ Jesus. (Romans 6:3-11)

In a rush of evocative images Paul addresses the question of how those who are redeemed through Christ shall
live. Believers are baptized "into" Christ. In addition to
terminology describing experience "in" and "with" Christ
there is therefore the notion of Christ (also the body of
Christ) as a domain or a sphere of allegiance and relationships into which the believer enters or transfers. Baptism
therefore is not just a religious ritual with personal significance; it signifies the individual's entry into the community of those who participate with Christ within that realm
in which Christ reigns. This experience involves being "co-
crucified," "co-buried," and "co-raised" with Christ.

As Paul sees it, such participation with Christ clearly
has moral implications. No longer can those who have
died to sin and been raised to new life as part of the body
of Christ behave in ways that contradict their new allegiance. Those who have died to sin no longer live under
the reign of sin. Those who have been raised with Christ
walk in newness of life. This implies deliberate choice. The
initiative of God's gracious intervention in Christ leads to
liberation, but people still need to choose how they will
live out their loyalty, because sin still seeks to exercise sovereignty over people who yield to its power. Paul exhorts
those who have died to sin and been raised to new life not
to allow themselves to be enslaved again:

Therefore, do not let sin exercise dominion in your
mortal bodies, to make you obey their passions. No
longer present your members to sin as instruments of

wickedness, but present yourselves to God as those
who have been brought from death to life, and present
your members to God as instruments of righteousness.
For sin will have no dominion over you, since you are
not under law but under grace. (6:12-14)

Paul goes on to say in 6:15-23 that, quite paradoxically, all
must choose between two allegiances: either to sin, which
leads to death, or to obedience, which leads to righteousness (6:16). In fact, he reassures them that they have
already chosen the latter (6:17-19). What remains for them
is to continue in their participation with Christ. What they
already are they need to continue to become.

Before leaving this theme Paul graphically spells out
the consequences of their ongoing alignment with the way
of Christ. He does so by contrasting their former life under
sin with their current reality in Christ:

When you were slaves of sin, you were free in regard
to righteousness. So what advantage did you then get
from the things of which you now are ashamed? The
end of those things is death. But now that you have
been freed from sin and enslaved to God, the advantage you get is sanctification. The end is eternal life.
For the wages of sin is death, but the free gift of God
is eternal life in Christ Jesus our Lord. (6:20-23)

Paul outlines a distinct "before" and "after": Before Christ,
they were captivated by the dominating power of sin. The
ultimate outcome of sin's enslaving work is death. But,
thanks to God's liberating work, in Christ the believer is set
free: free from sin and free to serve God. And the outcome
of God's freeing work is life: the free gift of eternal life in
Christ Jesus the Lord!

The Body of Christ

Closely related to Paul's emphasis on believers participating with Christ is his image of the church as the body of Christ. This metaphor appears in Ephesians 4:11-16 and in Colossians 1:18-20. However, it is developed most prominently in 1 Corinthians 12 and Romans 12. These texts all bring out the corporate nature of the "in Christ" experience. Individuals enter the realm in which the crucified and risen Christ is Lord, and their allegiance is expressed among other people who are also allied with the same head.

Paul's agenda in 1 Corinthians 12 is to respond to a query from the church in Corinth about the exercise of spiritual gifts within the congregation. First he warns them about rival spirits in their culture clamoring for their allegiance, and he reminds them that the Holy Spirit inspires their foundational confession, "Jesus is Lord!" (12:1-3). Then he underscores in a triadic formula the many gifts, services, and activities manifest within the church, all of which have a common source of empowerment: the same Spirit, the same Lord, the same God (12:4-6).

After illustrating this variety and highlighting the divine source (12:7-11), Paul moves into an extended elaboration of the image of the church as the body of Christ. Here again he emphasizes both "one" and "many": the unity of the body, yet also the diversity within the body. We note Paul's key theological affirmation:

> For just as the body is one and has many members, and all the members of the body, though many, are one body, so it is with Christ. For in the one Spirit we were all baptized into one body—Jews or Greeks, slaves or free—and we were all made to drink of one Spirit. (12:12-13)

One might expect Paul to have explained the application of his body metaphor in 12:12 by noting "so it is with the church." Instead he says, "so it is with Christ." Christ is seen corporately, and the church is viewed with reference to Christ. Furthermore, given the propensity within the Corinthian congregation toward emphasizing the gifts of the Spirit and boasting about the more showy gifts, Paul here also reminds them that they were all baptized in the one Spirit into one body. This unity transcends ethnic and economic difference: "Jews or Greeks, slaves or free." (Gender issues are touchy in Corinth, and Paul chooses not to add, as he does in Galatians 3:28, "male and female.") In a possible reference to their common meals or to the Lord's Supper, Paul also reminds the Corinthian believers that "we were all made to drink of one Spirit." Life in Christ involves life within the church as the body of Christ. And life in Christ is guided and enlivened by the ministry of the Spirit, available to all.

Paul enlarges on his body metaphor with considerable detail in 1 Corinthians 12:14-26. He begins by stating the obvious: "Indeed, the body does not consist of one member but of many" (12:14). This introduces the ridiculous scenario of various parts of the human body disowning or disparaging other parts. The thrust of this somewhat pedantic realism is that within the body of Christ no one is more equal than others. All members are needed, and there is a dynamic interaction among its members, all united in a common loyalty in one Christ and the one Spirit. In 12:27 Paul summarizes by repeating himself: "Now you are the body of Christ and individually members of it."

In Romans 12 Paul also draws on the body metaphor in ways designed to address dismissive tendencies expressing themselves within and between various congregations in Rome. Only in this case it is not the quest for showy spirituality but the phenomena of Gentile arrogance and Jewish exclusivism that invite the use of this image of the church. Having appealed to the believers in Rome to present their bodies as a living sacrifice (12:1), Paul reminds them that they are all part of a body, the body of Christ, where each one makes a contribution toward the welfare of others:

> For by the grace given to me I say to everyone among you not to think of yourself more highly than you ought to think, but to think with sober judgment, each according to the measure of faith that God has assigned. For as in one body we have many members, and not all the members have the same function, so we, who are many, are one body in Christ, and individually we are members one of another. (Romans 12:3-5)

Both Colossians and Ephesians develop the body of Christ metaphor further. Both of these letters make explicit what is implicit in 1 Corinthians and Romans: namely, that Christ is the head of the church and the source of the church's life.

In Ephesians 4 an eloquent appeal to unity (4:1-6) introduces reminders about how the church body can grow in maturity through the exercise of various ministries (4:7-14). Then in 4:15-16 we hear an injunction toward loving truth-telling within the body of Christ:

> But speaking the truth in love, we must grow up in every way into him who is the head, into Christ, from whom the whole body, joined and knit together by every ligament with which it is equipped, as each part is working properly, promotes the body's growth in building itself up in love. (Ephesians 4:15-16)

In a hymn about Christ and his role in both creation and the new creation (Colossians 1:15-20) Paul also testifies concerning Christ: "He is the head of the body, the church" (1:18a). Here too he is quick to emphasize the ethical implications of being intimately connected to the church's head, Jesus Christ. (See chapter 11.)

The Spirit as God's Presence

Along with Paul's participation metaphors and his image of the body of Christ one should consider his understanding of the ministry of the Holy Spirit. Paul appears to move quite freely from talking about life "in Christ" to his reflections about life "in the Spirit." As we have just seen, imbedded in Paul's teaching about unity and diversity within the body of Christ in 1 Corinthians 12 is his declaration about being baptized into one body by one Spirit and about drinking together from the one Spirit (12:12-13).

Whole books have been devoted to the theme of the Holy Spirit in Paul's letters. An impressive example is Gordon Fee's 1994 book entitled *God's Empowering Presence*, which exceeds nine hundred pages! His book illustrates how difficult it is to isolate Spirit themes in Paul's letters from other aspects of his theology. Even though Paul nowhere explicitly outlines a trinitarian view of God, his reflections about the deity often mention God, Christ, and the Spirit in dynamically intertwined ways. For him, following his life-transforming encounter with the risen Christ, to speak of God is to share Christ and to testify concerning Christ is also to talk about the ministry of the Spirit.

Paul's reflections on the role of the Spirit therefore have been (and will be) noted throughout each chapter in which we interact with one after another of his letters. A few samples can illustrate some of his emphases.

Paul recalls vividly that when he and his partners in Thessalonica preached the gospel "in power and in the Holy

Spirit and with full conviction," their hearers in that city received the word "with joy inspired by the Holy Spirit" (1 Thessalonians 1:5, 6). Both the proclamation of the gospel and its reception are enabled by the work of the Spirit of God.

Paul also utilizes creative imagery to recount the Spirit's ongoing role in the believer's life. After dealing with the exercise of spiritual gifts in 1 Corinthians, his later letter to Corinth retells these believers' (and his own) earlier experiences with the Spirit. For example, in 2 Corinthians 1:21-22 he explicitly names God, Christ, and the Spirit, and he talks about the gift of the Spirit with images that tumble out one after another:

> But it is God who establishes us with you in Christ and has anointed us, by putting his seal on us and giving us his Spirit in our hearts as a first installment.
> (2 Corinthians 1:21-22)

Similar images are deployed in Ephesians. The Spirit is a pledge, a down payment, the promissory seal, which guarantees the future inheritance already broadcast in the gospel:

> In him you also, when you had heard the word of truth, the gospel of your salvation, and had believed in him, were marked with the seal of the promised Holy Spirit; this is the pledge of our inheritance toward redemption as God's own people, to the praise of his glory. (Ephesians 1:13-14)

In Romans 8:1-17 we find Paul's most extensive pastoral meditation on the role of the Spirit. After pondering the disabling power of sin (note especially Romans 7:7-12) he marvels at the divine enabling available through the Spirit to those who are in Christ Jesus, for whom there is no condemnation (8:1). Repeatedly throughout this section Paul affirms both what God has already accomplished in behalf of those liberated through Christ and what the recipients of such freedom need to do in order to continue within the relationship thus established. "For the law of the Spirit of life in Christ Jesus has set you free from the law of sin and of death," he says (8:2). He explains that Jesus, God's Son, condemned sin in the flesh by taking on human flesh (8:3).

In the meantime, humans, still in the flesh though already freed, have ongoing decisions to make. Will their "walk" (i.e. their behavior in daily life) be "according to the flesh" or "according to the Spirit" (8:4)? Clearly all believers are still "in the flesh" (with "flesh" a neutral description of human bodily existence). They need, however, to discern in ongoing ways whether or not they will live "according to the flesh." Here "the flesh" symbolizes the impulses and temptations of the present age, which continues, even though the era of the new creation has been launched. Though living in bodies, believers do not need to yield to fleshly impulses and desires. In their daily lives they can align themselves with the impulses and the promptings of the Spirit.

Paul expands on this ongoing tension between life "according to the flesh" and life "according to the Spirit." He does so in ways that both encourage and reassure the hearers of this letter. He essentially asks, On what do you set your minds? Things of the flesh, or things of the Spirit? (8:5). He notes that one's mindset matters. A fleshly mindset results in a life that does not please God, indeed a life that is hostile to God, and it ultimately leads to death, while being Spirit-minded leads to life and peace (8:6, 7).

Paul is quick to reassure the recipients of this pastoral counsel that indeed they have entered into the realm of God's embrace:

But you are not in the flesh; you are in the Spirit, since
the Spirit of God dwells in you. Anyone who does not
have the Spirit of Christ does not belong to him. But if
Christ is in you, though the body is dead because of
sin, the Spirit is life because of righteousness. If the
Spirit of him who raised Jesus from the dead dwells in
you, he who raised Christ from the dead will give life
to your mortal bodies also through his Spirit that
dwells in you. (8:9-11)

Paul's reassuring words here speak about the realm or
sphere into which believers have entered through identifying with Christ's death: "You are in the Spirit" and "the
Spirit of God dwells in you" (8:9). The mutual indwelling
of the believer in the Spirit and the Spirit within the believer closely parallels the believers' experience in Christ (8:10:
"if Christ is in you"). In 8:10-11, Paul's two conditional
statements describe not a hypothetical scenario but a situation that already exists. These verses would be better
translated by changing the "if" to "since": "[since] Christ
is in you" (8:10), and "[since] the Spirit of him who raised
Jesus from the dead dwells in you" (8:11).

Yet Paul does continue both to reassure and appeal. In
8:12-13 we hear a repeat, though with some variation, of
his earlier warning against living "according to the flesh."
Then in 8:14-17 he recycles some of the rich adoption
imagery from Galatians 4:1-7, complete with an echo of
the cry of the heart that bursts forth from among those
who were formerly enslaved who have now become the
children of God. During Spirit-inspired worship they call
out, "Abba! Father!" as they glimpse already their guaranteed future inheritance:

So then, brothers and sisters, we are debtors, not to
the flesh, to live according to the flesh—for if you live

> according to the flesh, you will die; but if by the Spirit
> you put to death the deeds of the body, you will live.
> For all who are led by the Spirit of God are children of
> God. For you did not receive a spirit of slavery to fall
> back into fear, but you have received a spirit of adop-
> tion. When we cry, "Abba! Father!" it is that very
> Spirit bearing witness with our spirit that we are chil-
> dren of God, and if children, then heirs, heirs of God
> and joint heirs with Christ—if, in fact, we suffer with
> him so that we may also be glorified with him.
> (Romans 8:12-17)

In these tender and reassuring words, Paul paints the glorious big picture of the life of the children of God: life in Christ, life led by the Spirit of God. The Spirit of God prompts the children of God to put to death the fleshly impulses, the deeds of the body. The same Spirit also testifies that, as God's heirs and as joint heirs with Christ, the children of God participate with Christ in his death, so that they will participate with Christ in glory!

10

IN TRANSFORMED RELATIONSHIPS

The shortest of Paul's extant letters is addressed to Philemon, Apphia, Archippus, and the church that meets in their house. Behind this personal communication lurks a remarkable story involving a slave named Onesimus, his master, other members of the master's household, and the apostle Paul.

In the two narratives below we attempt to reconstruct the events that led to Paul's writing of the letter usually known simply as Philemon. That brief letter is the primary source for the narratives below. An additional resource is the epistle to the Colossians, especially 1:3-8, where Paul mentions the circumstances that led to the emergence of a church in Colossae, and 4:7-17, where a person named Onesimus is identified as a member of that congregation (4:9). Though proof remains elusive, this Onesimus may be the slave about whom Paul writes the letter to Philemon.

As we enter into the drama involving a slave and his master, we will be hearing directly only from the apostle Paul. However, by listening beneath the surface and exercising our imagination we may be able to discern the basic plot of this unfolding drama. In this case we need to make the effort to hear from both Onesimus the slave and Philemon his master before we follow Paul in his attempted intervention into their relationship with each other.

A STORY: Behind the Scenes with Onesimus

First we listen to the story as Onesimus might have remembered it.

Onesimus was born as the son of slaves. From his earliest days he heard family stories about how his father had sold himself into slavery because he was so deeply in debt. Onesimus always reflected sadly about this painful decision, though with an undercurrent of contentment and gratitude. They had stayed together as a family, and life in the Philemon household had largely been pleasant.

For Onesimus, thoughts about what might have been were never far away. Yet his childhood years were largely carefree and happy. He even managed to get a basic education. Philemon was a kindly master who recognized in the young Onesimus the potential to be trained to take on major responsibilities in managing his properties and his business efforts. Onesimus, for his part, eagerly pursued whatever learning opportunities that came his way. As he learned to read and write he also sometimes dreamt about what he would do if he were free.

Onesimus had been entrusted with many of his master's business matters. He learned to know Philemon's business associates and other friends, and would sometimes accompany his master on business trips out of Colossae. One memorable excursion took them to Ephesus, where he became acquainted with the Jewish missionary Paul. It was nigh impossible to remain unaffected by Paul, his passion for God, and his testimony about a dramatic encounter that he had had with the living Christ. Onesimus was not surprised when he learned that on a subsequent visit to Ephesus Philemon converted to Christ and became active in supporting Paul's ambitious missionary efforts.

What happened next was something of a blur for Onesimus. Some of Paul's preaching about freedom in Christ put him in touch with his own dream of freedom. In a moment of weakness Onesimus took advantage of his access to Philemon's resources and helped himself to some money. Then he bolted. As soon as he left, he panicked, realizing that not only had he taken money (which he fully intended to return), he had wronged Philemon as a "stealer of himself" from this kindly master's cadre of slaves. Desperate to redeem himself, Onesimus considered returning directly to the only home he had known. Ultimately, however, he decided rather to ask Paul to intercede for him.

Miraculously Onesimus managed to obtain passage on a ship bound for Rome, where he heard Paul was a prisoner. The long journey afforded him an opportunity to weigh the significance of what he had done and to ponder the possible outcome of this venture. As he sought his master's mentor, Onesimus wondered whose cause Paul would advocate. Would he be moved by the slave's predicament as a fugitive? Or would he regard mainly the legitimate interests of Philemon, his friend and this fugitive slave's master?

Their time together in Rome turned out to be beneficial for both Onesimus and Paul. For starters, Onesimus became a believer himself, which began a new relationship with the apostle, who evidently also needed him. The two men become emotionally close. And Onesimus began to sense that, though legally he still belonged to Philemon, morally and spiritually he was also valuable to Paul during his ongoing detention in Rome.

After one of their heart-to-heart conversations, it was clear that Paul had framed a response to this dilemma. He reached for his quill and parchment and began to write a letter.

ANOTHER STORY: Behind the Scenes with Philemon

Philemon had a story that deserves to be heard as well.

The news that his trusted slave Onesimus had vanished stunned and angered Philemon. Loyal slaves were valuable assets, and Onesimus had previously been reliable in every way. The news of Onesimus' sudden departure also raised suspicions in Philemon's community and among his business associates. When a slave like Onesimus abruptly leaves, the neighbors often wonder if the master might had been abusing that slave. So in addition to the economic loss, Philemon had to cope with this social stigma among his peers.

There was another dimension. Under the ministry of Paul in Ephesus, Philemon and Epaphras had accepted Jesus as Messiah. Epaphras later established the church in Colossae, a congregation that came to include both slaves and their masters. The home of Philemon, Apphia, and Archippus became the gathering place for a community of believers who accepted Paul's gospel of the crucified and risen Christ. This group also encompassed both masters and their slaves. So the faith community had become a natural extension of the household, which had within it women and men, rich and poor, masters and slaves.

Philemon knew that Onesimus had had a number of heart-to-heart conversations with Paul about the faith. Had Onesimus also committed himself to the way of Christ? If so, why did he run away? Surely such irresponsibility was unthinkable for a slave who had become a brother in the Lord. Harsh punishment seemed warranted. But what would Apphia, Archippus, and all the other members of the faith community think? And what, for that matter, would Paul say if he became aware of this turn of events? Did a relationship in Christ transform social and family relationships? What were the personal consequences and social outcomes of the glorious freedom realized through Christ?

What might Onesimus have been up to, and what was Philemon to do?

An Appeal on the Basis of Love

> I preferred to do nothing without your consent, in order that your good deed might be voluntary and not something forced. (Philemon 14)

Paul's images sometimes seem to collide with one another. In Galatians, as we have seen, Paul urges believers to view themselves as slaves who are freed in order to serve each other in love (Galatians 5:13). And that admonition comes on the heels of a warning not to be enslaved again after having been freed in Christ (5:1). Paul draws on the slavery metaphor both to warn against certain kinds of enslavement and to advocate an ethical posture of loving service.

In his epistle to Philemon Paul addresses a slave owner about his wayward slave. Later readers of this brief personal letter often ask about its relevance for slavery as a social reality in the first-century Roman world. What does the rhetoric of freed slaves serving each other in love mean for actual slaves and their masters?

The epistle to Philemon is one of two letters linked to the Christian community in Colossae. It is a short and deeply personal appeal, which names Philemon, Apphia, and Archippus as recipients, but it is also addressed to the congregation meeting in Philemon's home. Despite its brevity, this communication hints at a lively underlying saga involving the apostle Paul, a slave and his owner, and other people in their lives. An examination of this letter with its appeal for individual and congregational action in a particular domestic and social situation reveals an operational theology and its ethical warrants. A study of the epistle to Philemon affords an opportunity to discern whether and how the big story of God's redemptive activity as climaxed in Jesus Christ shapes an ethic in relation to the deeply entrenched social reality of slavery in the first century.

Paul writes his letter to Philemon from prison, but unfortunately (at least for his later readers), he leaves no return address. Nor is his letter dated. Likely he wrote from Rome, where he did face a period of captivity, and the year was probably around 60. An alternative possibility sometimes advocated is that he penned this letter from Ephesus, the premise being that he might have been in prison there at some point also.

In a departure from his normal routine of dictating letters, Paul writes this letter in his own hand (Philemon 19), even though Timothy is apparently nearby. Onesimus is evidently also close at hand, preparing himself to return to his home and his master, yet also apprehensive about what faces him there.

Paul starts writing to Philemon, his friend and patron, and to the church that meets in his house, about Onesimus, the fugitive slave. The beginning of the letter flows easily, "Grace to you and peace from God our Father and the Lord Jesus Christ" (3). But the rest is not so simple. What are the implications of God's grace and peace for this situation? On which narrative should Paul draw in offering counsel? And how should he approach Philemon, his beloved co-worker, about this domestic concern, which has now also become a congregational issue?

The Simple Facts

On one hand, the facts are straightforward and the verdict is clear. Paul muses that, at least from the perspective of the way things normally operate in such matters, the data make judgment easy. A slave runs away from his master and seeks help from a third party. Paul could presumably be guided in his ethical discernment by the law requiring runaway slaves to be returned to their owners. On the basis of this law it is self-evident that the slave needs to return home and face the consequences of his actions.

Another factor also enters in. Philemon is much more to Paul than an aggrieved businessman who feels that he has been personally wronged and economically injured by a turncoat slave in whom he had placed his trust. Philemon has also become a valued ally and fellow worker in Paul's apostolic mission to the Gentiles. More than once in the past, Philemon had left his business interests to trusted workers (like Onesimus) in order to join Paul in his evangelistic endeavors. Paul enjoys the help of influential and wealthy benefactors like Philemon, who generate the base of support from which his global mission can continue to flourish. Would Paul's letter turn Philemon off, the result being a reduction or even the end of that support?

But there is yet another side. At great risk to himself Onesimus has come to Paul in prison. He ministers to Paul's needs. And in the course of events he became a believer, acknowledging Jesus Christ as Lord. So should Paul send Onesimus back to his owner, as the law requires? According to prevailing law, Onesimus could expect to be beaten, branded, chained, or even killed. Paul has come to view Onesimus like a son, and so the prospect of sending him back to face the music does not sit well. Besides, might Onesimus not actually be more helpful to the mission if he stayed with Paul? As even his name suggests, Onesimus is indeed "useful." Perhaps the crucial question is, Would Onesimus continue to be useful to Philemon as his slave or useful to the larger cause through active participation in Paul's apostolic mission to the Gentiles?

Something Has Changed

Paul's opening thanksgiving clearly declares that the relationships of those who are in Christ are no longer what they once were:

> When I remember you in my prayers, I always thank my God because I hear of your love for all the saints and your faith toward the Lord Jesus. I pray that the sharing of your faith may become effective when you perceive all the good that we may do for Christ. I have indeed received much joy and encouragement from your love, because the hearts of the saints have been refreshed through you, my brother. (Philemon 4-7)

In prayer Paul remembers Philemon and finds himself moved to offer thanksgiving to God for Philemon's love and his faith. Philemon's lifestyle in Christ is summed up as "love" and "faith," with both love and faith oriented toward both the Lord Jesus and all the saints. This is better expressed by the RSV translation: "I hear of your love and of the faith which you have toward the Lord Jesus and all the saints" (5). The preposition *toward* signals Paul's conviction that believers participate in the way of Jesus. Faith is not static assent to propositions about God. It is dynamic faithfulness toward the God made known in Jesus the faithful one. And love toward all the saints becomes the primary social manifestation of this faithfulness.

Such faith expresses itself in dynamic relationships

among "the saints," the people of faith. In verse 6 Paul
employs the rich notion of fellowship (Greek: *koinonia*,
referring to sharing and mutual participation) as he gives
voice to his longing for the outcome of a fruitful faith for
Philemon and the other addressees. N. T. Wright identifies
Philemon 6 as "the driving heart of the letter." His para-
phrase of this verse articulates the dynamic character of
participation in Christ:

> "I am praying that the mutual participation which is
> proper to the Christian faith you hold may have its full
> effect in your realization of every good thing that God
> wants to accomplish in us to lead us into the fullness of
> Christian fellowship, that is, into Christ." (1991:203)

Here Paul underscores the participatory character of
Christlike love and faithfulness, which is patterned after
the way of Christ. A shared commitment toward Christ
leads partners on the journey of faith to do good, specifically to relate to each other within the community of faith
and to behave toward others in light of that still unfolding
future. Philemon's love, which has already refreshed the
saints, therefore gives Paul deep joy and encouragement
(7). Later in the letter (15-22) Paul hints broadly at what
is "the good" that Philemon might do in relation to
Onesimus and himself.

Although he might have commanded Philemon to take
a particular course of action (8), Paul approaches him
from within their shared relationship in Christ:

> For this reason, though I am bold enough in Christ to
> command you to do your duty, yet I would rather
> appeal to you on the basis of love—and I, Paul, do this
> as an old man, and now also as a prisoner of Christ
> Jesus. (8-9)

Paul frames his appeal "on the basis of love" or, more literally, "for love's sake" (RSV). His plea comes not from a vantage of power but in weakness: "I, Paul, do this as an old man and now also as a prisoner of Christ Jesus" (9). The RSV reads "an ambassador" instead of "an old man," but this rendering is based on a conjecture that the underlying Greek word is *presbeutes* ("an ambassador") rather than the word that is best supported in the available manuscripts (*presbutes*, meaning "an old man"). The conjectural change reflected in the RSV translation seems to be built on the premise that Paul would make his appeal on the basis of his apostolic authority. He actually appeals instead from his vulnerable status as an old man who is now also a prisoner.

With gentle persuasion and artful tact Paul makes a series of moves toward Philemon. His letter is a literary masterpiece in which he portrays a complex set of present and anticipated future relationships between himself and Philemon and his slave Onesimus. A linear analysis of Paul's persuasive rhetoric unveils several dynamic interrelationships in Christ.

First, this is the story of two children and their father. Paul testifies to his own deep relationship to Onesimus, noting that in prison he had become spiritual father to him, whom he calls "my child":

> I am appealing to you for my child, Onesimus, whose
> father I have become during my imprisonment. (10)

Paul also lets it be known that the imminent departure of Onesimus causes his fatherly heart to break: "I am sending him, that is, my own heart, back to you" (12). A few verses later he obliquely reminds Philemon that he also is Paul's child: "I say nothing about your owing me even your own self" (19b). Within the kinship relationship established in Christ, therefore, Onesimus the slave and Philemon the master are brothers, with Paul as their father.

Second, this story involves an imprisoned apostle, a potential co-worker, and an aggrieved master. It is clear that Paul would value Onesimus' continued presence with him:

> I wanted to keep him with me so that he might be of service to me in your place during my imprisonment for the gospel but I preferred to do nothing without your consent, in order that your good deed might be voluntary and not something forced. (13-14)

Paul's desire for help does not preempt Philemon's claim on Onesimus. Nor does Onesimus' new status in Christ release him from meeting his prior social obligations. Accordingly, Paul sends Onesimus back to his master, knowing that legally Philemon could severely punish Onesimus for forcibly removing himself from service. Paul therefore urges that Philemon receive Onesimus back, and he does so by intimately identifying himself with this runaway slave: "So if you consider me your partner, welcome him as you would welcome me" (17).

Third, as recounted in this narrative there are two partners with Paul in God's mission: Philemon and Onesimus. Actually Paul might have insisted there were three active partners. He hints broadly that God has a larger plan within which this slave's act of defiance actually turns out ultimately for good, both for Paul and for Philemon:

> Perhaps this is the reason he was separated from you for a while, so that you might have him back forever, no longer as a slave but more than a slave, a beloved

> brother—especially to me but how much more to you,
> both in the flesh and in the Lord. (15-16)

Paul's use of the passive tense verb *was separated* subtly conveys the conviction that in the larger scheme of things not the slave but God is the primary actor. Something definitely has changed. Philemon's short time of separation from Onesimus would be more than made up by his return, because Onesimus would come "no longer as a slave but more than a slave, a beloved brother" (16). This was certainly true for Paul, but even more for Philemon, and that at two levels: "both in the flesh and in the Lord."

As if to underscore an ongoing ethic of social responsibility (i.e. relationships "in the flesh") Paul puts his own credit on the line, offering to pay back to Philemon whatever Onesimus owes him (18, 19). In a broad hint at the anticipated benefit accruing to Paul himself from Onesimus' new status "in the Lord," Paul also says, "Yes, brother, let me have this benefit from you in the Lord! Refresh my heart in Christ!" (20). He concludes the main body of his letter by expressing his confidence in Philemon: "Confident of your obedience, I am writing to you, knowing that you will do even more than I say" (21). This kind of expression of confidence would, of course, raise the pressure on Philemon even more!

Finally, the story line includes the vision of a new household, with master and slave in a reconciled new relationship, a household soon to be joined by a guest. Expressing the hope that he would be released soon Paul reserves a guestroom for himself in Philemon's household (22). Still in prison, with Onesimus about to leave with his letter, Paul envisions that he will soon be joining Philemon, Apphia, and Archippus (plus Onesimus!) in an emotional reunion with the church that meets in that house.

How Does the Christian Story Relate?

In this brief letter Paul attacks no heresies, and he pronounces no specific theological affirmations. A slave runs away, and a third party tries to make peace between the slave and his master. The letter shows glimpses of the plot and the characters in a lively story, but it hardly qualifies as profound theology, at least as theology is usually understood. How does the Christian story relate? Does Paul's foundational theological narrative come into play here?

Throughout Paul's letters are allusions to the foundational story about what God has done in Christ and continues to do through the community of those who participate in the way of Christ. This foundational narrative is nowhere told in detail but in his letters to congregations Paul repeatedly provides glimpses into that grand story. But is this also the case in the letter to Philemon?

Nowhere in Philemon does Paul recall any of the stories about Abraham and Sarah or any of the characters in Israel's history. Jesus's story is not retold, nor any congregational stories about pain or joy, conflict or unity. Yet his references to Christ (eight times in this short letter) recall the story of Jesus the faithful one who was sent by God to liberate people from their bondage and incorporate them into God's people.

Several times Paul mentions the love (5, 7, 9) and the faith (5, 6) that characterize those who are in Christ. These words also recall the Christian story. In faithfulness to God, Jesus died on the cross, an act of grace and love whereby liberation and forgiveness are made available potentially to all people. God raised Jesus from the dead, thereby vindicating the faithful one. Jesus's faithfulness unto death on the cross and God's vindication of Jesus through the resurrection exhibit God's gracious love, a love which elicits a responsive faith and love. Those who respond with trust in God belong to Christ.

Another signal regarding the theological narrative underlying Paul's letter to Philemon is the use of the words *koinonia*, translated "sharing" in verse 6, and *koinonos*, translated "partner" in verse 17, as reminders that those who belong to Christ also participate in the way of Christ. They find themselves in tension between Already and Not Yet because they are both "in the flesh" and "in the Lord" (16). They live in the era between the climax of the story and its ultimate consummation. In the midst of their suffering and the ambiguities arising from tensions with prevailing cultural and social values, this community seeks to live in faithfulness and love under the empowerment of the Holy Spirit as it awaits with hope God's final assured triumph.

The church is the social embodiment of God's future, which is still breaking into the present. Freedom and love characterize this future, as do faithfulness, forgiveness, mutuality, and fellowship. When Onesimus presents Paul's letter to Philemon, which introduces him no longer as a slave but as a brother in the flesh and in the Lord, a new relationship develops between them. Of course, the social institution of slavery in the ancient world continues, with Christians as both slaves and masters. Even if Onesimus experienced manumission and forgiveness and even if he later became a bishop in Ephesus, as some have claimed, this remains anecdotal change rather than deeply transformative change. Nonetheless, each time the new creation breaks into human experience there is a hopeful sign that all social, racial, and economic barriers can be transcended within the new relationships established in Christ. When apostle, slave master, and slave are all part of one family in Jesus Christ, a dynamic is unleashed that undermines the oppressive institution of slavery and eventually leads to its abolition. Liberation from bondage through Jesus Christ has become social reality even while this movement toward true freedom continues to unfold.

Freed to Serve

We have been exploring the complex ethical decision-making processes needed to sort things out between a runaway slave and his aggrieved master. Numerous ethical themes are explicitly named in the epistle to Philemon, and others have also come to the surface as we have tried to follow this story. These themes include freedom, responsibility, service, love, partnership, and faithfulness.

We take the occasion now to conduct a more systematic survey of several major ethical themes in Paul's letters. We begin with some general introductory comments about his approach to ethical discernment. Then we look specifically at freedom and love as moral categories. And we pause to ponder further the question of his views concerning slavery in light of his convictions about God's still unfolding future.

Our survey of ethical themes continues in chapter 11, where we will focus on Paul's teaching about household relationships, sexuality, and holiness. In chapter 12, we look at the church and its relationships with the powers.

Theology and Ethics in Paul

First we need to give attention to the relationship between theology and ethics in Paul's thought. Some readings of his letters that emphasized the doctrine of "salvation by grace through faith alone" led to a corresponding de-emphasis on the dimension of "works."

A phrase that Paul employs in both the introduction and the conclusion of his epistle to the Romans presents an

intriguing case study into his conception of faith and obedience. In Romans 1:5 he declares that the purpose of his
apostleship is "to bring about the obedience of faith among
all the Gentiles for the sake of his name." Paul reiterates
this claim as part of his closing doxology in 16:26. What
does he mean by "the obedience of faith," this phrase that
appears prominently in the introductory and concluding
material bracketing the entire letter? Many interpret this as
"the obedience which is faith" on the premise that faith
alone is what is required of people. Another more likely
rendering is "faithful obedience" (as in NIV, for example:
"the obedience that comes from faith"), because Paul elsewhere (e.g. Romans 6:12-23) expresses the conviction that
obedience grows out of a living faith.

Interpreters of Scripture, including Paul's letters,
appear at times to assume that "theology" is to "ethics"
what "theory" is to "practical application." Or the presumption is sometimes expressed that first one "believes"
and then one will know how to "behave."

The "therefore" pattern, which is prominent in Paul's
correspondence, tends to reinforce these perceptions.
Several of his letters seem to be organized into a theology
section followed by an ethics section. For example,
1 Thessalonians 4:1, Romans 12:1, Colossians 3:5, and
Ephesians 4:1 appear to be points of transition from theology to morality. In terms of the structure of these letters
and the broad movement of Paul's thought, as he relates
the gospel to the life situations of his addressees, this distinction rings true. His letter to the churches in Rome illustrates this pattern. In Romans 1–11 he has been wrestling
theologically with many issues, especially the question of
the relationship between Jews and Gentiles within the people of God. Moved by the mercy and mystery of God's
ways ("O the depth of the riches and wisdom and knowl-

edge of God" 11:33), Paul begins at Romans 12 to explore answers to the question, So what? How then shall God's people behave toward each other and within the world? On the basis of God's mercy he urges his readers to present themselves sacrificially to God. The experience of God's grace moves inevitably to the requirement to make ethical choices in line with God's will:

> I appeal to you therefore, brothers and sisters, by the mercies of God, to present your bodies as a living sacrifice, holy and acceptable to God, which is your spiritual worship. Do not be conformed to this world, but be transformed by the renewing of your minds, so that you may discern what is the will of God—what is good and acceptable and perfect. (12:1-2)

At 12:3 then Paul begins to deal successively with a variety of aspects of life among the believers in Rome, including their relationship to each other and how they should respond to the existing authorities and powers (12:3–13:14). (See "Obedient to God, Submissive to Authorities" in chapter 12.)

Having recognized that the broad structures of some of Paul's letters conform to the "first theology then ethics" pattern, we need to be aware that it is misleading to make a sharp distinction between his theology and his ethics. Paul includes ethical guidance throughout his letters, and he repeatedly conveys the theological grounding for his moral appeals. "Therefore" statements occur frequently throughout his correspondence. There is only one "therefore" in the epistle to Philemon (verse 17), but it demonstrates Paul's pastoral strategy. He is applying subtle pressure on Philemon to act in ways that give lived concrete testimony to a new set of relationships in the Lord.

"Therefore" clauses are prevalent in Paul's letters, especially as part of his reminders that an experience of God's grace leads directly to the expectation of obedience to God's will. There is a dynamic interrelationship between the indicative (God's grace) and the imperative (a responsive faithfulness). In Galatians 5:1 Paul begins with the indicative of God's liberating work and then moves to an ethical injunction, and in Philippians 2:12-13 he begins with a command and then reminds his readers of God's enabling work among them. In both examples (and there are many others) Paul underlines both God's gracious initiative and the necessity of human response to that initiative:

> For freedom Christ has set us free. Stand firm, therefore, and do not submit again to a yoke of slavery. (Galatians 5:1)

> Therefore, my beloved, just as you have always obeyed me, not only in my presence, but much more now in my absence, work out your own salvation with fear and trembling; for it is God who is at work in you, enabling you both to will and to work for his good pleasure. (Philippians 2:12-13)

As these two samples show, Paul consciously imbeds the moral imperative within the indicative of God's liberating and enabling work. Now we ask, What then is "the will of God" (Romans 12:2)? What does Paul include under the category of God's "good pleasure" (Philippians 2:13)?

"That You May Discern What Is the Will of God"

In part 2, God's Unfolding Story, we attempted to document how Paul grounds his theology, including his ethical teachings, in the Scriptures. After his Damascus road encounter with the living Christ, he sees all of Scripture through the lenses of God's climactic revelation in Jesus Christ, whereby the scriptural ethical traditions have also been transformed. Much of our attention has focused on how Paul views the Torah in light of the Christ event. The relationship between God's will and God's law has been significantly altered by the coming of Christ.

Despite what seems at times to be Paul's dismissal of the law now that Christ has come, he does not advocate that the Torah be abandoned as a norm for faithful living. The law still illuminates the path of obedience. However, now that Christ has come, there is a new creation (Galatians 6:15; 2 Corinthians 5:17), and in Christ through the Spirit, people are empowered to walk in newness of life. The law and the commandments are thereby both fulfilled and transcended.

We can illustrate the transcending and fulfilling of the law by citing in parallel three texts in which Paul asserts that neither circumcision nor uncircumcision have any value in comparison to the new reality now launched in Christ:

> For in Christ neither circumcision nor uncircumcision counts for anything; the only thing that counts is faith working through love. (Galatians 5:6)

> For neither circumcision nor uncircumcision is anything; but a new creation is everything! (Galatians 6:15)

> Circumcision is nothing, and uncircumcision is nothing; but obeying the commandments of God is everything. (1 Corinthians 7:19)

For a Jew like Paul to dismiss circumcision as nonessential would have been jarring to the sensibilities of fellow Jews. Equally puzzling for his later readers, who (unlike the original audiences) have the opportunity to view these texts side by side, is the fact that whereas in Galatians he promotes an ethic of "faith working through love," in 1 Corinthians he advocates "obeying the commandments of God." In Corinth, where Jewish identity issues are less pressing than in Galatia, he affirms the abiding importance of the commandments as guidelines for living.

In 1 Corinthians 7:19 Paul does not mention which specific commandments he has in mind, but in Romans 13:9 he lists four of the Ten Commandments (Exodus 20:13-17; Deuteronomy 5:17-21):

> The commandments, "You shall not commit adultery;
> You shall not murder; You shall not steal; You shall
> not covet"; and any other commandment, are summed
> up in this word, "Love your neighbor as yourself."
> (Romans 13:9)

Evidently the Ten Commandments are viewed by Paul as norms for faithful living. The fact that Paul here and in Galatians 5:13-14 quotes the love commandment from Leviticus 19:18 also indicates that he recognizes the abiding validity of the law, especially the law as summed up and fulfilled in love.

In addition to the commandments of the law, Paul at times goes to Jesus's teachings for ethical norms for daily living. There are several instances of this in the exhortation section of Romans (12:1–15:13):

> Bless those who persecute you; bless and do not curse
> them. (Romans 12:14; cf. Luke 6:27-28; Matthew 5:44)

> I know and am persuaded in the Lord Jesus that noth-
> ing is unclean in itself; but it is unclean for anyone
> who thinks it unclean. (Romans 14:14; cf. Mark 7:15)

In 1 Corinthians 7, where Paul deals with marriage, celibacy, divorce, and other sexuality themes, he explicitly specifies that his ruling on divorce is rooted in Jesus's teachings:

> To the married I give this command—not I but the Lord—that the wife should not separate from her husband (but if she does separate, let her remain unmarried or else be reconciled to her husband), and that the husband should not divorce his wife. (1 Corinthians 7:10-11; cf. Matthew 5:31-32; Mark 10:11-12; Luke 16:18)

Immediately following these instructions is a word of counsel regarding a situation apparently not reflected in any of Jesus's recorded teachings. Paul explicitly makes this differentiation: "To the rest I say—I and not the Lord" (1 Corinthians 7:12). It is clear that, if Jesus's explicit teachings are to function as norms for discovering the will of God within various circumstances of life, the supply soon runs out, and other means of discerning God's will need to be implemented.

On a number of occasions Paul commends the imitation of Christ. Sometimes he correlates the imitation of Christ with the imitation of his own model of following Christ. In his first letter to the church at Thessalonica, he testifies gratefully that in their early response to the gospel the Thessalonian believers had become imitators both of the missionaries who had shared the gospel with them and of the Lord:

> And you became imitators of us and of the Lord, for in spite of persecution you received the word with joy inspired by the Holy Spirit, so that you became an example to all the believers in Macedonia and in Achaia. (1 Thessalonians 1:6-7)

378 Remember the Future

Paul commends the Thessalonians believers, noting that their experience of joyfully receiving the word despite persecution followed the path of Jesus's suffering and that of the apostles. What had happened to Jesus and to the apostolic missionaries was also now unfolding in their lives. In 2:14 Paul widens the angle of view by noting that the Thessalonians were suffering in identification with the churches in Judea, who were also being persecuted at the hands of their own compatriots. When he says, "You became imitators of the churches of God in Christ Jesus that are in Judea" (2:14), he does not mean that the Thessalonians deliberately copied the conduct of their sister churches in Judea. Jewish believers in Judea and believers in Thessalonica in their common allegiance to Jesus Christ share together in the fellowship of Christ's suffering.

Paul at times also exhorts his people both to imitate Christ and to follow his example. At the conclusion of his pastoral counsel to the church in Corinth on the issue of food sacrificed to idols (1 Corinthians 8:1–11:1), he says, "Be imitators of me, as I am of Christ" (11:1). The Thessalonian congregation, whom he commends as imitators of Christ, also includes people whom he commands to imitate Christ. In his first letter Paul identifies them as needing admonition: "Admonish the idlers" (1 Thessalonians 5:14). By the time of his second letter the problem of the unruly and disruptive enthusiasts in Thessalonica has apparently gotten worse. Not only were they not working to support themselves and contribute toward the common good. They were also busybodies who were burdening the congregation and leaving a negative impression in their city. In this case he issues a series of clear commands addressed both to the unruly idlers themselves and to the congregation about how to deal with the situation:

Now we command you, beloved, in the name of our
Lord Jesus Christ, to keep away from believers who
are living in idleness and not according to the tradition
that they received from us. For you yourselves know
how you ought to imitate us; we were not idle when
we were with you, and we did not eat anyone's bread
without paying for it; but with toil and labor we
worked night and day, so that we might not burden
any of you. This was not because we do not have that
right, but in order to give you an example to imitate.
For even when we were with you, we gave you this
command: Anyone unwilling to work should not eat.
For we hear that some of you are living in idleness,
mere busybodies, not doing any work. Now such persons we command and exhort in the Lord Jesus Christ
to do their work quietly and to earn their own living.
(2 Thessalonians 3:6-12)

We note that Paul's vigorous exhortations are reinforced
by repeated references to the teaching and the modeling
that he and his co-workers had done during their initial
visit in Thessalonica. In this case we notice that he does
not specifically commend imitation of Christ. He does
exhort these believers "in the name of the Lord Jesus
Christ" (3:6) and "in the Lord Jesus Christ" (3:12). And
he reminds the Thessalonians of the ethical tradition transmitted by the teaching and lifestyle of the ones who had
brought the gospel to them, and he urges them to conform
to that tradition (3:6).

When Paul refers to the tradition that he and his co-
workers had taught and modeled he might have had in
mind some of Jesus's specific instructions, as he does, for
example, in 1 Corinthians 9:14 on the issue of the apostle's
right to be supported by the church. It is more likely that he
has in mind the self-giving pattern of Jesus's life and his

death for the sake of others. Gorman entitles his 2001 book
Cruciformity to convey the notion of conformity to Jesus's
way of costly service. Richard Hays uses the expression
"the christomorphic life" and identifies three "focal
images" (cross, new creation, and community), all of which
serve as paradigms for the church in its ethical discernment
(1996:43; cf. 19-36; 193-200). We cite Hays' summary:

> The distinctive shape of obedience to God is disclosed
> in Jesus Christ's faithful death on the cross for the sake
> of God's people. That death becomes metaphorically
> paradigmatic for the obedience of the community: to
> obey God means to offer our lives unqualifiedly for the
> sake of others. Thus, the fundamental norm of Pauline
> ethics is the christomorphic life. To imitate Christ is
> also to follow the apostolic example of surrendering
> one's own prerogatives and interests.
>
>   Within the world shaped by the story of Jesus Christ,
> the community wrestles with the constant need for
> spiritual discernment to understand and enact the obe-
> dience of faith. Ethics cannot be sufficiently guided by
> law or by institutionalized rules; instead, Spirit-
> empowered, Spirit-discerned conformity to Christ is
> required. The community is called to act in creative
> freedom in order to become "a living sacrifice, holy
> and acceptable to God" (Romans 12:1). In so doing,
> the community discovers *koinonia* with one another in
> the sufferings of Christ and in the hope of sharing his
> glory. (1996:43, italics original)

How then does the community of faith discern the will
of God? The church decides what is the good, acceptable,
and perfect will of God (Romans 12:2) not primarily by
the law, or even by Jesus's moral instructions, but by participating with Christ in conformity to his life of service
and his sacrifice on the cross.

Freedom and Love

After this overview of the character of Paul's ethics, we shift to a consideration of some of the prominent ethical categories evident in his pastoral correspondence. At this point we focus on the themes of freedom and love. It is abundantly apparent that Paul views these two moral values as being in some tension with each other.

In his struggles with advocates of law observance among Gentile churches, Paul in various ways espouses freedom as a counterpoint to life under the law. In 2 Corinthians, where he compares the old and new covenants, he asserts, "Where the Spirit of the Lord is, there is freedom" (3:17). In Romans, where he appeals to Jews and Gentiles in Christ to express their unity within a shared awareness of God's welcoming justice, he emphasizes freedom: "For the law of the Spirit of life in Christ Jesus has set you free from the law of sin and of death" (Romans 8:2).

In our treatment of Paul's letter to the Galatians (see chapters 8 and 9) we have noted that he employs the rhetoric of liberation to describe the outcome of God's invasion of grace through Jesus Christ. His retelling of the stories of Hagar and Sarah and their sons ends with the declaration, "So then, friends, we are children not of the slave but of the free woman" (Galatians 4:31). Immediately he adds, "For freedom Christ has set us free" (5:1). A little later he echoes this assertion: "For you were called to freedom, brothers and sisters" (5:13). Near the heart of Paul's understanding of the gospel is the metaphor of liberation. Among the narratives that shape this metaphor are the exodus of Israel from their bondage in Egypt and a variety of stories in the Greco-Roman world about slaves being freed through the practice of manumission.

As we have already noted, in Galatians 5 Paul articulates

both the indicative of God's liberation through Christ and the imperatives that flow from it. He is concerned that the believers in Galatia might return to the kind of bondage from which they have already been rescued. He urges them not to give up their freedom in Christ by giving in to the demand that they take on law observance: "Stand firm, therefore, and do not submit again to a yoke of slavery" (5:1). Paul also warns about the slippery slope of fleshly indulgence whereby liberty in Christ can degenerate into license: "Do not use your freedom as an opportunity for self-indulgence" (5:13). Freedom attained through Christ calls for clear moral choices both to avoid certain kinds of behavior and to live in obedient faithfulness to the way of Christ. In Galatians 5:13 he calls for a servanthood kind of love: "Through love become slaves to one another." In 5:14 he elaborates on this call to love one another by recalling Leviticus 19:18:

> For the whole law is summed up in a single commandment, "You shall love your neighbor as yourself."

Paul in his ethical exhortations often identifies love as the way believers are called on to respond to God's grace made known in Christ. The following are a few of the many instances where this is the case:

> Let love be genuine; hate what is evil, hold fast to what is good; love one another with mutual affection; outdo one another in showing honor. (Romans 12:9-10)

> I therefore, the prisoner in the Lord, beg you to lead a life worthy of the calling to which you have been called, with all humility and gentleness, with patience, bearing with one another in love, making every effort to maintain the unity of the Spirit in the bond of peace. (Ephesians 4:1-3)

Therefore be imitators of God, as beloved children,
and live in love, as Christ loved us and gave himself up
for us, a fragrant offering and sacrifice to God.
(Ephesians 5:1-2)

Shun youthful passions and pursue righteousness,
faith, love, and peace, along with those who call on
the Lord from a pure heart. (2 Timothy 2:22)

Paul's celebrated poem about love (1 Corinthians 13) is
situated within his response to the issue of spiritual gifts,
including the high value being placed on the more showy
gifts. As an antidote to the self-promoting exercise of glos-
salalia Paul promotes a more excellent way, the way of love:

If I speak in the tongues of mortals and of angels, but
do not have love, I am a noisy gong or a clanging cym-
bal. And if I have prophetic powers, and understand all
mysteries and all knowledge, and if I have all faith, so
as to remove mountains, but do not have love, I am
nothing. If I give away all my possessions, and if I hand
over my body so that I may boast, but do not have
love, I gain nothing. Love is patient; love is kind; love is
not envious or boastful or arrogant or rude. It does not
insist on its own way; it is not irritable or resentful; it
does not rejoice in wrongdoing, but rejoices in the
truth. It bears all things, believes all things, hopes all
things, endures all things. (1 Corinthians 13:1-7)

There is in Paul's mind a dialectical relationship
between freedom as a gift made available through Christ
and love as the Christlike way of living. In Galatians 5 he
articulates this relationship paradoxically, urging his followers to exercise their freedom in the slavery of love. To
explore this intersection between liberty and love further
we turn to Paul's pastoral counsel to the church at Corinth

on the issue of food offered idols (1 Corinthians 8–10) and the section in Romans with similar themes (Romans 14:1–15:13).

In chapter 3 we featured Paul's pastoral interaction with the church in Corinth around the issue of whether or not it was appropriate for them to eat food that had been previously sacrificed to idols. Some among the Corinthian believers were apparently flaunting their freedom from superstitious beliefs about idols. "All of us possess knowledge," they said, "no idol in the world really exists" (1 Corinthians 8:1, 4). In his reply, Paul expresses his basic agreement. "We know," he says; but then he adds, "Knowledge puffs up, but love builds up" (8:1). He urges the Corinthians not to let the exercise of their personal freedom scandalize those whose consciences on this matter make them vulnerable: "But take care that this liberty of yours does not somehow become a stumbling block to the weak" (8:9). The underlying word here translated "liberty" is *exousia*, which conveys the notion of a personal right or authority to choose (as in the NIV: "the exercise of your freedom").

First Corinthians 9 seems to interrupt the flow of Paul's treatment of the issue at hand. Before he resumes his direct discussion of idols and food (10:1–11:1), he inserts an extended reflection about his personal rights and his deliberate choice to use his freedom in service of others.

Paul opens with several rhetorical questions: "Am I not free? Am I not an apostle?" (9:1). This launches him into a series of arguments and appeals by which he establishes his apostolic right to receive support from the congregations he serves (9:3-14). He appeals on the basis of the example of other apostles (9:5-6) and the analogy of the soldier, the farmer, and the shepherd, all of whom derive benefits directly from those among whom they labor (9:7, 10). He quotes the Mosaic law (9:8-9), recalls the way people involved in temple service receive life sustenance (9:13), and rehearses Jesus's commandment that "those who proclaim the gospel should get their living by the gospel" (9:14).

Having established his right to receive support from people among whom he proclaims the gospel, however, Paul makes a stunning about-face:

> Nevertheless, we have not made use of this right, but we endure anything rather than put an obstacle in the way of the gospel of Christ. (9:12)

> But I have made no use of any of these rights, nor am I writing this so that they may be applied in my case. Indeed, I would rather die than that—no one will deprive me of my ground for boasting! (9:15)

As a free person himself, he declares that he has made himself a slave in the ministry of proclaiming and teaching the gospel of Jesus Christ:

> For though I am free with respect to all, I have made myself a slave to all, so that I might win more of them. (9:19)

As "a slave to all," Paul determines to preach the gospel free of charge. He relinquishes his rights in order to reach as many people as possible. He adapts his strategy to the people among whom he works. Paul goes to people where they are, on their terms, and engages them in love. Toward Jews and Gentile proselytes under the law he respects the Torah including its rituals. For Gentiles, however, he resists imposing food laws and other observances. In 9:21 he seeks to articulate his adaptive strategy, and he does so with the use of a word play. Because such word plays rarely survive the translation process we have inserted the underlying Greek words into the NRSV text:

> To those outside the law [*anomois*] I became as one outside the law [*anomos*] (though I am not free from God's law [*anomos*] but am under Christ's law [*ennomos*]) so that I might win those outside the law [*anomous*]. (9:21)

Here is the key to understanding Paul's flip-flop concerning financial support. He insists that he is not *anomos*, lawless before God, even though he has been freed from the compulsion to impose observance of all of the law's commandments. Rather he is *ennomos*, under the law of Christ. And, as in Galatians 6:2, the law of Christ points not to an additional legal code, or even to Jesus's teachings as normative guidance for faithful living. Rather, Paul views Jesus's life of obedience and his faithfulness to God even unto his death on the cross as the pattern for his ministry and as the model for life and relationships within the church.

Paul too has rights, but he does not insist on exercising these rights. Rather he chooses to do what is right. In Corinth he identifies himself with the weak, the low and despised, rather than with the strong and those of noble birth (cf. 1:26-29). He adjusts to the scruples of the weak concerning idol meat. He identifies with the poor by joining them in working with his own hands. All of this also invites the upwardly mobile Corinthians, who love to network in the temples with the rich and the strong, to relinquish their rights for the sake of others. Paul's way of life also challenges the spiritual elite in Corinth who seek the showy gifts of tongues and miraculous powers to pursue instead the way of love and those gifts that build up the church.

In 10:23-24 Paul recapitulates his counsel for the Corinthians, and in 10:33–11:1 he refers them to his own example as one who seeks to imitate Christ:

> "All things are lawful," but not all things are beneficial. "All things are lawful," but not all things build up. Do not seek your own advantage, but that of the other. (10:23-24)

> I try to please everyone in everything I do, not seeking my own advantage, but that of many, so that they may be saved. Be imitators of me, as I am of Christ. (10:33–11:1)

One of his final exhortations in 1 Corinthians says it succinctly: "Let all that you do be done in love" (16:14).

In this consideration of the interplay between the moral themes of freedom and love in Paul's writings, we turn finally to a brief exploration of the grand finale in his epistle to the Romans: 14:1–15:13. His exhortation there is highly reminiscent of his climactic appeal to the Corinthians:

> We who are strong ought to put up with the failings of the weak, and not to please ourselves. Each of us must please our neighbor for the good purpose of building up the neighbor. (15:1-2)

The weak appear to be attentive to Jewish ritual observances, such as food laws, festival days and circumcision. The strong are likely mainly Gentile believers, although Paul, a Jew, includes himself within this group; they demonstrate a certain level of freedom from purity laws

388   *Remember the Future*

and rituals. But what kind of behavior does Paul call for, and why?

In Romans 14–15 he refers repeatedly to the work of Christ as warrant for the way in which they are summoned to relate to each other:

> We are the Lord's. (14:8)
> Christ died and lived again. (14:9)
> Do not let what you eat cause the ruin of one for whom
>   Christ died. (14:15)
> Christ did not please himself. (15:3)
> Christ has welcomed you, for the glory of God. (15:7)
> Christ has become a servant of the circumcised on
>   behalf of the truth of God. (15:8)

Paul's prayer for the church in Rome articulates his longing that the members might "live in harmony with one another, in accordance with Christ Jesus" (15:5). The life of the church needs to be shaped in conformity to the character of God as made known in Jesus Christ.

Paul becomes quite directive in spelling out what kind of behavior within the community would conform to the way of Christ. He urges them not to quibble with each other over opinions (14:1). He repeatedly calls on them neither to condemn each other nor to despise each other (14:3, 4, 10). In 14:13 he elaborates:

> Let us therefore no longer pass judgment on one
> another, but resolve instead never to put a stumbling
> block or hindrance in the way of another.

Clearly he desires that the church as a body manifest a Christlike character. This entails "walking in love" (14:15) and "mutual upbuilding" (14:19).

Paul wants his Roman hearers to relate to each other

in ways that are coherent with the big story of God's creative and redemptive work climaxing in Jesus Christ. He
warns them about the coming judgment: "We will all stand
before the judgment seat of God" (14:10b); and he cites
Isaiah looking toward the time when every knee will bow
to the Lord and every tongue will praise God (14:11, echoing Isaiah 45:23). And he reminds them about the nature
of God's reign:

> The kingdom of God is not food and drink but right-
> eousness and peace and joy in the Holy Spirit. (14:17)

In sum: Paul urges the church to view its life and relationships from within the cosmic perspective of God's
reign, already inaugurated in Jesus Christ, yet still moving
toward consummation. Likely that is what he has in mind
when he urges, "Do not let your good be spoken of as evil"
(14:16). Paul explains in terms of God's reign. The expression "your good" goes way beyond any notion of freedom
or tradition. God's still unfolding reign is characterized by
"righteousness and peace and joy in the Holy Spirit"
rather than by prescribed practices ("food and drink").
When the people of God embody kingdom values, the
communities among whom they live begin to glimpse
God's grand intention for all.

But What About Slavery?

We began this chapter with the story of Philemon, his
freedom-seeking slave, and the apostle who tried by means
of letter to mediate between them. Even though we do not
know exactly how things developed for Onesimus, we do
know that slavery as a social and economic institution continued. Paul himself and those of his followers who per-
petuated his theological legacy seemed to assume that a

slaveholding master and his slave would remain within that relationship, even though in some cases they were now also kin through Christ.

In the remaining chapters we will have occasion to comment about the household codes in Colossians and Ephesians as well as some directives in the Pastoral Epistles (1 and 2 Timothy and Titus). These texts seem to be on the conservative side of the social and political spectrum with reference to slavery. In our examination of all of these letters, however, we will ask whether the underlying momentum is toward the dismantling of slavery or the justification of its continuation.

There is another text in Paul's writings that connects directly with the issue of slavery: 1 Corinthians 7:17-24. As he communicates his pastoral counsel concerning marriage and celibacy and other sexuality themes, he pauses to articulate what he calls his rule in the churches:

> However that may be, let each of you lead the life that
> the Lord has assigned, to which God called you. This
> is my rule in all the churches. Was anyone at the time
> of his call already circumcised? Let him not seek to
> remove the marks of circumcision. Was anyone at the
> time of his call uncircumcised? Let him not seek cir-
> cumcision. Circumcision is nothing, and uncircumci-
> sion is nothing; but obeying the commandments of
> God is everything. Let each of you remain in the con-
> dition in which you were called. Were you a slave
> when called? Do not be concerned about it. Even if
> you can gain your freedom, make use of your present
> condition now more than ever. For whoever was called
> in the Lord as a slave is a freed person belonging to
> the Lord, just as whoever was free when called is a
> slave of Christ. You were bought with a price; do not
> become slaves of human masters. In whatever condi-

tion you were called, brothers and sisters, there remain
with God. (1 Corinthians 7:17-24)

Paul illustrates his "rule" with reference to Jew/Gentile
and slave/free issues, even though the subject at hand has
to do with relationships between women and men. He
underscores the priority of God's calling. People are urged
to stay within their primary calling, regardless of their sta-
tion in life. Jews already circumcised should not attempt to
undo the marks of their circumcision, and Gentiles are
advised not to seek circumcision. For Jews and Gentiles in
Christ, their new reality within God's calling goes beyond
the physicality of their participation (or nonparticipation)
in the circumcision ritual.

With reference to slavery, Paul is equally persuasive
about giving ultimate priority to God's calling (7:21, 24).
However, the syntax of 7:21, where he directly addresses
slaves, is difficult to disentangle. Paul appears to convey
either a benign tolerance of slavery or a sense of resignation
that, at least for most slaves, change will be slow at best.
Freedom through manumission will be a possibility for
some, but there is little prospect for deep systemic change
any time soon. Available translations of 7:21 demonstrate
the vexing dilemma of interpreting Paul's instructions.
Compare the NRSV rendering with the RSV:

Were you a slave when called? Do not be concerned
about it. Even if you can gain your freedom, make use
of your present condition now more than ever. (NRSV)

Were you a slave when called? Never mind. But if you
can gain your freedom, avail yourself of the opportunity.
(RSV)

What is abundantly evident in this articulation of Paul's guiding rule regarding relationships between people whose social status is unequal is that their status in the Lord matters more. He expresses himself paradoxically. In the Lord the slave is actually free, and the free person is enslaved to Christ. Both slaves and their masters know that the high price of their manumission has been paid: "You were bought with a price" (7:23). Through Christ's death on the cross they have been set free.

11

IN HOUSEHOLDS OF A NEW ORDER

Our next visit to a congregation counseled by one of Paul's letters takes us to the city of Colossae. It seems appropriate to feature Colossians at this point, because this epistle has significant similarities to the letter to Philemon, which we explored in the previous chapter. Both letters come from Paul and Timothy (Philemon 1; Colossians 1:1). The persons conveying greetings in the two letters are largely the same: Epaphras, Mark, Aristarchus, Luke, and Demas (Philemon 23-24; Colossians 4:10-15). And there is significant common agenda, especially because Colossians includes a household code (3:18–4:1) with guidelines for relationships between wives and husbands, children and fathers, and slaves and their masters. It is the last of these relationships, of course, that is most prominent in Paul's short epistle to Philemon, Apphia and Archippus, and the church gathered in their household.

Some scholars judge Colossians to have been written not by Paul but by a Pauline disciple following the apostle's death. But references to Epaphras and other individuals known both to the Colossians and to Paul make it more likely the letter was written in Paul's lifetime. It is possible that, because of Paul's circumstances in prison, Timothy, who is listed as coauthor, might have written the letter. But what is the underlying story?

We'll hear the story in the way that Epaphras, himself

a member of the church at Colossae, might have experienced the events leading up to the writing of this letter. Besides the Colossians and Philemon texts noted above, our sources for this narrative include the thanksgiving section (Colossians 1:3-8), Paul's asides about his experiences of suffering (1:24–2:5), his oblique references to an ascetic philosophy being promoted in Colossae (1:16-23), his reference to the ethnic composition of the congregation and the surrounding community (3:11), and his personal references (4:7-9, 16-18). As for previous stories, so again here, some of the details have been imaginatively developed beyond what can be established in the texts themselves.

A STORY: Epaphras Remembers

Growing up in the fertile Lycus River valley, Epaphras often watched ships making their way from the Aegean Sea along the Meander and Lycus rivers to Colossae and the nearby cities of Hierapolis and Laodicea. Figs and olives from the groves nestled along the river went to market on these ships. Their cargo also included textiles woven from the wool of the sheep that grazed along the slopes of the river. Many of the fabrics had been dyed the rich red color for which the region was widely known. Medicines and herbs drawn from the roots and shoots of various native plants also found their way downriver to people near and far.

The population of Colossae and neighboring regions included Phrygians and Greek settlers and a sprinkling of other ethnic and religious groups from around the Mediterranean world. The Greek-speaking residents tended to regard all others as barbarians who were not as cultured as they were. The Scythians from the hinterland were viewed as the lowest of the barbarians, often caricatured as uncouth, not much better than wild beasts; typically they were slaves in households of those higher on the social ladder.

A significant Jewish minority in the Lycus valley also made its presence known, especially through their synagogues. The postures of the Jewish people toward their neighbors varied. Some Jews sharply separated themselves from people of different cultures, while other Jews accommodated their lifestyles to that of the people around them. Some synagogues warmly welcomed the *goyim* (Gentiles), and Gentiles occasionally joined in synagogue gatherings to study the Scriptures and for social interaction. A few Gentiles became proselytes, though most of them participated in synagogue worship and other activities without formally converting through circumcision or adopting ritual observances and devotion to the Torah.

Epaphras too had found his way into a synagogue in Colossae. He found the social life there stimulating, and the readings and discussions of the ancient texts edifying. A whole new world opened up for him as he heard the stories and participated in the Jewish festivals. Then on one of his business trips to Ephesus he became acquainted with an itinerant Jewish teacher named Paul. Paul's preaching and teaching from the sacred texts captivated him, especially when Paul shared his personal experience with a Jew named Jesus, who had been crucified in Judea but restored to life again. Epaphras recalled with deep emotion the time when he responded to Paul's preaching by acknowledging Jesus Christ as his Lord. Following his conversion Epaphras spent further time with Paul, being nurtured in his newly discovered faith.

Soon Epaphras himself began to share the gospel of Jesus Christ not only back home in Colossae but also in nearby Laodicea and Hierapolis. As a result, congregations emerged with Epaphras as their spiritual leader and guide. Believers gathered in homes for worship. In Laodicea a woman named Nympha opened her home to new believers and gave leadership to the group gathered there.

Most of the people who confessed their faith through baptism came from Gentile backgrounds. Many were formerly associated with the synagogues as God-fearers. Over and over, Epaphras was deeply moved by the life transformation that occurred when individuals abandoned various traditional religions and mystery cults for life in the church. They were dramatically transported from one kingdom to another. Even Scythian slaves from some of the households began to demonstrate a genuine personal faith, which was a surprise to many and an offense to some. The process of welcoming and incorporating these people into their life together as a congregation proved a major challenge.

There were some upsetting developments as well. Epaphras was uneasy about some of the bewildering practices and beliefs advocated by zealous representatives from some of the synagogues. These teachers endorsed a lifestyle of strict self-abasement and urged new believers to deny themselves through fasting and the observance of strict rules and guidelines. They introduced ritualistic practices that they claimed would result in visionary experiences of a lofty world of angels. They invited their neighbors to join in celebrating various festivals and Sabbath rituals. To Epaphras and many others in the community, these beliefs and practices seemed to be unnecessary, if not dangerous, additions to their life and worship. He was chagrined that some of the new believers, ever enthusiastic and eager to experience more of the fullness of God's grace and power, were tempted to seek these spiritual highs.

Epaphras decided to contact his mentor and spiritual father, Paul. During a business-related journey to Rome, he caught up with the apostle, who was in a Roman prison.

Paul was naturally eager to hear what had been happening as a result of the evangelistic efforts of this co-worker from the Lycus valley. Epaphras shared the good news that by God's grace new congregations had emerged in Colossae and nearby Laodicea and Hierapolis. The imprisoned apostle and his younger representative rejoiced as they reflected on the way that the gospel of Jesus Christ had flourished in these congregations and beyond.

But Epaphras also needed to convey his concerns about the ascetic and visionary philosophy that had influenced some in the church. What might the apostle have to say about these developments?

By the time Epaphras needed to depart on his journey home he had received a letter from Paul and his younger co-worker, Timothy, addressed to the church in Colossae. It was clear on first reading that Paul also intended this communication to be shared with the church in Laodicea.

Two others joined Epaphras for the trip back to the Lycus valley. Tychicus, another of Paul's associates, turned out to be valuable as an additional interpreter of Paul's letter. And Onesimus, though anxious about going back to Colossae, also seemed genuinely relieved that he could travel in company.

Transformed Relationships Within the Household of Faith

> As you therefore have received Christ Jesus the Lord, continue to live your lives in him, rooted and built up in him and established in the faith, just as you were taught, abounding in thanksgiving. (Colossians 2:6-7)

Paul's short letter to Philemon holds within it the seed of the coming liberation of slaves. The relationship between a slave and his master begins to be transformed when both are in Christ. Even when the social reality of slavery remains intact, slaves and masters who are relating as kin within the body of Christ catch a preview of the germination and glorious flowering of that seed, the future equality and unity assured in Christ. The social realities in the flesh and the assured oneness in the Lord may coexist in tension, but within the expanding vision of God's reign the latter eventually wins over the former.

But what then is the case for other relationships within the household, especially that between women and men, or specifically between husbands and wives? Is there in Christ a transformation of relationships between the sexes, or do the established values and understandings within the society at large also prevail within the church?

The societal standard for relationships within the home in the Greco-Roman world was rooted in Aristotle's description of a foundational hierarchy, an order of things deeply inscribed by nature, reason, and the gods. Children growing up would have been socialized into this way of viewing normal relationships within the home. Aristotle identifies three basic pairs of dominant and submissive partners within the household: master and slave, husband and wife, and father and children. The person in the dominant position (a male as master, husband, and father) functions as protector and provider as well as the household's representative to the outside world.

Political rhetoric during the time of Caesar Augustus and later promoted a hierarchical ideology in which the household is viewed as a microcosm of the empire. In the Roman world the emperor is at the top of the hierarchy. Divinely chosen by the gods to be keeper of the peace and guarantor of security, he was regarded as a benefactor who was deserving of honor, loyalty, and obedience. Beneath the emperor were the governors of the various provinces of the empire as well as the military leaders, who were charged with the responsibilities of maintaining order and suppressing rebellion.

Relationships within the home were therefore understood to be rooted in what was regarded as "the natural order of things" as expressed in the empire as a whole. In the household, the male as husband, as father, and as master of the slaves exercised control, just as the emperor did over the citizens and the subjugated peoples of the empire. The wife, children, and slaves were required to submit. One admittedly extreme expression of these understandings of the nature of things is the following: "A man has the rule of the household by nature, for the deliberative function in a woman is inferior, in children it does not yet exist, and in the case of slaves, it is completely absent" (quoted in Osiek and Balch, 1997:119).

Some of the letters within the New Testament (prominently Colossians and Ephesians in the Pauline corpus, and 1 Peter) include instructions about life within the household. Interpreters have disagreed about how they are to be interpreted. Are these guidelines for life in the household taken from the standard societal expectations of how the household should operate? Or are they shaped more by the relationships now made possible in Christ? We will come to this issue in due course, as we follow the argument of this letter to the church at Colossae.

It is the slave/master relationship that gets more attention in Colossians than relationships between women and men within the household. The reader of this letter needs to note, however, that right from the beginning it has in interpersonal relationships in mind. The opening is addressed "to the saints and the faithful brothers and sisters in Christ in Colossae" (1:2). The letter as a whole invites reflections about life in Christ for people within all of life's circumstances.

Before dealing specifically with relationships in the household, Paul builds the groundwork by pondering the big picture of what God has accomplished in Christ.

Transferred into the Kingdom of God's Son!

As Paul weighs what Epaphras has shared with him, he finds himself instinctively moved to pray, first offering thanksgiving, and then speaking his heartfelt petition to God. In a similar way he begins his letter by thanking God for the faith and the love evident among the saints in Colossae and acknowledging the hope laid up for them in heaven (1:3-5), a hope now growing and bearing fruit among them (1:6a). With Epaphras likely still nearby, Paul also ponders with gratitude the ministry of this faithful servant from Colossae and the ways in which his witness has taken root and borne fruit in the Lycus valley (1:6b-8).

Paul reassures the Colossians that he has been praying for them. He prays that they might be filled with the knowledge of God's will in all wisdom and that they might live in a way that is worthy of the Lord (1:9-10). He prays that they might be strong in the power that God supplies, so that they can endure patiently whatever comes their way (1:11).

He also reminds these new believers about their inheritance as saints (1:12). Their story features a rescue and transfer achieved by God. The result is a distinct "before" and a "now":

> He has rescued us from the power of darkness and transferred us into the kingdom of his beloved Son, in whom we have redemption, the forgiveness of sins. (1:13-14)

What God has accomplished is described using warfare imagery. The Colossian saints have been rescued from malignant powers and escorted into another realm, the kingdom of God's Son. Paul also draws on the language of redemption, which has its roots in the practice of the manumission of slaves or the release of prisoners of war. And he talks about the forgiveness of sins. Even here the underlying notion is that of release, the act of freeing those who are bound by the power of sin. Redemption, release, and admission into the kingdom are all part of the "already" of the inheritance of the saints.

This present "inheritance of the saints in the light" (1:12) is emphasized to such an extent that some later interpreters of this letter have wondered whether Paul could have written it. Was this letter written by the same apostle who authored the letters to Thessalonica and Corinth, in which he emphasizes that the consummation of God's redemption is still to be awaited in the future? In Colossians the future inheritance seems already to have arrived. Yet, as will be evident later (especially in 3:4), even in this letter Paul also recognizes a period "in the meantime" during which the saints still await their glorious full inheritance, a future already realized though not yet present in perfect fullness.

Their inheritance is rooted in what God has done in Christ. Before he speaks directly to the intrusive philosophy making its inroads into the Colossian church (2:8-23), and before he instructs them concerning life in the household (3:1–4:1), Paul offers a reminder regarding what is foundational for their life of faith. The dynamic center of his pastoral word to the saints at Colossae is an exalted hymn or poetic narrative about Christ (1:15-20). This poem is bracketed by the transitional summary in 1:13-14 (discussed above) and its recapitulation in 1:21-23, both of which remind these believers that they are participants with Christ. This hymn depicts Christ as the twice first-born, "the firstborn of all creation" (1:15), and "the first-born from the dead" (1:18):

> He is the image of the invisible God, the firstborn of
> all creation; for in him all things in heaven and on
> earth were created, things visible and invisible, whether
> thrones or dominions or rulers or powers—all things
> have been created through him and for him. He him-
> self is before all things, and in him all things hold
> together. He is the head of the body, the church; he is
> the beginning, the firstborn from the dead, so that he
> might come to have first place in everything. For in
> him all the fullness of God was pleased to dwell, and
> through him God was pleased to reconcile to himself
> all things, whether on earth or in heaven, by making
> peace through the blood of his cross. (1:15-20)

Scholars frequently note that this poem utilizes the language of Jewish wisdom literature to affirm Jesus's role as God's partner in creation (see Witherington, 1994a:266-72). A personified Wisdom speaks in Proverbs 8:22: "The Lord created me at the beginning of his work, the first of his acts of long ago." She takes her place as co-creator: "When he marked out the foundations of the earth, then I was beside him, like a master worker; and I was daily his delight" (8:29-30). Other images may be derived from the Wisdom of Solomon: "She is a breath of the power of God, and a pure emanation of the glory of the Almighty" (Wisdom of Solomon 7:25). Wisdom reflects God's image: "She is a reflection of eternal light, a spotless mirror of the working of God, and an image of his goodness" (7:26). Yet Wisdom also seems to be all powerful and divine: "Although she is but one, she can do all things, and while remaining in herself, she renews all things" (7:27).

Paul seems to have been influenced by these and other Jewish Wisdom motifs. However, he does more than borrow proof texts to help him articulate theological convictions about the relationship between Jesus and God. Drawing on a poetic confession, which may have been recited or sung in worship, he tells the story of Jesus Christ as the central player in God's grand story, a story beginning in creation and climaxing in the new creation. And Paul shares this narrative in ways that both affirm the continuity with God's creating and redeeming activity in the past and testify concerning God's dramatic new initiative in the reconciling work of Christ accomplished on the cross. The same God who created the world and entered into covenant with Israel has now intervened climactically in Christ. Through this saving initiative, God in Christ extends redemption, the forgiveness of sins, reconciliation, and peace, not only to Israel but potentially also to all the world. A rupture in the relationship between the creator God and the created world calls for a new beginning. Christ, "the firstborn of all creation" (1:15) inaugurates this beginning through his resurrection as "the firstborn from the dead" (1:18).

In the following chart we present in parallel columns a literal translation of what this poem says about Jesus Christ (adapted from Wright, 1992:104). We note a roughly parallel series of affirmations concerning Christ and his role in both creation and the new creation.

Creation (1:15-18a)	New Creation (1:18b-20)
. . . who is the image of God, the invisible, firstborn of all creation:	. . . who is the beginning, firstborn from the dead:

Creation (1:15-18a)	New Creation (1:18b-20)

For
in him were created all things
  in heaven and earth,
  things seen and unseen
  whether thrones or
    lordships
  whether rulers or
    authorities,
all things **through him** and
for **him** were created.
	so that
	he might become in all
	  things himself preeminent
	for **in him** all the fullness
	  was pleased to dwell
	and **through him** to recon-
	  cile all things to himself

He is before all things
and all things **in him** hold
  together
	making peace by the blood
	  of his cross (**through him**)
	  whether things on the earth
	  or things in heaven.

and He is the head of the body, the church.	

What this exalted poem celebrates about Jesus Christ has contributed to later attempts at formulating doctrinal affirmations about the triune God. With reference to creation, Christ is the sphere, the agent, and the goal: "In him, through him, for him" all things were created. The outcome of the resurrection is that Christ becomes the preeminent Lord of all. This relationship is again described in terms of sphere ("in him all the fullness was pleased to dwell") and agency ("through him to reconcile all things to himself"). Acknowledged as having been "before all things," Christ is also the one who sustains all things: "All things in him hold together."

Situated between the two strophes about creation and new creation is a striking assertion concerning the relationship of Christ to the church: "He is the head of the body, the church" (1:18a). Christ is head of the church both as ruler and as source, both as the one who guides and the one whose crucifixion and resurrection establishes and nurtures the community.

Because the worshipful poetry of Colossians 1:15-20 has inspired later doctrinal formulations, the significance of its claims within its own cultural and political context have often been underplayed. Inadequately acknowledged is the fact that this eulogy to Christ subverts and deeply undermines the claims prominently made about the Roman Caesar. Jesus Christ is the image of the invisible God, before whom all authorities and rulers (including Caesar) must submit. In the popular imagination fanned by imperial mythology, Caesar is the head of all things, the one bearing the image of the divine, whose benevolent power maintains order and peace throughout the world. "Not so!" declare those who confess Jesus Christ in the rhetoric of this hymn. Jesus makes peace by the blood of his cross, not by the violent strategies of the Roman peace. Jesus as head of the church and as Lord of all renounces such violence and extends an embrace that potentially includes all (see Walsh & Keesmaat, 2004).

Following the poem about Christ, Paul goes on to describe what he sees as the implications for the church:

> And you who were once estranged and hostile in mind, doing evil deeds, he has now reconciled in his fleshly body through death, so as to present you holy and blameless and irreproachable before him. (1:21-22)

As in 1:13-14, here Paul reminds the church at Colossae about the "before" and the "now" of their status before God. They were once among the estranged and hostile who have now been reconciled through Jesus's death on the cross; the words "in his fleshly body through death" (1:22a) emphasize the incarnation and especially his real suffering. The outcome for those reconciled is that they are presented "holy and blameless and irreproachable before him" (1:22b). However, there is a proviso, namely, that they abide in the faith and the hope of the gospel (1:23).

To illustrate what is involved in this kind of participation in Christ, Paul draws his readers' attention to his own model of ministry (1:24–2:5). He even refers to himself as a co-sufferer with Christ:

> I am now rejoicing in my sufferings for your sake, and in my flesh I am completing what is lacking in Christ's afflictions for the sake of his body, that is, the church. (1:24)

Paul also dwells on the grand sweep of God's self-revelation through Christ, a mystery now made known through the glorious riches of the gospel (1:25-26). The aim of his ministry, he says, is their maturity in Christ: "Christ in you, the hope of glory" (1:27). In striving to build up the believers in Colossae (as well as in Laodicea and elsewhere) (1:29; 2:1), Paul expresses the longing that they will be knit together in love, and he reminds them to keep their sights on the exalted Christ:

> I want their hearts to be encouraged and united in love, so that they may have all the riches of assured understanding and have the knowledge of God's mystery, that is, Christ himself, in whom are hidden all the treasures of wisdom and knowledge. (2:2-3)

The Christ of the hymn therefore defines their unity as believers and unveils the wisdom and knowledge of God.

Living in Kingdom Ways

Paul offers a transitional summary to introduce a series of images describing life within the kingdom of God:

> As you therefore have received Christ Jesus the Lord, continue to live your lives in him, rooted and built up in him and established in the faith, just as you were taught, abounding in thanksgiving. (2:6-7)

The indicative of God's grace and redemption, as received through Christ, leads to the imperative of living in Christ. In a fast-paced series of vivid word pictures (2:9-15), Paul underscores the triumph made known to the Colossian believers through Jesus Christ the crucified and risen Lord.

He addresses the Colossian believers directly in several declarations about what they have received through Christ. He draws on metaphors and images from the political realm and from Jewish ritual practices. He reminds them that Christ is the one in whom "the whole fullness of deity dwells bodily" (2:9). He adds, "You have come to fullness in him, who is the head of every ruler and authority" (2:10). Therefore, no emperor or provincial governor can claim ultimate authority, because Christ is the head. Paul also spiritualizes the Jewish ritual of circumcision in order to make his point that believers participate in the death, burial, and resurrection of Christ. Circumcision rituals among Jewish people and baptismal practices in the early church lie behind this claim:

> In him also you were circumcised with a spiritual circumcision, by putting off the body of the flesh in the circumcision of Christ; when you were buried with him in baptism, you were also raised with him through faith in the power of God, who raised him from the dead. And

when you were dead in trespasses and the uncircumcision of your flesh, God made you alive together with
him, when he forgave us all our trespasses. (2:11-13)

In addition to these "you" statements in which Paul
underscores by means of a variety of metaphors what the
Colossian believers have already experienced in Christ, he
offers several further picturesque portrayals of what God
has done. He employs the legal and financial image of the
erasure of a record of indebtedness, or the dismissal of
such a record by pinning it to the cross:

[God] forgave us all our trespasses, erasing the record
that stood against us with its legal demands. He set
this aside, nailing it to the cross. (2:13b-14)

By means of yet another dramatic image Paul clinches his
point. He imagines a triumphal procession in which the
victorious general parades prisoners of war down the
streets of his capital city. In this case, however, the rulers
and the authorities responsible for the crucifixion of Christ
have been disarmed and publicly disgraced through his
death on the cross. These rulers and authorities are pictured as being shamed in a victory parade in which they
are not victorious heroes being honored but prisoners in
shackles on public display:

He disarmed the rulers and authorities and made a
public example of them, triumphing over them in it.
(2:15)

Through these dramatic word pictures, Paul reassures
the Colossians that they have no need for any of the
philosophies, ascetic rituals, or mystic practices which are

being commended to them as providing added value to their life in Christ (2:16-23). These philosophies and practices only deceive and enslave, whereas life in Christ frees and nurtures and sustains. Paul reassures them, "These are only a shadow of what is to come, but the substance belongs to Christ" (2:17). There was no need for the believers in Colossae to fear "the elemental spirits of the universe" (2:8). Their relationship to Christ as "the head of every rule and authority" (2:10) and as "the head of the body, the church" (1:18) guarantees both their life of faithfulness in the present and their inheritance in the future.

Having remembered the story of Christ and the believers' future in Christ, Paul reminds the Colossians what it means for them to participate in the way of Christ in their relationships in Christian community life and in their daily lives within the household (3:1–4:6). What constitutes fullness of life in the kingdom into which they have been transferred through Christ?

Up There: Life with Christ

In 3:1-4 Paul helps the believers in Colossae remember the future already opened up to them through Christ:

> So if you have been raised with Christ, seek the things
> that are above, where Christ is, seated at the right
> hand of God. Set your minds on things that are above,
> not on things that are on earth, for you have died, and
> your life is hidden with Christ in God. When Christ
> who is your life is revealed, then you also will be
> revealed with him in glory. (3:1-4)

In this series of statements Paul identifies for believers what already is, what believers need to do, and what still lies in the future. What happened to Christ has occurred in their lives as well: "You have died" (3:3), and "you have been raised with Christ" (3:1). They in turn need to respond in faithfulness: "Seek the things that are above. . . . Set your minds on things that are above" (3:1, 2). Their glorious future in Christ has already been unveiled, even though it has not yet been fully realized: "When Christ who is your life is revealed, then you also will be revealed with him in glory" (3:4). Even though Paul definitely puts the accent on the present status of persons in Christ he also signals clearly that the future has not yet fully arrived.

The employment of spatial categories ("the things that are above" and "the things that are on earth") is sometimes seen as evidence that the author has taken over Greco-Roman philosophical categories. Within Hellenistic thought, including early Gnosticism, there was a tendency to emphasize a vertical dualism, with an earthly material realm below and the spiritual domain of heavenly things above. Has this earth/heaven framework preempted the linear framework that is more typical of a Hebraic view of history and chronology and a movement into the future?

A vertical (earth/heaven) dualism is certainly evident here. However, it is appropriate to recognize that Paul's thought still fits into the narrative structure and chronology within which he views what God has done and will yet do in Christ and his body the church. This story encompasses Jesus's death and resurrection as well as the anticipation of his future glory. As Paul goes on to illustrate, believers also have active roles within this redemptive narrative. He urges them to "put to death whatever is earthly" (3:5-11) and to "put on" the virtues that cohere with life in Christ (3:12-17). Those who participate with Christ in his death and resurrection do so from the perspective of a horizontal chronological movement from "before" to "now" rather than a vertical shift from "here below" to "up there." Life "up there" with Christ who is seated at the right hand of God is primarily by identification with the forward future-opening trajectory of Jesus's life, death, resurrection and exaltation.

Those who have died with Christ still need to make ethical choices in line with their new status in him. In 3:5-8 Paul identifies the deliberate steps that the individual needs to take:

> Put to death, therefore, whatever in you is earthly: fornication, impurity, passion, evil desire, and greed (which is idolatry). On account of these the wrath of God is coming on those who are disobedient. These are the ways you also once followed, when you were living that life. But now you must get rid of all such things—anger, wrath, malice, slander, and abusive language from your mouth. (3:5-8)

Even though believers have already died and been raised with Christ, they also still need to make decisions that align with the new reality into which they have been transferred. Paul lists several earthly impulses, particularly some inappropriate sexual and economic practices that may have characterized their former life. These impulses need to be "put to death" (3:5). He warns that "the wrath of God" comes on people who live in these ways. Paul appears to name some abusive and hurtful attitudes and activities from a general list of vices prevalent among people. He also may have in mind the negative values and enticements of the empire, which continued to threaten to entrap even people who have viewed their glorious future in Christ.

In 3:9-11 Paul reminds the Colossians about the transformation that they have experienced:

Do not lie to one another, seeing that you have
stripped off the old self with its practices and have
clothed yourselves with the new self, which is being
renewed in knowledge according to the image of its
creator. In that renewal there is no longer Greek and
Jew, circumcised and uncircumcised, barbarian,
Scythian, slave and free; but Christ is all and in all!

The language here suggests that Paul is recalling their baptism, often pictured as the shedding of old clothes and the
donning of new (3:9-10). Drawing on the vision of their
participation in the new humanity in Christ, Paul invites
the Colossian congregation to celebrate the fact that
potential barriers among them have been demolished. The
baptismal confession quoted in Galatians 3:27-28 has been
enlarged in terms of ethnic categories. In addition to Greek
and Jew Paul mentions circumcised and uncircumcised, as
well as barbarian, Scythian, slave and free (3:11). Their life
together therefore reflects the image of the Creator (recall
"he is the image of the invisible God," 1:15). Christ has
deeply formed their communal identity: "Christ is all and
in all" (3:11). Here is yet another echo of the cosmic work
of Christ celebrated in the earlier hymn in 1:15-20.

Once again, imperatives follow. Having named the
kinds of behaviors and attitudes that believers should
remove from their moral wardrobe, Paul describes the
behavior and mindset believers are summoned to wear:

As God's chosen ones, holy and beloved, clothe yourselves with compassion, kindness, humility, meekness,
and patience. Bear with one another and, if anyone has
a complaint against another, forgive each other; just as
the Lord has forgiven you, so you also must forgive.
Above all, clothe yourselves with love, which binds
everything together in perfect harmony. And let the

peace of Christ rule in your hearts, to which indeed
you were called in the one body. And be thankful. Let
the word of Christ dwell in you richly; teach and
admonish one another in all wisdom; and with gratitude in your hearts sing psalms, hymns, and spiritual
songs to God. (3:12-16)

Activities and attitudes like "compassion, kindness, humility,
meekness, and patience" are likened to clothing which a person chooses to put on (3:12). Others highlighted here include
forgiveness, love, peaceableness, gratitude, and worship. As
the Lord has forgiven (recall 1:14), so they also are to extend
forgiveness (3:13). The supreme virtue is love, whereby the
community is bound together in perfect harmony (3:14).
Paul enjoins the believers: "And let the peace of Christ rule
in your hearts. . . . And be thankful" (3:15). And he urges the
community to express their gratitude in worship through
teaching, admonition, and the singing of psalms, hymns, and
spiritual songs to God (3:16). In these ways they allow "the
word of Christ" to indwell them richly (3:16).

The Colossian believers hearing Paul's admonition to
cultivate these various virtues and qualities will not have
failed to notice his repeated reference to Christ as the
source and norm for their life together. He sums up by
pointing to Jesus Christ:

And whatever you do, in word or deed, do everything
in the name of the Lord Jesus, giving thanks to God
the Father through him. (3:17)

The thrust of these injunctions is clear. The Christ of the
hymn (1:15-20) is the one in whom and through whom
and for whom they are called to live in all of their relationships.

How then does Christ inform relationships within the household? Ironically 3:18–4:1 is often read as evidence that, when Paul counsels appropriate patterns of relating among members of the household, the values and way of life espoused in 3:1-17 recede into the background. But is this actually the case?

Down to Earth: The Household

In 3:18 Paul abruptly begins to share some pastoral teaching regarding relationships within the household. The following quotation of the Colossian household code is arranged in a way that shows clearly what is said to each of several groups within the household:

Wives, be subject to your husbands, as is fitting in the Lord.

Husbands, love your wives and never treat them harshly.

Children, obey your parents in everything, for this is your acceptable duty in the Lord.

Fathers, do not provoke your children, or they may lose heart.

Slaves, obey your earthly masters in everything, not only while being watched and in order to please them, but wholeheartedly, fearing the Lord. Whatever your task, put yourselves into it, as done for the Lord and not for your masters, since you know that from the Lord you will receive the inheritance as your reward; you serve the Lord Christ. For the wrongdoer will be paid back for whatever wrong has been done, and there is no partiality.

Masters, treat your slaves justly and fairly, for you
know that you also have a Master in heaven.
(3:18–4:1)

Because this section is not introduced by any of the
usual transitional linking words (such as *therefore*) it has
sometimes been considered to be an ethical tradition simply copied and pasted from elsewhere. We have already
noted that Aristotle's description of the natural order of
things in the empire and the household has sometimes been
viewed as a primary source for Paul's ethical counsel here.
Does he promote an understanding of the home as a
microcosm of the empire?

Scholars have been sharply divided in their approach
to this material. Some authors (for example, Carolyn
Osiek and David Balch) see the instructions included here
to be the imposition of prevailing societal expectations
into the life of the church. According to their reading, a
later disciple of Paul has taken a significant step away
from the radically egalitarian relationships evidenced in
Paul's letters toward a socially conservative ethic more
aligned with the values of the surrounding culture
(1997:118-21). A variant of this view is that, in response
to eager claims of freedom and equality by slaves and
women moved by the Spirit, Paul introduced these household guidelines in order to restrain such destabilizing
enthusiasm.

Other interpreters of the household code in Colossians
assert that instead of baptizing the status quo Paul actually subverts it. Ben Witherington III, for example, includes
discussion of Colossians 3:18–4:1 under the subtitle "Paul
the Radical." Within his view, the household is called to be
a microcosm not of the empire but of the church as the
body of Christ, a diverse community united by their com-

mon participation in the way of Christ. (1998:184-202.)

Several signals in this text testify to Paul's conviction that relationships within the household need to echo relationships within the body of Christ. He names the traditionally subordinate members first (the wives, children, and slaves) and addresses them as moral agents in their own right. Notably, slaves are described as heirs whose ultimate loyalty is given not to their earthly master but to the Lord. Paul advocates a liberating interdependence among members of the household, including an inheritance for the slaves. The most significant hint that he views all relations within church-related homes as patterned after the way of Christ is the recurring mention of the Lord: "in the Lord" (3:18, 19), "fearing the Lord" (3:22), "done for the Lord" (3:23).

When the household instructions are read within the context of Paul's overall argument in Colossians, it becomes clear that the references to "the Lord" all intend to recall the whole story of Jesus Christ as a persuasive model for human relations within the body of Christ. The love of husbands for their wives participates in the self-giving nature of divine love in Christ. When masters treat slaves with justice and equality they let the peace of Christ prevail over the impulse of self-interest. Selfless service partakes of the suffering of Jesus who in his death gained victory over every rule and authority. And in a significant sense Paul is addressing the entire faith community as servants when he speaks to the slaves. Both slave and master are under the same Lord, and before the Lord all are called to serve the other.

The way in which Paul follows up on the household instructions (4:2-6) is also instructive. He brings out the missional intention of the church, not only in the request for prayer (4:2-4) but also in the admonition "Conduct yourselves wisely toward outsiders, making the most of the time" (4:5). The conduct and relationships within the community of Jesus's followers need to intersect wisely with the realities of its cultural context. Christ-honoring households and congregations are located in the world and therefore they resemble other households and social gatherings. They are, however, not of the world. They participate already in the future of God's new order being made known in inviting ways to the world. Life "up there" with Christ leads to the kind of "down to earth" living that opens up a promising future for all who commit themselves to living in the way of Christ.

Households, Holiness, and Sexuality

We have been listening to Paul's reminders to the church at Colossae concerning their life in Christ. Their worship and their communal relationships are to reflect the dynamic life-giving character of being rooted and grounded in Jesus Christ, who is their head. Our thematic focus has called for attention to household relationships, specifically those between wives and their husbands. In the next chapter, we focus on Ephesians and attend to the other major household code (Ephesians 5:21–6:9). At this point, we attempt a survey of themes related to households, holiness, and sexuality in Paul's other pastoral letters.

No Longer Male and Female

In Galatians 3:28 Paul quotes what is widely recognized as a baptismal confession. That this was used during baptisms is suggested by his introductory declaration in 3:27:

> As many of you as were baptized into Christ have
> clothed yourselves with Christ. There is no longer Jew

> or Greek, there is no longer slave or free, there is no longer male and female; for all of you are one in Christ Jesus. (3:27-28)

He testifies that persons distinguished from each other by ethnic, economic, and gender difference are incorporated into Christ through baptism into a unity that transcends all such distinctions. Yet he also recognizes that such differences remain, despite the unifying dynamic of incorporation into Christ. However, in the grand scheme of things among those living into the future already opened up in Christ, such distinctions ultimately do not matter. Paul finds himself navigating between the "already" of that future and the "not yet" character of present realities.

As we have seen, Paul works passionately for unity between Jews and Gentiles, recognizing that they still retain their ethnic identities (see chapter 4). He mediates between a slave and his master on the basis of their common allegiance to Christ, but the master-slave relationship apparently remains intact, at least for a time (see chapter 10). What then does Paul take to be the relationship between women and men, now that in Christ "there is no longer male and female"?

The impulse toward unity and mutuality between women and men at times led some people, especially women, to make exuberant claims that sexual distinctions had already been erased through Christ. For a variety of reasons Paul feels compelled to restrain such enthusiasm. As a consequence, he sometimes seems to downplay the unity and equality of women and men in Christ. For example, in 1 Corinthians 12:13 Paul consciously omits reference to male/female unity, even though here, as in Galatians 3:28, he is talking about how baptism unites diverse people into the body of Christ:

> For in the one Spirit we were all baptized into one
> body—Jews or Greeks, slaves or free—and we were all
> made to drink of one Spirit. (1 Corinthians 12:13)

Paul would have been expected to include "male and female," as in Galatians 3:28. However, he does not, likely because strident voices from some Corinthian women tended (from Paul's perspective) to destabilize the congregation and create negative impressions within their culture. In their call for gender equality these women appeared to be blurring sexual distinctions, and Paul reacts in ways that seem to reinforce traditional patriarchal patterns.

This tension within Paul between patriarchal and egalitarian perspectives on the relationships between women and men is abundantly evident in 1 Corinthians 11:2-16. He assumes here that women as well as men pray and prophesy in public worship gatherings. Women participate along with men as equals in the Spirit-inspired activities of worship. However, Paul's burden in this part of the letter is to emphasize gender distinctions, presumably over against what he perceived to be a boundary-blurring emphasis on their unity in Christ. He appeals to social conventions about style of hairdo or head covering for women and men (11:4-10) and length of hair (11:14-15). He recalls motifs from the creation stories (11:7-9) and an enigmatic reference to the angels (11:10). All of these arguments are designed to undergird his opening articulation of a hierarchical relationship between a woman and her husband, a relationship that reflects the relationship between Christ and God (11:3). Yet imbedded within these hierarchical assertions about female/male (specifically wife/husband) relationships is an emphatic statement about mutuality and interdependence between women and men:

> Nevertheless, in the Lord woman is not independent of
> man or man independent of woman. For just as
> woman came from man, so man comes through
> woman; but all things come from God. (11:11-12)

Even here, when he asserts the mutual interdependence of
woman and man, Paul does not recall the baptismal confession, "There is no longer male and female" (Galatians
3:28). Rather he grounds this emphasis in the Genesis 2 creation narrative ("woman came from man") and in the natural birthing process ("man comes through woman"), and
he sums up that "all things come from God." Paul's avoidance of the baptismal confession seems motivated by his
desire not to fan still further the flames of freedom, especially for women tending (again, from Paul's perspective) to
take their emancipation in Christ to dangerous lengths.

That Paul affirms women as valued equal partners in
the life and work of the church is shown in striking ways in
the greetings at the conclusion of his epistle to the Romans.
In Romans 16:1-2 he commends Phoebe as a minister of the
church at Cenchreae and as a leader of many others, including Paul himself. Likely Phoebe delivered and helped to
interpret this letter to the churches in Rome. Paul also
greets Prisca and Aquila (note that Prisca is named first) as
his dedicated co-workers in Christ; they are leaders of the
church that meets in their home (16:3-5a). Paul greets
Mary, who has worked hard among the believers in Rome
(16:6). And he extends greetings to Andronicus and Junia,
whom he describes as "my relatives who were in prison
with me" (16:7a). It is noteworthy that Paul adds, "They
are prominent among the apostles, and they were in Christ
before I was" (16:7b). Here are a man and a woman (likely husband and wife) who are identified as apostles and as
persons who had affirmed Christ as Messiah before Paul

did so. Scribes copying this text frequently changed the name Junia to that of a male, Junias. In all these greetings, as well as those to Tryphaena and Tryphosa (16:12), to Rufus's mother (16:13), and to Julia and to Nereus's sister (16:15), Paul obliquely yet eloquently testifies that he affirms these women as Spirit-gifted pastoral leaders.

Another testimony to Paul's inclusive attitude toward women as full partners in the work of the church is his use of kinship imagery to talk about his own apostolic ministry. It is not surprising that he would employ the image of father when he talks about his relationship to people in the churches under his pastoral care. "I became your father through the gospel," he reminds the Corinthians (1 Corinthians 4:15). What is startling is that in referring to himself he also draws on other family metaphors. Particularly striking is a cluster of the images of child, mother, and orphan in his first letter to the church in Thessalonica. A literal translation of 1 Thessalonians 2:7-8 shows how Paul portrays himself in his apostolic role:

> Although able to be demanding as apostles of Christ, yet we came into your midst as little children. As a nursing mother cherishes her own children, so, longing for you, we were pleased to give to you not only the gospel of God but also our own souls, because you had become beloved to us. (1 Thessalonians 2:7-8; translation adapted from Elias, 1995:65)

In a jarring juxtaposition of word pictures, Paul depicts himself and his missionary partners both as little children and as a mother. He, Silvanus, and Timothy had entered into their relationship with the Thessalonians not as demanding or authoritarian apostles but as children. And their stance toward these new believers had been akin to that of a nursing mother who cherishes and nourishes her own children. To round out the picture Paul in 2:11 also likens himself and his partners to a father who exhorts and encourages his children. However, in 2:17 he resorts to another household metaphor, which again depicts the apostles in childlike terms: "We were made orphans by being separated from you." It is his unabashed use of maternal and filial images that eloquently testifies to his conviction that in Christ there is no longer male and female. Coming from a person otherwise concerned, especially in his later letters, about the risk of blurring gender distinctions, this kind of imagery is remarkable indeed.

Holiness

Another theme that arises frequently when Paul confronts sexual issues is sanctification as a process, or its result, namely holiness. In his greetings he often addresses his recipients as saints (literally, "holy ones"): Romans 1:6; 1 Corinthians 1:2; 2 Corinthians 1:1; Philippians 1:1; Colossians 1:2; Ephesians 1:1. One dimension of the life of saints is holiness in their sexual relationships. We turn to two of his letters where these ethical themes emerge prominently: 1 Thessalonians and 1 Corinthians.

Shortly after picturing himself and his apostolic colleagues as children, mother, and father in their relationships with the believers in Thessalonica (1 Thessalonians 2:1-12), Paul sums up his prayer for them:

> And may the Lord make you increase and abound in
> love for one another and for all, just as we abound in
> love for you. And may he so strengthen your hearts in
> holiness that you may be blameless before our God
> and Father at the coming of our Lord Jesus with all his
> saints. (1 Thessalonians 3:12-13)

This prayer both recapitulates concerns already dealt with in the letter and announces the topic that he now wants to pick up. It is the concern for holiness that gets attention first (4:1-8).

Paul begins the exhortation section from within their shared relationship in Christ: "Finally, brothers and sisters, we ask and urge you in the Lord Jesus" (4:1a). He both commends them for what they are already doing and exhorts them to grow in their "walk." The imagery underlying the expression "how you ought to live" is the typical Hebraic notion of *halakah*, faithfulness as "walking" in obedience to God. Paul also puts his longing in terms more understandable to Greek-speaking Thessalonians: "how you ought to . . . please God" (4:1b). In 4:2 he reminds them that the subject of holy sexual behavior had come up in his earlier pastoral teaching: "For you know what kind of instructions we gave you through the Lord Jesus."

In 4:3-6a Paul lays out his ethical directives. The opening statement announces God's will as sanctification:

> For this is the will of God, your sanctification:
> that you abstain from fornication;
> that each one of you know how to control your own
>   body in holiness and honor,
>   not like the Gentiles who do not know God;
> that no one wrong or exploit a brother or sister in
>   this matter. (4:3-6a)

The will of God is described in most translations (as in the NRSV above) as "your sanctification," with the accent on the process of becoming holy. Paul may also be viewing the outcome of the sanctifying process: "your holiness." What this entails is described in a series of three clauses.

The first clause defines holy sexual practice in terms of

what needs to be avoided: "that you abstain from fornication" (4:3). The underlying Greek word *porneia* can have the narrow meaning of "fornication," that is, sexual intercourse between a woman and man not married to each other (as in 1 Corinthians 5:1). It can also refer to sexual immorality more generally. There are no clear indications here whether Paul knows about an actual situation in Thessalonica or whether this is a precautionary warning in light of the rather lax moral climate in this Macedonian seaport city.

The second clause (4:4-5) is more difficult to disentangle, especially because Paul uses the Greek word *skeuos* (literally, "jar" or "vessel") in a metaphorical sense. Interpreters waver between trying to suggest what Paul might have meant by *skeuos* or simply leaving it uninterpreted. The KJV has done the latter: "that every one of you should know how to possess his own vessel in sanctification and honour." Most translations supply an interpretation, but no agreement exists about whether Paul intends *skeuos* to refer to the wife (whom a man acquires or possesses) or the body (whose sexual urges each one, both male and female, needs to control). The RSV opts for the former: "that each one of you know how to take a wife for himself in holiness and honor." The NIV sides with the latter: "that each of you should learn to control his own body in holiness and honor." The NRSV (cited in the layout above) promotes a similar view, although expanding it to include both women and men as needing to know how to control their sexual urges: "that each of you know how to control your own body in holiness and honor." All in all, the NIV/NRSV reading (*skeuos* equals "body") best coheres with Paul's apparent intention here. He makes a clear distinction between the morality prevailing in the Greco-Roman world and those patterns of morality that need to be evident in the Lord. A Christlike union between a man and a woman needs to reflect holiness and honor, both the sanctity of a committed sexual relationship and a relationship characterized by mutual honor. Holiness and honor, not lustful sexual indulgence, characterize marriages in Christ.

The third clause functions as a reminder of the social consequences when sexual boundaries are transgressed: "that no one wrong or exploit a brother or sister in this matter" (4:6a). Sexual infidelity not only implicates the two persons involved in adultery. It is also a sin against each adulterous partner's spouse.

Having called for an ethic of sexual purity and faithfulness Paul enumerates three motivating principles for such holy and honorable conduct: God's judgment on transgressors (4:6b), God's call to holiness not impurity or uncleanness (4:7), and God's enabling Holy Spirit (4:8). These motivating principles emphasize that though God judges people whose actions contravene the divine will for holy living, God continues to call women and men to holy relationships and graciously supplies the empowering Holy Spirit that makes such holy living possible. Paul appears to have such divine enabling in mind as he concludes this first letter to the church in Thessalonica with a prayer for their sanctification:

May the God of peace himself sanctify you entirely;
and may your spirit and soul and body be kept sound
and blameless at the coming of the Lord Jesus Christ.
The one who calls you is faithful, and he will do this.
(1 Thessalonians 5:23-24)

In his correspondence with the church at Corinth he also includes a significant amount of material on sexuality themes, both in response to disturbing reports about a blatant case of sexual immorality in their midst (5:1-13) and in reply to a query from a group in the Corinthian congregation (7:1-40).

Paul recoils with horror at a reported case of sexual immorality in Corinth: "A man is living with his father's wife" (5:1), and he urges strong disciplinary action: "Drive out the wicked person from among you" (5:13). His call for the expulsion of the offender is reminiscent of the code of justice in Deuteronomy 22:21-24, although there the penalty for both the man and the woman is death. The purpose of such severe discipline is to "purge the evil from the land" (Deuteronomy 22:22, 24). Paul shows concern about the salvation of the sinning individual (1 Corinthians 5:5, "so that his spirit may be saved in the day of the Lord"), but he is also anxious about the unity and the holiness of the body of believers in its ongoing witness in the world. He diagnoses the pernicious consequence of communal tolerance of such behavior by using the metaphor of leaven: "Do you not know that a little yeast leavens the whole batch of dough?" (5:6). Paul therefore urges a purging and cleansing process so that the congregation can faithfully live out the implications of Jesus's sacrificial death as the paschal lamb:

> Therefore, let us celebrate the festival, not with the old yeast, the yeast of malice and evil, but with the unleavened bread of sincerity and truth. (1 Corinthians 5:8)

In 1 Corinthians 7 he begins to craft his reply to a letter that he had received from some leaders within the Corinthian church. Having sounded the alarm about both sexually immoral behavior and a tolerating attitude toward it, Paul now addresses another group in the Corinthian church. When he says, "It is well for a man not to touch a woman" (7:1b), he is quoting the position of a subgroup in Corinth that was advocating the practice of marital asceticism, the abstinence from sexual intercourse within marriage. Even though Paul himself is a celibate man, he strongly promotes sexual intimacy as the mutual submission of husbands and wives to each other (7:2-4), with the possible exception of brief periods of sexual abstinence for the sake of prayer, if such an arrangement is mutually desired (7:5-6). He endorses marriage as one of God's good gifts among other gifts (7:7). His preference for the single life comes from his assessment of the eschatological urgency of the times (7:26-28, 29-31). He also knows (perhaps from previous personal experience) that having a mate can at times distract from undivided devotion to the Lord (7:32-35). Because of his conviction that time was growing short (7:29), Paul seems at times to depict marriage as only for weaklings (7:8-9, 36-38). It is important to observe that he is here engaged in responding to advocates of sexual abstinence, and that he recognizes that the rigors of sexual abstinence imposed unilaterally by some persons were creating temptations for their spouses to engage in illicit sexual activity. He responds to a group that has picked up on his personal model of celibacy and sought to impose that model on others, including, in some cases, their spouses. His response dramatically underscores the fact that despite his agreement with some aspects of such asceticism he solidly affirms marriage and sexual expression within the sanctity of a mutually affirming marriage.

Paul's pastoral counsel in this part of his letter to the church at Corinth also makes evident one dimension of his understanding of holiness. In 7:10-16 he speaks to the issue of divorce. First he echoes Jesus's teachings prohibiting divorce (7:10; cf. Mark 10:11-12). He recognizes that despite such a prohibition, divorce does happen; in cases where divorce occurs he envisions either reconciliation or remaining unmarried (7:11). Next he moves into a scenario not covered by Jesus's teaching. In the case of a believer whose wife or husband has not become a believer, Paul urges that the believing spouse should not initiate divorce (7:12-13). His rationale gives testimony to the underlying notion of holiness:

> For the unbelieving husband is made holy through his wife, and the unbelieving wife is made holy through her husband. Otherwise, your children would be unclean, but as it is, they are holy. (7:14)

He does not describe holiness as vulnerable to the corrupting or contaminating power of unbelief. Rather, Paul, as it were, views holiness as contagious. The power of the holy as it were "contaminates" the realm of the unholy and begins to transform and sanctify it. God's holiness therefore calls believers to a redemptive continuing relationship with those who have not yet made the choice to align themselves with that calling.

The other side of Paul's counsel here is that if the unbelieving partner desires to separate, the believer should let it be. "In such a case the brother or sister is not bound. It is to peace that God has called you" (7:15). Nevertheless, he repeats his reminder of the sanctifying power of the faithful example of the believing spouse: "Wife, for all you know, you might save your husband. Husband, for all you know, you might save your wife" (7:16).

We conclude these explorations into Paul's views concerning sexuality and holiness by examining an earlier section in 1 Corinthians. After his initial comments about the circumstances involving the man living with his stepmother (5:1-8), he recalls an earlier letter, in which he demanded that they not associate with sexually immoral persons (5:9). He hastens to correct what appear to have been some misperceptions of what he wrote. In the process of clarifying what he meant, Paul provides a cumulative listing of vices that are characteristic of the world. His point is that these are not to be evidenced in the church, and if they are, there needs to be firm discipline:

> I wrote to you in my letter not to associate with sexually immoral persons—not at all meaning the immoral of the world, or the greedy and robbers, or idolaters. . . . But now I am writing to you not to associate with anyone who bears the name of brother or sister who is sexually immoral or greedy, or an idolater, reviler, drunkard, or robber. (5:10a,11)

> Do you not know that wrongdoers will not inherit the kingdom of God? Do not be deceived! Fornicators, idolaters, adulterers, male prostitutes, sodomites, thieves, the greedy, drunkards, revilers, robbers—none of these will inherit the kingdom of God. And this is what some of you used to be. But you were washed, you were sanctified, you were justified in the name of the Lord Jesus Christ and in the Spirit of our God. (6:9-11)

Each of these three lists is longer than the previous one. All of them include references to the sexually immoral (Greek term *pornoi*), idolaters, the greedy, and robbers. Adulterers are mentioned in two of these lists. And the final list mentions *malakoi* (NRSV translates "male prostitutes") and *arsenokoitai* (NRSV translates "sodomites"); within the New Testament the first appears only in Luke 7:25 in a reference to soft garments and the latter only in a comparable list in 1 Timothy 1:10.

There is no doubt that Paul condemns certain patterns of sexual and economic behavior as being unworthy of those who claim to have entered the realm of the reign of God. His primary intention here is to rebuke those people in Corinth who consider themselves to have achieved a spiritually superior status in which moral guidelines supposedly no longer apply. "All things are lawful for me," they say (6:12). Paul responds, "But not all things are beneficial" and "I will not be dominated by anything" (6:12). They say, "Food is meant for the stomach and the stomach for food, and God will destroy both one and the other" (6:13). Paul replies, "The body is meant not for fornication but for the Lord, and the Lord for the body. And God raised the Lord and will also raise us up by his power" (6:13b-14).

Clearly Paul's responses are designed to point out to some people with an "anything goes" sexual ethic that indeed what one does in the body does matter. Both life in Christ now and a future bodily resurrection attest to the importance of sexual fidelity and an ethic of faithfulness and purity in life in the body here and now.

But Paul's intention is also to reassure the faithful in Corinth: "This is what some of you used to be" (6:11a). He adds a reminder of their conversion and their baptism in identification with Jesus Christ and in the Spirit of God: "But you were washed, you were sanctified, you were justified" (6:11). As he wraps up this pastoral reflection on reported sexual immorality in Corinth as well as the pious rationalizations underlying an attitude of tolerance toward it, Paul echoes this reassuring reminder and he reissues his admonition, "For you were bought with a price; therefore glorify God in your body" (6:20).

12

AS WARRIORS WITH GOD

Paul's short personal letter to Philemon and his epistle to the Colossian congregation were written to individuals and congregations situated in the western regions of Asia Minor. Turning now to the epistle to the Ephesians, we keep our focus on congregations within that general geographical area. We lack, however, some of the expected specific clues regarding the underlying story. Many questions about that story are much debated. What might have been the writer's situation? Was Paul the author, or might this epistle have been written by his mission partners, or even by someone writing in his name after his death? And what were the circumstances facing the congregations to whom this document was originally addressed?

Even the letter's normal address line is unclear. The earliest extant manuscripts do not name a place. This fact has led many scholars to suggest that it was originally addressed generally "to the saints who are also faithful in Christ Jesus" (Ephesians 1:1, RSV) rather than more specifically "to the saints who are in Ephesus and are faithful in Christ Jesus" (1:1, NRSV).

In an effort to identify with what some first-century hearers of the epistle to the Ephesians might have heard, we imagine ourselves in the following narrative as members of a congregation in Laodicea in about A.D. 85. This congregation recalls its beginnings in the home of Nympha

(Colossians 4:15-16). Some of the hints in Ephesians about the author's circumstances and the situation in Ephesus and the surrounding region have been taken into account in telling this story: Ephesians 1:15; 2:1, 11; 3:1, 7; 4:17; 5:3-5, 6-14; 6:21-22. Once again, however, the details of the narrative have been elaborated imaginatively beyond what can be reconstructed from the text.

We listen to the memories and reflections of Adolphos and Eleria, who are giving leadership to the congregation. They recall their first twenty-five years of congregational life and mission.

A STORY: Parades, Prosperity, and the Powers

Life in Laodicea at times resembled the eddies and crosscurrents where the Meander River emptied into the Lycus. The devastation of a regional earthquake in A.D. 60 created major chaos, but those scars were all but masked by the vigorous rebuilding programs of businesspeople and homeowners who were eager to get things back to normal. Cargo-laden barges on the Lycus River and merchant caravans wending their way along the Iconium-Ephesus highway gave vivid testimony to the prosperity of the region. Textile products made from the local black wool were in demand in markets near and far.

The congregation in Laodicea included people who had generously benefited from this prosperity and the peaceful circumstances throughout the Roman province of Asia. Yet Adolphos and Eleria realized that underneath the surface calm of life within this bustling region were deeper issues that confused and divided. Some of those tensions rose to the surface as the congregation celebrated its beginnings in Nympha's household.

Concerns had emerged about a drift in moral standards in society as a whole and even among some who were baptized into participation in the church. All remembered the rousing refrain of the baptismal hymn: "Sleeper awake! Arise from the dead, and Christ will shine on you." Some in the congregation suggested that even when shameful sexual relationships and various old habits persist following baptism the believer continued to experience the gift of new life in Christ. Several seemed to think that what one did in the body ultimately did not matter much; what did matter is that one's spirit be in union with the divine mystery and the wisdom made known in Christ. So Eleria and Adolphos sometimes wrestled with what new life in Christ meant in daily patterns of living in the household, in business dealings, and in sexual relationships.

But issues regarding individual moral faithfulness often connected to other questions. What did it mean to be part of this community called the church? What was the big picture? And how did this vision compare with the ideology of the empire, which was touted as deserving ultimate loyalty? To Adolphos and Eleria it sometimes seemed futile to tell the story of their beginnings in ways that would unite young and old, Jews and Gentiles, established families and migrants within a common vision. It seemed right and appropriate to celebrate twenty-five years, but how could the church compete with all the civic festivals being sponsored both by Asians and by Roman citizens with connections all the way to the emperor?

Out of the disruption of an earthquake came renewed order and economic vitality. Even more dramatic was the story often told about how Caesar Augustus created stability and order in the empire after many years of civil war. The "Roman Peace" secured by the great Augustus throughout the vast empire continued to be guaranteed by his successors in Rome, recently Vespasian and Titus, and now the great Emperor Domitian. And the local city and provincial officials eagerly planned for lavish annual festivals, parades, and games to celebrate this peace. Town criers navigated the roads and market areas, inviting the populace to show honor to city politarchs, to provincial governors and senators, and to the emperor himself. Images of Domitian were everywhere on statues and friezes, not to mention the coins specially minted for such occasions.

Festivals also brought out the gods. In Ephesus it was the goddess Artemis. From Anatolia came the deity Mēn Karou with many devotees in Laodicea. And Zeus featured prominently, along with the gods and goddesses of numerous mystery cults with origins throughout the territory of the Great Sea. With the emperor's visage displayed prominently in coins and statues alongside the statues of the gods, the aura of the divine pervaded all patriotic festivities. And when the festivals continued for several days, drawing people from the rural areas as well as the town, the spirit of such celebrations conveyed a clear message: "In the emperor and the gods of the empire we stand in glorious unity. We thank you, Domitian, for peace, stability and opportunity!"

For the church these seasons of public festival posed a dilemma. Eleria and Adolphos knew how the spectacular displays of patriotic devotion attracted the population, including Jews and the faith communities of Jews and Gentiles who acknowledged Jesus Christ as Lord. Some Jews, whose readings in the synagogues enjoin their obedient devotion to the sovereign God, offered sacrifice on behalf of the emperor, though not *to* him.

But what could those who continued in the faith lineage of Paul, Epaphras, and Nympha do to remain faithful to the gospel of Jesus Christ? How could their worship of

God and devotion to Christ as Lord coexist with all this religious and political hoopla on the streets and public squares in their city and at the imperial palaces throughout the province? In the midst of heady manifestations of the empire's splendor, which attempted to woo the loyalty of its diverse people and unite them into one happy family, how should the church shape its life?

Another issue haunted Adolphos and Eleria: some of the believers in Laodicea were beginning to lose the memory of their Jewish origins. The older members of the congregation remembered Epaphras, who first shared the gospel in Laodicea, Hierapolis, and nearby Colossae. Some knew Nympha, in whose home the congregation first met. Both Epaphras and Nympha told stories about Paul, the famed Jewish apostle with the burden to preach the gospel of Christ to the nations. And Adolphos and Eleria kept reminding their people that, even though there were few Jews in their group, they all had Jewish roots. Jesus was a Jew, and he had lived in the eastern provinces of Galilee and Judea. Jews in synagogues scattered throughout all the provinces of the empire studied the very same Scriptures that were read in their congregation.

But there were some who had lost interest in the unique history of the Jewish minority in their midst. A few who seemed to be in the loop concerning such things grumbled about the closed attitudes of some past Jewish Christian leaders toward Gentiles who had joined the church. What then should the congregation do to bring unity across this ethnic divide?

The time seemed right to read a letter bearing the name of Paul. This letter had been circulating among congregations in the region for some time. What would Paul say to the circumstances they were facing?

God and the Powers

> Our struggle is not against enemies of blood and flesh,
> but against the rulers, against the authorities, against
> the cosmic powers of this present darkness, against the
> spiritual forces of evil in the heavenly places.
> (Ephesians 6:12)

We followed Paul's pastoral interaction with a master whose slave has absconded. We heard how his vision of the crucified and exalted Christ shaped household relationships within the congregation at Colossae. In line with the epistle to the Ephesians we now explore the cosmic dimensions of the gospel in intersection with the prevailing powers and principalities. We join in exalted worship with first-century congregations being built up for their mission in the Asia Minor communities of Caesar's vast empire.

As already noted, the words *in Ephesus* do not appear in the opening salutation (1:1) of the earliest copies of this letter. This epistle might have been a circular letter written for use in the worship gatherings of congregations in and around Ephesus and elsewhere in western Asia Minor. Some commentators have proposed that the epistle to the Ephesians was written as an introduction and placed at the head of a collection of Paul's letters. Some scholars even nominate the freed slave Onesimus as the later bishop of Ephesus who superintended this process of gathering Paul's specific letters for general use in the church. But it seems best simply to recognize Ephesians as a general letter initially circulating among various congregations and eventually being incorporated along with the other of his letters into the New Testament canon. (See Yoder Neufeld, 2002:32-5.)

The epistle to the Ephesians begins with a eulogy in

praise of the God made known in Jesus Christ (1:3-10). It concludes with a rousing call to the faith community to don "the whole armor of God" as defense and offense against malignant worldly and spiritual powers (6:10-20). Whether Paul wrote this letter with assistance from mission partners when he was being held captive in Rome, or whether a disciple drafted it following Paul's death, it is easy to see why it has had staying value in the life of the church. Ephesians offers lofty prose, moving prayers, and fervent admonition, all framed from within the breathtaking drama of God's ongoing work in the cosmos.

How might this profound theological epistle have been heard as it circulated among churches in first-century Roman Asia?

Blessed be God!

To Jews and others accustomed to synagogue routines, the opening blessing in Ephesians 1:3-14 would have been reminiscent of the *berakah*, an ascription of praise to God for the blessings of creation, redemption, and sustenance. However, such expressions of worship might have startled non-Jewish citizens of Roman Asia, who were accustomed to hearing eulogies honoring the emperor as the chief benefactor who supplies rich benefits to his adoring people. Here the adulation is voiced toward the God of the universe who has graciously intervened in Jesus Christ:

> Blessed be the God and Father of our Lord Jesus Christ, who has blessed us in Christ with every spiritual blessing in the heavenly places. (1:3)

A majestic narrative underlies the exalted prose of this blessing. It begins before creation and extends into all eternity. Already "before the foundation of the world" God chose the saints "to be holy and blameless in love" (1:4). Through Christ they have experienced "adoption as his children" (1:5). As children they have already "obtained an inheritance" (1:11) for which the Holy Spirit is the "seal" (1:13) and "pledge" (1:14). Indeed, in Christ God has set forth "a plan for the fullness of time, to gather up all things in him, things in heaven and things on earth" (1:10).

That grand plan is still unfolding. In the meantime, those who have set their hope in Christ are called to live "to the praise of his glorious grace that he freely bestowed on us in the Beloved" (1:6; cf. 1:12). From creation to the consummation of all things, God has acted and is acting in Christ and now also in his heirs who have experienced lavish grace and forgiveness (1:7-8). Through the gospel of salvation in Christ, God unveils the mystery of the divine will to a people whose future inheritance is already sealed and guaranteed by the Holy Spirit:

> In him you also, when you had heard the word of
> truth, the gospel of your salvation, and had believed in
> him, were marked with the seal of the promised Holy
> Spirit; this is the pledge of our inheritance toward
> redemption as God's own people, to the praise of his
> glory. (1:13-14)

Reminders of their past, present, and future are gathered up within the grandeur of the God whom they worship: God the Father, Jesus Christ the Beloved, and the promised Holy Spirit.

This grandiose vision of the exalted God of the universe gives way to a personal prayer in behalf of the church (1:15-23), a prayer for "wisdom and hope and power." The theme of hope is emphasized in the reminder concerning "the riches of his glorious inheritance among the saints" (1:18), but the motif of power receives the heaviest accent (1:19-21). The church is invited to remember the future already opened up through Jesus Christ whom the almighty God raised up from the dead and exalted to God's right hand. God has unveiled in Jesus Christ an immeasurable power:

> God put this power to work in Christ when he raised him from the dead and seated him at his right hand in the heavenly places, far above all rule and authority and power and dominion, and above every name that is named, not only in this age but in the age to come. (1:20-21)

For those who believe, the panorama of God's majestic power is breathtaking. The story of Jesus Christ features his resurrection from the dead and his exaltation above all powers and authorities and names, including the power, authority, and name of Caesar. And, whereas emperors rise and fall, and empires crumble, Christ's dominion is established not only in this age but also into the age which will yet come in glorious fullness!

For believers in Roman Asia, often dazzled by the power of Caesar and his empire, the implications of this dramatic proclamation of the lordship of Christ are provocatively spelled out. What has been claimed concerning him also pertains to his body the church. "God has put all things under his [Christ's] feet" (an echo of Psalm 8:1). Furthermore, God has established Christ as head over all things through Christ's body, the church (1:22-23). The church is therefore viewed as the body of Christ through which God works in the world. God's power is made known to all the powers through the church. And what is the church? The church is Christ's body, "the fullness of him who fills all in all" (1:23). Within this grand and glorious vision, the pageantry of Caesar and his deputies is trumped by the humble and often fragile communities of faithful saints gathered for worship, fellowship, and mission in the name of Christ in Asia Minor and throughout the vast Roman Empire.

From Death to Life, from Aliens to Citizens

What God has done for Christ in raising him from death is replicated in the church, whose story also includes a transformation from death to life (2:1-10). This story features their rescue from the forces of death and sin and their transfer into new life as participants with Christ in his resurrection and exaltation. The way of life characteristic of the age is graphically portrayed both as a living death and as subservience to malignant powers:

> You were dead through the trespasses and sins in
> which you once lived, following the course of this
> world, following the ruler of the power of the air, that
> spirit that is now at work among those who are dis-
> obedient. (2:1-2)

The plight of all humanity is painted with a universal brush: "We were by nature children of wrath, like everyone else" (2:3). But salvation is available to all who accept God's mercy, love, and grace as demonstrated in Jesus Christ. Another breathtaking story elucidates the high points of God's past, present, and future salvation through Christ:

> But God, who is rich in mercy, out of the great love
> with which he loved us even when we were dead

> through our trespasses, made us alive together with
> Christ—by grace you have been saved—and raised us
> up with him and seated us with him in the heavenly
> places in Christ Jesus, so that in the ages to come he
> might show the immeasurable riches of his grace in
> kindness toward us in Christ Jesus. (2:4-7)

A summary follows: "For by grace you have been saved through faith" (2:8). God's grace is the hinge that opens the door to the future. It is "through faith" that the dramatic divine reversal comes. Salvation is "not the result of works." For this reason, any boasting about salvation status is inappropriate (2:9). However, salvation does issue in obedience among those created anew as part of the new humanity: "For we are what he has made us, created in Christ Jesus for good works" (2:10). Even these good works, viewed within the cosmic narrative of God's sovereign activity in creation and redemption, are declared to have been "created beforehand to be our way of life" (2:10). Anyone hearing this reminder would have realized anew that genuine belief is evidenced in doing good.

In Christ there is also a social transformation, again with a distinct "before" and "after" (2:11-22). Gentiles are reminded of their prior status before God as aliens in contrast to the status of Israel as God's chosen nation:

> Remember that you were at that time without Christ,
> being aliens from the commonwealth of Israel, and
> strangers to the covenants of promise, having no hope
> and without God in the world. (2:12)

But now in Christ the aliens have also become citizens:

> But now in Christ Jesus you who once were far off
> have been brought near by the blood of Christ. (2:13)

What leads to this change in relationships? Through the cross of Christ a wall of hostility has come tumbling down. Jews and Gentiles, two peoples previously separated from each other by many generations of animosity and ethnic pride, are now united into "one new humanity" (2:15), "one body" (2:16). The result is peace, not the Roman peace attained through warfare and domination but the peace of free, open, and equal access in one Spirit to God through the death and resurrection of Christ.

The new community that has come into being through God's initiative in Jesus Christ is described using imagery from life in the household (2:19-20) and worship in the temple (2:21). In the household language, the citizens of Roman Asia would have heard echoes of the imperial propaganda that intended to cultivate a united family feeling in the empire, with the emperor as the patriarch at the head. The church as "the household of God" is structured differently, under Jesus Christ as the head:

> So then you are no longer strangers and aliens, but you are citizens with the saints and also members of the household of God, built upon the foundation of the apostles and prophets, with Christ Jesus himself as the cornerstone. (2:19-20)

Not Caesar and his deputies but Jesus Christ and his apostles and prophets provide the paradigm for the church. Through the church as his body, Jesus Christ also supplies an alternative model for the world.

The reference to the church as "the holy temple in the Lord" in 2:21 would especially have connected with Jews, who would have visualized the Jerusalem temple. The temple lay in ruins, but the people now connected to each other through Christ constitute another temple. With Jesus

Christ as the cornerstone and the apostles and prophets constituting the foundation, a renewed entity emerges:

> In him the whole structure is joined together and
> grows into a holy temple in the Lord; in whom you
> also are built together spiritually into a dwelling place
> for God. (2:21-22)

As "a dwelling place for God in the Spirit" (2:22, RSV), the church embodies the reconciling message of God's peace in the midst of the hostility, brokenness, and hopelessness of the present age.

In 3:1-13 are reflections about Paul's life and ministry. Imbedded within these reflections are some of the most exalted of all the claims concerning what God is about. Paul is described as "a prisoner for Christ Jesus for the sake of the Gentiles" (3:1). This mystery of the inclusion of the Gentiles is further elaborated in a sweeping portrayal of the salvation drama, in which the proclamation of the gospel has a strategic role:

> In former generations this mystery was not made
> known to humankind, as it has now been revealed to
> his holy apostles and prophets by the Spirit: that is, the
> Gentiles have become fellow heirs, members of the
> same body, and sharers in the promise in Christ Jesus
> through the gospel. (3:5-6)

After further reflections about Paul's role in bringing the gospel of Christ to the Gentiles (3:7-9), the grandiose intention of God ("who created all things" 3:9) is articulated, "So that through the church the wisdom of God in its rich variety might now be made known to the rulers and authorities in the heavenly places" (3:10).

What the author describes as "the eternal purpose" being accomplished "in Christ Jesus our Lord" (3:11) obviously includes a strategic role for the church!

This dizzying glimpse into God's intent introduces an eloquent prayer report recalling "the breadth and length and height and depth" of God's power (3:14-19). A moving benediction commends the hearers to God's power and expansively ascribes glory to God "in the church and in Christ Jesus to all generations, forever and ever. Amen" (3:20-21).

The stage is now set for the letter's fervent appeal and encouragement regarding the church's daily life and faithfulness in the world.

Living Within God's Victory

An "I therefore" statement in 4:1 signals the transition to ethical exhortation. The moral appeal in Ephesians 4:1–6:20 is framed within the traditional dynamic so characteristic of Paul's letters, namely, the interplay between the indicative of God's initiating grace and an accompanying set of ethical imperatives. What God has graciously given in Christ Jesus calls for a responsive lifestyle that harmonizes with this divine gift.

Heirs and citizens are summoned to live worthily of their inheritance and calling. Life within God's household calls for certain attitudes and commitments: humility, gentleness, patience, and love (4:1, 2). Particular effort is commended toward maintaining "the unity of the Spirit in the bond of peace" (4:3), all in view of God's character made known as the "one God and Father of all, who is above all" (as creator) "and through all" (Christ as God's pervasive fullness) "and in all" (the Spirit) (4:6). The vital source of the church's life and identity is Christ, who is the head of the whole body (4:15). Life within that body of which Christ is the head involves growth toward Christlikeness as various ministry gifts are employed for the mutual benefit of all (4:7-16).

But what does conformity to Christ look like?

In 4:17-32 Paul enumerates the moral consequences of the believers' transfer from darkness to light. There is a stark contrast between their former lifestyle (one that still prevails in the surrounding culture) and the moral qualities that characterize their new life in Christ. The language here is that of sheer prohibition: "You must no longer live as the Gentiles live" (4:17). Darkened understanding and an alienation from the life of God are identifying marks of their former way of life characterized by licentiousness and impurity (4:18-19). All of this is (or at least should be) in the past: "That is not the way you learned Christ!" (4:20). Their transformation of life includes being taught about Christ and being nurtured in him (4:21). Such teaching not only shapes the mind, it also leads to moral choices publicly attested in baptism and lived out in righteousness and holiness. Baptismal imagery likely lies behind the imperatives here: "put away your former way of life" (4:22), "be renewed in the spirit of your minds" (4:23), and "clothe yourselves with the new self" (4:24). When individuals experience the transforming power of Christ and become active participants in the body of Christ, they shed old clothes and don new garments. Some elaboration follows in 4:25-32. Several behaviors are clearly to be "put away": falsehood, anger, stealing, evil talk, wrangling, and slander. Instead members of the body of Christ are summoned to manifest the qualities demonstrated by God in Jesus Christ: "Be kind to one another, tenderhearted, forgiving one another, as God in Christ has forgiven you" (4:32).

The admonitory tone continues in chapter 5, where

strikingly the believers are urged as beloved children to imitate God (5:1). What this means specifically is spelled out again in terms of the way of Christ:

> Walk in love, as Christ loved us and gave himself up
> for us, a fragrant offering and sacrifice to God. (5:2,
> RSV)

Once again the intention seems to be to remind the hearers of their calling to live in conformity to the Christ whom they had professed in baptism as part of their transfer into the new community. It is likely that 5:14 cites a baptismal hymn:

> Sleeper, awake!
> Rise from the dead,
> And Christ will shine on you. (5:14)

What it means to have joined the company of those awakened from their moral stupor to experience new life and enlightenment in Christ is articulated in a list of some of the pagan ways needing to be renounced: "fornication, impurity, greed, obscene or silly or vulgar talk" (5:3). Such behaviors are not in conformity to their "inheritance in the kingdom of Christ and of God" (5:5). Paul reminds them of their past, their present, and the consequences for their life in the future: "For once you were in darkness, but now in the Lord you are light. Live as children of the light" (5:8). Among other things they are challenged to expose the works of darkness with the light of Christ (5:11).

Believers are also to avoid getting drunk with wine (5:18). In addition to its literal meaning, drunkenness appears to serve as a metaphor for the foolish, unfruitful, and shameful life that is contrary to the will of the Lord

(5:10-14, 15-17). Those who are wise, who recognize that "the days are evil," will experience another kind of high: that which comes from being "filled with the Spirit" (5:18). In short, imitators of God walk in the kind of love that Christ demonstrated in his death (5:1-2), and they in turn are filled with the Spirit (5:18).

And what characterizes this Spirit-filled community? Translations often blur the fact that four participial clauses enlarge on this experience of being filled with the Spirit. The first and the last deal with horizontal relationships within the community and the other two focus on the vertical dimension of the worship of God:

> Be filled with the Spirit
> > speaking to one another with psalms and hymns and songs,
> > singing and making melody in your hearts to the Lord,
> > giving thanks to God the Father at all times and for everything in the name of our Lord Jesus Christ,
> > being subject to one another out of reverence for Christ.
> > > (5:18-21, author's translation)

What constitutes evidence for the Spirit's work within the community of faith? The telltale marks of the infusion of God's Spirit into the community include brotherly and sisterly counsel in harmony with Scriptures, spirited singing, grateful praying, and mutual submission in Christ.

What it means for members of the body of Christ to "be subject to one another out of reverence for Christ" (5:21) is developed in the "household code" in 5:22–6:9. The Ephesians version of this code makes even more explicit than the one in Colossians 3:18–4:1 that relationships in Christ are not based on the hierarchical exercise of power but on mutual submission as sisters and brothers in Christ.

On the surface the guidance that is here given to wives and husbands, children and fathers, and slaves and masters seems to conform to the imperial pattern. As the emperor wants to be viewed as benevolent benefactor worthy of obedience and honor, so the father in each household seems to be expected to provide for the family and to rule his wife, children, and slaves firmly, thereby doing his part to keep the social fabric stable. At a deeper level, however, the ethical admonition given to the various members of the household reflects not the power relations of the dominant toward the subservient but the mutuality of relations among persons whose roles differ but whose equality derives from their common allegiance to Christ.

Christ is the head of the church, and yet the emphasis is not on his authority over but on his sacrifice for the church, "the body of which he is the Savior" (5:23). That is also what it means for the husband to be "the head of the wife" (5:22, 24). As Christ selflessly gave himself up for the church, so husbands are to love their wives (5:25); this theme is elaborated in a variety of ways in 5:26-32. Children are to obey their parents "in the Lord" (6:1-3); fathers need to bring up their children in "the discipline and instruction of the Lord" (6:4). Slaves are urged "as slaves of Christ" to be obedient to their earthly masters (6:5-8), and masters are reminded that they too are subject to the same impartial heavenly Master (6:9).

In sum, all the relationships within the household are potentially transformed in Christ. Social structures, even oppressive ones such as slavery, may continue, but in Christ the dynamics of change are unleashed whereby the selfless love made manifest in his sacrificial death eventually overcomes the forces of domination, subservience, and fear. The hierarchical relationships modeled and promoted by the empire are therefore profoundly challenged and undercut by the church as an alternative community formed by Christ.

Warriors Called Up and Equipped for Battle

The climax of this letter's emphasis on divine power comes in a rousing concluding call in 6:10-20 for the church to join God's holy war against the malevolent powers pitted against them. Hearers are urged to recognize the nature of their struggle:

> For our struggle is not against enemies of blood and
> flesh, but against the rulers, against the authorities,
> against the cosmic powers of this present darkness,
> against the spiritual forces of evil in the heavenly
> places. (6:12)

This language reflects awareness not only of cosmic spiritual forces but also their earthly manifestations in political and social structures (see Wink, 1992:3-10). Especially pertinent for our understanding of Ephesians is the need to recognize the pervasive spirit of empire, the imperial ideology maintained through a complex maze of patronage relationships from the emperor on down. Within this ideology, the emperor confers benefits and protection on citizens and subject peoples throughout the empire. The recipients of these benefits, in turn, are expected to demonstrate their gratitude by showing honor and expressing their allegiance.

The opening entry in the concluding admonitions in Ephesians displays a striking emphasis on God's power: "Finally, be strong in the Lord and in the strength of his power" (6:10). Yoder Neufeld notes that three "power" words are strung together: "Be *empowered* with the *strength* of the Lord's *might*!" (2002:293, emphasis his). The admonitions continue in ways strongly reminiscent of early baptismal liturgies, which feature the image of putting off the old and putting on the new (as in 4:22, 24-25; also Colossians 3:5-17; Romans 13:11-14). Here there is an elaboration of what the faithful put on:

> Put on the whole armor of God, so that you may be
> able to stand against the wiles of the devil. (6:11)

Being incorporated into the body of Christ through baptism, believers are urged to don God's whole armor. This armor equips the church not only for a defensive battle against a wily enemy, the devil, but also for an offensive struggle in the ongoing skirmishes, the victorious outcome of which has already been assured.

Such confidence in the future triumph of those who align themselves with God does not diminish the ferocity of the struggle in the meantime. After Paul identifies the spiritual dynamic lurking behind the antagonistic powers (6:12), the church hears another reminder to be equipped with the full arsenal of God's weaponry:

> Therefore take up the whole armor of God, so that
> you may be able to withstand on that evil day, and
> having done everything, to stand firm. (6:13)

Yoder Neufeld has demonstrated convincingly that this is an admonition for the church to engage in an active struggle against the forces marshaled against them rather than merely to seek protection from them. He argues that the outcome of being equipped with God's armor should be phrased differently: "so that you may be able to resist on the evil day, and having conquered completely, to be standing" (2002:297-8). Victors are the ones still standing when the battle finally comes to an end.

Another utterance of the injunction to stand launches a series of appeals, in which various parts of the soldier's armor and weapons metaphorically represent what God provides the believers for engaging the powers. The imagery of Isaiah 59:17-19 (also used in 1 Thessalonians 5:8) stands behind this extended appeal:

> Stand therefore, and fasten the belt of truth around your waist, and put on the breastplate of righteousness. As shoes for your feet put on whatever will make you ready to proclaim the gospel of peace. With all of these, take the shield of faith, with which you will be able to quench all the flaming arrows of the evil one. Take the helmet of salvation, and the sword of the Spirit, which is the word of God. (6:14-17)

With what weapons are believers equipped to vanquish the powers? First on this list is "truth" (6:14). Believers are summoned to declare the wisdom of God to rulers and authorities (3:10) and within the church to speak the truth in love (4:15; cf. 4:25). Next comes "righteousness" (6:14), rightly understood as justice at work in active intervention in behalf of victims. Closely related is the readiness to announce "the gospel of peace" (6:15). This text echoes Isaiah 52:7, where a messenger arrives announcing news of peace; within Ephesians this mention of peace recalls the earlier testimony to the peacemaking death of Christ whereby peoples once hostile toward each other are reconciled (2:14-18). Mentioned next is "faith" (6:16). The word *faithfulness*, however, better represents the active dimension implied here; it implies not just trust in God but also trusting participation in Christ's faithfulness in the face of opposition and death. "Salvation" (6:17a), already assured by grace through faith (2:8), is also to be shared with others in ministries of liberation. And "the word of God" (6:17b) is the Spirit-driven revelation of divine power. (For more on each aspect of this armor, see Yoder Neufeld, 1997:131-45.)

As defense and offense against the powers aligned in opposing the church, the author therefore urges the believers to equip themselves with God's armor for the continuing struggle. The church is envisioned as a corporate warrior participating with God in the battle against the powers. The believing community joins this battle knowing that ultimate victory is assured. With these weapons the community not only defends itself against but also engages an offensive struggle with the idolatrous and oppressive spiritual powers and their social incarnations.

As this epistle ends, Paul appears as "an ambassador in chains" urging perseverance in prayer (6:20). Hearers are urged to pray "for all the saints," because their corporate role as God's warriors against the powers calls for the Spirit's empowerment (6:18). Hearers are also enjoined to pray for Paul himself in continuing to make known "the mystery of the gospel" (6:19). As has been declared earlier in the letter (3:10), the anticipated outcome of this bold proclamation is that the good news of God's variegated wisdom will become fully known through the church to all rulers and authorities and the spiritual powers that undergird them.

God's power is therefore wielded through the prayerful community. Through the exercise of truth, justice, peace, and faithfulness the saints announce salvation and proclaim God's word. Empowered by the Spirit and watchful in prayer they announce the good news and live already within God's assured victory.

Here is a lofty and inspiring vision for the church's witness in the world!

The Church's Witness in the World

This soaring view of the church giving testimony among the powers that God reigns supreme clearly calls for a reality check. What in actuality is the status of the church among the varied political, economic, and cultural powers that provide the social matrix for the church? We need to attend to Paul's counsel and instructions about relations with the governing authorities (notably Romans 13:1-7); our examination of that text includes attention to its larger context in Romans 12:1–13:14. In addition we focus on Paul's gospel of peace and specifically on his use of the reconciliation metaphor both for what God has done in Christ and as a description of how believers need to behave within hostile environments.

Ephesians is not alone in its testimony to Paul's wide-angle perspective of the church's witness to rulers and authorities. There are remarkable parallels between the prayer report in Ephesians 3:14-19 and the triumphant climax to his reflections on life in Christ in Romans 8:37-39. Ephesians 3:14-17 pictures the saints strengthened by the Spirit, indwelled by the living Christ, and rooted and grounded in the love of God. Being firmly grounded the saints can pray:

> I pray that you may have the power to comprehend, with all the saints, what is the breadth and length and height and depth, and to know the love of Christ that surpasses knowledge, so that you may be filled with all the fullness of God. (Ephesians 3:18-19)

This reference to the four dimensions ("breadth and length and height and depth") serves to convey the claim that all of reality is subject to God's sovereign rule now made fully known in Christ. God has in Christ displayed a plan to gather up all things, both "things in heaven and things on earth" (1:10). Believers therefore see already on grand display the vista of all reality gathered up within the cosmic Christ, who embodies the very fullness of God (cf. Colossians 1:19-20).

It is this vision of an all-pervasive fullness already glimpsed in Christ that Paul also puts forward in Romans 8. He seeks to inspire confidence and hope for believers who are suffering during the interim season of waiting, praying, and working for the realization of this fullness:

> For I am convinced that neither death, nor life, nor
> angels, nor rulers, nor things present, nor things to
> come, nor powers, nor height, nor depth, nor anything
> else in all creation, will be able to separate us from the
> love of God in Christ Jesus our Lord. (Romans 8:38-39)

In this listing, the dimensions ("nor height nor depth") have the penultimate position following the mention of "powers." Also mentioned are other realities with which the believing community has to contend: "death, life, angels, rulers, things present" and "things to come." The all-encompassing final phrase, "nor anything else in all creation," sums it all up. None of these realities can ultimately drive a wedge separating the believing community from "the love of God in Christ Jesus our Lord."

This triumphant acclamation is set within a section that provides distinct clues about the harsh political situation on the ground for the congregations in Rome. In 8:35 Paul asks,

> Who will separate us from the love of Christ? Will
> hardship, or distress, or persecution, or famine, or
> nakedness, or peril, or sword? (8:35)

It is not possible to know for sure whether he has actual
circumstances in mind. "Hardship" and "distress" might
refer to experiences of opposition. The "famine" reference
hints at natural disasters. "Persecution," "nakedness," and
"peril" may refer to hostility inflicted by local or imperial
authorities. At the mention of "sword" Paul breaks in with
a quotation from Psalm 44:22, which gives voice to all
those who (like Jesus himself) in their faithfulness to God
are slandered, condemned, and threatened with death:

> As it is written, "For your sake we are being killed all
> day long; we are accounted as sheep to be slaugh-
> tered." (8:36)

In view here appears to be especially the Jewish community in Rome, which had been evicted by Claudius Caesar a
few years earlier. Members of the house churches in Rome
may also have encountered open official hostility in face of
their refusal to participate fully in the imperial cult.

Obedient to God, Submissive to Authorities

Paul's thundering announcement that nothing "will be
able to separate us from the love of God in Christ Jesus our
Lord" (Romans 8:39) introduces his wrestling with the
question whether ethnic Israel is included among the "us"
for whom God continues to "be" (9:1–11:36). His personal and theological reflections and his grappling with
Scripture on this question preoccupied us in this book's
chapter 6. In 11:32 Paul wraps up these reflections by pondering the mystery of God's mercy: "For God has impris-

oned all in disobedience so that he may be merciful to all."
With that he breaks out into a rousing accolade lauding
God, whose riches, wisdom, and knowledge are being
made known (11:33-35). And he closes with a doxology:
"To him be the glory forever. Amen" (11:36).

God's incredible mercy not only elicits praise; it also
solicits obedience. In 12:1-2 Paul connects the mercies of
God with the will of God. It is this intersection between
the indicative of God's lavish mercy and the imperative of
doing God's will that Paul explicates further in
12:1–13:14. In the middle of this exhortation section is his
pastoral word regarding relationships with governing
authorities (13:1-7). In our deliberations about the church
in its relationship to the powers it is important to consider what might be the underlying story behind Paul's counsel in 13:1, "Let every person be subject to the governing
authorities." Having noticed how he in Romans 8 sees
principalities and powers as threatening entities whose
dominion has been broken through Christ, the reader of
Romans 13 is startled to run across a positive picture of
worldly authorities before whom believers are called to be
subject. Does Paul here sing a different tune, one that actually calls for unquestioned loyalty toward rulers?

Before attempting to discern the narrative within
which the meaning of Romans 13:1-7 comes to light, we
need to examine this text in its literary context. A literary
analysis of 12:1–13:14 helps to highlight the theological
movement within which 13:1-7 can be understood. As
Wright has shown, there is a chiastic structure here. This
layout follows Wright's lead, although the headings have
been restated (1992:703):

A 12:1-2   Transformed nonconformity to this age
  B 12:3-13   An appeal for unity and love
    C 12:14-21   Living as citizens of God's kingdom
    C′ 13:1-7   Living within the present world
  B′ 13:8-10   An appeal for love
A′ 13:11-14   Living in light of the salvation still to come

In A and A′ Paul portrays the eschatological space in which the faith community lives. B and B′ articulate the ethic of love, expressed both within the body of Christ and toward the neighbor. And the parallel material in C and C′ highlights the kind of behavior incumbent respectively upon citizens of God's kingdom and people living in the kingdoms of this world. It is especially the center sections (C and C′) that dramatize the tension for believers living within the overlapping eras of this age and the age to come.

The "therefore" in 12:1 signifies a transition to Paul's ethical appeals, which come with a clear reminder of the gift of God's abundant mercies:

> I appeal to you therefore, brothers and sisters, by the mercies of God, to present your bodies as a living sacrifice, holy and acceptable to God, which is your spiritual worship. (12:1)

What Paul calls for is sacrifice: not the bloody sacrifice characteristic of some cultic rituals, both Jewish and pagan, but "a living sacrifice." The words "your bodies" point to the believers' physical existence both individually and corporately in the midst of the structures of this world. Their relationship to God rests on Jesus's faithfulness, which Paul has illustrated earlier by using sacrificial imagery ("a sacrifice of atonement," 3:25). In response, the beneficiaries of Jesus's sacrifice are also to give themselves to God as "a living sacrifice, holy and acceptable." Such giving of themselves is worship, often described as "spiritual" (NRSV, NIV), but more accurately "reasonable" (given as alternate reading in NRSV and NIV; KJV has "reasonable service"). Their lives are to be given in reasonable service and worship of God, not in irrational superstition toward the pagan gods or uncritical allegiance to any earthly ruler.

Paul continues his appeal in 12:2 with reference to the grand framework of God's still unfolding reign. He urges nonconformity to the prevailing patterns of the present age:

> Do not be conformed to this world, but be transformed by the renewing of your minds, so that you may discern what is the will of God—what is good and acceptable and perfect. (12:2)

Paul calls for a transformative spirituality that renews the mind, and he espouses an ethic that resists conformity to the values of this age. (The NAB rendering "this age" is more accurate than "this world" in NRSV.) Paul reflects the apocalyptic conception of the overlap of "this age" and "the age to come." People whose minds are renewed and whose bodies are presented as living sacrifices are already in this age living the transformative vision of the coming age. Careful communal discernment of God's will is therefore called for. In circumstances that the church confronts in the world, what is the "good and acceptable and perfect" toward which they are to be oriented as they live within the will of God?

In 12:3-13 Paul speaks to internal processes within the congregations: the need for healthy self-assessment, the valuing of various gifts within the body of Christ, and the many ways that genuine love expresses itself in relationships. (For further discussion, see "The Body of Christ" in chapter 9.)

In 12:14-21 his angle of vision widens to include the church's social and political context. He enlarges on the theme of loving relationships, doing so in ways that reflect Jesus's ethical teaching about how to deal with enemies (Luke 6:27-28; Matthew 5:44):

> Bless those who persecute you; bless and do not curse them. Rejoice with those who rejoice, weep with those who weep. Live in harmony with one another; do not be haughty, but associate with the lowly; do not claim to be wiser than you are. Do not repay anyone evil for evil, but take thought for what is noble in the sight of all. If it is possible, so far as it depends on you, live peaceably with all. (Romans 12:14-18)

Clearly this ethical counsel is relevant to Jews and Gentiles within the Roman house fellowships, whose relationships with each other were rancorous at times (cf. 14:1–15:13). Here, however, as the further directives in 12:19-21 demonstrate, Paul has in mind the open hostility and occasional acts of violence that the believers endure from their neighbors and the authorities.

For the first and only time in this letter, Paul addresses his hearers as "beloved." His use of this affectionate term indicates that he recognizes how deep their feelings of hurt, anger, helplessness, and desire for revenge must be:

> Beloved, never avenge yourselves, but leave room for the wrath of God; for it is written, "Vengeance is mine, I will repay, says the Lord." (12:19)

Paul cites Deuteronomy 32:35, pointing out to the believers in Rome that vengeance is God's prerogative, not

460 Remember the Future

theirs. However, reliance on God's vindicating justice does not invite passive waiting. As expressions of their faith and confidence in God, believers are urged to extend hospitality by offering food and drink even to their enemies. He quotes Proverbs 25:21-22:

> No, "if your enemies are hungry, feed them; if they are thirsty, give them something to drink; for by doing this you will heap burning coals on their heads." (Romans 12:20)

When enemies eat together, they take a major step toward reconciliation with each other. Even the image of burning coals on the head may come from ancient practices of hospitality. Carrying live coals on the head in a well-insulated container was the normal way of transporting them. This action may therefore be a necessary preparatory stage toward a meal of reconciliation (Klassen, 1984:119-21). Paul envisions gestures of hospitality and practical helpfulness whereby enemies can be transformed into friends. He sums up his admonition: "Do not be overcome by evil, but overcome evil with good" (12:21).

As Paul continues his pastoral counsel for the saints living in the capital city of the empire, he speaks next about their relationship to the ruling authorities (13:1-7). This text has sometimes been interpreted as though it provides a comprehensive theology of the state and an abiding ethic describing how believers should respond to any and all governments. Neil Elliott has described this passage as "the reef that threatens to capsize every Christian liberative project" but he adds, "The fault has not been Paul's" (1994:217). Some scholars regard this text as alien material that was inserted here by later scribes, though there is no proof for this theory. Instead, this text needs to be seen in its literary context, where it parallels Paul's ethical counsel regarding relationships to the larger culture (12:14-21). It is also important to try to reconstruct the underlying story.

To this point in the ethical instructions that began at 12:1, Paul has commended a posture of nonconformity to the world for those who align themselves with the will of God. Why then would he abruptly advocate in 13:1-7 a submissive posture toward governing authorities and why would he do so by asserting that such authorities are God-ordained? It seems as though Paul here locates compliance with the imperial and local rulers within the categories of "the good and acceptable and perfect" (12:2):

> Let every person be subject to the governing authorities; for there is no authority except from God, and those authorities that exist have been instituted by God. Therefore whoever resists authority resists what God has appointed, and those who resist will incur judgment. (13:1-2)

There have been numerous attempts to reconstruct the circumstances that would have moved Paul to draft these instructions, which appear not to be congruent with the perspectives he enunciates elsewhere (for example, 1 Corinthians 2:6-8: "The rulers of this age . . . crucified the Lord of glory").

Some scholars' explanations highlight the plight of Roman Jews. Elliott mentions three scenarios featuring, respectively, simmering anti-Judaism, a grassroots tax revolt, and growing Jewish nationalism within the empire (1997:184-86).

First: Claudius Caesar had expelled Jews from Rome in A.D. 49. Even though Nero later reversed this expulsion edict, anti-Jewish sentiment continued, and so any perceived belligerence by the Jewish population might bring serious repercussions. Even in the churches (as we have seen in chapter 6) dismissive Gentile attitudes toward Jews also surfaced. These were often reinforced by theological claims that God had finally given up on the Jews.

Second, during Nero's reign there was general discontent about tax increases, and occasionally tax revolts erupted. Jews also felt the tax burden and may have considered joining such tax resistance efforts. Among Jewish privileges negotiated over the years was the payment of a temple tax in lieu of some imperial taxes; this privilege was resented by the populace, leaving the Jews all the more vulnerable to charges of tax evasion.

Third, Jews throughout the Mediterranean, including Rome, were keenly aware of the brewing Zealot militancy in Galilee and Judea, where groups of revolutionaries increasingly looked for ways to expel the hated Roman occupying forces from their regions. Whether or not Jews in Rome openly expressed their support for the Jewish nationalistic movements in the east, the political leaders undoubtedly viewed them with some suspicion. Any public endorsement of Zealot nationalism and any support of tax resistance movements could bring the ire of the imperial authorities down on the heads of the Jewish people yet again.

For one or more of these reasons (so these portrayals of the situation in Rome suggest), Paul urges that especially the Jews among the believers in Rome maintain a politically realistic stance. In a word, they should submit to governing authorities and pay their taxes, knowing that the might of Rome could crush them if they tested the limits too far. Prudence would suggest the kind of lifestyle that does not arouse suspicion or invite reprisals:

For rulers are not a terror to good conduct, but to bad.
Do you wish to have no fear of the authority? Then do
what is good, and you will receive its approval; for it is
God's servant for your good. But if you do what is
wrong, you should be afraid, for the authority does
not bear the sword in vain! It is the servant of God to
execute wrath on the wrongdoer. (13:3-4)

As Elliott puts it, Paul's positive characterization of the
Roman authorities has an important function, namely "to
encourage submission, for now, to the authorities, rather
than desperate resistance; and thus to safeguard the most
vulnerable around and among the Roman Christians,
those Jews struggling to rebuild their shattered community in the wake of imperial violence" (1997:203).

Some other efforts at reconstructing the background
situation focus on how members of the house churches and
synagogue groups in Rome were summoned to express
their loyalty to the emperor. Luise Schotroff notes that the
Roman Caesars generally sought to unite the empire by a
policy of tolerance toward various religions while also
insisting that Roman civil religion be integrated into such
distinctive religious practices. This made it necessary for
Jews and Christians to discern how far they could go in
showing honor to the emperor without compromising
their allegiance to God. What Paul writes in Romans 13:1-
7 is therefore designed to equip believers, both Jews and
Gentiles, to pass the test of loyalty when officials interro-
gated them. It helped them to express a level of loyalty that
did not contravene either God's sovereignty or the lordship
of Christ (Schotroff, 1992:224-30).

What remains intact is the conviction that God is sovereign and that Christ is Lord. Indeed, even when believers
submit to authorities they testify that their ultimate alle-

giance is to God, who puts the rulers and authorities in order and will finally judge all. Schotroff notes:

> It is considered highly self-evident that the authorities in power are unjust and that they oppress the people. But unjust rulership is also God's servant. Its power, however, is borrowed and limited, and it will end before long. In their confrontation with unjust power, Christians practiced a peculiar behavior: refusal to pay retribution, prophetic announcement of God's judgment against the enemy, and loving the enemy. (1992:250)

According to Schotroff, such "peculiar behavior" is actually an expression of resistance against the unjust powers and ultimately resistance against Satan and the power of sin. In the spirit of the suffering Jesus they renounced violent retaliation, leaving vengeance to God. The saints demonstrated by their lifestyle that their deepest loyalty is to God alone.

Whom then do believers seek to honor? Their allegiance is ultimately reserved for God. Nevertheless, within their commitment to the sovereignty of God they also discern what levels of submission they can offer to their rulers:

> Therefore one must be subject, not only because of wrath but also because of conscience. For the same reason you also pay taxes, for the authorities are God's servants, busy with this very thing. Pay to all what is due them—taxes to whom taxes are due, revenue to whom revenue is due, respect to whom respect is due, honor to whom honor is due. (13:5-7)

According to Paul in his further counsel in 13:8-10, there is, when all is said and done, but one "debt" that matters among recipients of God's mercies: "Owe no one anything, except to love one another" (13:8a). Love for the neighbor, including the enemy, sums up all the commandments (13:9-10). In 13:8-10, therefore, he creates a bracket around his counsel concerning their relationship to the authorities. It parallels his earlier words of encouragement about the way of love in the life of the church (12:3-13).

In 13:11-14 Paul also recalls an earlier motif: the eschatological framework within which the church exists (parallel to 12:1-2). The hour of the consummation of God's salvation begun in Christ is near:

> Besides this, you know what time it is, how it is now
> the moment for you to wake from sleep. For salvation
> is nearer to us now than when we became believers;
> the night is far gone, the day is near. (13:11-12a)

Paul goes on to evoke the memory of the believers' baptisms, described earlier in this letter as dying and rising with Christ (6:3-4). Here he speaks about "taking off" certain patterns of behavior ("works of darkness") and then "putting on" the weapons of righteousness ("the armor of light"):

> Let us then lay aside the works of darkness and put on
> the armor of light; let us live honorably as in the day,
> not in reveling and drunkenness, not in debauchery and
> licentiousness, not in quarreling and jealousy. Instead,
> put on the Lord Jesus Christ, and make no provision
> for the flesh, to gratify its desires. (13:12b-14)

Having been baptized into God's infantry, the members of the community, whose Lord is Jesus Christ, are galvanized into the kind of action that befits their primary citizenship. Certain behaviors, which conform to the present age, need to be abandoned. Some attitudes and activities ("debauchery and licentiousness" and "quarreling and jealousy") are not in keeping for people who have already through Christ made the transfer into the age to come.

The faith community's stance can therefore be described as reliance on God while submitting to authorities to the extent that does not violate their primary loyalty. Such devotion to God may, despite their measured submission to their rulers, still lead to suffering. In John Howard Yoder's words, such suffering is "participation in the character of God's victorious patience with the rebellious powers of his creation. . . . We subject ourselves to government because it was in so doing that Jesus revealed and achieved God's victory" (Yoder, 1994:209).

The Gospel of Peace and Reconciliation

Each of Paul's letters opens with a greeting that features peace, always also combined with grace: "Grace to you and peace from God our Father and the Lord Jesus Christ" (Romans 1:7). How does he understand peace?

Gordon Zerbe describes Paul's understanding of the gospel as centered around a "vision of cosmic peace":

> At the core of Paul's gospel is his vision of cosmic restoration—the eschatological redemption of the entire created order. This coming order of peace and righteousness (a) will be fully realized by the final triumph of God over the hostile and destructive powers of this age, which includes judgment and wrath against all unrighteousness and opposition to God, (b) has been proleptically inaugurated by God in Christ through the resurrection, and (c) is realized provisionally in the life of the believer and the church where Christ already reigns as Lord. (1992:181)

In short, *peace* (Greek: *eirene*; Hebrew: *shalom*) is Paul's shorthand for salvation, God's wholeness, known already in the present yet still to be experienced more fully in the future.

Ephesians 6:15 mentions "the gospel of peace." The reign of God, according to Paul in Romans 14:17, is characterized by "righteousness and peace and joy in the Holy Spirit"; people living in accordance with kingdom values are therefore urged to "pursue what makes for peace and mutual upbuilding" (14:19). In a number of Paul's benedictions, God is acknowledged as "the God of peace" (Romans 15:33; 16:20).

Such peace has personal, social, and cosmic dimensions. At the personal level, Paul asserts, "Since we are justified by faith, we have peace with God through our Lord Jesus Christ" (Romans 5:1). He clearly recognizes the communal aspect of such peace, which expresses itself in a welcoming embrace across ethnic barriers. The benediction that wraps up Paul's appeal to Jews and Gentile in Christ to welcome one another (15:7-12) refers to such communal peace:

> May the God of hope fill you with all joy and peace in
> believing, so that you may abound in hope by the
> power of the Holy Spirit. (Romans 15:13)

Realizing peace as a gift from God at the personal and communal levels, the faith community also glimpses cosmic peace. The eye of faith already glimpses it, as we have seen in Ephesians. The community of faith lives "in the unity of the Spirit in the bond of peace" (Ephesians 4:3). The church as Christ's body participates in living out of that vision. Christ is our peace! (2:14). Knowing that God has already put all things under Christ's feet, the church as the body of Christ experiences "the fullness of him who fills all in all" (1:22-23).

One of Paul's rich metaphors expresses how the individual and the community, having received the gift of God's peace, are invited to engage in making peace. This is an image from the realm of diplomacy. The church is pictured as the community of the reconciled who engage as ambassadors in ministries of reconciliation. In Romans 5 Paul emphasizes reconciliation as a gift of God's grace:

> For if while we were enemies, we were reconciled to
> God through the death of his Son, much more surely,
> having been reconciled, will we be saved by his life.
> But more than that, we even boast in God through our
> Lord Jesus Christ, through whom we have now
> received reconciliation. (5:10-11)

In 2 Corinthians 5 Paul enlarges on the gift character of reconciliation to highlight the ways in which the recipients of this gift participate as God's ambassadors in a ministry of reconciliation:

> All this is from God, who reconciled us to himself
> through Christ, and has given us the ministry of recon-
> ciliation; that is, in Christ God was reconciling the
> world to himself, not counting their trespasses against
> them, and entrusting the message of reconciliation to
> us. So we are ambassadors for Christ, since God is
> making his appeal through us; we entreat you on
> behalf of Christ, be reconciled to God. (5:18-20)

As enemies now reconciled to God through the peace-restoring death of Jesus Christ, believers are enlisted into the diplomatic corps whose mandate is to seek reconciliation: between God and estranged humanity, and among peoples alienated from each other. God longs for peace!

Part 4

Therefore, Remember the Future!

INTRODUCTION

At this point in our journey, we ponder the enduring fruit of Paul's apostolic ministry.

Through an apocalypse of Jesus Christ, Paul had come face-to-face with God's preemptive grace. He caught a vision of a glorious future, already realized, yet still unfolding. This vision powered his evangelistic endeavors and inspired his pastoral care for the congregations that emerged in the cities and regions where he preached the gospel. Paul read the Scriptures with new eyes. The grand story of God's creating, calling, covenanting, correcting, and consummating handiwork took on new meaning and relevance in light of Jesus Christ. Paul also entered into the stories of varied congregations, from Thessalonica and Philippi in Macedonia to Corinth and Cenchreae in Achaia, from Galatia, Ephesus, and Colossae in the east to Rome in the west. In his pastoral letters to these churches, he has been drawing on Scriptures and revelation in ways that intersect with their local stories. And in his eagerness to communicate effectively with these congregations, he has been creatively employing metaphors and images from their worlds.

In this concluding unit, we get in touch with a later generation in the church, with an older Paul, and with some of the co-workers carrying his missionary and theological enterprise into the next generation. We visit the three Pastoral Epistles, one addressed to Titus and two to Timothy.

Many scholars consider these letters to have come not

from Paul but from others writing on his behalf during his lifetime or in his name following his death. We will not attempt to resolve the issue of authorship. However, we do ask whether these letters continue the rich, future-creating narrative that we have discerned in the other letters bearing Paul's name.

Some suggest that Paul's earlier dramatic vision for the future has become blurred or that his successors have domesticated the prophetic message of the apostle. According to these interpretations of the Pastoral Epistles, worship has shifted away from dynamic doxology to a concern to articulate static propositions and root out heresies. Community relationships have evolved from egalitarian understandings into the hierarchical patterns reflected in guidelines for life in the household, which call for the strict subordination of women and slaves. And the sense of the church's urgent mission has dissipated into a quest for respectability. In a word, the church has moved from subverting the status quo to accommodating to it. According to this reconstruction of the contextual realities within which the Pastoral Epistles need to be interpreted, by the beginning of the second century a bourgeois establishment ethic had taken over within the church. In a word, the movement that was rooted in the ministry of Jesus, who identified with the poor and the marginalized, has now been co-opted by a concern for stability rooted in a ruling hierarchy.

The question is acute. What kind of future do Paul and his successors commend? Do the Pastoral Epistles lay the foundation for the emerging "church catholic" seeking accommodation with the empire? Or do these letters give ongoing testimony to the dynamic vision of God's still unfolding peace-restoring and justice-creating reign? Do they continue to inspire and empower congregations to model an alternative to the status quo of life within the empire?

13

SUFFERING, HOPE, AND
THE CHURCH'S MISSION

Our attempt to discern narratives that will illuminate the Pastoral Epistles—Titus and 1 and 2 Timothy—is beset with significant uncertainty and ambiguity. We will try, however, to enter into the stories of congregations in Crete and Ephesus, as their lives are mirrored in these letters.

The actual chronological sequence of the letters is difficult to establish. Titus and 1 Timothy are similar in their focus on congregational organization, but it is not clear which one came first. Second Timothy has the aura of a last testament, so it could arguably have been the final letter. In both the opening narrative and the following discussion of these letters, we begin with the letter to Titus and then follow up with the two letters to Timothy.

There are two introductory narratives. First we visit a young Christian community in Crete. Paul left Titus in Crete to bring some order and to appoint leaders. What is the story in Crete? In "Church Life in Crete" we meet Jason, whom we imagine to be a member of one of the Jewish communities on the island. He has recently become a believer in Christ. Our sources are several texts in Titus that provide some clues: 1:5, 10-16; 2:1-10; 3:1-3, 9. We also acknowledge the account of Paul's travel to Crete in Acts 27:1-12.

In "Church Life in Ephesus" we get in touch with established congregations in Ephesus, a city where Paul

*spent several years, according to Acts 19:10. There is some
background information about subsequent events in several
texts in 1 and 2 Timothy: 1 Timothy 1:3-7, 19-20; 2 Timothy
1:15-18; 2:9, 16-18; 3:6-7; 4:9-21. Apparently Paul had visited Ephesus following his release from his imprisonment in
Rome. When he departed Ephesus for Macedonia he asked
his co-worker Timothy to stay behind. In this story we check
in with some natives of Ephesus who have long connections
to the church: Onesiphorus and his household.*

A STORY: Church Life in Crete

Travelers making their way along the coast of the
island of Crete were treated to breathtaking views of the
Great Sea. To the north lay the Aegean Sea; its waters often
bore cargo and passenger ships from distant harbors like
Cenchreae in Achaia or Ephesus in Asia. Jason recalled
that it was one of these ships that had delivered the missionary Paul to Crete. He discovered later that Paul had
previously made a stopover on the island as a prisoner on
his way to Rome. Jason speculates that something about
that rest stop at Fair Havens might have sparked Paul's
desire to make a return trip. Upon his release from prison
some time later, he chose to revisit Crete on a preaching
mission. Paul's living testimony concerning Christ had
moved Jason to join Jews and native Cretans in confessing
Jesus Christ as Lord.

By the time Paul departed Crete, a congregation was
growing there, and his co-worker Titus was left behind to
take care of things.

"It won't be easy," Jason mused. Cretans had a reputation as an independent and stubborn bunch. Residents of
Crete even quoted a memorable line from Epimenides, one
of their own poets of a bygone era: "Cretans are always

liars, vicious brutes, lazy gluttons." Such characterization would have smarted if it were spoken by an outsider, but the people of Crete seemed to get a cynical kind of pleasure from perpetuating this self-deprecating caricature among themselves. Many Cretans were notorious for raucous oratory, drinking too much wine, and the pursuit of sexual pleasures. Jason wondered whether the isolation, especially during the winter when travel was risky at best, led to their rough-and-tumble attitude toward life.

Some of these Cretan qualities seemed to have rubbed off on people in the Jewish colonies. After traveling to Jewish communities elsewhere, Jason noticed a distinctive level of contentiousness among his own people in Crete, especially in arguments about some of their founding myths and the interpretation of their traditional laws. And now with the emergence of groups of Jews and Gentiles acknowledging Jesus as the Messiah, the arguments and debates had intensified. Some families on the wild island province of Crete had become quite distressed by it all. Jason wondered how soon the Roman authorities would begin to investigate and take action, and what Titus might do to bring stability among converts to Paul's gospel.

ANOTHER STORY: Church Life in Ephesus

Along with other residents of Ephesus, Onesiphorus marveled at the economic and cultural vigor of their city. Served by a major harbor into the Aegean Sea and by the trans-Anatolian highway, Ephesus had a well-deserved reputation as "the gateway to Asia." Dredging operations were needed to keep the harbor open to marine traffic, but such efforts were well rewarded by prosperity in the city and the surrounding region. Onesiphorus was also aware that travelers who made their way to the city often brought more than material prosperity. Various philosophies and religious movements came with them. Indeed that is how the gospel of Jesus Christ took root and bore fruit in the emergence of different congregations in and around Ephesus and from there into other centers such as Colossae and Laodicea in the Lycus River valley.

Onesiphorus and his household had been taking active leadership roles within the church in Ephesus nearly from its beginning, when the apostle Paul preached the gospel there. Paul made Ephesus his base of operations for several years. For his part, Onesiphorus made an effort to keep in touch with Paul during his extensive missionary travels. On one occasion Onesiphorus even launched an extensive search in Rome until he discovered Paul as a prisoner in chains.

Onesiphorus knew firsthand the challenges facing a leader involved with congregations in a teeming urban center like Ephesus. Many religions made their inroads into the community and developed their cult centers. The grand architecture of the temple of Artemis attracted admiring glances from all visitors to the city, and the devotees of the goddess were always eager to capitalize on fascination with the Ephesian deity. Throughout the city were shrines with carved relief depictions of Cybele the Phrygian mother goddess escorted by the male deity Zeus. The temple of Sarapis with its water basins and canals attested to the presence of Egyptian mystery rites. And prominent on the main street into the heart of the city was the imperial temple dedicated to the veneration of Augustus Caesar and his successors in Rome.

With so many religious options and with the ever-present reminder to give homage to Rome, Onesiphorus realized that the church needed to be clear in its focus on the God made known in Jesus Christ. Yet it never seemed sim-

ple. Even some of the church's leaders had drifted away,
including Phygelus, Hermogenes, and Alexander.
Hymenaeus and Philetus, still active within the church,
promoted the notion that the resurrection was already
past. Some ardent evangelists targeted whole households,
and particularly the women in them, to accept new ver-
sions of the gospel. Some women and men emphasized
ascetic practices as a means of removing themselves from
the world. Through rigorous self-denial they sought to
gain favor with God. Some advocated a celibate lifestyle as
more faithful than marriage and domestic life. In some
cases, married women were convinced that they should
abandon their families for a life of higher devotion. With
so much diversity within and among congregations,
Onesiphorus found himself thinking that a more autocrat-
ic style of leadership was needed to bring order and unity.

Still other professed believers in Ephesus and the surrounding area seemed to see nothing wrong with a self-
indulgent lifestyle that was hardly distinct from the way
people outside the church lived. On the issue of morality
also, Onesiphorus pondered the nature of effective leadership within the church.

"What will it take," Onesiphorus wondered, "to bring
some order to all of this chaos? If only Paul were back in
town!"

The Gospel, Godliness, and the Church's Mission

> The grace of God has appeared, bringing salvation to
> all, training us to renounce impiety and worldly pas-
> sions, and in the present age to live lives that are self-
> controlled, upright, and godly. (Titus 2:11-12)

> Remember Jesus Christ, raised from the dead, a
> descendant of David—that is my gospel, for which I

> suffer hardship, even to the point of being chained like
> a criminal. But the word of God is not chained.
> Therefore I endure everything for the elect, so that they
> may also obtain the salvation that is in Christ Jesus,
> with eternal glory. (2 Timothy 2:8-10)

What vision for the future sustains and builds up faith communities when the founder disappears from the scene? We have visited a young congregation in Crete and some established congregations in and around Ephesus. Now we identify with Titus and Timothy in their roles as leaders guiding these churches into the future.

The epistles addressed to Titus and Timothy assume a period when Paul was engaged in further missionary activity following his release from the Roman imprisonment described in Acts 28. The tide of scholarly opinion favors the view that these letters were written in Paul's name to update his theological legacy for a later generation. The personal details concerning his further ministry before he was imprisoned again are then regarded either as fictional or as reconstructed by his colleagues, perhaps partly on the basis of fragmentary notes from Paul smuggled out of prison before his death. (For a discussion of the authorship of these letters, see commentaries such as Johnson, 1996:1-36; Collins, 2002:1-14.)

The pastoral letters to Titus and Timothy tackle circumstances that can no longer be fully discerned or placed chronologically. It is evident, however, that internal dynamics and external pressures in Crete and Ephesus call for clear intervention by leaders designated and equipped for this assignment. Timothy previously had a similar role as co-worker with Paul in Thessalonica (1 Thessalonians 3:1-6), Corinth (1 Corinthians 4:17; 2 Corinthians 1:19), and Philippi (Philippians 2:19-24), and he is listed as a co-sender of the letters addressed to these congregations. Titus had functioned as Paul's delegate to Corinth (2 Corinthians 2:13; 7:5-16; 8:6, 16-24). That Paul should write official letters to these close colleagues should occasion no surprise.

We cannot here disentangle the complex issue of authorship. Nevertheless, we can with other readers of these letters attempt to hear and understand the rebuke, counsel, and teaching proffered by or in the name of Paul. We call the author Paul in the recognition that, whether he actually wrote them or not, these pastoral writings speak solidly from within the trajectory of his apostolic tradition.

A Pastoral Word for the Church in Crete

Even the salutation of the epistle to Titus (1:1-4) seems to bear in mind the trademark incivility of the people of Crete among whom the church struggles for a clear sense of its identity in Christ. Paul cites as the goal of this apostolic letter not only the "faith of God's elect" (1:1) and "the hope of eternal life" (1:2) but also "the knowledge of the truth that is in accordance with godliness" (1:1). The gospel is truth lived out by people of faith within godly relationships sustained by the reassurance of their everlasting hope. Such godliness derives from the nature and the redemptive activity of God our Savior (1:3), who is made known through Christ Jesus our Savior (1:4). The promises of God as one "who never lies" (1:2) are trustworthy and sure.

The letter opens with practical counsel and warnings. It outlines the desired character qualities of elders and overseers (1:5-9), warns about the corrupting influence of deceptive speech (1:10-16), and exhorts members of the households concerning appropriate behavior and relationships (2:1-10). The Cretans' rough-and-tumble moral ethos necessitates firm and even harsh correctives, many of which leave later readers of this letter feeling quite uncomfortable. It is important, however, to note the redemptive and missional intention of these directives.

Elders and bishops need to be rooted in the trustworthy word, so that they not only preach in accord with truth but also correct those who contradict the truth of the gospel (1:5-9). Deceivers who upset families with their teachings need to be rebuked sharply (1:10-12), "so that they may become sound in the faith" (1:13). Older women are to model reverent behavior and teach young women to show love to their husbands and children (2:3-5a), "so that the word of God may not be discredited" (2:5b). The urgency for young men to exercise self-control calls for Titus to show himself to be a model of good works and integrity of speech (2:6-8a): "Then any opponent will be put to shame, having nothing evil to say of us" (2:8b). Even the submission and fidelity of slaves to their masters (2:9-10a) is advocated, "so that in everything they may be an ornament to the doctrine of God our Savior" (2:10b). In a situation beset by significant chaos, the witness of the church must include attention to orderly relationships, a commitment to the basic values of hard work and love within the family, and an eagerness to do good.

In 2:11-14 and 3:4-7, Paul supplies the narrative framework that informs and motivates the living of the gospel for the sake of the mission of the church. The gospel's implications for the church coming of age within the disarray of first-century Crete may not be the same as in other situations. But the big story, the gospel of Jesus Christ, remains dynamically the same.

As a pastor drawing on the living gospel tradition to address these local circumstances, Paul recounts the story of salvation. This telling of the story features the imagery of epiphany: the process of making visible what had been hidden. In fact, the gospel's narrative plot involves two manifestations of divine mystery, one past epiphany, the other still future. During the period between these two revelatory moments the church is summoned to live within its current social and political reality in light of what has already been unveiled and in the hope of its future consummation. The following table depicts how 2:11-14 portrays these past and future epiphanies and the life and witness of the community that finds itself in between:

The Past Epiphany	Life and Witness in the Interim	The Future Epiphany
The grace of God has appeared bringing salvation to all >	training us to renounce impiety and worldly passions and in the present age to live lives that are self-controlled, upright, and godly >	while we wait for the blessed hope and the manifestation of the glory of our great God and Savior Jesus Christ.>
He it is who gave himself for us that he might redeem us from all iniquity >	and purify for himself a people of his own who are zealous for good deeds.	

This confession lifts up both the people-formation and the educative functions of God's gracious salvation, which is potentially available to all people through Christ's self-sacrificing, redemptive love. Given the prevailing ethos in the surrounding culture, it is noteworthy that Paul fixes first on the corrective training required among people who need to "renounce impiety and worldly passions" (2:12a). Such training entails the formation of virtuous character in individuals who "live lives that are self-controlled, upright, and godly" (2:12b). Character formation, however, also has a communal dimension. God's salvation liberates the faith community from lawlessness (from all iniquity) and cleanses a people as God's own possession (an echo of Exodus 19:5), a people who express their covenant faithfulness through their zeal for doing good ("zealous for good deeds") (2:14).

The language of epiphany would have been quite familiar to the original hearers of this letter. Within the imperial cult, the emperor was venerated as a manifestation (an epiphany) of the divine. Here it is the redeemer God who has appeared in Jesus Christ, not the god Apollos made manifest in Caesar. God's people are invited to anticipate the glorious future manifestation not of Caesar as liberator and benefactor but of "our great God and Savior Jesus Christ" (2:13). This confession of God in Jesus Christ as the Savior flies in the face of imperial proclamations announcing the emperor as savior.

When Paul echoes a confession that preempts imperial claims, the question about the relationship between the church's confession of the gospel and its life within the empire is posed sharply. What obligations do the people of God then have toward the imperial authorities? A group of people who confess God as the Savior through Jesus Christ would have seemed subversive to Roman officials. Strikingly, however, Paul continues his instructions to Titus by counseling submission and obedience toward the authorities:

> Remind them to be subject to rulers and authorities, to be obedient, to be ready for every good work, to speak evil of no one, to avoid quarreling, to be gentle, and to show courtesy to everyone. (3:1-2)

How should these instructions be understood? We need once again to follow the grand story whose plot helps the reader to make sense of this pastoral counsel.

Here too Paul develops the narrative framework that undergirds faithfulness. He does so first with a graphic sketch of their former life (3:3). What follows is another poetic litany of what God has done (3:4-6). The story reaches its climax in a reference to the future and their hope of eternal life (3:7).

Former life (3:3)	What God Has Done (3:4-6)	The Future (3:7)
For we ourselves were once foolish, disobedient, led astray, slaves to various passions and pleasures, passing our days in malice and envy, despicable, hating one another.	But when the goodness and loving kindness of God our Savior appeared, he saved us, not because of any works of righteousness that we had done, but according to his mercy, through the water of rebirth and renewal by the Holy Spirit. This Spirit he poured out on us richly through Jesus Christ our Savior >	so that, having been justified by his grace, we might become heirs according to the hope of eternal life.

Several observations about this marvelous version of the grand salvation story will need to suffice. The depiction of their past appears in a generic sense rather than specifically with reference to their situation in Crete. Paul includes himself representatively in this chronicle concerning sinful humanity (3:3). The emphasis here lies on the saving and renewing power of God our Savior, whose philanthropy has appeared not because anyone deserves it or has earned it but because of God's mercy (3:4-5). Once again the language of the ruler-cult has been co-opted, not only in the vocabulary of epiphany but also in the reference to God's loving kindness. The underlying Greek word translated as "loving kindness" could be left untranslated: *philanthropy* was a word used to describe the benevolent activity of rich

and powerful benefactors such as the emperor, who give
benefits to their subjects and who then expect their subjects to show honor and allegiance in return. The reference
to "the water of rebirth and renewal by the Holy Spirit"
may allude to the ritual of water baptism, which symbolizes the believers' conversion and inner renewal (3:6).
Through justification by God's grace the members of this
family remember their future as "heirs according to the
hope of eternal life" (3:7).

How then does this telling of the gospel story inform
the ethical counsel about submission and obedience to the
authorities?

To those who have experienced rebirth, renewal, and
incorporation as heirs into God's family, it goes without
saying that their ultimate allegiance belongs to God. God's
heirs will therefore not submit to rulers in ways that violate their primary loyalty to God. Through exemplary
character and behavior, including the kind of submission
to ruling authorities that makes clear that emperors and
governors too are accountable to God, the members of
God's household give testimony to God. As with the
household instructions in 2:1-10, so here with reference to
their relationships to rulers and authorities, their compliance with these guidelines has a missional goal:

> I desire that you insist on these things, so that those
> who have come to believe in God may be careful to
> devote themselves to good works; these things are
> excellent and profitable to everyone. (3:8)

Attention to good works does not however imply con-
formity with the status quo in ways that contravene their
Christian confession. A congregation formed through
God's redeeming initiative in Jesus Christ lives within its

culture in ways that conform to those values that are in harmony with the gospel. However, actions and attitudes that do not echo the way made known in Jesus Christ need to be confronted, first of all within the church:

> Avoid stupid controversies, genealogies, dissensions, and quarrels about the law, for they are unprofitable and worthless. (3:9)

As a people of God's own, a people eager to reflect God's philanthropy ("loving kindness") within their culture (cf. 2:14; 3:4), the church therefore needs to discipline sinners (3:10-11). The church must also demonstrate a commitment to mutual aid:

> And let people learn to devote themselves to good works in order to meet urgent needs, so that they may not be unproductive. (3:14)

A missional stance toward the surrounding culture invites the church both to confess faith and to maintain a lifestyle that confronts sin.

A Word to the Church in Ephesus

What is Paul's pastoral word to his delegate Timothy regarding the congregations in Ephesus? We turn our attention to the first of two letters addressed to Timothy.

In 1 Timothy Paul warns about people whose teaching is aberrant and behavior unfaithful (1:3-11; 4:1-5; 6:3-10). He offers personal encouragement to Timothy (1:18-20; 4:6-16; 6:11-21) and instructions for the church's life (2:1-15). He outlines the character qualities desired in various congregational leaders and other groups within the church (3:1-13; 5:1–6:2). However, these warnings and lists and instructions do not convey the heartbeat of the letter.

Pastoral passion pulses through various renditions of the gospel story interspersed throughout the letter: especially 1:15; 2:5-6; 3:16; 4:9-10; 6:13-16. Frequently Paul also shares from his own story (1:12-16; 2:7; 3:14-15). These rich gospel narratives accented by vivid glimpses into Paul's own life experiences need to shape how we read the letter's warnings, encouragement, and guidance for leaders.

Even a casual reading of this letter makes it apparent that a struggle has erupted within the church about what is its defining story. From Paul's perspective, some teachers disseminate "myths and endless genealogies that promote speculations rather than the divine training that is known by faith" (1:4; cf. 4:7). He laments that some would-be teachers of the law have recklessly departed from true faith: "Some people have deviated from these and turned to meaningless talk" (1:6). Paul longs that Timothy and the church will adhere to "the sound teaching that conforms to the glorious gospel of the blessed God" (1:11). This gospel, which has been entrusted to Paul and the church, is summarized in a profoundly simple story: "Christ Jesus came into the world to save sinners" (1:15).

This telling of the gospel story is accentuated by a formula used frequently elsewhere in the Pastoral Epistles: "The saying is sure" (1:15; cf. 3:1; 4:9; 2 Timothy 2:11; Titus 3:8) "and worthy of full acceptance." However, the gospel is authenticated in another way, through Paul's testimony to his own transformation and call. Formerly "a blasphemer, a persecutor, and a man of violence" he has experienced the mercy and grace of God (1:13, 14) and God's appointment to service (1:12-14). He therefore presents himself as verification of the truth of the gospel story that he shares (1:16). He invites the faithful to join him in doxology: "To the king of the ages, immortal, invisible, the only God, be honor and glory forever and ever" (1:17).

Situated within Paul's instructions for prayer and worship (2:1-15) is another gospel confession, which buttresses his call for the church to pray that society's leaders will ensure structures conducive for quiet and peaceable living. Peace and quiet are desired, not as ends in themselves but for the sake of the church's mission, because God "desires everyone to be saved and to come to the knowledge of the truth" (2:4). This gospel confession echoes the Shema, the Deuteronomy 6:4 affirmation of the sovereignty of God, and it continues with brief articulations of the story of Jesus:

> There is one God;
> There is also one mediator between God and humankind,
> Christ Jesus, himself human, who gave himself a ransom for all. (2:5, 6a)

This creed highlights the incarnation of Jesus Christ, his mediating role, and ransom imagery to describe the significance of his death. Each of these plot lines in the gospel story has a rich trajectory, none of which is elaborated here. Paul only lets it be known that his ministry as "herald, apostle, . . . a teacher of the Gentiles in faith and truth" gives timely testimony to this gospel (2:6b-7).

Included in his instructions regarding prayer and worship are words of counsel addressed to men (2:8) and to women (2:9-15). The directive silencing the woman (more likely, the wife) (2:11-12) draws support from a hierarchical reading of the Genesis 2 and 3 story of the creation of Adam and Eve and their disobedience in the garden (2:13-14). It is possible that certain religious claims being promoted in Ephesus regarding Artemis, Cybele, or other goddesses led to this strategy of silencing wives, lest the mission of the church be hindered (see Kroeger & Kroeger, 1992).

Later readers of this part of the letter are still drawn into
one dimension of a first-century struggle between two con-
tending stories. Will relationships between men and women
in the church be guided by the story of creation and human
transgression echoed in 2:13-14? Or will they be informed
more by the story of salvation rehearsed in 2:5-6? Likely
the bewildering and upsetting assertion in 2:15, "She will
be saved through childbearing," has to do with refuting
ascetics who prohibit marriage (see 4:3). What endures,
also for those who marry and for women who bear children, is the foundational story of salvation through the
"one mediator between God and humankind, Christ Jesus,
himself human, who gave himself as a ransom for all" (2:5-
6). For both women and men, salvation is through Christ.
The new relationship between them makes it possible for
them to transcend the legacy of transgression that goes
back all the way to Eve and Adam in the garden.

The character and lifestyles of bishops (3:1-7) and deacons (3:8-13) also have centrally to do with "the faith that
is in Christ Jesus" (3:13). This faith is modeled by behavior in God's household, "the church of the living God, the
pillar and the bulwark of the truth" (3:15). Individual
faithfulness and communal witness are again grounded in
the story, here called "the mystery of our religion."

> He was revealed in flesh,
> vindicated in spirit,
> seen by angels,
> proclaimed among Gentiles,
> believed in throughout the world,
> taken up in glory. (3:16)

This gospel litany again highlights the incarnation and
exaltation themes within the story of Jesus, but it adds

allusions to the proclamation and reception of the gospel throughout the world. This understanding of the gospel corrects the creation-negating impulse of the ascetics' defining story (4:1-5), and it nurtures the quest for the kind of godliness that holds promise both for this life and the life to come (4:6-10). Paul testifies,

> The saying is sure, and worthy of full acceptance. For to this end we toil and struggle, because we have our hope set on the living God, who is the Savior of all people, especially of those who believe. (4:9-10)

In the rest of the letter, he offers general counsel regarding Timothy's personal life and public ministry (4:11-16) and rather detailed instructions for various groups, including widows (5:1-16) and slaves (6:1-2). Again he warns about those who contradict "the sound words of our Lord Jesus Christ and the teaching that is in accordance with godliness" (6:3). There are warnings about conceited and contentious people, and active encouragement toward contentment (6:3-10). Paul wraps up with a striking personal charge to Timothy, urging him to remain true to his confession (6:11-12). In doing so, Timothy joins Jesus, who himself made the good confession before the Roman governor Pilate and is now exalted above all as cosmic Lord:

> In the presence of God, who gives life to all things, and of Jesus Christ, who in his testimony before Pontius Pilate made the good confession, I charge you to keep the commandment without spot or blame until the manifestation of our Lord Jesus Christ, which he will bring about at the right time—he who is the blessed and only Sovereign, the King of kings and Lord of lords. (6:13-15)

This rousing charge leaves no doubt that Timothy and the church are challenged to remember the assured future epiphany of the exalted Christ "at the right time." In the meantime, even as Jesus himself had done before Pilate, they are invited to give witness to the God who is sovereign over all.

Victorious Summons from Death's Door

The second epistle to Timothy qualifies as Paul's final testament. What does the apostle have to say as he faces his own death?

Readers of 2 Timothy both then and now are moved by the picture of a shackled apostle reaching out from his prison cell to his beloved co-worker Timothy and through him to the church. As in Titus and 1 Timothy the apostle shares stern warnings (3:1-9) and tender words of encouragement (1:3-18; 2:1-7; 3:14-17) and instructions for the life of the church (2:14-25; 4:1-5). This letter also incorporates several creed-like summaries of the gospel (1:9-10; 2:8-13). However, the most poignant dimension of 2 Timothy is the way that the suffering apostle participates in the passion and death of Christ in joyous anticipation of sharing in the victory of the resurrection (3:10-13; 4:6-8, 9-18). For his younger colleague and for the church, both then and now, the gospel story of Jesus Christ is replicated when the faith is lived out by individual believers and by communities of faith within the exigencies of their daily lives.

Recalling the legacy of faith passed on to Timothy by his grandmother, Lois, and mother, Eunice (1:3-5), and through the laying on of hands (1:6-7), Paul invites Timothy: "Join with me in suffering for the gospel, relying on the power of God" (1:8). One of this letter's gospel summaries is cited here to validate the gospel as divine empowerment for lived testimony even unto death. This summary of the gospel story identifies past and present and future scenarios (1:9-10):

Past (1:9)	Present (1:10a)	Future (1:10b)
[God] saved us and called us with a holy calling, not according to our works but according to his own purpose and grace. This grace was given to us in Christ Jesus before the ages began, >	but it has now been revealed through the appearing of our Savior Christ Jesus, >	who abolished death and brought life and immortality to light through the gospel.

Jesus's story, rooted before the ages, not only unveils God's grace. The manifestation of Christ also results in the abolition of death and the gracious offer of the gift of life and immortality. To underscore these implications of the gospel, Paul reflects on his own life, particularly his appointment as herald, apostle, and teacher, and his suffering (1:11-12). In response to God's initiating grace made known in Jesus Christ, Paul expresses confidence in God for the future: "I am sure that he is able to guard until that day what I have entrusted to him" (1:12). And he encourages Timothy to hold to sound gospel teaching, indeed to guard it as a treasure while relying on the Holy Spirit to empower him for his ministry (1:13-14). Paul adds, "Be strong in the grace that is in Christ Jesus" (2:1), and to illustrate the qualities needed, he cites the examples of soldier, athlete, and farmer (2:2-7).

But the prime exemplar for faithful witness is none other than Jesus Christ. Another short reminder of the story of Jesus is inserted here: "Remember Jesus Christ, raised from the dead, a descendant of David" (2:8). "That is my gospel," Paul adds, as he relates the story of Jesus to his own suffering ("chained like a criminal" 2:9) and his willingness to endure in light of the promise of salvation in Christ "with eternal glory" (2:10).

This interplay between the believers' present suffering and future glory leads Paul to quote another confession (again introduced with the expression "The saying is sure"), which highlights the believers' participation with the passion and resurrection of Jesus Christ (2:11-13):

Believers' Participation in Suffering	Promise of Participation in Resurrection
The saying is sure: If we have died with him >	we will also live with him;
If we endure, >	we will also reign with him;
If we deny him, >	he will also deny us;
If we are faithless, >	he remains faithful—for he cannot deny himself.

The promise and threat linked to the believers' participation or nonparticipation in the way of Christ reassures Timothy in his own suffering (note 2:3), in his ministry of correcting troublemakers (2:14, 16-18), and in modeling faithfulness (2:15, 19). A dangerous version of the gospel story ("like gangrene," 2:17) denies the future promise, and therefore also the threat, of the true gospel: "Among them are Hymenaeus and Philetus, who have swerved from the truth by claiming that the resurrection is past already" (2:18). An understanding of the gospel that alleges that future glory has already become full reality in the present potentially leads to the contentiousness and ungodly behavior that needs to be confronted and rebuked (2:20–3:9).

As Paul wraps up this letter he recalls his own life and

current situation (3:10-11; 4:6-8) and articulates urgent appeals to Timothy regarding his ministry (3:12-17; 4:1-5). No gospel summary is cited here, but there are dynamic gospel "sound bites" that recall the larger gospel narrative. Of particular prominence in Paul's mind is God's climactic saving action in Christ: "You have known the sacred writings that are able to instruct you for salvation through faith in Christ Jesus" (3:15). The phrase as translated above, "salvation through faith in Christ Jesus," points to the responsive faith elicited by God's initiating grace. However, this phrase also testifies to the story of Jesus's faithfulness, even unto death on the cross: "salvation through the faith which is in Christ Jesus" (author's literal translation). This salvation is to be viewed within the whole story of God's restorative activity in the past. Paul reminds Timothy and the church about the importance of staying tuned to the "sacred writings," the ancient text, the law and prophets, and the writings:

> All scripture is inspired by God and is useful for teaching, for reproof, for correction, and for training in righteousness, so that everyone who belongs to God may be profitable, equipped for every good work. (3:16-17)

In addition to attending to the Scriptures with their stories of God's activity in the past, the church needs to be mindful of the future, as indicated both in Paul's urgent charge to Timothy (4:1-2) and in his personal testimony as he faces his own death (4:7-8):

> In the presence of God and of Christ Jesus, who is to judge the living and the dead, and in view of his appearing and his kingdom, I solemnly urge you: pro-

claim the message; be persistent whether the time is
favorable or unfavorable; convince, rebuke, and
encourage with the utmost patience in teaching. (4:1-2)

I have fought the good fight, I have finished the race, I
have kept the faith. From now on there is reserved for
me the crown of righteousness, which the Lord, the
righteous judge will give me on that day, and not only
to me but also to all who have longed for his appearing. (4:7-8)

As Paul's final testament comes to a close in 4:9-18, his
readers catch sight of the apostle huddled in a cool, damp
prison, wishing for his warm cloak, missing his books,
waiting for visitors. We observe him as he rehearses his
losses but without nursing resentment, as he identifies his
opponents and prays for God to forgive them. Above all,
as we join Paul at death's door, we hear grateful testimony,
inspiring expressions of confidence, and doxology:

But the Lord stood by me and gave me strength, so
that through me the message might be fully proclaimed
and all the Gentiles might hear it. So I was rescued
from the lion's mouth. The Lord will rescue me from
every evil attack and save me for his heavenly kingdom. To him be the glory forever and ever. Amen!
(4:17-18)

Here is a stirring testimonial to the One who led the
way through suffering and death on the cross. As Jesus
forgave his executioners, so does Paul. As Jesus surren-
dered himself to God and the heavenly kingdom, so does
Paul. Participation with Christ can lead to dying with
Christ. And dying with Christ leads to ongoing life with
Christ. To God be the glory forever!

Communal and Individual Quests for a Hopeful Future

We have caught glimpses of congregational life both on the island of Crete and in and around the city of Ephesus. Each of the three letters to Paul's delegates, Titus and Timothy, also helps us to see how the pastor (Paul or a representative) recalls the church's hymns and confessions. We have reflected on how these hymns and confessions shape ongoing life and relationships within the congregations. In addition we have been privy to some of this pastor's most intimate thoughts as he rehearses his life, including the stunning revelation of God's grace to him through Jesus Christ, and as he anticipates the church's future and wonders about his own.

At this point we expand our angle of vision, first, to explore how the gospel moves each of these congregations—in their search for a hopeful future—to engage their cultural and political context. In particular this discussion will include how the church negotiates two competing agendas: maintenance and mission. Second, we attend to a closely related theme, namely, an understanding of leadership and authority in the church's quest for order and direction. And, finally, we ponder the broad theme of hope.

Participating in God's Mission, Maintaining the Church

In both Crete and Ephesus a generation of believers whose parents had been part of the church presents new challenges for congregational life. As the first generation of converts leaves the scene, how shall congregations work at maintaining their life together while participating in God's mission within their social and political context?

There is a tension between the desire to maintain order and the call to participate in God's mission. Maintenance instincts at times lead to accommodation with the status quo, resulting in compromise. Mission dynamics challenge certain dimensions of the culture, sometimes leading to instability, even suffering.

One way of understanding this tension in the life of the church is to focus broadly on relationships between gospel and culture. The chart below attempts to picture how the congregation that confesses the gospel relates to its cultural context in ways that to varying degrees conform to that culture or confront that culture:

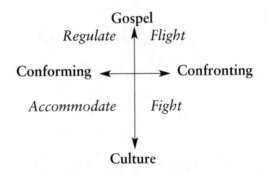

A few interpretive comments may show how this diagram can illuminate the dynamics operative behind the epistles 1 and 2 Timothy and Titus.

As we have seen, each of the three Pastoral Epistles includes formal confessional materials (hymns, confessions, and recitals) that articulate the gospel of Jesus Christ. Each of these letters also provides glimpses into the political, social, religious, and cultural context in which the community of faith finds itself. Redeemed and formed by God's intervening grace through Jesus Christ, the faith community finds itself summoned to live in harmony with that dynamic gospel within its real life context. The lifestyle of the faith community conforms in certain ways with the values of the surrounding culture. At other points that lifestyle confronts those cultural values.

Four different possibilities suggest themselves for the congregation that seeks to negotiate the extent to which they conform or confront. To some degree, each of these tendencies is evident in Crete and Ephesus, as reflected in these three letters. Each tendency can also have problematic aspects.

One is the tendency to take flight, either physically (through migration) or virtually (by escaping into esoteric and fanciful spiritual realms), thereby removing the congregation from its social setting or leaving it disconnected from that setting. Ascetic denial of sexual instincts and the disavowal of marriage, as attested in 1 Timothy 4:1-5, are examples of such attempts to escape normal life. Paul warns women not to flee into an ascetic lifestyle on the premise that they will thereby attain a higher level of spirituality. He assures these women that while bearing children and participating in the normal life of the household they remain among those who will be saved (2:15).

Another is the instinct to fight, thereby leading to a destabilized relationship with the surrounding culture. This option seems not to be actively entertained in the congregations being addressed by these letters. However, Timothy is urged to fight the good fight (1 Timothy 1:18; 6:11). Might this be an indication that, in the author's judgment, faithful missional engagement should involve Timothy and the congregation in a more assertive confrontation with some prevailing cultural values?

A strong tendency seems to have been to accommodate with the culture, resulting in a compromised position in relation to the gospel. First Timothy 6:2-10 includes a strongly worded warning addressed to people driven by a consuming desire to acquire riches. Paul laments that "in their eagerness to be rich some have wandered away from the faith and pierced themselves with many pains "(6:10b). Even though wealth is not in itself a negative, "the love of money is a root of all kinds of evil" (6:10a).

A fourth tendency is to regulate, to define obligations and state rules for conduct, a process that can make people feel constrained to behave in certain narrowly defined ways. In 1 Timothy there are rather lengthy instructions regarding bishops (3:1-7), deacons (3:8-13), and widows (5:3-16), plus some counsel for slaves (6:1-2). In Titus there are also guidelines regarding bishops (1:7-9) and slaves (2:9-10). The Pastoral Epistles definitely tend toward the regulation of behavior in an effort to define carefully how life within the faith community can be distinct from the lifestyle prevailing in the surrounding culture.

We have identified two instincts that compete with each other: the desire for stability and the urge to stimulate change. An impulse toward stability can lead the church to overemphasize its conformity to the dominant culture. Such quest for respectability will de-emphasize missional engagement. A zealous impulse to create change can upset relationships with that culture, leading to an unhealthy disconnect between the church and its context. The Pastoral Epistles are sometimes seen to manifest a dominant quest for respectability, employing a hierarchical process of regulation to assure stability and safety. However, as our discussion of each of the Pastoral Epistles has shown, even these letters testify to a dynamic interplay between the gospel and the culture within which these congregations exist.

The congregation's lived confession of the formative and transforming dynamic of God's grace manifest in Jesus Christ elicits a communal character somewhere between a compromising conformity and a destabilizing confrontation. As part of the process of guiding and shaping that communal character in conformity to Christ, there is also the need within the redeemed community to confront the invasive power of sin, from which God in Christ has brought redemption. As congregations demonstrate Christlike qualities in their life together, God's saving intent through Jesus Christ is made known in transformational ways to the people among whom they live.

Leadership and Church Order

Closely related to the dialectic between an inward-looking maintenance agenda and an outward-oriented missional stance are the issues of ministry and authority within the congregation. Paul himself offers pastoral care as itinerant apostle through visits and letters to the congregations within his orbit. At times he feels compelled to defend his own authority to exercise that kind of ministry. Each of these congregations also had developed internal leadership patterns, whether formal or informal, to teach, address needs, and set direction.

Scholars attempting to delineate the emergence of congregational leadership structures have reached divergent conclusions. Was there a gradual evolution in the early church from informal charismatic beginnings toward later institutional ministry offices? Or did charismatic and official leadership patterns coexist and evolve in parallel fashion? The evidence in Paul's letters points toward the latter. Like the Jewish synagogue and various guilds and voluntary associations in the Mediterranean world, the church designated persons with specific authority to lead. The church also benefited from spontaneous movements of God's Spirit in individuals and within the gathered community as a whole. (See Elias, 2004:85-104.)

Several ministry offices are mentioned in Paul's letters.

He addresses a letter to "all the saints in Christ Jesus who are in Philippi, with the bishops and deacons" (Philippians 1:1). As we have already noted, in Titus 1:7-9 and 1 Timothy 3:1-7, there are instructions regarding "bishops" (*episkopoi*, literally "overseers"). The word translated "deacons" (*diakonoi*) occurs fairly frequently in the Pauline literature to describe individuals who have congregational leadership responsibilities; strikingly, it also occurs with reference to Christ himself (Romans 15:8) and even to governing authorities as God's ministers (Romans 13:4). Another title, "elders" (*presbuteroi*), is employed often in Acts but in the Pauline literature only in the pastoral epistles (1 Timothy 5:1, 2, 17, 19; Titus 1:5). Some scholars see the synagogue leadership structure behind the elder system, while others understand the term "elders" to be equivalent to the honorific title used in households for respected heads of families.

A particular instance where Paul names and describes a person with reference to her ministry office is found in Romans 16:1-2. He commends Phoebe, likely the carrier of his letter, to the congregations in Rome. He describes her as a *diakonos* in Cenchreae, but the translations are unclear about what *diakonos* means: NIV has "servant," RSV "deaconess," and NRSV "deacon." When this same word occurs with reference to a man (as in 1 Timothy 4:6 and Colossians 1:7) it is normally translated "minister" (so also in the NRSV marginal reading of Romans 16:1). Clearly Paul wants the churches in Rome to recognize Phoebe as "a minister of the church at Cenchreae." In Romans 16:2 he adds to his commendation of Phoebe by employing the noun *prostatis*, rendered as "helper" (RSV, NIV) or "benefactor" (NRSV). More appropriately this noun could be translated as "leader," in line with 1 Timothy 3:4, 5, 12, where the corresponding participle points to a leading or managing function. In short, Paul testifies that Phoebe as "a minister of the church in Cenchreae" has been "a leader of many and of myself as well" (Romans 16:2, author's translation).

In 1 Thessalonians, possibly the earliest of his letters, Paul counsels the believers to respect and esteem their congregational leaders because of their work among them:

> But we appeal to you, brothers and sisters, to respect
> those who labor among you, and have charge of you
> in the Lord and admonish you; esteem them very high-
> ly in love because of their work. (1 Thessalonians
> 5:12-13)

Instead of using titles, Paul here describes church leaders with reference to their activity among the people. They "labor among you," he says. Elsewhere in this letter he expresses his anxiety lest his labor among them might turn out to have been in vain (3:5); the word *labor* here clearly refers to his evangelistic efforts among them. In Romans Paul employs similar terminology as he greets house church leaders:

> Greet those workers in the Lord, Tryphaena and
> Tryphosa. Greet the beloved Persis, who has worked
> hard in the Lord. (Romans 16:12)

The way that the NRSV renders Paul's second depiction in 1 Thessalonians 5:12 ("have charge of you") calls for some modification, because it implies a hierarchical relationship that does not fit with their mutual relationship "in the Lord." A better reading is the literal one: "Those who stand before you in the Lord" (author's translation); here is an instance of the participle (mentioned above) that describes the leading or managing function, as in 1 Timothy 3:4, 5, 12. In their evangelistic and teaching labors among and in behalf of their brothers and sisters in the Lord, pastors have a representative function in the Lord. As leaders in the Lord, who stand before the people who are also in the Lord, they serve as models of faithfulness and as persons called by God to speak for God.

One more dimension of the work of the individuals called to special ministry is admonition (5:12). This activity is also highlighted in 5:14 in a list that appears to enumerate some mutual care activities commended for all members of the congregation, namely "to admonish the idlers, encourage the faint hearted, help the weak, be patient with all of them" (5:14). These and other ministries are to be engaged by all members, not just the designated leaders. All of the members of the body are also urged to avoid retaliation (5:15) and to rejoice and pray and give thanks within all the circumstances of their lives (5:16-18).

As part of the ministry of all there is also opportunity for spontaneous Spirit-inspired speech, including prophecy. However, any such charismatic activity needs to be accompanied by processes of spiritual discernment:

> Do not quench the Spirit. Do not despise the words of prophets, but test everything; hold fast to what is good; abstain from every form of evil. (5:19-21)

It is apparent therefore that, already in Thessalonica in the A.D. 50, Paul envisioned inspiration for worship and guidance for daily living to come from both formally designated leaders and persons experiencing the spontaneous empowerment of the Spirit of God within the gathered community. In an environment in which unruly enthusiasts (*ataktoi*, "the idlers," 5:14) were creating disruption within and negative impressions beyond the congregation, he carefully articulates a balanced view, urging love and respect for official leaders while also encouraging discerning openness to the ministrations of the Spirit active among them all.

This commitment to recognize both designated formal leaders and charismatic Spirit-led prophets came to be severely tested in the young Thessalonian congregation. In 1 Thessalonians 4:11-12 Paul already hints broadly about the need for a subgroup within the congregation to tone down their frenetic spiritual enthusiasm in favor of a down-to-earth work ethic. He urges them "to be ambitious to be quiet, to mind your own affairs, and to work with your own hands" (4:11, author's translation). In 4:12 Paul clarifies a two-prong rationale for his counsel: his desire for a positive witness among outsiders and the need for a healthy self-sufficiency through gainful employment by those who are able to work. The spiritual frenzy of some people anticipating the imminent triumph of God's reign seems to have led them to an irresponsible and disruptive style of life.

The dilemma posed by the teaching and activity of the *ataktoi* ("idlers") is also mentioned in Paul's second letter to the church at Thessalonica (3:6-15). This text therefore makes for an intriguing longitudinal study concerning congregational leadership and order. It is apparent that the unruly enthusiasts became more disruptive as time went on. How would the congregation and its leaders deal with the situation?

Paul felt compelled to lay down the law and to call for the exercise of communal discipline. Rather than appealing to the church, he in this case issues a command:

> Now we command you, beloved, in the name of our
> Lord Jesus Christ, to keep away from believers who

are living in idleness and not according to the tradition
that they received from us. (2 Thessalonians 3:6)

As he continues to address the situation in Thessalonica,
Paul reminds the people about his lifestyle and teaching
when he lived among them:

For you yourselves know how you ought to imitate us;
we were not idle when we were with you, and we did
not eat anyone's bread without paying for it; but with
toil and labor we worked night and day, so that we
might not burden any of you. This was not because we
do not have that right, but in order to give you an
example to imitate. For even when we were with you,
we gave you this command: Anyone unwilling to work
should not eat. (3:7-10)

Assessing the congregational situation where the behavior
of some members has departed from the normative tradition, he also has some sharp words, including commands
addressed directly to the unruly people in their midst:

For we hear that some of you are living in idleness, mere
busybodies, not doing any work. Now such persons we
command and exhort in the Lord Jesus Christ to do
their work quietly and to earn their own living. (3:11)

Beyond these words of rebuke and strict instruction that
target the unruly "busybodies," he also counsels the congregation as a whole. He commends a process of restorative discipline:

Brothers and sisters, do not be weary in doing what is
right. Take note of those who do not obey what we
say in this letter; have nothing to do with them, so that

they may be ashamed. Do not regard them as enemies,
but warn them as believers. (3:13-15)

In the exercise of his apostolic authority, Paul therefore
prescribes congregational discipline on those whose behavior does not measure up to accepted norms. The discipline
that he recommends calls for patience, so he pleads with
the congregation not to become weary of doing what is
right. The desired outcome of disciplinary avoidance is to
shame people whose aberrant lifestyle is problematic.
However, he does not want to stigmatize these persons as
enemies but rather warn them as fellow believers, ostensibly in the hope that they will change their ways and be
restored to fellowship.

Here is a situation in which Paul follows a pastoral
instinct to regulate congregational life with firm guidance.
In a situation marked by people taking flight into other-
worldly spiritual enthusiasm, he issues pastoral directives
and invites constructive change. In this case, the change
being sought is toward greater conformity to a normal cultural expectation: that people will work for their own
keep. Hope for the future includes ongoing relevance for
the present.

Hope

Paul's pastoral approach is deeply imbued by a theology of hope. His hopefulness flows from his stunning preview of a glorious future guaranteed through Jesus Christ.
Such hope motivated his apostolic labors among congregations throughout the Mediterranean region. Even fragile
and often conflicted bodies of believers embody an alternative hopeful vision for the future. But Paul's reflections
about hope also had a deeply personal dimension. In the
midst of his struggles as apostle, Paul was also dealing

with his own mortality. He looked beyond his death to a future resurrection.

In his correspondence with the church at Corinth, he dwells at length on the themes related to the resurrection and life after death. In 1 Corinthians 15 he rehearses the church's witness to the resurrection of Christ, and in the process he includes testimony to his own encounter with the risen Lord, an experience that propels him in his apostolic labors (15:1-11). Paul also confronts a pattern of denial regarding the resurrection; he points out that both the preacher of the gospel and those who believe the gospel are to be pitied if their hope in Christ is limited only to this life (15:12-19). To deny the resurrection is to negate the foundational story of Jesus Christ:

> that Christ died for our sins in accordance with the
> scriptures, and that he was buried,
> and that he was raised on the third day in accordance
> with the scriptures, and that he appeared to Cephas,
> then to the twelve. (15:3-5)

To deny the resurrection is also to contravene the Scriptures' attestation of this foundational story, as shown by the repetition of the phrase "in accordance with the scriptures" in 15:3, 4.

We have already explored Paul's exegetical and eschatological thought in 1 Corinthians 15:20-28, 35-49 (see chapter 3). At this stage in our investigation of his theology we need to acknowledge how Paul extrapolates from the fact of the resurrection to the implications of the resurrection hope for his own life and his ministry. If there were no resurrection, he says, he and his hearers would lack the backbone to face opposition and possibly even lose their motivation for upright living. As it is, he boasts about his weakness and his suffering, and he shames some in Corinth whose morality did not conform to their confession:

> And why are we putting ourselves in danger every hour? I die every day! That is as certain, brothers and sisters, as my boasting of you—a boast that I make in Christ Jesus our Lord. If with merely human hopes I fought with wild animals at Ephesus, what would I have gained by it? If the dead are not raised, "Let us eat and drink, for tomorrow we die." Do not be deceived: "Bad company ruins good morals." Come to a sober and right mind, and sin no more; for some people have no knowledge of God. I say this to your shame. (15:30-34)

Paul's comments about wrestling with beasts in Ephesus provide evidence that he has had difficulties in his ministry in that city. As he concludes this letter, he announces his upcoming travel plans: "I will stay in Ephesus until Pentecost" (16:8). At this point he is optimistic, commenting that "a wide door for effective work has opened to me" (16:9a). He is also realistic, noting that "there are many adversaries" (16:9b). Resurrection hope translates into confidence in the face of death. Resurrection hope also inspires and enables persistence in ministry even when times are tough.

Paul's confident persistence in the face of suffering and opposition comes to its most dramatic expression in 1 Corinthians 15:50-58, the rousing conclusion to his extended excursus on the resurrection. In verse 50 he wraps up the rather thick discourse about the nature of the resurrection body in 15:35-49. What follows is a rhapsody introduced with the exclamation "Listen, I will tell you a mystery!" (15:51). In a series of poetic declarations, including citations from Isaiah 25:8 and Hosea 13:14, Paul discloses the marvelous mystery of the future transformation anticipated by both the living and the dead. He appears to envision himself among those who will be transformed while alive, rather than raised from the dead, at the sounding of the last trumpet:

> We will not all die, but we will all be changed, in a moment, in the twinkling of an eye, at the last trumpet. For the trumpet will sound, and the dead will be raised imperishable, and we will be changed. For this perishable body must put on imperishability, and this mortal body must put on immortality. When this perishable body puts on imperishability, and this mortal body puts on immortality, then the saying that is written will be fulfilled: "Death has been swallowed up in victory." "Where, O death, is your victory? Where, O death, is your sting?" (15:51-55)

In this privileged preview of the future, Paul sees that God achieves victory over the tenacious powers of sin and death. This divine triumph over the malevolent powers reassures him and all those in his audience who in their fragility and suffering place their ongoing trust in God. There is a future life, which transcends death, a life that is continuous with the relationship already established in Christ, a life that is also gloriously transformed. The mortal and perishable body gives way to an immortal and imperishable body. Death's sting recedes, and life in the fullness of resurrection glory begins.

This assured triumph of God through Christ not only reassures Paul and others facing their own mortality. It also inspires hopefulness for ongoing ministry and witness in the confidence that the church will survive and thrive. Paul wraps up with an enigmatic assertion about sin, death, and the law (15:56) and an ardent expression of thanksgiving to God (15:57). He also appends a pastoral word of encouragement (15:58). Adversity and setbacks continue, including the threat of death, as sin's sting, and the divisiveness of the law, as coopted by sin's power. Nevertheless, in the Lord, victory is assured. Hence labor in the Lord is never in vain:

> The sting of death is sin, and the power of sin is the law. But thanks be to God, who gives us the victory through our Lord Jesus Christ. Therefore, my beloved, be steadfast, immovable, always excelling in the work of the Lord, because you know that in the Lord your labor is not in vain. (15:56-58)

In 2 Corinthians we catch more glimpses into Paul's hopeful ministry as he corresponds further with the same congregation. The circumstances for Paul in Ephesus had in the meantime become even more grievous. As he begins this letter to the Corinthian church he rehearses his experiences, sharing his conflicting feelings of both despair about his circumstances and ongoing confidence in the God who raises the dead:

> We do not want you to be unaware, brothers and sisters, of the affliction we experienced in Asia; for we were so utterly, unbearably crushed that we despaired of life itself. Indeed, we felt that we had received the sentence of death so that we would rely not on ourselves but on God who raises the dead. He who rescued us from so deadly a peril will continue to rescue us; on him we have set our hope that he will rescue us again. (2 Corinthians 1:8-11)

As we have seen (chapter 5) in 2 Corinthians 2–7 Paul engages in a spirited defense against what he regards as a misguided caricature of his ministry as lackluster and ungrounded. The theological exposition in 3:1-18 of the story of Moses and the second giving of the Torah (cf. Exodus 34) is part of this defense. In 4:1 he begins to enlarge on the theme of his hopefulness in ministry despite difficult circumstances: "Therefore, since it is by God's mercy that we are engaged in this ministry, we do not lose heart." In 4:16 he repeats, "So we do not lose heart." Between these parallel assertions he chronicles his apostolic trauma in ways that heighten the paradox between outer appearances and the deeper reality. Arranging 4:8-12 in parallel columns illuminates Paul's conviction that resurrection hope overwhelms the forces of death:

Forces of Death	Resurrection Hope
We are afflicted in every way, >	but not crushed;
perplexed, >	but not driven to despair;
persecuted, >	but not forsaken;
struck down, >	but not destroyed;
always carrying in the body the death of Jesus, >	so that the life of Jesus may also be made visible in our bodies.
For while we live, we are always being given up to death for Jesus' sake, >	so that the life of Jesus may be made visible in our mortal flesh.
So death is at work in us, >	but life in you.

In Paul's listing of his hardships, the expression "but not" always emphasizes God's sustaining and life-restoring presence in the midst of his suffering (4:8-9). Paul's affliction replays Jesus's death, and his endurance of affliction displays Jesus's resurrection life (4:10). Even within his life-threatening circumstances Jesus's resurrection life is made visible (4:11). Paradoxically death's ominous work in the circumstances of Paul's ministry leads to life for the Corinthians. They are the direct beneficiaries of this lived witness to the crucifixion and resurrection of Jesus (4:12).

Paul's ongoing confidence, rooted in the death and resurrection of Jesus, is explicitly articulated in what follows. He gives his testimony, and he augments his testimony with Scripture: "'I believed, and so I spoke'—we also believe, and so we speak" (4:13b). The citation comes from Psalm 116:10 (in the LXX: Psalm 115:1), a psalm that testifies to divine deliverance from death. Having alluded to this Scripture, Paul echoes the church's resurrection hope:

> because we know that the one who raised the Lord Jesus will raise us also with Jesus, and will bring us with you into his presence. (4:14)

Here again Paul reiterates his assurance that his witness as suffering apostle results in God's bountiful grace being made available to more grateful people: "So that grace . . . may increase thanksgiving, to the glory of God" (4:15).

This note of grace, thanksgiving, and abounding glory even leads Paul to minimize the severity of his affliction. In comparison to the glory yet to come, his suffering turns out to be "slight momentary affliction" (4:17a). The glory yet to be unveiled promises to be "an eternal weight of glory beyond all measure" (4:17b). His mind moves from pondering the lesser (the setbacks in the present) to contemplating the greater (unsurpassed glory in the future).

Paul employs multiple metaphors to further this contrast between present affliction and eternal glory. One of these images is introduced already in 4:7:

> But we have this treasure in clay jars, so that it may be
> made clear that this extraordinary power belongs to
> God and does not come from us.

Portrayed by interlopers as a weak and battered apostle,
Paul appropriates their caricature of him in ways that
highlight the power of the resurrection. Though his body
is fragile, like an earthen vessel, his participation in the
death and resurrection of Jesus points beyond that mortal
reality to the treasure of the gospel. In 4:16-18 this point
is made in a variety of ways:

Experiences in the Present	These Experiences Viewed in Light of the Future
Even though our outer nature is wasting away, >	our inner nature is being renewed day by day.
For this slight momentary affliction is preparing us >	for an eternal weight of glory beyond all measure,
because we look not at what can be seen >	but at what cannot be seen;
for what can be seen is temporary, >	but what cannot be seen is eternal.

In 5:1-5 Paul elaborates on the contrast in 4:16 between
the outer nature (now wasting away) and the inner nature
(already being renewed). This language has sometimes been
viewed as symptomatic of his use of Platonic categories,
with the body represented as disposable shell containing the
inner self. However, even though he accommodates himself
to some extent to the language apparently employed by
some Corinthians, he is actually thinking more about a
chronological movement from present to the future than

about an anthropological dualism between outer and inner natures. Underlying the word *nature* in 4:16 is the Greek word *anthropos,* "human." Perhaps Paul wants the Corinthians to think about the transition from the epoch of the first human, Adam, to the epoch of the new creation through Christ, the new human or second Adam (Shillington, 1998:107). Perhaps he elicits a recollection of the apocalyptic shift already accomplished through Christ, namely, the present age, while still continuing, now invaded by the future age, as dramatically attested in Christ's resurrection as first fruit of the future general resurrection still to come (Wright, 2003:364-70).

Another chart can illustrate the overlapping ways in which Paul in 5:1-4 reflects on his present experience (here imaged as life within a tent) which already includes a foretaste of future resurrection life (pictured both as dwelling in an eternal house and as being clothed with a heavenly garb):

Present Experience	Future Hope
For we know that if the earthly tent we live in is destroyed, >	we have a building from God, a house not made with hands, eternal in the heavens.
For in this tent we groan, >	longing to be clothed with our heavenly dwelling—if indeed, when we have taken it off we will not be found naked.
For while we are still in this tent, we groan under our burden, >	because we wish not to be unclothed but to be further clothed, so that what is mortal may be swallowed up by life.

Clearly Paul is here talking about life in the face of imminent death. Groaning precedes death, the destruction of the body. What is not so clear is how he intends to have his hearers understand his earnest desire to avoid nakedness after taking off the earthly tent. His images pile into each other here. Does he hint at an intermediate state between earthly life and the future life following the resurrection? Perhaps he does, although few details are given. What is clear is that Paul envisions a future in a transformed body rather than as a disembodied spirit. And this future is already guaranteed by the gift of God's Spirit: "He who has prepared us for this very thing is God, who has given us the Spirit as a guarantee" (5:5).

Paul concludes this part of his appeal to the Corinthians with another expression of confidence, in which he essentially rests his case (5:6-10). At the final tribunal, faithfulness will ultimately be rewarded:

> So we are always confident; even though we know that
> while we are at home in the body we are away from
> the Lord—for we walk by faith, not by sight. Yes, we
> do have confidence, and we would rather be away
> from the body and at home with the Lord. So whether
> we are at home or away, we make it our aim to please
> him. For all of us must appear before the judgment
> seat of Christ, so that each may receive recompense for
> what has been done in the body, whether good or evil.
> (2 Corinthians 5:6-10)

In the meantime, Paul says, "We walk by faith, not by sight" (5:7). As he anticipates the future, he ponders two possible scenarios, both good. Either he will die soon, or he will continue his apostolic ministry for a while longer. Life makes possible continued apostolic ministry. Death leads to being home with the Lord.

Living into the Future with Hope

What then is Paul's ongoing word for the church, now that more than two thousand years have elapsed since God's coming to the world through Jesus Christ? What is the roadmap into that future announced by God through Christ and the church?

Paul views a glorious future already announced and embodied by God in and through Jesus Christ. The grand biblical narratives concerning God's sovereign care climax in a preemptive invasion of God's grace. God's love is put on public display through the cross of Christ. The death of the Messiah on the shameful cross, and God's vindicating resurrection of the Messiah, supply dramatic previews of the ultimate triumph shared by all who trust God.

Paul reminds the church always to stay tuned to God's future-creating initiative in Christ, always as it were to keep the cross within the rearview. However, the church needs always to incarnate that future in the present, always as it were to keep their eyes on the road. Through the empowerment of the Spirit, the church participates in God's ongoing restorative mission of reclaiming the world and its peoples from the powers of sin and death.

Even though years and centuries have passed, the passion of Paul's vision of this future opened through Christ continues. Neither Paul nor any of his companions, then and now, has deciphered God's time line, still known only to God. But the roadmap into the future has been made known. As dynamic alternative communities of the future, congregations scattered around the world can in their worship, community life, and bold witness live into that future with hope.

Paul's benediction near the end of his letter to house churches in imperial Rome continues to inspire twenty-first-century congregations in their life and witness around the world:

> May the God of hope fill you with all joy and peace in believing, so that you may abound in hope by the power of the Holy Spirit. (Romans 15:13)

BIBLIOGRAPHY

Abbreviations

AusBR	Australian Biblical Review
CBQ	Catholic Biblical Quarterly
JTS	Journal of Theological Studies
JSNT	Journal for the Study of the New Testament
NovT	Novum Testamentum
NTS	New Testament Studies

Aageson, James W.
    1993   *Written also for Our Sake: Paul and the Art of Biblical Interpretation.* Louisville, KY: Westminster John Knox Press.

Adams, Edward
    2002   "Paul's Story of God and Creation: The Story of How God Fulfills His Purposes in Creation." In *Narrative Dynamics in Paul: A Critical Assessment*, edited by Bruce W. Longenecker. Louisville, KY: Westminster John Knox Press, 19-43.

Adams, Edward, and David G. Horrell, eds.
    2004   *Christianity at Corinth: The Quest for the Pauline Church.* Louisville, KY: Westminster John Knox Press.

Adams, Edward
    2000   *Constructing the World: A Study in Paul's Cosmological Language.* Studies of the New Testament and its World. Edinburgh: T & T Clark.

Arnold, Clinton E.
  1989   *Ephesians: Power and Magic. The Concept of Power
          in Ephesians in Light of its Historical Setting. JSNT*
          Monograph Series 63. Cambridge: Cambridge
          University Press.
Aune, David E.
  2002   "The Judgment Seat of Christ (2 Corinthians 5:10)."
          In *Pauline Conversations in Context: Essays in
          Honor of Calvin J. Roetzel*, eds. Janice Capel
          Anderson, Philip Sellow, and Claudia Setzer. London,
          New York: Sheffield Academic Press, 68-86.
Badenas, Robert
  1985   *Christ the End of the Law: Romans 10:4 in Pauline
          Perspective. JSNT* supp. 10. Sheffield: JSNT Press.
Banks, Robert
  1994   *Paul's Idea of Community*. Rev. ed. Peabody, MA:
          Hendrickson Publishers.
Barclay, John M. G.
  1991   *Obeying the Truth: Paul's Ethics in Galatians*.
          Edinburgh: T & T Clark, 1988; Minneapolis:
          Fortress Press.
  2001   "Ordinary but Different: Colossians and Hidden
          Moral Identity." *AusBR* 49:34-52.
  2002   "Paul's Story: Theology as Testimony." In *Narrative
          Dynamics in Paul: A Critical Assessment*, edited by
          Bruce W. Longenecker. Louisville, KY: Westminster
          John Knox Press, 133-56.
Bassler, Jouette M., ed.
  1991   *Pauline Theology*. Vol. 1, *Thessalonians, Philippians,
          Galatians, Philemon*. Minneapolis: Augsburg
          Fortress.
Benhayim, Menahem
  1985   *Jews, Gentiles, and the New Testament Scriptures*.
          Jerusalem: Yanetz Ltd.
Beker, J. Christiaan
  1980   *Paul the Apostle: The Triumph of God in Life and
          Thought*. Philadelphia: Fortress Press.

Best, Ernest
1997   *Essays on Ephesians*. Edinburgh: T & T Clark.
Bieberstein, Sabine
2000   "Disrupting the Normal Reality of Slavery: A Feminist Reading of the Letter to Philemon." *JSNT* 79:105-16.
Bosch, David J.
1991   *Transforming Mission: Paradigm Shifts in Theology of Mission*. Maryknoll, NY: Orbis Books.
Boyarin, Daniel
1994   *A Radical Jew: Paul and the Politics of Identity*. Berkeley, Los Angeles, & London: University of California Press.
Bruce, F. F.
1977   *Paul: Apostle of the Heart Set Free*. Grand Rapids, MI: Eerdmans.
Burtchaell, James Tunstead
1998   *Philemon's Problem: A Theology of Grace*. Grand Rapids, MI: Eerdmans.
Campbell, Douglas A.
2002   "The Story of Jesus in Romans and Galatians." In *Narrative Dynamics in Paul: A Critical Assessment*, edited by Bruce W. Longenecker. Louisville, KY: Westminster John Knox Press, 97-124.
2005   *The Quest for Paul's Gospel: A Suggested Strategy*. London & New York: T. & T. Clark International.
Collins, Raymond F.
2002   *1 & 2 Timothy and Titus: A Commentary*. The New Testament Library. Louisville, KY: Westminster John Knox Press. Cornfeld, Gaalya, ed.
1982   *Josephus: The Jewish War*. Grand Rapids, MI: Zondervan.
Cosgrove, Charles H.
1988   *The Cross and the Spirit: A Study in the Argument and Theology of Galatians*. Macon, GA: Mercer University Press.

Cotter, Wendy, CSJ
1993   "Our *Politeuma* is in Heaven: The Meaning of Philippians 3:17-21." In *Origins and Method: Towards a New Understanding of Judaism and Christianity*, *JSNT* supp. 86, edited by Bradley H. McLean. London, New York: Sheffield Academic Press.

Cousar, Charles B.
1990   *A Theology of the Cross: The Death of Jesus in the Pauline Letters*. Minneapolis: Augsburg Fortress.

Crossan, John Dominic, and Jonathan L. Reed
2004   *In Search of Paul: How Jesus' Apostle Opposed Rome's Empire with God's Kingdom. A New Vision of Paul's Words and World*. San Francisco: HarperSanFrancisco.

Das, A. Andrew
2001   *Paul, the Law, and the Covenant*. Peabody, MA: Hendrickson Publishers.

Donaldson, Terence L.
1997   *Paul and the Gentiles: Remapping the Apostle's Convictional World*. Philadelphia: Fortress Press.

Donfried, Karl Paul
2002   *Paul, Thessalonica, and Early Christianity*. Grand Rapids, MI: Eerdmans.

Dunn, James D. G.
1996a   *The Epistles to the Colossians and to Philemon*. The New International Greek Testament Commentary. Grand Rapids, MI: Eerdmans.
1996b   *Paul and the Mosaic Law*. Grand Rapids. MI: Eerdmans.
1998   *The Theology of Paul the Apostle*. Grand Rapids, MI: Eerdmans.
2000   "The First and Second Letters to Timothy and the Letter to Titus." In *The New Interpreter's Bible*. Vol. 11. Nashville: Abingdon Press, 773-880.
2002   "The Narrative Approach to Paul: Whose Story?" In *Narrative Dynamics in Paul: A Critical Assessment*, edited by Bruce W. Longenecker. Louisville, KY: Westminster John Knox Press, 217-30.

Elias, Jacob W.

1995   *1 & 2 Thessalonians*. Believers Church Bible Commentary. Scottdale, PA: Herald Press.

2000   "Faithfulness and Unity in Romans." In *Without Spot or Wrinkle: Reflecting Theologically on the Nature of the Church*. Occasional Papers 21, edited by Karl Koop and Mary Schertz. Elkhart, IN: Institute of Mennonite Studies, 45-64.

2002   "Confessing Faith, Confronting Sin." *Vision: A Journal for Church and Theology* 3:67-76.

2003   "The New has Come! An exegetical and theological discussion of 2 Corinthians 5:11–6:10." In *Beautiful upon the Mountains: Biblical Essays on Mission, Peace, and the Reign of God*, edited by Mary Schertz and Ivan Friesen. Elkhart, IN: Institute of Mennonite Studies; Scottdale, PA, and Waterloo, Ontario: Herald Press, 197-213.

2004   "A New Testament Model for Ministry and Leadership." In *The Heart of the Matter*, edited by Erick Sawatzky. Telford, PA: Cascadia Publishing House, 85-104.

Elliott, Neil

1994   *Liberating Paul: The Justice of God and the Politics of the Apostle*. Maryknoll, NY: Orbis Books.

1997   "Romans 13:1-7 in the Context of Roman Imperial Propaganda." In *Paul and Empire: Religion and Power in Roman Imperial Society*, edited by Richard A. Horsley. Harrisburg, PA: Trinity Press International, 184-204.

Fee, Gordon D.

1987   *The First Epistle to the Corinthians*. The New International Commentary on the New Testament. Grand Rapids, MI: Eerdmans.

1994   *God's Empowering Presence: The Holy Spirit in the Letters of Paul*. Peabody, MA: Hendrickson Publishers.

1995   *Paul's Letter to the Philippians.* The New
        International Commentary on the New Testament.
        Grand Rapids, MI: Eerdmans.

Fowl, Stephen E.
1990   *The Story of Christ in the Ethics of Paul. JSNT* supp.
        36. London, New York: Sheffield Academic Press.

Frederickson, Paula
1991   "Judaism, the Circumcision of Gentiles, and
        Apocalyptic Hope." *JTS* 42:532-65.

Gaventa, Beverly Roberts
1986   *From Darkness to Light.* Philadelphia: Fortress Press.

Gibbs, John G.
1971   *Creation and Redemption: A Study in Pauline
        Theology.* Leiden, The Netherlands: E. J. Brill.

Goodwin, Mark J.
2001   *Paul, Apostle of the Living God: Kerygma and
        Conversion in 2 Corinthians.* Harrisburg, PA: Trinity
        Press International.

Gorman, Michael J.
2001   *Cruciformity: Paul's Narrative Spirituality of the
        Cross.* Grand Rapids, MI: Eerdmans.
2004   *Apostle of the Crucified Lord: A Theological
        Introduction to Paul and His Letters.* Grand Rapids,
        MI: Eerdmans.

Grieb, A. Katherine
2002   *The Story of Romans: A Narrative Defense of God's
        Righteousness.* Louisville, KY: Westminster John
        Knox Press.

Griffith-Jones, Robin
2004   *The Gospel according to Paul: The Creative Genius
        who Brought Jesus to the World.* San Francisco:
        HarperSanFrancisco.

Hafemann, Scott J.
1995   *Paul, Moses, and the History of Israel.* Tübingen,
        Germany: J. C. B. Mohr (Paul Siebeck).
1997   "Paul and the Exile of Israel in Galatians 3-4." In
        Exile: Old Testament, Jewish, and Christian

Conceptions, edited by James M. Scott. Leiden, The Netherlands: E. J. Brill, 329-71.

Harink, Douglas
    2003   *Paul among the Postliberals: Pauline Theology beyond Christendom and Modernity.* Grand Rapids, MI: Brazos Press.

Hays, Richard B.
    1987   "Christology and Ethics in Galatians: The Law of Christ." *CBQ* 49:268-90.
    1989   *Echoes of Scripture in the Letters of Paul.* New Haven & London: Yale University Press.
    1991   "Crucified with Christ: A Synthesis of the Theology of 1 and 2 Thessalonians, Philemon, Philippians, and Galatians." In *Pauline Theology.* Vol. 1. *Thessalonians, Philippians, Galatians, Philemon*, edited by Jouette M. Bassler. Minneapolis: Augsburg Fortress, 227-46.
    1996   *The Moral Vision of the New Testament: Community, Cross, New Creation: A Contemporary Introduction to New Testament Ethics.* San Francisco: HarperSanFrancisco.
    1997   *First Corinthians.* Interpretation: A Bible Commentary for Teaching and Preaching. Atlanta: John Knox Press.
    2000   "The Letter to the Galatians." In *The New Interpreter's Bible.* Vol. 11. Nashville: Abingdon Press, 181-384.
    2002   *The Faith of Jesus Christ: The Narrative Substructure of Galatians 3:1-4:11.* 2d ed. Grand Rapids, MI: Eerdmans.

Hengel, Martin
    1983   *Between Jesus and Paul.* Philadelphia: Fortress Press.

Hengel, Martin, and Anna Maria Schwemer
    1997   *Paul between Damascus and Antioch: The Unknown Years.* Louisville, KY: Westminster John Knox Press.

Hofius, Otfried
    1990   "'All Israel will be Saved': Divine Salvation and Israel's Deliverance in Romans 9–11." *The Princeton*

Seminary Bulletin, supp. 1: "The Church and Israel: Romans 9–11," 19-39.

Hooker, Morna D.
2002   "'Heirs of Abraham': The Gentiles' Role in Israel's Story: A Response to Bruce W. Longenecker." In *Narrative Dynamics in Paul: A Critical Assessment,* edited by Bruce W. Longenecker. Louisville, KY: Westminster John Knox Press, 85-96.

Horbury, William
1998   *Jewish Messianism and the Cult of Christ.* London: SCM Press Ltd.

Horrell, David G.
2002   "Paul's Narratives or Narrative Substructure? The Significance of 'Paul's Story.'" In *Narrative Dynamics in Paul: A Critical Assessment,* edited by Bruce W. Longenecker. Louisville, KY: Westminster John Knox Press, 157-71.

Horsley, Richard A., ed.
1997   *Paul and Empire: Religion and Power in Roman Imperial Society.* Harrisburg, PA: Trinity Press International.
2000   *Paul and Politics: Ekklesia, Israel, Imperium, Interpretation. Essays in Honor of Krister Stendahl.* Harrisburg, PA: Trinity Press International.
2004   *Paul and the Roman Imperial Order.* Harrisburg, London & New York: Trinity Press International.

Hurtado, Larry W.
1988   *One God, One Lord: Early Christian Devotion and Ancient Jewish Monotheism.* Philadelphia: Fortress Press.
1999   "The Binitarian Shape of Early Christian Worship." In *The Jewish Roots of Christological Monotheism.* Supplements to the Journal for the Study of Judaism, vol. 63, edited by Carey C. Newman, James R. Davila, and Gladys S. Lewis. Leiden, The Netherlands: E. J. Brill, 187-213.

2003   *Lord Jesus Christ: Devotion to Jesus in Earliest Christianity*. Grand Rapids, MI: Eerdmans.

Jervis, L. Ann
  1999   "Paul the Poet in First Timothy 1:11-17; 2:3b-7; 3:14-16." *CBQ* 61:695-712.

Jewett, Robert
  1970-71 "The Agitators and the Galatian Congregation." *NTS* 17:198-212.
  1979   *A Chronology of Paul's Life*. Philadelphia: Fortress Press.
  1986   *The Thessalonian Correspondence: Pauline Rhetoric and Millenarian Piety*. Philadelphia: Fortress Press.

Johnson, E. Elizabeth
  1995   "Romans 9-11: The Faithfulness and Impartiality of God." In *Pauline Theology: Volume 3: Romans*, edited by David M. Hay and E. Elizabeth Johnson. Minneapolis: Augsburg Fortress, 211-39.

Johnson, Luke T.
  1996   *Letters to Paul's Delegates. 1 Timothy, 2 Timothy, Titus*. The New Testament in Context. Valley Forge, PA: Trinity Press International.
  1997   *Reading Romans: A Literary and Theological Commentary*. New York: The Crossroad Publishing Co.

Keesmaat, Sylvia C.
  1996   "Paul and his Story: Exodus and Tradition in Galatians." *Horizons in Biblical Theology* 18:133-68.

Klassen, William
  1984   *Love of Enemies: The Way to Peace*. Philadelphia: Fortress Press.

Klausner, Joseph
  1943   *From Jesus to Paul*. Translated by W. F. Stinespring. New York: Macmillan.

Kroeger, Richard Clark, and Catherine Clark Kroeger
  1992   *I Suffer not a Woman: Rethinking 1 Timothy 2:11-15 in Light of Ancient Evidence*. Grand Rapids, MI: Baker Book House.

Lewis, Naphtali, and Meyer Reinhold, eds.
  1955   *Roman Civilization.* Vol. 2, *The Empire.* New York, London: Columbia University Press.
Lincoln, Andrew T.
  1999   "The Household Code and Wisdom Mode of Colossians." *JSNT* 74:93-112.
  2002   "The Stories of Predecessors and Inheritors in Galatians and Romans." In *Narrative Dynamics in Paul: A Critical Assessment*, edited by Bruce W. Longenecker. Louisville, KY: Westminster John Knox Press, 172-203.
Longenecker, Bruce W.
  1998   Longenecker, Bruce W. *The Triumph of Abraham's God: The Transformation of Identity in Galatians.* Nashville: Abingdon Press.
  2002   "Sharing in their Spiritual Blessings? The Stories of Israel in Galatians and Romans." In *Narrative Dynamics in Paul: A Critical Assessment*, edited by Bruce W. Longenecker. Louisville, KY: Westminster John Knox Press, 58-84.
Longenecker, Richard N.
  1997   "A Realized Hope, A New Commitment, and a Developed Proclamation: Paul and Jesus." In *The Road from Damascus*, edited by R. N. Longenecker. Grand Rapids, MI: Eerdmans, 18-42.
Marshall, I. Howard
  1999   *The Pastoral Epistles.* International Critical Commentary. Edinburgh: T & T Clark.
Martin, Ernest D.
  1993   *Colossians, Philemon.* Believers Church Bible Commentary. Scottdale, PA: Herald Press.
Martin, Ralph P.
  1986   *2 Corinthians.* Word Biblical Commentary, no. 40. Waco, Texas: Word Books.
  1991   *Ephesians, Colossians, and Philemon.* Interpretation: A Bible Commentary for Teaching and Preaching. Atlanta: John Knox Press.

Martin, Ralph P., and Brian J. Dodd, eds.
    1998   *Where Christology Began: Essays on Philippians 2.* Louisville, KY: Westminster John Knox Press.

Martyn, J. Louis
    1997a   *Galatians.* The Anchor Bible, vol. 33A. New York: Doubleday.
    1997b   *Theological Issues in the Letters of Paul.* Nashville: Abingdon Press.

Minear, Paul S.
    1990   "Singing and Suffering in Philippi." In *The Conversation Continues: Studies in John and Paul,* edited by R. Fortna and Beverly R. Gaventa. Nashville: Abingdon Press, 202-19.

Murphy-O'Connor, Jerome
    1996   *Paul: A Critical Life.* Oxford: Oxford University Press.
    2004   *Paul: His Story.* Oxford: Oxford University Press.

Nanos, Mark D.
    1996   *The Mystery of Romans: The Jewish Context of Paul's Letter.* Minneapolis: Fortress Press.
    2002a   *The Galatians Debate: Contemporary Issues in Rhetorical and Historical Interpretation.* Edited by Mark Nanos. Peabody, MA: Hendrickson Publishers.
    2002b   *The Irony of Galatians: Paul's Letter in First-Century Context.* Minneapolis: Augsburg Fortress.

Neufeld, Tom Yoder
    1997   *Put on the Armour of God: The Divine Warrior from Isaiah to Ephesians.* JSNT supp. 140. London, New York: Sheffield Academic Press.
    2002   *Ephesians.* Believers Church Bible Commentary. Waterloo, Ontario, and Scottdale, PA: Herald Press.

Newton, Derek
    1998   *Deity and Diet: The Dilemma of Sacrificial Food at Corinth.* JSNT supp. 169. London, New York: Sheffield Academic Press.

Osiek, Carolyn, and David L. Balch
    1997   *Families in the New Testament World: Households and House Churches.* Louisville, KY: Westminster John Knox Press.

Penner, Erwin
    1990   *The Power of God in a Broken World.* Winnipeg, Manitoba: Kindred Press.

Peterson, Norman
    1985   *Rediscovering Paul: Philemon and the Sociology of Paul's Narrative World.* Philadelphia: Fortress Press.

Pheme, Perkins
    1991   "Philippians: Theology of the Heavenly Politeuma." In *Pauline Theology.* Vol. 1, *Thessalonians, Philippians, Galatians, Philemon.* Edited by Jouette Bassler. Minneapolis: Augsburg Fortress, 89-104.

Polaski, Sandra Hack
    2005   *A Feminist Introduction to Paul.* St. Louis, Missouri: Chalice Press.

Richardson, Neil
    1994   *Paul's Language about God. JSNT* supp. 99. London, New York: Sheffield Academic Press.

Riesner, Rainer
    1998   *Paul's Early Period: Chronology, Mission Strategy, Theology.* Grand Rapids, MI: Eerdmans.

Sanders, E. P.
    1977   *Paul and Palestinian Judaism: A Comparison of Patterns of Religion.* Philadelphia: Fortress Press.

Schotroff, Luise
    1992   "'Give to Caesar what belongs to Caesar and to God what belongs to God': A Theological Response of the Early Christian Church to its Social and Political Environment." In *The Love of Enemy and Nonretaliation in the New Testament,* edited by Willard M. Swartley. Louisville, KY: Westminster John Knox Press, 223-57.

Schweitzer, Albert
    1931   *The Mysticism of Paul the Apostle.* London: Black.

Segal, Alan F.
  1990   *Paul the Convert: The Apostolate and Apostasy of Saul the Pharisee.* New Haven & London: Yale University Press.
Shillington, V. George
  1998   *2 Corinthians.* Believers Church Bible Commentary. Scottdale, PA: Herald Press.
Siker, Jeffrey S.
  1991   *Disinheriting the Jews: Abraham in Early Christian Controversy.* Louisville, KY: Westminster John Knox Press.
Sloan, Robert B.
  1991   "Paul and the Law: Why the Law Cannot Save." *NovT* 33:35-60.
Snodgrass, Klyne
  1988   "Spheres of Influence: A Possible Solution to the Problem of Paul and the Law." *JSNT* 32:93-113.
Standhartinger, Angela
  2000   "The Origin and Intention of the Household Code in the Letter to the Colossians." *JSNT* 79:117-30.
Stanton, Graham N.
  2002   "'I Think, When I Read That Sweet Story of Old': A Response to Douglas A. Campbell." In *Narrative Dynamics in Paul: A Critical Assessment*, edited by Bruce W. Longenecker. Louisville, KY: Westminster John Knox Press, 125-32.
Stendahl, Krister
  1976   "St. Paul and the Introspective Conscience of the West." In *Paul among Jews and Gentiles, and other essays.* Philadelphia: Fortress Press, 78-96.
Toews, John E.
  1982   "Some Theses toward a Theology of the Law in the New Testament." In *The Bible and Law.* Occasional Papers, edited by Willard M. Swartley. Elkhart, IN: Institute of Mennonite Studies, 43-64.
  2004   *Romans.* Believers Church Bible Commentary. Scottdale, PA, and Waterloo, Ontario: Herald Press.

Towner, Philip H.
   1989   *The Goal of Our Instruction: The Structure of Theology and Ethics in the Pastoral Epistles*. JSNT supp. 34. London, New York: Sheffield Academic Press.

Walsh, Brian J., and Sylvia C. Keesmaat
   2004   *Colossians Remixed: Subverting the Empire*. Downers Grove, IL: InterVarsity Press.

Walters, James C.
   1993   *Ethnic Issues in Paul's Letter to the Romans: Changing Self-Definitions in Earliest Roman Christianity*. Valley Forge, PA: Trinity Press International.

Watson, Francis.
   2002   "Is There a Story in These Texts?" In *Narrative Dynamics in Paul: A Critical Assessment*, edited by Bruce W. Longenecker. Louisville, KY: Westminster John Knox Press, 231-39.

Watson, Francis.
   2004   *Paul and the Hermeneutics of Faith*. London, New York: T & T Clark.

White, John L.
   1999   *The Apostle of God: Paul and the Promise of Abraham*. Peabody, MA: Hendrickson Publishers.

Wiefel, Wolfgang
   1991   "The Jewish Community in Ancient Rome and the Origins of Roman Christianity." In *The Romans Debate*. Rev ed. Edited by Karl P. Donfried. Peabody, MA: Hendrickson Publishers, 85-101.

Williams, David J.
   1999   *Paul's Metaphors: Their Context and Character*. Peabody, MA: Hendrickson Publishers.

Wink, Walter
   1992   *Engaging the Powers: Discernment and Resistance in a World of Domination*. Minneapolis: Augsburg Fortress.

Witherington, Ben III
  1994a *Jesus the Sage: The Pilgrimage of Wisdom.* Minneapolis: Augsburg Fortress.
  1994b *Paul's Narrative Thought World: The Tapestry of Tragedy and Triumph.* Louisville, KY: Westminster John Knox Press.
  1998 *The Paul Quest: The Renewed Search for the Jew of Tarsus.* Downers Grove, IL: InterVarsity Press.

Wright, N. T.
  1991 "One God, One Lord, One People: Incarnational Christology for a Church in a Pagan Environment." *Ex Auditu* 7:45-58.
  1991 "Putting Paul Together Again: Toward a Synthesis of Pauline Theology." In *Pauline Theology.* Vol. 1, *Thessalonians, Philippians, Galatians, Philemon,* edited by Jouette M. Bassler. Minneapolis: Augsburg Fortress, 183-211.
  1992 *The Climax of the Covenant: Christ and the Law in Pauline Theology.* T & T Clark, 1991; Minneapolis: Fortress Press.
  1994 "Gospel and Theology in Galatians." In *Gospel in Paul. JSNT* supp. 108, edited by L. Ann Jervis and Peter Richardson. London, New York: Sheffield Academic Press, 222-39.
  1995 "Romans and the Theology of Paul." In *Pauline Theology.* Vol. 3, *Romans,* edited by David M. Hay and E. Elizabeth Johnson. Minneapolis: Augsburg Fortress, 30-67.
  1997 *What Saint Paul Really Said: Was Paul of Tarsus the Real Founder of Christianity?* Grand Rapids, MI: Eerdmans.
  2002 "The Letter to the Romans." In *The New Interpreter's Bible.* Vol. 10. Nashville: Abingdon Press, 393-770.
  2003 *The Resurrection of the Son of God.* Philadelphia: Fortress Press.

2005   *Paul: In Fresh Perspective*. Minneapolis: Fortress Press.

Yoder, John Howard
1994   *The Politics of Jesus*. 2d ed. Grand Rapids, MI: Eerdmans.
1997   *For the Nations: Essays Public and Evangelical*. Grand Rapids, MI: Eerdmans.

Young, Frances
1994   *The Theology of the Pastoral Letters*. New Testament Theology. Cambridge: Cambridge University Press.

Young, Frances, and David F. Ford
1987   *Meaning and Truth in 2 Corinthians*. Grand Rapids, MI: Eerdmans.

Zerbe, Gordon
1992   "Paul's Ethic of Nonretaliation and Peace." In *The Love of Enemy and Nonretaliation in the New Testament*, edited by Willard M. Swartley. Louisville, KY: Westminster John Knox Press, 177-222.
2003   "The Politics of Paul: His Supposed Social Conservatism and the Impact of Postcolonial Readings." *Conrad Grebel Review* 21:82-103.

INDEX

533

ABOUT THE AUTHOR

Jacob W. Elias is author of *1 & 2 Thessalonians* in the Believers Church Bible Commentary series. He was born in Rosthern, Saskatchewan. He studied at the University of Saskatchewan, and graduated in 1968 from Mennonite Biblical Seminary. He began pastoral ministry at Mountainview Mennonite Church, Vancouver, and in 1978 earned a ThD in New Testament from the Toronto School of Theology. He has been teaching at Associated Mennonite Biblical Seminary since 1977. Since 2001, Jacob and his wife, Lillian, have worked as co-pastors of Parkview Mennonite Church in Kokomo, Indiana. They have three children and seven grandchildren.